Seventeen and Oh

Also by the author:

A Terrible Splendor:
Three Extraordinary Men, a World Poised for War,
and the Greatest Tennis Match Ever Played

A Backhanded Gift

With David E. Fisher:

Tube: The Invention of Television

Strangers in the Night:
A Brief History of Life on Other Worlds

SeventeenandOh

Miami, 1972, and the NFL's Only Perfect Season

Marshall Jon Fisher

Abrams Press, New York

Library of Congress Control Number: 2022932223

ISBN: 978-1-4197-4850-9
eISBN: 978-1-64700-005-9

Printed and bound in the United States
10 9 8 7 6 5 4 3 2 1

Abrams books are available at special discounts when purchased in quantity
for premiums and promotions as well as fundraising or educational use.
Special editions can also be created to specification. For details, contact
specialsales@abramsbooks.com or the address below.

Abrams Press® is a registered trademark of Harry N. Abrams, Inc.

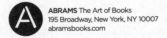
ABRAMS The Art of Books
195 Broadway, New York, NY 10007
abramsbooks.com

For Ron

and for Dad: quarterback for both teams

CONTENTS

Introduction

Every football season for the past fifty years, there has come a weekend when the last undefeated NFL team finally loses a game. More than half the time, it's been in the first half of the season. Usually, it's over before Thanksgiving. In 2007, it didn't happen until February of the next year. Whether in early fall or midwinter, though, it always happens. And when it does, there is a group of old football players who can't help but smile. They don't, as rumor once had it, gather together and share a glass of champagne when the final zero disappears from the NFL Standings loss column. But how could they not feel a twinge of satisfaction? They are the surviving members of the 1972 Miami Dolphins, the only team in NFL history to go from opening day to the league championship without losing or tying a game.

The greatest season ever took place in a setting made for Hollywood. Miami in 1972 was a steamy cauldron of politics and sex and culture wars. As both national party conventions came to town that summer, the sidewalks and parks of Miami Beach filled with hippies, Zippies, Yippies, activists, protesters, and tourists gawking at it all. Meanwhile, the Vietnam War raged through the final bloody months of U.S involvement and Richard Nixon spent more and more time at the "Winter White House," his modest compound on Key Biscayne, just off the Miami coast.

The relatively new Miami football team, running through its seventh preseason during the conventions, reflected the social dichotomy of the times. There were long-haired, bell-bottomed party animals with historically specific facial hair, like Jim "Mad Dog" Mandich and Manny Fernandez, along with active liberals like Marv Fleming and Marlin Briscoe—not to mention Curtis Johnson with his supernova Afro—sharing the locker room with quiet, conservative, straight-laced men, such as the quarterbacks Bob Griese and Earl Morrall. But unlike the fractious society seeming to unravel around them, this diverse group found a way to meld seamlessly into a team. The perfect team.

I was nine years old and finally on board with the Dolphinmania rising all around South Florida. My father and brother had gotten interested in the team the past couple of seasons, especially when it won what is still the longest NFL game ever, against Kansas City in the playoffs the year before, and made it to the Super Bowl (where they were humbled by the Dallas Cowboys).

Over the decades since, I have often wondered if it was merely nostalgia that made me think of this team of my childhood as unique, as having some inimitable combination of talent and character that led it to the greatest gridiron achievement ever. But no, after examining it again over the past few years, I believe this was not just another excellent NFL team. It was a rare combination of mental capacity and toughness, discipline and playfulness, youth and experience, that made for the perfect team. Above all, though, this was an unusually intelligent football team. They later became a doctor, a state senator, a mayor, lawyers, successful businessmen. A sports psychologist who tested them declared that no team had ever scored higher in motivation. And one player who was traded to Green Bay the next year recalled, comparing playbooks, that he felt like he'd gone from Harvard back to high school.

Not that they weren't tough as nails. During pregame strategy sessions, star fullback Larry Csonka would finally have enough of the subtle strategizing, crinkle his nose, already contorted by a long history of breaks, and say, "Let's just line up and knock them on their asses." Another player who was later traded was shocked to find new teammates who wouldn't play with injuries. "Our guys would crawl across broken glass with no clothes on to get to the field," he said. "That made that team what it was." The Dolphins played the perfect season with chipped teeth, a splintered forearm, a bruised liver, a slipped disc, and broken ribs—and that was just one guy, defensive end Bill Stanfill. Others had broken arms, broken noses, you name it. Time would reveal a dark side to such intrepidness. Middle age and beyond would become a minefield of dementia and other concussion-related brain disorders, not to mention constant musculoskeletal pain to remind them of their old job.

It was a team with the poorest owner in the league, a team composed largely of castoffs and has-beens. One of the greatest offensive lines ever was assembled almost wholly from parts other teams had jettisoned. A number of crucial starters shared the scouts' dismissal: "too small and too slow." One defensive starter almost went to veterinary school instead; another, the son of physicians, arrived via the unlikely NFL breeding ground of Amherst College. It was a team saved by a thirty-eight-year-old over-the-hill quarterback, coached by a forty-two-year-old wunderkind with a leviathan chip on his shoulder. It's noteworthy how often players echoed a similar refrain: "I wasn't a gifted athlete," "We weren't the greatest athletes. . . ." This wasn't really true, but it reflected an emphasis on intelligence, teamwork, and a work ethic forged in the struggles of many of their parents, immigrants in the American Midwest.

The fruits of that labor unfolded in the unlikeliest of places. The Greater Miami area was a quiet, relatively uncrowded sprawl of communities, a far cry from what it would become in the 1980s and beyond. The name "Miami" still evoked snowbirds in polyester suits playing shuffleboard on the beach, rather than fashion models and cocaine. Previous attempts at pro football in Florida had failed miserably, and the Dolphins franchise, the state's only major professional sports team, was still so young that most elementary school kids could remember its first season.

Nineteen seventy-two, despite ever-present racial and political tensions and continued national divisiveness about the war in Vietnam, was a simpler time in America. A simpler era in football, too, free of the trappings of a billion-dollar business. Not that the early seventies was a utopia of peace and harmony. The Dolphins marched to perfection in a season of war, political corruption, and barely veiled racism. But Don Shula managed to integrate his team—at least during business hours—and instill a sense of dedication and purpose that blinded them to anything that might distract them from his obsession, which became *their* obsession: to win every game until it was January 14, 1973, and their Super Bowl debacle was supplanted by triumph.

· · ·

"They went 17–0, and it won't happen again," wrote a prescient Dave Anderson in the *New York Times*, just days after the Super Bowl. "The chemistry is too involved, and impossible to repeat, as if the test tube shattered before Don Shula had time to analyze the formula." Shula's laboratory assistants included offensive and defensive coordinators often compared to college faculty, an offensive line coach who played bass fiddle and taught his men psycho-cybernetics, and a lone-wolf scouting genius who gathered the parts no one else saw the value of. The spark to bring this perfect beast to life came the previous January in the form of a traumatic loss on football's biggest stage. When players and coaches all reassembled the next summer, they were joined in their leader's all-consuming drive to obliterate that failure and replace it with its opposite: ultimate victory. It all began, as every season did, with everyone running for twelve minutes in the sweltering soup bowl of July in Miami. While across the bay, as Neil Young would have it, freaks would soon streak down neon streets, podiums would rock, truth would leak, and even Richard Nixon had got soul.

Preperfect I: Who Are These Guys?

> Now is the winter of our discontent
> Made glorious summer . . .
> —*Richard III*

On the morning of July 9, 1972, fifty-four hopeful football players trotted out of the locker room at Biscayne College, a twenty-minute Sunday drive north of downtown Miami. It was the beginning of the seventh annual Miami Dolphins training camp, and these men were mostly rookies and free agents reporting a few days ahead of the rest of the team. Led by their coach, Don Shula, and his assistant coaches, they trotted down the sidewalk from the building to the practice fields, running a gauntlet of adulation through hundreds of fans packed tight on either side. Shula, the successor to Vince Lombardi as the most lauded coach in football, had arrived in Miami two years earlier and immediately turned a hapless expansion club into a playoff team. The next year, 1971, he took them all the way to the Super Bowl, which meant that this was the first training camp the Dolphins opened as champions—of their conference. But they had lost that Super Bowl in humiliating fashion, and so to Shula and most of the veterans who would return later in the week it was anything but a triumphant return. It had been the winter of Don Shula's smoldering furor, and his forced smile as he ran by the fans hid a blinding rage to make this year different.

There was a reason flights to Miami were cheap in summer. The vacation mecca, which for half a century had been promising soothing respite from the bone-chilling winters of New York, Boston, and Chicago, offered no such attraction in July. No need to waste time looking at the weather forecast each morning: ninety degrees, ninety percent humidity, and very likely a thunderstorm at three in the afternoon. If you lived in Miami and weren't lucky enough to escape to Cape Cod or the North Carolina mountains, at least your home and office were air-conditioned. Bad luck if you were a farmworker or a football player. For the latter, July meant brutal wind sprints and blocking and tackling drills in the midday steam bath. There should have been fifty-five players dripping sweat that morning, but one was missing. Eddie Jenkins, a rookie running back, was on Miami Beach, watching cars get turned over.

Jenkins was an African American from Queens who had been recruited, along with future Supreme Court justice Clarence Thomas and others, to the College of the Holy Cross up in Worcester as part of an initiative to boost Black attendance at the Jesuit college. Despite an injury-abbreviated career at a small school, he had somehow been drafted by the Super Bowl Dolphins in the eleventh round. This morning he'd caught an early flight from Jacksonville, where he had been working out in preparation for his shot at the NFL, and on the plane he had sat next to a young woman who was heading to Miami Beach to work for the Congressional Black Caucus at the Democratic National Convention. You wouldn't think that Miami would be a popular choice for mass congregations in summertime, but in 1972, for the last time—and the only time since 1952—both national political conventions took place in the same city, and the locale was Miami Beach. Jenkins had forged an interest in politics and government during his college years, a period of intense national unrest. After his football career, he would become a prosecutor, a private attorney, and a law professor. When his plane landed and the young woman suggested he ride over to Miami Beach with her and check out the scene, he jumped at the chance. It was only nine a.m., and he didn't need to check in at camp until noon.

The convention wasn't to begin until the following night, but when their taxicab crossed the MacArthur Causeway to the island city and began to make its way up Alton Road, Jenkins and his new friend could see that some proceedings had begun early. They passed Flamingo Park and gaped out the window at the village of tents that filled the softball fields. Two thousand self-designated "non-delegates"—those hippies and Zippies, etc.—had arrived from all over the country and saturated the park. Those who could afford it were in the cheap motels and boardinghouses in South Beach. The rest, mostly young, were camping out, sharing free pot, free love, and public nudity while protesting for peace, amnesty, abortion rights, and gay liberation, among other causes. There were fiddlers, flutists, lots of guitar players. There was self-proclaimed Holy Joe, preaching the gospel to anyone who'd listen. "Mescaline! Who wants mescaline?" came the shouts of one vendor. "Hey man," came another voice, "what you gotta see is that Kierkegaard said that the leap of faith can only be made by a cat who can really get into the world of the irrational."

Closer to the Miami Beach Convention Center it looked more like a war zone. The city was swelling not only with conventioneers and protesters and celebrities but also about seventy-five hundred media and ten thousand security forces: local and state police, federal troops, National Guardsmen, plus plainclothesmen from ten different federal agencies. Several hundred members of the Youth International Party were marching from the park up to the convention center for a marijuana "smoke-in," chanting, "We smoke pot, and we like it a lot!" Other groups were making the same march to demonstrate for more sober political causes. (Flying the length of the beaches and back down the bay side was a small plane carrying a banner: PEACE POT PROMISCUITY—VOTE MCGOVERN. A favorite little inspiration of Donald Segretti, head of the "dirty tricks" division of the Nixon campaign.)

Jenkins and the woman left the cab and went their separate ways, she to her meeting and he to take in the scene. In the park, there were gospel singers, folk singers, blues and rock and roll. Allen Ginsberg, unmistakable with his untethered black beard, was cross-legged on the grass, pumping Eastern chords through a harmonium, the smell of incense mixing with the "Om" chanted by the cross-legged crowd massed around him. Abbie Hoffman and Jerry Rubin were in town, Norman Mailer and Arthur Miller, Gloria Steinem and Germaine Greer, even Robert Redford, who had ridden down on a mock train-whistle tour to publicize his new political film, *The Candidate*. After an hour or so, Jenkins figured it was time to get to Dolphin camp, but doing so suddenly seemed a challenging proposition. Traffic was completely stalled, and demonstrators had gotten the idea to swarm the stranded cars and begin shaking them. As police arrived, everyone began running aimlessly, and Jenkins joined them. Finally he spotted an empty taxi in the line of stuck vehicles and jumped in. The cabbie was as invested in getting off the Beach as he was. "Demonstrators were starting fires," Jenkins remembered, "and the cabdriver says we better get the hell out of here, they may start closing bridges." After a heroic effort by the driver, squeezing through narrow alleyways and weaving along back streets, they finally made it across the Broad Causeway way up at Ninety-Sixth Street. Twenty minutes later, as they pulled into Biscayne College, Jenkins was surprised to see over a thousand fans filling the stands around the practice fields while football players were running offensive and defensive drills. When he finally changed and made it out to the field, everyone seemed to know who he was, but not in a good way: "Jenkins, you're late." "Jenkins, Shula's looking for you." Turns out he had read his letter wrong: first practice was ten o'clock, not one o'clock.

· · ·

If a Miami Dolphins football player was to be the object of someone's displeased concern, he might well pray it would be someone other than Coach Don Shula. Always fair and honest but stern, disciplined, perfectionist to a fault and expecting the same of his staff and players, Shula could sniff a missed block or a blown snap count in a practice drill from a hundred yards away. He certainly wasn't going to overlook a missing player on the first day of practice. And it didn't always take three strikes before you were out. No, the last thing a rookie eleventh-round draft choice wanted to do was get on Shula's bad side, especially in the summer of 1972. That soul-crushing defeat to Dallas five months earlier in Super Bowl VI had popped an unsightly dent in the remarkable rise of the Miami team and put fresh paint on the soubriquet no coach wants: the guy who can't win the big one. Now Shula had his team back to absorb the force of his mania, which had been building all winter and spring, and he wasn't going to gloss over any ingredient, however trivial, of a successful Super Bowl campaign.

He had always been a perfectionist, focused on every detail of the job at hand. Even as a kid, he said, "I couldn't understand why anyone else would goof up. On my high school team, I'd point out mistakes before the coach did. That didn't go over great, but I could handle it." "Shula was irritating," said his college coach Herb Eisele. "He insisted on knowing the assignment of every player and why. He wanted to know how it all fitted together, curious, inquisitive about every aspect of the game. He was as intense then as he is now."

When Shula became the Dolphins coach in 1970, the players, after four years under the collegial and easygoing George Wilson, were stunned by the new guy's Spartan regime. On one of the first days of training camp, the offense was running basic pass patterns. The offensive line wasn't even there, just backs and receivers. "Griese was throwing long patterns, where Kiick and I have to block," said Larry Csonka, already the team's star fullback in his third year, "and we would sort of step up to where we were supposed to be. Shula was forty yards downfield and yelled, 'Csonka, what the hell are you doing?' I didn't know what was going on. I thought one of my little boys had run on the field, or my shorts had fallen off or something. Then Shula came running over and explained I had moved out about a step too wide. 'How do you expect to get an angle on a linebacker from over there?' Six inches—that was 'over there' to Shula. That's when it dawned on me I better concentrate every second, because the time you least expect it is when you're going to get Shula's foot in your ass."

Shula's imposing profile, with the Dick Tracy jaw and the somewhat flattened nose from being broken four times in his playing years, became a famous emblem of the work ethic and attention to detail that brought greatness to the Dolphins. Everything "ran on Shula time," remembered Manny Fernandez. "He did everything on the minute, every detail was perfectly scripted." Every huddle in practice needed to end with a perfect clap. The quarterback would call the play—say, "Brown Right 19 Straight on 2, ready, break!"—then everyone clapped on "break," and it better sound like one person clapping: if you don't get the clap right, you know you're not going to get the play right. For years the Dolphins were always the least penalized team in the league. They didn't jump offsides in autumn because all summer long Shula's voice reverberated over the practice fields: "What the hell's wrong with our snap count? Come on, back in the huddle!" It was part of achieving what Shula liked to call the "winning edge." And it all began, each stultifying July, in training camp.

The early 1970s came long before the time when NFL players were, and were treated like, millionaires. They were more like indentured servants. "I'm twenty-six years old," said Csonka, "and I'm kept in training camp for six weeks like I'm a child or a convict—up at seven for breakfast, practice and meetings until ten o'clock at night, in my room at eleven for the check. I've got a wife and two sons that I'm responsible for, but I've got to be in my room at eleven o'clock." Linebacker Doug Swift echoed the atmosphere of incarceration: "The day before you went in was the worst day. It was like the ordeal before starting a jail term." And in 1972 prison camp was going to be even tougher. "This was the year," said Shula, "I wanted total emotional involvement from the players.

Nothing could interfere with what I wanted them to do. . . . I wouldn't permit any outside activities to take their minds away from their responsibilities."

It all began on day one with a Shula staple: the twelve-minute run. It was as simple as it sounds: you run around the perimeter of the practice field for twelve minutes in the middle of the day in Miami in July while coaches record how many laps you complete. Not surprisingly, some players—rookies hoping to impress, veterans who were fitness freaks—took it more seriously than others. Dick Anderson, the starting strong safety, was the reigning twelve-minute king but lost his crown in '72 to rookie John Crisp from UConn, who would never be heard from again. Right before the event, Jim Kiick complained loudly, "If I wanted to run cross-country I would have gone out for it in high school." He and Csonka, the starting backfield the past four years, proceeded to come in dead last as usual. "Csonka was on a sympathy strike with Kiick," deadpanned Shula, whose martinetish discipline always left room for humor. "The worst part," panted Kiick, the hard-partying city kid from New Jersey, sweat pouring off his Fu Manchu mustache, "is running past all those fans in the stands. Here we are supposed to be big pro football players in good shape, and we're dying out there, and the fans laugh at us. It's humiliating."

For others, embarrassment wasn't the worst part. Apparently feeling that hydration would pamper his players, Shula in these early years never allowed water on the practice field. Not after the twelve-minute run, not after the "gassers"—wind sprints from one sideline to the other and back, repeated over and over, making sure you bent and touched each sideline without fail. He later shrugged that policy off as "one of those outdated ideas. Everyone believed it. [Water] was supposed to give you cramps or something." His players remembered differently. "In six years, not a drop of water," recalled Mercury Morris. Said Csonka: "He told us we have two ways of looking at this heat thing down here. We can use it as a negative and hide behind it, or use it to our advantage and make it an asset. So if we can practice for two and a half hours without water in ninety-degree heat, we can become camel-like during the game, and when people come down here, we'll see in the fourth quarter who has their head up or head down. And that literally came to pass." Morris agreed: sometimes, he said, late in a game he would look over to the other side of the Orange Bowl and see the quarterback, his bottom half obscured by heat haze and the eighteen-inch curve of the playing surface, kneeling down, exhausted, with a wet towel over his head, "and we knew we had them. And that was the winning edge."

Early in the '72 camp two defensive linemen, both newcomers, passed out in the heat. Both were trying to get their weight down from the 280s to the 260s by the end of the week to avoid a fine of $10 per pound. Neither made the team. Offensive guard Larry Little collapsed, too, but he was more in the Csonka-Kiick school. "I didn't really pass out," Little said, "I faked it. I told my roommate the night before, I'm not going to let the SOB kill me. So I timed it, and about an hour and a half into practice I started reeling a little and suddenly hit the ground. Trainer put me in the old big red Chevy station wagon we had, took me to the locker room, started packing me in ice."

By this year, though, Shula's third training camp in Miami, the veteran players, despite a lingering complaint here and there, had bought into the program. They had seen the results—a 10–4 playoff year in '70 followed by a Super Bowl appearance the next year. To quarterback Bob Griese, Shula had become a father figure. (To Csonka even more so. "A true Hungarian," he said, "nothing but work. I know another one: my father. When my old man told us to build a barn in thirty days, it meant we'd damn well better have the thing up in twenty-eight days.") To Paul Warfield, Shula resembled nothing less than the famous generals of his boyhood: Eisenhower, Patton, and MacArthur. For a newcomer like Marlin Briscoe, who had been an All-Pro wide receiver on a losing team in Buffalo, coming to Shula's Dolphins was like moving up to a new league: "Shula was amazing. When I got to Miami, I realized that I didn't know the first thing about professional football. And I loved it, from the first day of training camp."

• • •

The fans of South Florida must have still found it hard to believe their team had become a paragon of professional football. It was only three years since they had been pathetic, and only six since they had had a team at all.

Well, there was the ill-fated Miami Seahawks, which played one year, 1946, in the All-America Football Conference (original home of the Cleveland Browns and San Francisco 49ers). Two Seahawks home games in Burdine Stadium—later renamed the Orange Bowl—were postponed by hurricanes, and several others were played in drenching rain before audiences of only a few hundred people. The owners had to concede that Miami was a tourist town, not a sports town, and folded after one year. Almost twenty years later, someone decided to try again: not a wealthy Miami businessman but rather a forty-eight-year-old Lebanese South Dakotan attorney with a Minneapolis practice, eleven children, and nothing resembling wealth.

Joe Robbie liked to say that people held it against him that his father came from the Middle East and he came from the Middle West. A rare bird among team owners, he was a liberal Democrat, a self-made man supporting his family on a comfortable but workingman's salary. His father had immigrated from Lebanon, all alone, at age eleven. Customs officials changed his name from Arabi to Robbie, and the boy made his way out to the little town of Sisseton, South Dakota, where his uncles had settled. Joe Robbie was born there in 1916 and lived a hardscrabble childhood, always working to help out his mother, who sold baked goods, and his father, who ran several small businesses and doubled as the town's police chief. He learned at a young age how to move people's minds with words, and he took a debating scholarship to Northern Normal and Industrial School (now Northern State University). Not long after he graduated, Pearl Harbor was attacked, and Robbie enlisted in the Navy, eventually participating in five Pacific invasions and earning a Bronze Star.

After the war, Robbie went to law school at the University of South Dakota and soon afterward got involved in politics, serving as minority leader in the state house of representatives for two years and winning the Democratic nomination for governor in 1950. At the urging of his friend Hubert Humphrey, whose father served with Robbie in the South Dakota House, Robbie moved his family to Minneapolis. He failed in his political campaigns there but built a successful law practice. And when the Minnesota Vikings were born in 1960, Robbie grabbed a choice five-dollar season ticket and became a fan.

Robbie loved sports, but, having grown up out in Dakota, this was the first time he'd had any particular interest in pro football. Professional team ownership was not even in the back of the mind of a man who'd never earned more than $27,000 in a year. But in early 1965, after working for Humphrey's vice presidential campaign and then at Lyndon Johnson's inauguration, he was in Miami Beach on vacation with his family when he became, in his words, "the beneficiary of venal circumstance." He ran into an acquaintance from the campaign who asked Robbie to represent him in a local lawsuit; a co-plaintiff in the case wanted to start a football franchise in Philadelphia and heard Robbie was old friends with Joe Foss. The former governor of South Dakota and a college buddy of Robbie's, Foss was now the commissioner of the American Football League, fast becoming a legitimate rival to the NFL. Foss told Robbie the AFL wasn't interested in competing with the NFL's Eagles, but he suggested Miami. The Seahawks fiasco was long forgotten, and Miami was growing into a city that could support more than hotels on the beach. Robbie's client was uninterested, so Foss told his old friend: Why not you?

Why not indeed? Robbie had a populous family to feed and not a lot of cash to throw into the venture, but he was a shrewd negotiator and "could squeeze more words into a split second than a tape recorder set on super fast." He began meetings with the league and soon agreed to buy an expansion franchise in Miami for seven and a half million dollars, a sum that he could only dream of. He quickly negotiated for a half million as his share of the AFL's new television deal, enough to pay the first installment of the purchase fee, and he went to visit his friend and fellow Lebanese American, showbiz personality Danny Thomas. Thomas didn't have seven million to throw away, either, but he was enthusiastic, and together they put together a team of investors, with Robbie in control of operations.

For five years, until the venture finally turned a profit, Robbie juggled an ever-changing roster of moneymen, replacing them when they either lost interest or got too interested. He kept them satisfied just long enough, while conducting a small orchestra of banks, surviving on a tangled web of credit. Somehow, when the dust settled, he was left standing with sole control of the team, and it eventually made him a very wealthy man. Until then, he ran the club the way his father had run his gas station: with an eye on every penny. In doing so, he forged a reputation for frugality that rivaled Jack Benny. You couldn't buy a pencil sharpener without him approving it. Phone bills were scrutinized like million-dollar contracts. Players swore they saw him counting towels in the locker room. He canned the caterer who was charging a hundred bucks a game to feed the press box: Let them eat hot dogs. As his counterpart in Houston, Bud Adams, put it, "He's running a two-million-dollar-a-year business like a fruit stand."

To his dismay, press and public scrutiny focused on his cheapness rather than his hard-won success and his many charitable acts. But although he complained about it, he was partly to blame. For instance, in 1972 he demanded that a reference to the $100,000 he had given to charity that year be stricken from his bio in the team yearbook. When the PR department asked why, he told them, "Because when I sit across from Csonka and his agent, I want them to think I'm the meanest son of a bitch in town."

"I liked Joe very much," said Larry King, a Miami radio and newspaper personality at the time, "but he was not likable." "He doesn't light up any rooms," as a *Sports Illustrated* profile went. "He's a shrewd manipulator of men and money, tough as a wharf rat, charming as a rent collector." He was also, both sadly and almost comically, an outrageous alcoholic—"a slovenly drunk," according to King. It was typical for visitors to the owner's box after a game to find him passed out in a chair or on a table, an empty bottle of Wild Turkey nearby. He drank on the plane to away games, drank all weekend, drank on the plane home. He ended most nights passed out on booze. When sober he was candid, outspoken, as likely to walk right by you without so much as a glance as he was to shake your hand. Robbie made plenty of enemies but still managed to be a formidable businessman. He more or less bluffed his way into owning a pro football team with a celebrity friend and a bagful of phantom money, always kept one step ahead of the banks and his fellow investors, and managed to turn a hopeless expansion team into the NFL's greatest team ever.

• • •

The Miami Dolphins started life with a slap and scream of almost twenty-seven thousand fans in the Orange Bowl: Joe Auer, a hometown boy from Coral Gables High, who had played for Georgia Tech and then the Buffalo Bills before being cut, ran back the opening kickoff of the opening game of 1966 for a touchdown. Danny Thomas sprinted down the sidelines with him for the last forty yards, right into the end zone, where he joyously pounded Auer's back. Behind the end zone, in a sixteen-thousand-gallon tank, Flipper the dolphin, on loan from the Miami Seaquarium out on Virginia Key, responded to the unexpected score (via a signal from his keeper) with a spectacular leap and flip. Auer, a civil engineer, artist, and owner of lions and gators, among more typical farm animals, also scored a touchdown on the final offensive play of that inaugural season, a thirty-eight-yard touchdown pass from John Stofa with thirty-eight seconds left that gave the Dolphins a 29–28 victory over the Houston Oilers. The cheers of twenty thousand fans echoed in a mostly empty stadium, and the Dolphins were 3–11. Auer, the team MVP that first year, was gone eighteen months later upon the arrival of Csonka and Kiick. Danny Thomas left even earlier, selling out his stake in the team in the first off-season.

The early foibles of Robbie's team became local lore. They held training camp in St. Petersburg, where Robbie got a cheap deal housing them in a motor inn and practicing on a slipshod field of loose sod thrown on top of seashells. There was no locker room; players dressed in their motel rooms. For their first exhibition game, they endured a hot, rickety eight-hour flight in an old DC-7 whose broken pressurization system forced them to fly no higher than twelve thousand feet. After their very first home game ever, an exhibition game in the Orange Bowl, the players found themselves locked out of their own locker room. They wandered the hallways exhausted, soaked in sweat, for fifteen minutes until a janitor could be found.

Joe Auer was just one of a cast of colorful players: rejects from other teams, free agents trying to jump-start a pro career by latching on to an AFL expansion team. Most notable among them was Wahoo McDaniel, a Choctaw Native American from Oklahoma and Texas, a fun-loving boozer and bruiser who had been a popular player for the New York Jets before being made available in the expansion draft. McDaniel led the partying in the strip-mall bars of St. Pete that first training camp and anchored the defense as middle linebacker for three years (sporting only his nickname, WAHOO, on the back of his jersey) before being finally let go after yet another carousing incident. In this case, after a night of barhopping, he backed his rental car into another car and got into a brawl with the owner, who happened to be an off-duty policeman. He later became a much bigger star as a professional wrestler, famously entering the ring with full Indian headdress and winning the National Wrestling Alliance heavyweight title five times.

It has become a bromide of South Florida sportswriters, and fans old enough to remember, to look back at the Dolphins' formative years with mockery, but in fact the team's first three seasons were fairly respectable. Three, four, and then five wins, ending that third year 5–8–1 and smack in the middle of the Eastern Division. An expansion team begins with rookies and only those veterans other teams were willing to give away for nothing; you can't expect a winning team in three years. Much of the credit for those decent seasons must go to the fact that they had a very respectable NFL coach. Robbie had managed to hire George Wilson, who had been Shula's boss while head coach of the Detroit Lions and who had led Detroit to the NFL championship in 1957—still the last time the Lions won the title.

Shula described him as a "man to man type of coach, who dealt with players like one player to another," and indeed Wilson's style was far from the Paul Brown teacher model, the aloof tactician Tom Landry of Dallas, or Shula's own all-consuming drive for perfection. His idea of preparing a game plan was to walk off the practice field with his arm over his quarterback's shoulders and ask, "So, Bobby, what are we going to cook up for Sunday?" On the most scorching day of training camp in Miami, when he saw his players flagging—or maybe when he'd had enough sun himself—he'd march them straight over to the pool and order them to jump in, commencing a practice-ending pool party. Once after a training camp meeting Wilson took aside Csonka and Kiick, already earning their reputation as carousers, and said, "If you got something good going somewhere and you're going to miss curfew, give me a call." As Csonka put it, that was the kind of guy you wanted to win for, if only so he kept his job.

Not surprisingly, the players loved him. Georgia country boy Bill Stanfill, the nation's top college lineman who was drafted number one by Miami in 1969, remembered thinking after his rookie year, "Lord help me, if this is what pro football is all about, playing under Wilson, I'd like to play here twenty or thirty years." Veterans like Nick Buoniconti, who arrived (also in 1969) after seven years playing linebacker for the Boston Patriots, was fond of him too. "It was a free atmosphere," said Buoniconti. "There was very little discipline. He tried to treat everyone as an adult. He believed if you're treated like a man, you'll act like a man." Of course, these were mostly very young men, and under Wilson there developed a fraternity-like atmosphere. Rookies were hazed like freshman pledges, including being thrown in the lake at Saint Andrew's School, where the team trained at the time. On "rookie night" they were taken to a seaside bar and forced to chew tobacco and then drink warm beer followed by pineapple wine. Mercury Morris, another '69 rookie, remembered crawling across the sand to the ocean to throw up and then being told he now had room for more beverage. By mid-August he'd had enough, and he even went public, writing in a diary for the *Miami News*, "We're all getting sick of the rookie bit. The harassment is not as bad as it was at first, but it's still here, and I hate it.

Most of it's high school stuff, and I'll probably get tossed in the lake for saying it in public." He did.

Morris was less impressed than others with good old George Wilson. When he heard the coach tell a local booster club that he was hopeful the team could win half their games that year, he got up afterward and declared, "Did I just hear Coach say that it's okay to lose seven games? Well, that's not okay with me. I'm here because I want to go fourteen and oh." That didn't go down well with Wilson, but it's what got Morris his column in the *News*. He remembered Wilson smoking during a pregame pep talk, saying, "'Well, if we get a few breaks, and the ball bounces our way, we might come out on top. So go out there and get 'em.' And five or six guys were smoking along with him, and they'd leave their stubs in the locker room so they could smoke the rest at halftime. And I'm thinking, this is pro football?"

Morris's dreams of perfection notwithstanding, a .500 year in 1969 would have continued the young team's ascent. But year four turned into a disastrous backward stumble. Even God couldn't help, it seemed. The Dolphins, alone among pro football franchises, from the very beginning preceded their home games with lengthy religious invocations. It wasn't the brainchild of Shula when he arrived, as some might have thought, considering that Shula was a gung-ho Catholic who attended Mass every morning of the week. Joe Robbie was an active Catholic, too, and from the beginning many fans, as well as players and sportswriters, were annoyed by the "increasingly boring, hypocritical and presumptuous . . . prayer meetings" (*Miami Herald*) followed by "displays of chauvinism": military bands banging out hymn after hymn.

Robbie had plenty of fodder for his prayers. Furiously shuffling bank loans to stay afloat, he was consumed in the off-season by an attempted mutiny by one of his fellow owners of the team who was trying to force Robbie out. Robbie prevailed, as always, but he kept putting off renewing Wilson's original three-year contract, which had expired. Finally, in March, he announced that Wilson and his staff would have their contracts renewed for the 1969 season. That was very different from a new multiyear contract, and Wilson's feathers were ruffled. "I don't know what, but something's up," he told a reporter. Indeed, Robbie was already thinking of how he could achieve a coaching upgrade. Although he acknowledged that the team's progress was above average for an expansion team, perhaps Wilson's good-old-boy style just wasn't enough for Robbie's unremitting drive for success. And if the one-year-renewal snub was intended to create a more obvious need for change, it worked like a charm.

Wilson was unusually short-tempered during the preseason, even before injuries began to cripple his team. "The boss is not himself," noted one assistant. Meetings were abruptly canceled. When Jim O'Brien of the *Miami News* wrote a story about linebacker Rudy Barber, who claimed he had been cut because he was Black, Wilson lashed out at O'Brien, even threatening him physically. He discontinued his daily press briefings, not to mention drinking at bars with reporters. Then his team began to fall apart. Offensive linemen Larry Little and Norm Evans sprained their knees. Even worse, it appeared Larry Csonka may have taken one too many shots to the head. Csonka finished an exhibition game with ice and cotton stuffed up his nose, which he'd broken yet again. He was then declared out indefinitely with a bone fracture in the base of his skull, pending medical examinations to "determine if his pro football career is at an end." And that was all in the preseason.

When the regular season began, things got worse—aside from the opening kickoff, which rookie Mercury Morris took 105 yards for a touchdown (the second time in its four years Miami had returned the season's first kickoff all the way). Later in the season, however, Morris bungled a punt return by running backward and getting tackled in his own end zone for a safety. "A high school play," Wilson snorted after the game. In another game, a perfect Bob Griese pass bounced off Stan Mitchell and into the hands of an Oakland Raider defender, who raced sixty-eight yards for a touchdown in a game the Dolphins barely lost. Slouched on a locker room bench like a man whose wife has left him, Wilson mumbled, "The Man upstairs says this isn't it, I guess." In the third game Mitchell, who had replaced Csonka, separated his shoulder and was done for the year. (Luckily, Csonka was able to come back the next week.) In the next game, wide receiver Howard Twilley dislocated his elbow and was gone for the season. A week after that their tight end was gone, and punter Larry Seiple, who had been a pretty good running back in college, was playing tight end in the NFL. (He led the team with forty-one catches that year.)

When they won their first game in seven tries, against the lowly Buffalo Bills, Wilson finally cheered up—and then some. But his prescient optimism sounded delusionary at the time. "This is gonna be a hell of a football team," he said. "It's a year or maybe two away from taking everything. We've got guys in the key positions like Griese and Csonka and Kiick and Buoniconti and Anderson. All we need are fill-ins to give us the strength and depth a championship team needs." The next week they barely lost up in New York to the Super Bowl champion Jets, and Larry King was right behind Wilson: "Has there ever been a better 1–6–1 team in pro football than the Dolphins? They could just as easily be 6–1–1. It's apparent the team is just one year away from championship caliber." Inspired, they went up to Boston and beat the Patriots at Boston College's muddy Alumni Stadium—but in the process lost Buoniconti for several weeks and Griese for the season, both with knee sprains. Now the wheels were really off, and the Dolphins lost badly the next three weeks to mediocre Buffalo, Houston, and Boston.

Wilson and the Dolphins' fourth season ended with a disappointing 3–10–1 record, although it looked worse than it was. Injuries had irrefutably sabotaged the year, but they had played the elite Jets and Raiders—twice each—as closely as could be. Still, your record is your record, and Wilson's gave Joe Robbie ever more justification for his quest for a new coach. The players were aware all year that Wilson was on his last legs, and they tried to stand up for him. "Wilson is a great leader," said Buoniconti. "He is respected by the players. Usually you get a coach who knows football but can't get along with the players, or one who is good with the players but isn't that good in football. Wilson is solid. This guy is tops." And when they won their third game near the end of the season, beating Denver in the Orange Bowl, Csonka swore that before the game the team had dedicated winning it for Wilson and his coaches.

But Wilson himself knew that the loyalty of the players wasn't going to keep him in his position. One Tuesday after a day off following one of those late-season losses, the players arrived at practice to find a trash can full of beer and ice. Wilson waited until they were all assembled around the can and just said, "You boys have a good practice." And he left.

· · ·

Things were getting almost as uncomfortable for Don Shula up in Baltimore. When his team slipped to 8–5–1 in 1969, after disgracing themselves in Super Bowl III the previous year, he was feeling a similar pressure from above and below. Owner Carroll Rosenbloom was enraged by the loss to smug Joe Namath

and the Jets of the supposedly inferior AFL, and Shula's relationship with his
players soured as well. He pushed them harder than ever, but this team of
veterans didn't appreciate being screamed at.

So when Shula got a phone call after that season asking if he'd be interested in moving to Miami to coach a losing expansion team, he didn't just hang
up. The caller, surprisingly, was an old college classmate named Bill Braucher,
who now was a sportswriter for the *Miami Herald*. Braucher and the *Herald*'s
sports editor, Edwin Pope, had been meeting with Joe Robbie, who was intent
on replacing George Wilson. Robbie had first offered the job, including a percentage of team ownership, to University of Alabama coaching legend Bear
Bryant, but Bryant had turned him down. Robbie was complaining to the
two sportswriters that he couldn't find the right coach, when Pope suggested
Shula: "Hell, why don't you go right to the top and get the best there is?" Robbie
pounded his fist down on his desk. "I remember him just about jumping out
of his seat," said Pope. "'That's the guy!'" Robbie hadn't considered Shula, as
he was under contract to Rosenbloom and apparently in a solid position. But
Braucher agreed to give Shula a call to see if he'd be interested. Robbie couldn't,
as it was against NFL rules to offer employment to another team's coach without
the owner's permission.

"Don, would you be interested in coming down to Miami as head coach
and also part owner?" It was an unusual conversation to be having, to say the
least. Sportswriters didn't usually offer NFL head-coaching jobs. "Are you
making me an offer, Bill?" "Well, let's just say that I have the authority to speak
about it." Well aware of NFL regulations, Shula told Braucher he would have to
ask the Colts' permission before he discussed possibilities with Robbie. Carroll
Rosenbloom, however, was traveling in Japan, so Shula instead called his
son, Steve Rosenbloom, who had recently been named president of the Colts
organization. Steve didn't mention his father's dissatisfaction with the coach
or his intention to replace him. He told Shula that he understood this was a
possibility for advancement and that the team wouldn't stand in his way. He
had permission to negotiate with Robbie.

Robbie, as soon as he learned of Shula's interest and the permission from
Steve Rosenbloom, arranged a meeting with Shula in Washington at the Marriott
Hotel, where they talked for three hours. Shula was impressed with Robbie's
sharp mind and even more so with his resolve to bring a championship to Miami.

He was also very attracted to the idea of having part ownership of the team, a perk that Braucher had mentioned and Robbie confirmed. One thing worried him, though: George Wilson was his friend and had given him his first NFL job at Detroit and then recommended him for the head coaching position at Baltimore. He hated the idea of usurping George's position. But Robbie assured him that no matter what his decision was, Wilson was out.

The next week Shula and his wife, Dorothy, flew to Miami well under press radar. Robbie had his wife, Elizabeth, meet them at the airport and inconspicuously whisk them off to their room at the Jockey Club, the newest and most prestigious establishment in downtown Miami. There was an awkward moment when they ran into sports columnist Elinor Kaine and the Coach himself, Vince Lombardi, at the restaurant there that night. But it was easy enough for Don and Dorothy to say they were vacationing in Miami too; that's what people did there, after all. The next day Elizabeth Robbie, who would have preferred to be at the horse track in Hialeah but who was apparently a cheaper alternative to hiring a car, picked up the Shulas again and ferried them back to the Robbie home in Miami Shores, an upscale neighborhood ten miles north of the city, where negotiations continued. Shula was all but convinced at this point. Robbie was offering him by far his biggest contract ever: five years at $70,000 a year plus an appointment as vice president and general manager, with ten percent ownership of the team, a deal that could well make him a millionaire in those five years. Even more important to Shula was that he would have complete control of all football-related decisions.

A week later, on February 18, 1970, just twenty-two days after that first phone call from Braucher, Don and Dorothy were back at the Jockey Club, an opulent setting for the official announcement. Reporters got a rare chance to rumble their old Ford Falcons and Chevy Novas down the sleek curving driveway off Biscayne Boulevard through tall, waving palm trees, then made their way to the pool deck, where a podium had been set up under clear skies and a rising full moon. Robbie, Shula, their families, and the team investors were all there. Robbie had told George Wilson of his firing and replacement only hours before, although certainly Wilson had known the writing was on the wall. Bitter and defensive, he had somehow agreed to be photographed shaking hands with his successor before the press conference, smiling and wishing him the best, before getting out of there. Robbie announced that George would always have a place in the Dolphins organization (though not necessarily a paid position—he made that clear), and he gave him a lifetime pair of season tickets. Wilson never used them.

At seven thirty p.m. Robbie introduced Don Shula to the Miami media. Doing his best to dispel any sudden Super Bowl fervor, Shula told them, "I'm no miracle worker. I don't have any magic formulas that I'm going to reveal if I ever write a book. I'm straightforward and rely on hard work." In a little preview of what the Dolphins had in store for them, he said, "First I plan to sit down and watch all the films of Miami's games last year. Then I'll grade every player on every play and see what I come up with at the end." Grade every player on every play? "Sure. I can do about three games, offense or defense, each day."

When Shula met forty-seven of his veteran players for a one-day get-acquainted workout in April, they were meeting not only their new head coach and a new coaching staff but also a completely new approach. One very large young man approached Shula, shook his hand, and said, "Coach, I'm your right guard, Larry Little." Shula looked him up and down and asked him his weight. "Two eighty-five, Coach." Shula just walked away. A week or two later, when Little received his letter telling him when to report to camp, it also designated what his weight should be that day: two sixty-five. Upon meeting Larry Csonka, Shula's first words were that when he saw him in July he wanted him fifteen pounds lighter: two thirty-five. "I haven't been that light since high school," Csonka retorted before Shula cut him off: "You will play better at that weight." "But I just ran a four-seven forty." "Lose fifteen and you'll run a four-five." Players felt like the team had been taken over by Weight Watchers rather than a new coach. This had been the major problem between Shula and Bubba Smith at Baltimore. "Bubba was a great athlete who was too fat," Shula said simply. "When the blubber came off, he became one of the finest players in the game—but it was hard on him, and he resented it." Smith never reconciled himself with Shula's style, but the young Dolphins in 1970 all reported to camp at the requested weight. They knew Shula was the big time, and they wanted to win—and keep their jobs.

Still, they were generally not happy about Wilson being axed. "I feel like I've lost a father, I really do" was Nick Buoniconti's reaction when he heard the news. "Wilson treated you like a man," not an overweight kid, said Jim Kiick. They weren't any happier when training camp began. For the veterans, that was two weeks later than normal. Buoniconti and other player reps had been in New York negotiating for better pensions and insurance benefits, and the players' union was on strike until the new contracts were signed. When the veterans finally reported, there were only five days of practice before the first exhibition game. At their first meeting, Shula said, "I know you guys are used to having a big party here. Well, the party's over. Look around the room. By the end of camp, half of you are going to be gone." He also announced a special practice schedule for this strike-shortened camp: instead of two practices a day, there would be four.

They'd begin at seven in the morning with a short workout. Then, after breakfast, a nine-thirty meeting to prepare for the ten a.m. practice, an hour and a half in full pads—and by ten a.m. in July the Miami sun is beating down hard. They practiced the running game and defending the running game. A break for lunch and rest until three, when they had another meeting and then another hour and a half at peak afternoon heat working on the passing game from both sides of the ball. Dinner at six, and then a final workout at seven thirty until dark to work on what hadn't gone perfectly during the day. A quick shower before a final nine-thirty meeting to review the day's work for an hour, including film.

"Until dark" was the official quitting time, but generally they kept running plays "until he was happy," as Csonka put it. All that would be left in the sky of the summer sunset was one of those magenta streaks that seem designed by a city of Miami marketing team. The few fans who remained couldn't tell who was on the field. Some weary player shouted out a request for miners' helmets, but Shula didn't even smile. "Okay, everybody! Once more. Let's get it right."

Lights-out was at eleven fifteen, but there was no real need for a bed check that year. One reporter described the players at the end of the day as resembling survivors of the Bataan Death March. "We were all so bushed," said Norm Evans, "that we'd run out of the classroom and race for the sack. Then it would start over again the next morning." On the other hand, said Mercury Morris, "Guys hated to go to bed at night because they knew when they woke up they were going right back to that field."

"You'd say to yourself skip breakfast," said Bob Griese. "After that seven a.m. workout you were afraid to eat because you knew the ten a.m. workout was going to be hot. Then you were too tired to eat lunch, and you told yourself you'd skip that one too and just wait for dinner. But by then you were so sore and hot and tired you just said to hell with it and went to bed." Surely they ate food, but joking about it eased the misery. Somebody piped up at a meeting that they felt more like strippers than football players, they were taking the clothes off and putting them back on so often. "We were bitching all the time," remembered Larry Seiple. "Screaming, 'We can't take it anymore . . .'" (They kept the outbursts to themselves. Shula had immediately made it clear that they had another option: "If it's too tough for you," he would say, "pack up and go home. We don't want quitters.")

"You and your goddamn Shula," Csonka said to Braucher as the team tottered off to their lunch break on the second day. Decades of distance did little to dull the memory. "As grueling as practices were, it was more grueling in the classroom than on the field," Csonka remembered long afterward. "We were completely sick of Shula in a matter of days. That guy was possessed. . . . But I think within a few weeks we started to show signs of becoming the team we were going to become."

Slowly, they were all coming around. Even Buoniconti, who had rued the loss of George Wilson, had to say, "This guy is something else. He's so thorough it's unbelievable." One player after another noted that under Shula things had changed overnight. Like going from sandlot ball suddenly to professional football, as one put it. Every minute of every day was planned in advance. "We were impressed," said Griese, despite the grumbling stomach. "He was always chomping at the bit to get on the practice field. I could tell from his intensity, this was going to be something good. A complete turnaround from what we had." If they didn't know it already, they got the idea during one of the first preseason games when the Dolphins were called for offsides, a penalty Shula apparently disagreed with. He kept haranguing the line judge, "Come over here! What kind of a call is that?" until finally the official looked back. "Come on, Don, it's only five yards." "Five yards?" Shula screamed back. "Five yards is my whole life!"

The arrival of Shula and the 1970s brought another welcome change. Even in the late sixties, the vacation land of sun and surf was no dream destination for Black players. In 1967, Ray Bellamy, the first ever Black player for the University of Miami football team, received a letter warning him to quit the team or be lynched. Larry Little, who grew up in Miami and played college football in Florida, never played against white players until he entered the

NFL. Though not as notorious as some of the cities of the Deep South, Miami was a bastion of Jim Crow. In 1968 and 1970, riots had broken out in the Black communities of Overtown and Liberty City in response to poor living conditions and perceived racist attitudes of the police, government, and local white business owners. As late as 1982, the *Economist* noted, "Miami is not a good city in which to be black."

African Americans had had a presence in Miami from the very beginning. In the nineteenth century, people who had escaped enslavement in Georgia and other Southern states made their way to what became Miami and Key Biscayne, where they could hope to gain passage to the British Bahamas and live free. When Henry Flagler was building the Florida East Coast Railway in the 1890s, some of the labor was provided by Black prisoners via "convict leasing," a system of forced penal labor that Florida was one of the last states to outlaw. But a number of Northern Blacks also worked on the railroad, and many of them then stayed in Miami to work construction or farm their own land. When 343 male residents, mostly workmen, voted for incorporation of the city of Miami in 1896, more than a third of the group was Black. Early in the twentieth century about forty percent of Miami's population was people of color, mostly Bahamians and African Americans, but they were crammed together by decree in a small section in the northwest quadrant of the city. "Colored Town," as it was called for decades, eventually became Overtown.

Throughout the first two-thirds of the century, Blacks mainly lived there and in the nearby housing project of Liberty City, built during the Depression. Miami was firmly segregated; in a seaside vacation paradise, Blacks were barred from all beaches until 1945, when they were given a sandy patch on Virginia Key, a small barrier island next to Key Biscayne. Even after the laws were reformed twenty years after that, Miami remained segregated culturally, and Blacks for a long time were uncomfortable at the big public beaches on Miami Beach and Key Biscayne. When Mercury Morris was in town for the college all-star game at the end of 1968, he found that on Miami Beach, "if you were Black and didn't have business there, you weren't welcome after dark." Six months later, as a new Dolphin, he learned that players looking for a house to rent were often told that Blacks were not allowed in that neighborhood.

When Shula arrived, he saw that the team ate separately, roomed separately in training camp and on the road, and even polarized themselves in the common shower room. Unfortunately, this was the norm in the NFL at the time. Mercury Morris had seen it on his first day of rookie camp: "There's a de facto segregation being practiced here, and it's as much my black brothers' fault as anyone else's." He did his best to mix up the dining tables and even the shower room but didn't dare once the veterans arrived. Marv Fleming, though, arriving in 1970 from Green Bay as a two-time Super Bowl champ, was having none of it. Unlike some teammates, he'd grown up and played football among whites in California, and as an extroverted young entrepreneur with "substantial oil, real estate and stock investments," he was used to doing business and socializing in the white world. He also happened to be coming from one of the only NFL teams where the coach, Vince Lombardi, had worked hard to create a color-blind team. As Dave Hyde reported, Fleming ridiculed the situation he saw when he was introduced to his new team in Miami. "All the blacks over here?" He pointed to the other side of the locker room. "All the whites over here? *You guys don't mind if I dress right here in the middle, do you?*"

Don Shula didn't need any more of a hint. He immediately embarked on his first project in Miami: the integration of the Dolphins. He rearranged the locker room into an offensive side and a defensive side to force racial mixing there and assigned Blacks and whites to room together on the road. "He even put afro picks, afro combs, and afro sheen in the locker room," said Mercury Morris. "He did it not to be a pioneer, but simply to do things the right way."

As Morris implied, Shula's motivation was not necessarily humanitarian: his concern was not equality but success. On the other hand, although as Shula's salary had grown over the years he had evolved from a Kennedy Democrat to a Nixon and Agnew man, players like Morris felt he was still "fairly liberal" when it came to race. He had no problem, for instance, inviting Otto Stowe and his white wife to his home for dinner, whereas the players had the strong suspicion that George Wilson had a thing against both Morris and linebacker Norm McBride, whom Wilson cut, because of their mixed marriages. Edwin Pope complained in a 1969 column that Morris, the NCAA's second-leading rusher, was barely being used and that the Dolphins were the only team in pro football without a Black offensive regular. (Larry Little was just beginning to take over the right guard spot).

Many players may have welcomed Shula's initiative to break up the "de facto segregation," but the forced mixing of roommates must have been awkward in some cases. Some matchups, like Griese and Warfield, seemed natural. Those two might have stayed up till all hours discussing the finer points of post patterns and umbrella defenses if they weren't both intent on getting a good night's sleep before a long day of practice. Others, though, seemed like odd couples. Maulty Moore, for instance, had grown up in a small, segregated Florida town, played for all-Black Bethune-Cookman College, and was a rookie defensive lineman in 1972. He'd never played with white players, much less roomed with them. And Vern Den Herder, his new roommate, didn't know much about Blacks, having grown up in Sioux City, Iowa. But despite competing for the same starting job, they got along fine. And the Curtis Johnson–Tim Foley room was like *The Mod Squad* meets *Bob Newhart*. But it all seemed to work out, and by 1972 the Dolphins felt and displayed a team unity that players would always remember, a feeling of togetherness that carried over onto the playing field. When Marlin Briscoe, a veteran who had experienced the NFL's racism in several cities, arrived in Miami, he said, "It was so different from any other team I'd played on or knew. No other team was like Miami's when I got there. It was the first time I saw black and white unite."

And yet, in 1972, Shula's third year, still only five of the Dolphins' twenty-two starters, and fourteen of the forty on the team roster, were Black. The defense had only one Black starter, Curtis Johnson. (Lloyd Mumphord did come in often in passing situations.) As surprising as this seems today, the Dolphins were about average in this regard. Equality was slow to come to pro football. The NFL had a number of Black players in its first decade, but in 1934 an unspoken agreement among the owners suddenly banned them from the league. Although the Rams began reintegration by signing Kenny Washington in 1947, most teams did not follow suit until 1952. The Washington Redskins' notoriously racist owner, George Preston Marshall, refused to have any Black players until forced to in 1962. In 1972, well after the 1964 Civil Rights Act and desegregation, only about a third of NFL players were Black. (By 2020, more than two-thirds were.) And in 1972 the University of Florida's first Black football player, Willie Jackson, was still a senior.

· · ·

The arrival of Don Shula in 1970 had South Florida football fans buzzing about a new era. Adding to the atmosphere was the advent, finally, of the AFL-NFL merger. The American Football League—the fourth league in history with that name—had been formed in 1960, giving birth to the future NFL teams the Jets (originally Titans), Patriots, Bills, Oilers, Chargers, Broncos, Raiders, and Chiefs (originally the Dallas Texans). Unlike all the previous rivals to the NFL, the AFL thrived, and by the middle of the decade bidding wars between the leagues for top prospects were financially straining both leagues. They finally agreed to a merger just before the Dolphins' first season in 1966. A new AFL-NFL World Championship Game between the champions of the two leagues would be held at the end of that season, the leagues would conduct a joint college draft beginning the next year, and in 1970 the junior league would be absorbed into the NFL. Of course, to call it the "world championship" was a bit overblown; football was played only in the U.S. But the phrase stuck, even after the name of the game went Super.

So as the new decade arrived the Dolphins were an NFL team, with the league's most heralded coach. The commencement of the exhibition season in August rewarded the anticipation. They won in Pittsburgh, and the next week over sixty thousand fans were in the Orange Bowl to see them beat Cincinnati. In their previous four seasons they were lucky to get half that many spectators for a regular-season game. No Miami team had ever won as many as three straight games, but soon they were going for four straight with Shula's old team, the Colts, visiting. In an era when preseason games were played to win, the resentment Shula had left behind in Baltimore and the enthusiasm he was catalyzing in Miami made this feel more like a playoff game. *Sports Illustrated* sent its top NFL guy down to cover it, and he noted that even the prostitutes on Collins Avenue were asking for tickets to the Friday-night game in lieu of cash. Joe Robbie had temporary bleachers from Biscayne College carted over to the Orange Bowl to boost capacity to 76,712 and giddily declared, "If we beat the Colts it'll blow the lid off this town." This may have sounded optimistic for an exhibition game, but fans filled every seat and the Dolphins' 20–13 victory shook the old stadium like it was December. No one seemed to notice, as one reporter did, that Baltimore coach Don McCafferty had treated it like the practice game it was: "Much of the second half he used a young offensive line, young linebackers and old Earl Morrall." Although Miami lost the final two preseason games, season ticket sales soared to more than twenty-six thousand, and average attendance that year almost doubled. Robbie's gambit was already paying off.

George Wilson would later claim that the nucleus of the Super Bowl team was already in place when he left. Wilson did have Griese, Csonka, Kiick, Morris, Twilley, Little, Evans, Buoniconti, Fernandez, Stanfill, Anderson, and Mumphord, although none of those exceptional players—with the possible exception of Buoniconti—had yet fulfilled their potential, either because of youth, weight, or coaching. But 1970 brought much more than Don Shula. To begin with, just a few weeks before Robbie began talking to Shula, renowned personnel director Joe Thomas made perhaps his greatest move. He convinced the Browns, who desperately needed a quarterback, to accept the Dolphins' number one draft pick in that week's college draft in exchange for the league's premier wide receiver, Paul Warfield. (Griese's eyes must have lit up like it was still Christmas.) Thomas then presided over what is certainly one of the best drafts for any team ever. In one day he acquired Jake Scott, Jim Mandich, Tim Foley, and Curtis Johnson, and the next day he added linebacker Mike Kolen. He also that spring traded for Fleming, Green Bay's excellent blocking tight end, and picked up a basketball player turned offensive lineman named Wayne Moore. When the dust settled on training camp, free agents Bob Kuechenberg, Doug Swift, and Garo Yepremian were also there. That's eleven new players in 1970 who would all be integral components of the Super Bowl teams.

And although Shula didn't have much—or anything—to do with most of these acquisitions, he had everything to do with who stayed. By the end of training camp, he had fulfilled his opening-day promise: about half of last year's team was gone. Only three players—Twilley, Evans, and Karl Noonan—remained from the 1966 expansion team. This was Shula's team now. Whether that was a good thing was not immediately apparent, as the 1970 season turned into a roller coaster that at times seemed like it might fly right off the rails. In the season opener against the Boston Patriots in Harvard's old stadium, the Patriots' home for just that year, Shula endured a 27–14 fiasco. Griese was sacked eight times, sending high-strung new offensive line coach Monte Clark to the hospital, fearful of a heart attack. Shula ripped into his new team in the locker room in a blue-streaked tirade, screaming that they would be objects of ridicule when they got back to Miami, and could only laugh later at the comment of a reporter, who'd overheard, that he shouldn't worry, the team had already been an object of ridicule for four years.

The team quickly responded to this poor performance and notched four straight wins, including first-ever victories against the Raiders and the Jets. The future was coalescing now as the offensive line began to dominate, Griese started relying on the running of Csonka and Kiick, and Paul Warfield brought transcendent grace to the Orange Bowl. Against Oakland, he gathered in a Griese pass crossing the middle of the field, faked out one defensive back, left another a motionless spectator by performing a full 360-degree pirouette without breaking stride, and finally cut between two more defenders and landed in the end zone. The home crowd was stunned for a moment and then broke into a standing ovation. "It happened instinctively," the professorial Warfield explained afterward. "There's really nothing to elaborate. But I'm pleased the crowd reacted so warmly."

When the Cleveland Browns visited in week six, the fans welcomed the Dolphins with their first-ever sellout crowd. Inexplicably, though, the four-game winning streak rubber-banded into a miserable skid worse than anything George Wilson and Flipper had seen. (The old porpoise disappeared a year before the coach, when Joe Robbie refused to pay the Seaquarium for the costs of transporting him and maintaining his tank.) Cleveland silenced the crowd 28–0, and when Shula returned to Baltimore the next week, the Colts avenged the preseason loss with a 35–0 thumping of their old coach. The Dolphins stumbled into Philadelphia the following week, sure of a respite against the struggling Eagles. But after three quarters they found themselves down 24–0, sufferers of an astonishing 0–87 score over the past three games. Griese was given a mercy benching in the fourth quarter, and backup John Stofa threw two long touchdown passes and made the game respectable. This led the fans, along with some of the press, to call for Stofa to replace Griese, but Shula stood firmly behind Griese and was rewarded, as his quarterback and team found themselves and wrapped up their season with six straight wins and an impressive 10–4 record. They flew out to play the Raiders in the playoffs, but their winning streak sank into a muddy field at the Oakland Coliseum. Griese hit Warfield crossing just in front of the goalpost for a 7–0 lead but had trouble moving after that. The ball slipped in his hand as he tried to hit Warfield for another one, resulting in a catastrophically underthrown ball easily intercepted by Willie Brown for a fifty-yard touchdown. A fourth-quarter touchdown pass brought them back to 21–14, but that was it. Shula had worked a minor miracle in Miami, but once again his season ended in a loss. Still, there was no question that after his disappointing final season in Baltimore, Don Shula had his winning edge back. Joe Robbie felt better than ever about his investment, and not a single Dolphins fan regretted the hoopla of last summer.

　　Shula's second training camp began with another tangle. In '70 it was the strike; in '71 it was the holdout of Butch and Sundance. Kiick and Csonka, that is. The starting backfield since their rookie year in 1968, the two runners—Kiick the city boy from Jersey and Csonka the Ohio farm boy—had become best friends, sharing a fondness for, shall we say, wine, women, and song, along with anti-authoritarianism and comedy in the line of duty. In December 1969 the *Herald*'s Bill Braucher heard the two running backs had been calling themselves after the characters in the new Robert Redford–Paul Newman hit, *Butch Cassidy and the Sundance Kid*, and wrote a funny column about it. Kiick was the leading rusher those first two seasons, as well as the more prolific catcher and scorer, so he was Butch. Csonka, the future Hall of Famer, was still the sidekick. While later it would primarily be vice versa, it was Csonka back then who had to do the blocking for Kiick. "If wily Butch Cassidy keeps using the Sundance Kid for a shield," wrote Braucher, "old Sundance soon will look like a Spanish-American War veteran.

　　"Your head keeps getting flatter," observed Butch.

　　"I can only get so ugly and no uglier," growled Sundance, who persists in using his head for a wrecking ball. . . . He missed the first three games when the wrecking-ball mechanism registered "tilt."

　　"Those guys were in a dangerous profession, being outlaws," said Kiick years later. "And they made light of it, had a good time. We made light of our job and had a good time also." They continued trading lines like Butch and the Kid. When Kiick found himself buried beneath a landslide of Los Angeles Rams, he looked up at Csonka staring down at him sympathetically and quoted the film: "Who *are* these guys?" They were photographed in period costume on the cover of *Esquire* and riding horses down Collins Avenue and along the beach, although in reality Csonka saddled up a Bentley, and Kiick a silver Continental Mark IV.

　　As a rookie, Kiick had signed a two-year contract for about $15,000 per year, and his performance allowed him to up that to $34,000 for the 1970 season. Csonka had played through a three-year deal at about $30,000 per. In the summer of 1971, the duo announced together that they had signed with an agent to get them a new deal and would not be reporting to camp until a contract was signed. "I'm no bargainer, and neither is Larry," explained Kiick. "We don't want to haggle. But we know we're worth more than we're being offered, so we decided to get an agent." Shula was incensed and announced a $200 fine on each of them for every day they missed. After two weeks they finally agreed to salaries in the $50,000 range, they happily paid the $2,800 fines, and Joe Robbie belied his cheapskate reputation by matching them and paying the total sum to a relief fund for a badly injured high school player. "Hell," said Kiick coyly upon reporting to camp, "we'd have played for nothing." But Butch and Sundance had made out like bandits, and the icing on the cake was that they'd been working out on their own instead of in Shula's boot camp.

The second year of the Shula era began in similar fashion to the first, with a fiasco on the road. In Denver, against a suspect Bronco team, Miami fumbled four times and missed three short field goals in a 10–10 tie. But they hit their stride in week four, rolled through eight straight victories, only two of them close, and finished the season 10–3–1.

And then it was Christmas Day, 1971. In Kansas City for the first playoff game, the Dolphins kept falling behind and coming back to tie it. The game went to overtime, with missed field goals on both sides, then a second overtime, and the Dolphins' second playoff game ever turned into what is still the NFL's longest game ever. Or rather: the Longest Game. Over eighty-two minutes of game time, until finally a long Csonka run set up a thirty-seven-yard field goal attempt. Players on both teams were almost too exhausted to care anymore. "Garo came out," said Csonka, "and he had played about three plays all game, and he just took two steps and went *plunk*."

Municipal Stadium was dead silent. In Miami, a few hundred thousand families, including mine, jumped out of their seats, screamed for joy, and finally sat down to Christmas dinner. A week later the Dolphins celebrated New Year's Day with a much easier win, 21–0 over the Colts in the AFC championship game in the Orange Bowl, and Joe Robbie's five-year-old turquoise-and-orange expansion team was in the Super Bowl.

• • •

Super Bowl week in New Orleans didn't start well, with George Wilson telling a reporter back in Miami that Shula had inherited "a ready-made team that any Joe Doakes could have coached to the Super Bowl." Shula tried to make light of it, starting his first press conference in New Orleans saying, "Hi, I'm Joe Doakes." But it couldn't have felt good to be attacked by his old mentor. He also noted later that he had felt his team wasn't feeling right in practice: guys who normally didn't crack a smile were forcing levity, and the regular jokers were quiet. Everyone seemed a little thrown off by the new sensation of playing in a Super Bowl.

The historical consensus on the Dolphins' failure in Super Bowl VI is that the young team was too satisfied just to have made the big game and that perhaps due to nervousness they made glaring errors. Larry Csonka fumbled for the first time all season. Bob Griese got trapped in a swirling backward double helix of a scramble and lost thirty yards. But in fact in the first half, when inexperience and nervousness would take their biggest toll, the Dolphins didn't look too bad. There were those two blunders, but neither really hurt the team that much. Csonka and Griese's mistiming of a handoff followed a strong twelve-yard run past midfield, and Dallas recovered on their forty-eight. But Miami held them to a field goal. On the next possession, Griese made his ill-fated backward odyssey: each time he spun around to scramble in a different direction, defensive tackle Bob Lilly seemed to anticipate his move, finally dragging him down at his own eight-yard line. (Griese must have thought the play would end like his almost identical scramble against Buffalo two years earlier, on which he finally found Kiick for a fifty-three-yard touchdown pass.) That made it fourth and thirty-nine, but Seiple got off a good punt to start the second quarter, and the Dolphins forced the Cowboys to punt in turn. Miami was down only 10–3 at the half. (It would've been 10–6 if Yepremian's forty-nine-yard attempt with the wind didn't fall a foot or two short.) It was in the second half that Dallas really dominated, embarrassing Shula and the Dolphins with a 24–3 blowout. A five-minute, eight-play touchdown drive to start the second half, and then, to start the fourth quarter, a forty-one-yard interception of Griese that led to an easy touchdown, and it was as good as over.

One Cowboy noted that it seemed like the Dolphins were just happy to be there, whereas Dallas had come to town to win the game. They'd been there the year before and lost and were now on a mission. There was something to that, as four of the first seven Super Bowl champions won it only after first experiencing a loss in the big game. But more than anything, the result was probably more due to the fact that Miami was a young team that had not quite reached its prime, and Dallas was simply better that day.

If the Dolphins had been happy just to be there, they weren't showing it as they trudged into the Tulane Stadium locker room afterward. The enormity of what they had lost, after coming so close, hit them. Larry Csonka sat uncharacteristically silent at his locker. When he did speak, he blamed himself for throwing early momentum away with his fumble, and he wouldn't listen to his teammates' consolation. Someone asked Tim Foley a question, and the undersized cornerback broke into tears. "I can't explain it," he managed to get out. "It's like a death in the family. . . . These guys all worked together since July, went through everything to get here, and then we played so bad. . . ." Manny Fernandez was a massive man with a drooping black mustache and heavy sideburns. As a defensive tackle he toiled in the trenches where brawny linemen fought in hand-to-hand combat, where you never dared show a hint of weakness. He managed to hold his pain in until the team bus returned to the hotel, but then he found himself sitting on the bumper of someone's car, unable to walk farther, crying his heart out. In the locker room, linebacker Doug Swift had sat stunned, like the others: "I don't think I've ever been more humiliated or depressed or just totally disconsolate after having played a game as I was that one. That's the stuff you never forget."

Shula didn't want them to. In the quiet interval before the press and the TV cameras invaded their locker room, he stood in front of his team and told them he was hurting as much as they were. "But I don't want you to forget how this feels. Take it with you everywhere. Remember it now and when you leave here. Remember it so when we get back to the Super Bowl next year, the highs of winning it will feel even greater. I want all of you to remember how we feel right now and I don't ever want to feel this way again." Larry Csonka never forgot what Shula said next: "You've got to remember, because in six months we're going to be back at camp, and we are going to re-dedicate ourselves. We're going to concentrate one week at a time, one game at a time, and we are going to win every game."

The general continued to rally the troops on the plane ride home. Vern Den Herder remembered him going around to players individually on the airplane and reminding them to remember how they felt after losing a Super Bowl. He promised them it would be different next year. Six months later, true to his postgame words, Shula began the first day of training camp after all the veterans had returned by showing films of the loss to Dallas. Then the lights came up, and Shula started to speak. "And he's reaming us out like it happened twenty-four hours ago," recalled Mercury Morris. "'You see how sick and sorry you feel now? Well, think how you're going to feel if you don't get back there and redeem yourselves.' And we were stunned. But we swore to a man that we would." Csonka had been sitting through the film in a sulk, in what he called his "usual head on elbow pose." Kiick was next to him, covertly leafing through a magazine. When Shula went into his peroration, both stared up at him. Then he repeated his mantra of taking the games one at a time . . . and winning each one. And, thinking of the camps they'd been through with Shula the past two years, Kiick turned to Csonka and said, "Oh, this is going to be a beauty."

Preperfect II: No Weakness

The commander of this crusade was the third of six children born to Hungarian immigrants in Painesville, Ohio. His father, who'd come to America as the six-year-old Dénes Süle, worked as a trap net fisherman for a Lake Erie fishing plant, and there was no money to send six kids to college. So when Shula graduated high school in 1947 and was offered a tuition-only football scholarship at little John Carroll University just outside Cleveland, he grabbed it and carpooled the thirty miles from home every day until he got a full scholarship his sophomore year. He played both sides of the ball, offense and defense, as many did at that time, and he continued, as he had in high school, to take a head coach's interest in all aspects of the game.

John Carroll football players didn't generally head to the NFL, but this year was different. For the first and only time, powerhouse Syracuse had put them on the schedule, agreeing to come play them at Cleveland Municipal Stadium. And legendary Cleveland Browns coach Paul Brown, who as it happened lived just a few blocks from the Carroll campus, came to watch, presumably to scout Syracuse players. Down 16–7 in the second half, Carroll came back behind the tremendous running and blocking by both Shula and his backfield teammate Carl Taseff to score twice and beat the Orangemen in an incredible upset, 21–16. Two months later, Brown drafted both Shula and Taseff, and they went from their small college to their NFL dream team without leaving town. When the Browns offered Shula a contract for the NFL minimum $5,000 salary, he wrote later, "I was afraid they'd pull it back before I could get my signature on it."

The friends and roommates continued to beat the odds, becoming the only two rookies to make the Browns that year. Shula played defensive back, and although he was too slow to keep pace with the wide receivers and too small to intimidate runners coming through the middle, he managed to hang on with intelligence and determination through seven NFL seasons. After suffering two NFL championship game losses with the venerable Browns, he (along with Taseff) was traded in 1953 to a brand-new team, the Baltimore Colts, where he became the defensive captain by virtue of sheer intensity. "What's the matter with you guys?" he'd berate his teammates in the huddle. "Dig in!" "A coach on the field," according to head coach Weeb Ewbank, Shula called the defensive signals instead of a linebacker. But guts and smarts can take you only so far, and in 1957 Shula was cut by the Colts in training camp. He found a spot on the Washington Redskins and hung on through the year, but by that point he could see that his future was in coaching, not playing.

The next year he was the defensive backs coach at the University of Virginia and constantly looking for the next step up—personally as well as professionally. He had been dating Dorothy Bartish, a girl from his hometown, in the off-seasons since meeting her around the time he graduated college. Now, beginning a new phase in life, he decided to ask her to marry him. The problem was, he was in Virginia and she was in Hawaii, teaching for a year. Also, she had met a pilot there and was getting serious with him. "You're making a terrible mistake," he wrote her, sounding like a head coach already. In letter after letter he began talking about marriage, and finally he proposed to her—in another letter. She accepted by return mail, and the following summer, July of 1958, they were married.

That fall they moved to Lexington, where Don had taken another defensive-back coaching position at the University of Kentucky, and a year later they were in Detroit, where Shula was back in the NFL, coaching the defensive backs of the Lions under head coach George Wilson. After a year he was promoted to defensive coordinator, and it was in that position that he played a major role in preventing the NFL's first perfect season. The 1962 Green Bay squad may have been the greatest of all the Packers teams, and they came into the Thanksgiving game in Detroit unbeaten after ten games. They had an almost unstoppable offense with quarterback Bart Starr and fullback Jim Taylor. Starr was so masterful at getting quick passes out to his receivers that the common wisdom was you couldn't blitz him. But Shula's defense not only held Taylor to forty-seven yards, it also blitzed at every opportunity, and from every angle, sacking Starr eleven times and intercepting twice. The crowd was cheering the defense even more than the offense as they ran up a 26–0 lead and handed the Packers their only loss in a championship season.

Detroit had strong teams those years, second only to Green Bay in the NFL West. But it helped the young assistant more than it did the head coach. George Wilson was fired a couple years later and his career was over, save for a few years coaching a lowly expansion team down in Florida. But those three years of great defenses in Detroit propelled Don Shula to his first head-coaching job in 1963 when he was hired by the Baltimore Colts to replace the very coach, Weeb Ewbank, who had cut him as a player only six years before.

In seven years in Baltimore, Shula built a reputation as the finest young coach in the league, despite the fact that even his best seasons ended with bitter losses. His second year the Colts went 12–2 but got pummeled in the NFL championship game by Paul Brown's Browns, featuring a terrific rookie receiver named Paul Warfield. The next year Shula's team lost an overtime playoff game to Green Bay on a field goal that was disputed and that led to the NFL making its goalposts higher: the "Baltimore extensions." In 1967 the Colts flirted with an unbeaten season of their own, going into the final game of the season 11–0–2, including a win over the Packers and a tie against their division rivals the Los Angeles Rams. In the season finale, the Rams, led by future Hall of Fame coach George Allen and the Fearsome Foursome (pass rushers Merlin Olsen, Deacon Jones, Lamar Lundy, and Roger Brown), deflated the Colts, 34–10, and Shula learned just what "unbeaten" will do for you. His quarterback Johnny Unitas was the league MVP, he himself was Coach of the Year (a tie with Allen), and they both watched the playoffs on television.

Worst of all, though, was the next year, 1968—even though the Colts finally won the NFL championship. Unitas was hurt most of the year, but Shula had brought in the old veteran quarterback Earl Morrall, who'd been the backup in Detroit when Shula was there, and Morrall took the Colts through the season like a superstar. But now, for the third year, the NFL champion had to play the AFL champion in a thing that this year was officially called the Super Bowl. The leagues were still separate, and their teams did not compete against each other during the season. So there was no data to argue that the NFL was not still the superior league, as most people thought; the Packers had won the first two "World Championship" games handily. After getting revenge on the Browns 34–0 in the NFL championship game, Shula and his Colts were almost three-touchdown favorites to dispatch the junior league's New York Jets and their playboy quarterback, Joe Namath. But Broadway Joe famously guaranteed victory and backed that up with a 16–7 win in Super Bowl III in Miami's Orange Bowl. Once again Shula had the league MVP (Earl Morrall this time), Coach of the Year honors, and a bitter off-season.

Dissent was growing in Baltimore. Though still widely considered one of the three best coaches in football, Shula was also starting to be known as the guy who couldn't go quite all the way. And his boss, Carroll Rosenbloom, was no longer a fan. "When you're a three-touchdown favorite and you get beat," he said after that Super Bowl, "you've been outcoached." Outcoached by whom? None other than the incomparably christened Weeb Ewbank, who had won two NFL championships for the Colts right after pretty much ending Shula's playing career by cutting him in 1957, and whom Rosenbloom had fired in favor of Shula six years later. Now Rosenbloom was (privately) looking toward a new coach (and a new city), and Shula could sense, if nothing else, tensions growing in his relationship with the team and its fans. The time was ripe for that phone call from his old classmate Bill Braucher in Miami: Would he be interested in talking to Joe Robbie?

• • •

Many years later Csonka said, "Every July, I think about the fact that I'm not in Miami. I don't have grass and sweat running down my neck and him standing on my stomach." There were no more four-a-days after the 1970 strike-shortened camp. But training camp under Shula was still no picnic. There was still the twelve-minute run, the gassers, the repetitions in the subtropical heat until you got it right. And this year, 1972, there was also the weight on every player's back of the nationally televised debasement in New Orleans. Every stretch in the morning, every drill they ran, every classroom lecture, seemed infused with one man's obsession to exorcise the demons of Super Bowl VI forever. And the compulsion infused from the coach to fifty-odd staff and players like nutrients to the branches of a tree. Nick Buoniconti had cut and saved a clipping from the day after the Super Bowl: the one where Cornell Green said that the difference was that Miami was just glad to be there. He put it up on the bulletin board in the locker room, and every player walked by it several times a day, all season long. That wasn't enough for Tim Foley. He took a newspaper photograph of the final scoreboard from Tulane Stadium and tacked it up in the den of his home. "The clock reads zero seconds," he said, "and the score reads Dallas 24, Miami 3. At least once a day since the Super Bowl I've taken a long, long look at that picture to help me remember what I felt like after that game, and how I don't want to feel that way again."

There was more of a professional attitude permeating the camp this year. Players were taking it on themselves to address weaknesses in their technique, and flaws were being uprooted like weeds. The rookies who remained when the veterans arrived were allowed to pursue their struggle for a position on the roster without being harassed like frat pledges. There was still a Rookie Night, with a variety show of music and skits, in which the young guys got a chance to make fun of their elders, but it was toned down from the Wilson era. Shula's first year, John Stofa recruited two local strippers for the cast, and their act was a bit much for Shula, who had been at Mass just hours earlier. He turned beet red and left the room, and now Rookie Night stuck mainly to comedy.

· · ·

Outside of the Biscayne College training camp, where Shula was marshaling his forces for his own fall run, Miami was unwinding from the turmoil of the Democratic National Convention. After a contentious few nights, marked by protracted battles between new young delegates promoting feminism, gay rights, and an antiwar platform on the one side and the old Democratic machine on the other, the party had finally chosen its candidate. Long after midnight on July 13, when most of the television audience had long since switched off and gone to bed, a weary Senator George McGovern—a minister's son from South Dakota and decorated bomber pilot in World War II—had ascended the stage and accepted the party's nomination for president. The convention had been so contentious and divisive that many later considered it a portent of a disastrous campaign. But now the invasion of protesting hippies was gone from Flamingo Park, where local retirees had recaptured their territory. T-shirts with tie-dyed designs or Day-Glo slogans (MAKE LOVE, NOT WAR) were replaced by Hawaiian-print button-downs from Burdine's. A corpulent white-haired lady wearing a pink shift and floppy green hat slowly made her way toward the shuffleboard courts where her husband, perhaps, was part of the games. "Far out," opined a young woman in blue jeans, sandals, and dark shades who looked like she had showed up a few days late.

Despite the car-shaking, the scattered fires, the disruption of some official events, Miami Beach officials were relieved that things hadn't gotten more out of hand. The previous Democratic convention, in Chicago in 1968, was the notorious scene of barbaric police suppression of protests. This year Miami Beach had been relatively peaceful. Compared to 681 arrests and 1,381 injuries in Chicago, here there had been only two arrests and two injuries. At least, that was the official police report. Miami Beach could not have been more different from Chicago, as the liberal mayor, Chuck Hall, and police chief Rocky Pomerance were eager to demonstrate. "Fellas," said Rocky to a contingent of Yippies, "I don't believe in trying to enforce what can't be enforced. If you guys smoke a little pot, I'm not going to send my men in after you." Mayor Hall even tried to join Abbie Hoffman and Jerry Rubin in leading the first march from the park to the Convention Center.

Meanwhile, the war in Vietnam dragged violently on. Since President Johnson had sent the first combat units to South Vietnam in 1964, more than fifty thousand American lives—and about a million overall—had been sacrificed to the conflagration. Richard Nixon had made his name as a fervent anticommunist crusader in the 1940s and 1950s. But by the time he won the presidency in 1968, four years of a jungle quagmire and snowballing numbers of American casualties—more than sixteen thousand were killed in that peak year of 1968 alone—had turned the American people against the war. Nixon came to power promising a policy of Vietnamization: training and supplying the South Vietnamese to fight their war without American soldiers. But he had found it easier said than done. Not until this year, 1972, had the U.S. managed to bring most of its boys home. And thousands were still there: more than five hundred imprisoned and five times that many missing in action. My sister wore one of several million copper or chrome-plated POW/MIA bracelets, the initiative of two California college students in 1970. You paid three bucks for the bracelet and swore to wear it until the soldier whose name and date of disappearance or capture was printed on it was either released or confirmed dead.

Even though far less American blood was being spilled in 1972, the carnage continued. The day after the convention ended, Miamians woke to the front-page headline, ENEMY SUFFERS HEAVY LOSS IN MASSIVE RAIDS BY B-52S. The bombers had flown more than a hundred missions over twenty-four hours, dropping over fifteen hundred tons of explosives in the area of Quang Tri, killing several hundred. The southern provincial capital had been the object of fierce fighting since North Vietnamese troops captured it in May. As usual, the Pentagon claimed the dead were enemy combatants, while Hanoi reported that many were simply peasants caught in the aggression.

The day before, peace talks had reopened in Paris between North Vietnam and the U.S. after a ten-week break. (The North refused to negotiate with a South Vietnam government they did not recognize.) It was, unbelievably, the 1,505th session of negotiations between the two entities. But it was an open secret that these sessions reported in the press were merely a public façade for the secret meetings between the real negotiators: North Vietnamese Politburo member Le Duc Tho and U.S. national security advisor Henry Kissinger. The two had been undergoing this shadow diplomacy since February 1970. Now Kissinger was back in Paris and Tho was reportedly on his way from Peking. The public demands of each side had not changed since a proposal from the Nixon administration in May that set a ceasefire and the return of all American prisoners as a condition for any political agreement. Hanoi, though, insisted on the resignation of South Vietnamese president Nguyen Van Thieu, a controversial figure the U.S. had been supporting. Eight years after the Gulf of Tonkin Resolution and the beginning of official U.S. military operations in Vietnam, the war raged on.

Unlike in past wars, very few NFL players served in Vietnam. Many were deemed unfit physically, with bad knees and backs, even as they continued to play football. A number of players did take part in USO tours. Larry Csonka went after the Super Bowl loss and, as he put it, got a different perspective on his broken nose and "Poly-Turf toe" after visiting soldiers in the hospital who had had parts of their bodies blown away. The next year, visiting troops via helicopter near Da Nang and in the Mekong Delta, Manny Fernandez ran into a college teammate. He didn't recognize him at first; his fellow defensive lineman, who had weighed 270 pounds, was down to 190 in the jungle. Marv Fleming was able to visit an old friend—a young Packers fan he'd gotten to know well in Green Bay—in a military hospital just before he died. Most of the Dolphins had friends who had gone; many knew someone who had died.

Two players did miss the first week of camp this year while serving in uniform: Paul Warfield and Garo Yepremian were both busy with their National Guard units on Miami Beach during the convention. Fleming was late, too, but not because of the convention, although he had been elected as a delegate from his native California after stumping for McGovern in six states during the off-season. Shula joked to reporters he'd heard the missing Fleming was considering an offer to join McGovern on the ticket as his running mate. Turned out he had just bungled his travel plans and arrived at camp a day late, ready to pay his fine.

Training camp was well in swing by now, and players were trying to get every edge they could to deal with the ordeal. From the room shared by odd couple Yepremian and Doug Swift wafted the lunchtime aroma of freshly baked black bread, along with a dizzying admixture of fruits. Each week Swift, the surprise third-year starting linebacker out of Amherst, hauled back to camp twenty-five pounds of carrots, a bushel of oranges, powdered nutritional supplements, and ingredients to use in his yogurt-making machine: instant dry milk, yogurt culture, and flavorings. "It's easily digestible, low on fat, and all protein," Swift explained to a reporter unfamiliar with the exotic fermented-milk specialty. "I eat it with raspberries or straight. Garo likes it with garlic, cucumbers, and a touch of mint." Swift mixed the yogurt with the fruit to make smoothies, and he wasn't the only one. Mercury Morris was working on perfecting his own concoction involving predigested protein and gland protein. "There are half a dozen blenders and portable ice boxes around here," said Swift. "It's like we're practicing a bit of sorcery. Everybody mixes up his own potion."

Around the corner, four men huddled over a chessboard set up on a bench. Newcomer Marlin Briscoe had become a devotee of the game in college and carried a board with him on road trips. He'd struck up a friendship with the rookie Eddie Jenkins, and they played often on breaks. Curtis Johnson and Hubert Ginn were also players and sometimes joined in. "We liked to joke," said Jenkins, "that the Black guys played chess, and the white guys played checkers." The four of them were also following, via newspaper reports, the world chess championship in Reykjavík, Iceland. The brash young American Bobby Fischer was challenging Russian champion Boris Spassky in what aficionados were already calling the Match of the Century. Briscoe liked to set up the pieces on his board to match the day's situation in Reykjavík, and the four of them would debate what Fischer's next move should be.

Despite Shula's ongoing drive for a championship, forged to an even more maniacal edge by the debacle in New Orleans, there was, paradoxically, a countercurrent of calm running through his third Miami training camp, personified perhaps by the four men hunched over the chessboard. Younger players like Morris had matured, growing into their prime; older veterans like Buoniconti and Fleming lent an unspoken mentorship. Offensive guard Bob Kuechenberg, a whipping boy for Shula the last two years for his frequent mental errors, hadn't heard his name screamed all camp. A truck of a man with thin blond hair, he looked like rock star Stephen Stills after a year in the gym. "Kooch" was the son of a rugged ironworker—and erstwhile human cannonball—and had only played semipro ball before catching on with the Dolphins in 1970. He'd showed up during rookie week this year of his own accord to get in extra work, and it had paid off. "In the past," said Shula, "chewing him out from top to bottom was almost a daily ritual. This year, like the other veterans, he knows what's expected of him. There hasn't been the need for corrections." It was true all across the roster. Shula watched with a visitor as the offense practiced a short pass over the middle to Jim Mandich. Offensive tackle Doug Crusan hit the defensive lineman low and brought him down so he couldn't get his hands up to block the ball. For the benefit of his visitor, Shula called to Crusan, "You didn't fire out at him, did you?" "No, sir," came the reply. "I didn't want to push him into Mandich's path." Shula nodded with satisfaction. He pointed out how players like Griese and Warfield were so professional, they hardly needed coaching. They both knew just where their progress needed to be at each step of camp. All around the campus, an atmosphere of excellence prevailed.

One of the young players coming into his own in 1972 was Jim Langer. A small-town kid from Royalton, Minnesota, he'd been a linebacker and also a baseball star (his favorite sport) at South Dakota State and had not been drafted in 1970. He ended up another new player on Shula's first Dolphins team, claimed off of Cleveland's waivers list. (The Browns wanted Langer for their taxi squad, a roster of seven who practice with the team but don't suit up for games, and had assumed no one would take him off waivers.) Like Warfield, barely visible to him up there at the top of the Browns totem pole, he was aghast at the thought of leaving the cream of the NFL to go join the lowly Dolphins down in the swamp. And he had been guaranteed $500 a week in Cleveland! In fact, two hours before he got the news of his relocation, he had called his wife, Lynn, back in Minnesota and told her to pack up and join him in Cleveland: "I think I'm going to be around here a little bit. I feel real good about it." Next thing he knew, he was in Miami, where again he barely made the team—on its taxi squad—and Joe Thomas came to his room at training camp and offered him $350 a week. In an attempt at negotiation, Langer said he was getting $500 at Cleveland. "Well, this isn't Cleveland," said Thomas. "This is what we're going to pay you." "But God, I don't have any money," said Langer. "Can I at least get a little extra to get my family down here?" Thomas relented and signed him at $375. And for two years he barely stayed on the team, as a backup guard who mainly played on special teams. But now, in his third training camp, like fellow guard Kuechenberg, he was starting to get some practice time in at center, though the Dolphins were solid at that position with veteran Bob DeMarco. Shula even started Langer at center in the first team scrimmage, a competition between the offense and defense, and liked what he saw.

• • •

In late July, just a couple weeks after the convention, George McGovern's campaign reached its first crisis and faltered terribly, an inauspicious sign of what was to come. His running mate, Tom Eagleton, acknowledged on July 25, after the press discovered it while investigating his medical history, that he had been hospitalized for depression three times in the 1960s and had even undergone electroshock therapy. McGovern immediately held a press conference and declared his unwavering confidence in Eagleton's ability to serve as vice president and even step in as president should it become necessary. Two days later, though, McGovern was wavering. And on July 31 McGovern, apparently having decided that admitting a vetting oversight was better than sticking with a potential liability, announced that Eagleton had agreed to leave the ticket. Whichever decision he had made, it would have been a poor way to start an uphill campaign against a popular president in a booming economy.

President Nixon, though, had his own ghosts stirring in the closet. The same day McGovern made his announcement, a young *Washington Post* reporter named Carl Bernstein was in Miami getting the runaround from the Dade

County state attorney's office. Seven weeks earlier, on June 17, five men had been arrested in a burglary at Democratic national headquarters in the Watergate Hotel in Washington. Four of the five were from Miami, including Bernard Barker, who had been a Cuban revolutionary, a B-17 crewman for the U.S. in World War II (and a prisoner of war in Germany), a loyal agent for Batista's secret police, the FBI, and the CIA, and a participant in the ill-fated Bay of Pigs Invasion. In July the *New York Times* had reported that Barker had made a number of calls from Miami to the Committee for the Re-election of the President, in Washington. In Miami, after a long day of being avoided by the state attorney and his assistant, Bernstein finally conned his way into the office and was allowed to dig into the records of their investigation into Barker. He phoned his haul to his partner back in Washington, and the next day readers of the *Miami Herald*—along with the *Post* and papers around the country—got their first look at a particular double byline: Carl Bernstein and Bob Woodward. The article, a small opening column on the front page, beneath larger headlines announcing Eagleton's resignation and the U.S. Navy's bombardment of a shipyard at Haiphong, began: "A $25,000 cashier's check, apparently earmarked for the campaign chest of President Nixon, was deposited in April in the bank account of Bernard L. Barker, one of the five men arrested . . ."

· · ·

This opening salvo of a campaign that would bring down a president caused little stir at the time, less than anywhere at the Dolphins camp, where players and coaches were hell-bent on a mission and preparing to begin the first stage of competition: the exhibition season. Unlike today, when even the most zealous fans care little about the results of preseason games, back then the games were taken seriously. "First and foremost is winning," said Shula when asked about his goals for the preseason. Evaluating new players, giving second-stringers the chance to compete for positions, and tuning up the stars were all important, but only secondarily. He proudly mentioned his stellar exhibition record in seven seasons at Baltimore: 32–4–1.

Even so, he kept Griese out of the first game, up in Detroit, letting new backup Earl Morrall get some work in against one of his old teams. Shula had acquired the thirty-eight-year-old Morrall off of waivers during the off-season. He certainly wasn't expected to play much, but it would be good to have an experienced veteran around just in case. In this, his first outing as a Dolphin, though, Morrall was rusty, to be generous—he completed only four of thirteen passes, with two costly interceptions—and the Dolphins lost their first tune-up, 31–23. The folksy Morrall was philosophical: "Ol' Lem always seems to get one on me every year," he said of the first interception, and of the other, "I just underthrew it. Couldn't get it out there." The bright spot was Garo Yepremian, who'd been eager to do well against *his* old team, who had given him his first chance in the NFL in 1966 but then cut him a couple years later. The last time Detroit played Miami, they'd had 250-pound Rocky Rasley chase Yepremian after every kickoff, and the diminutive Armenian had run for his life, straight to the sidelines, every time. Garo had been oh for six in field goal tries in team scrimmages this summer, but he came through with three out of three in Detroit, including a fifty-two-yarder, and was just as pleased with his kickoffs. "If you noticed," he said, "I didn't run off the field this time."

Morrall was given a few days to visit with his wife and kids in their permanent home near Detroit, and the rest of the team flew home. During the season, a player returned from a road trip to the sanctuary of his own home, but in preseason it was back to the grind. "There's no way I can say anything good about training camp," said Larry Csonka during a break from the sweat-soaked drills. In the middle of practice under the Miami sun, his mind would drift far away, like that of a prisoner dreaming of freedom. "It comes to me that I'm sitting on the porch of my A-frame house up in the mountains in Franklin [North Carolina]. A breeze is blowing across. No humidity. I'm on a peak. I'm looking down at the clouds tumbling through the valley below. It's so peaceful that wildcats will come right up onto the patio." He let loose a sigh. "So serene. So different from training camp."

At least there were the games. NFL players were negotiating for fewer meaningless games and more that counted, and they'd get that in 1978, but even the exhibition games were something to look forward to. The second one this year was at home in the Orange Bowl, on a sultry August Saturday night. Dolphin fans finally had a chance to see their team again after the breakout Super Bowl year, and the atmosphere that evening was electric. Two hours before the eight p.m. game time, the grass parking lot off Fourth Street began filling with cars, campers, even bicycles, for tailgating dinners. During the regular season, when players drove themselves to home games, they parked in that same lot. Csonka remembered folks having to move their picnic chairs so he could pull his car in. "And they'd be there after the game. And of course they want to talk to you about the game, and you do that . . . and you get to know people on a first-name basis. Other players would already be out there, and we'd have two or three thousand people out there at a tailgating party." Sometimes, after a late game, the partying would go on long past midnight, and at some point the police would come by to disperse it. But more often than not, the players would convince them to join in, and the cops would sit down and have a beer with them.

Their fame notwithstanding, in that era pro football players were not so far removed economically from those cops and fans. Only a few of the biggest stars on the Dolphins earned more than $40,000 a year, and half the roster had contracts for less than $20,000 (the equivalent of about $125,000 today). Although that might sound better than a police officer's or schoolteacher's salary, and the average price of a home in South Florida in 1972 was $34,000, consider that the average NFL career was five or six years. And that that average home price had doubled in the past decade. Most of the players had off-season employment. Jim Langer was a bank teller; Manny Fernandez worked carpentry jobs his first few off-seasons. Larry Little was a substitute teacher until he made the Pro Bowl and got a big raise. On the other hand, Jim Kiick avoided work like a kid on summer vacation. Even after he won a Super Bowl—and scored a touchdown in it—he recounted: "My wife Alice wants me to get a job, and I'll go out in the morning. But then I'll play basketball for a while and have a few beers, then come home and tell her, 'Nothing today, honey.'"

With ordinary salaries, the players lived not in gated mansions but right among the community. Howard Twilley lived with his wife and small children in a ranch house in the Cherry Grove development in Kendall, where a number of my school friends lived. Occasionally, some of them would get their courage up, knock on his door, and ask him if he'd throw a football around with them. "We'd show up in our full Dolphin uniforms, with pads and all," said one friend. "And he was too nice to say no. I think his wife was kind of annoyed with us."

The Dolphins players considered themselves just a bunch of ordinary working guys, and the people of South Florida, in turn, had taken them to heart. Now the Green Bay Packers were in town for the first home game, and more than seventy-five thousand "Dolfans," as they'd begun calling themselves, filled every freshly painted seat in the old stadium. They were thrilled by Griese hitting Warfield for six passes in the first half, although one of those ended in a fumble at the Green Bay five-yard line, which halted a long drive. In the second half, second-year quarterback Jim Del Gaizo, who had played well in the first game, got another chance and led the team on two good drives that might have won the game but for some kicking-unit woes.

Yepremian's holder was Karl Noonan, a wide receiver and one of the three remaining original Dolphins but facing extinction with the arrival of Otto Stowe and Marlin Briscoe. Noonan had been particularly pleased with the field goals up in Detroit: "I think Garo and I and [center] DeMarco have a unique thing going." But he and DeMarco must have noticed, too, that the surprise starter at center, in Detroit and again against Green Bay, was young Jim Langer. And as for the kicking unit, Yepremian first bounced a thirty-five-yard field goal attempt off the goalpost. Then, after Del Gaizo led a long touchdown drive in the closing minutes for the apparent tie, the extra-point attempt landed like the *Hindenburg*. DeMarco, perhaps looking over his shoulder while peering back through his legs, due to the fact that he only got to replace Langer for one series, tossed back a wild snap that sailed over holder Noonan's head. "I hoped it would bounce into my arms and I'd run all the way for an extra point," said Yepremian bravely after the fact, but at the time he stood and watched as Noonan chased the ball down and was crushed by an avalanche of Packers. He suffered a separated shoulder and was taken to the hospital, and the twenty-eight-year-old receiver, who'd been a starter in '68 and '69 and was the only player to have appeared in every Dolphins game ever, never played another down. By the time he recovered, the team was just fine with Warfield, Twilley, Briscoe, and Stowe.

DeMarco felt awful after the game, sitting dejected in front of his locker, and said he'd never bungled a snap like that in his entire twelve-year career. A three-time Pro Bowler (best in conference) and twice All-Pro (best at his position in the entire league) in his years in St. Louis, the balding, hulking DeMarco was about to turn thirty-four but had started almost every game for Miami the past two years and had no thought of his blooper affecting his future. He just felt bad for Noonan. A sportswriter wrote the next day that there was still "no competition for DeMarco's job." Langer himself blurted out to a reporter after the game, "He's the best darned center in pro football." However, Langer had played most of the game and played well. Offensive line coach Monte Clark was still telling the press, "DeMarco's age and experience are what make him so valuable right now. He's our stabilizer." But in private Clark had been gently pushing for Langer all camp, and now he said to Shula, "We ought to think about starting Langer—I believe he has an edge on Bob." "Not this again," said Shula and moved on to other topics. But he had heard.

Noonan's injury, which rendered him "white as a ghost" and writhing with pain on the sideline before they carted him off, wasn't even the worst of the night. Bob Heinz, who'd become a mainstay of the defensive line the year before, left the game in the fourth quarter with a head and back injury and a few days later learned he had a fractured vertebra and would be out at least two months. The same day, veteran Jim Riley, a regular defensive end since 1968, pulled up lame in practice with a bum knee. "Luckily, it popped right back into place," he said hopefully, but the coaches looked at each other. If it didn't stay there, they were going to have to look extra closely at young Vern Den Herder, who'd played mainly special teams his first year. Starting offensive tackle Doug Crusan had torn his calf muscle in the Detroit game and was out indefinitely. Observers were starting to compare the situation to the medical devastation of George Wilson's final year, and Braucher joked that maybe Shula should stop cutting players—he was going to need them.

Although Crusan and Riley were out for the next game, up in Cincinnati, they took over when the flight home was delayed several hours with mechanical problems. Crusan for several years had been the self-appointed judge of the "Ugliest Dolphin" award on Rookie Night, and as the team sat around the airport, he and Riley compiled a list of the all-time "All-Ugly" team, featuring the immortal Wahoo McDaniel. Shula sat nearby smiling with a sandwich and a beer. His team had finally showed their form, beating the Bengals and his old coach, Paul Brown. The flight delay, not to mention the next week of practice, might not have been so relaxed if the team were 0–3. Fans seemed to take these games as seriously as the coach: when the Dolphins arrived at Miami International at three in the morning, more than two hundred were there to cheer them—after an exhibition game.

The Dolphins were finally starting to look like a returning Super Bowl team. Bob Griese had led the offense to touchdowns on all five of the drives he played, including two touchdown passes to Warfield and another to Briscoe. Mercury Morris, getting more playing time than ever in his fourth preseason, was taking advantage of it. He rushed seven times in Cincinnati for fifty-three yards and caught two passes for another seventy-one. He now had twenty carries for 135 yards, and Shula knew he was going to be faced with the problem of splitting time between Morris and Kiick. "However, I'm enjoying that problem," he smiled at practice.

· · ·

The exhibition season was half over and training camp nearing its end, but out on Miami Beach another camp was just opening—or reopening. With the Republican National Convention about to take its turn at the Miami Beach Convention Center, the "non-delegates" were back at Flamingo Park. Or, as Hunter S. Thompson called them, "a useless mob of ignorant, chicken-shit ego-junkies . . . who embarrassed the whole tradition of public protest." How he must have smirked when handed a piece of paper at the entrance by a heavy-bearded, shirtless young man: "Welcome to Flamingo Park, the people's liberated zone of revolutionary living, organizing and nonviolent direct action. Here we shall work to expose, confront and defeat the oppressive Nixon Administration." A path known as the "Ho Chi Minh Trail" led into the park and past various encampments: the "Women's Tent," the "Free Berkeley Booth," the "Neo-American Church," the "Free Gays," the "Jesus Freaks," the "Society for the Advancement of Non-Verbal Communication," "Yippie Headquarters," "Zippie Headquarters," and finally "The People's Pot Park."

The day the Dolphins flew back from Cincinnati, Jane Fonda, home from her infamous visit to Hanoi, was at Flamingo Park with thousands of others for an antiwar protest. A presentation by the Miami Women's Coalition was disrupted by a group of twenty-two American Nazi Party members who stormed the stage, grabbed the mike, and began disparaging Jews, protesters, and other "anti-Americans we're really fighting." Fortunately, the park was home not only to the Jesus freaks and the nonverbal society but also the Vietnam Veterans Against the War. The vets encircled the stage, formed a corridor to the parking lot, and forced the Nazis off the stage after a fifteen-minute fistfight that left seven Nazis, four vets, and two CBS cameramen injured. Meanwhile, 250 "Zippies and friends" marched to the convention hall for a "Dishonor Amerika" demonstration: a pot smoke-in and mass urination on deodorant bottles, textbooks, and other "Amerikana" symbols. That evening, five hundred

members of the Students for a Democratic Society made the same march carrying a bloody corpse of a stag to protest outside a $500-a-plate dinner at the
Fontainebleau Hotel.

Another day, the veterans group marched to the Fontainebleau, the site
of convention headquarters, led by three comrades in wheelchairs, including
Ron Kovic, who would gain fame as the author of *Born on the Fourth of July*.
Miami Beach cops carried the three wheelchair-bound vets up the steps, where
they entered the hotel and read a letter to President Nixon pleading for an end
to the "insanity" of the war. That night, three thousand antiwar demonstrators marched to the convention hall, many in death masks or faces painted
deathly white, others in Nixon masks covered with fake blood. After a while,
many broke off and began filling the streets nearby, shoving delegates, breaking store windows, burning flags they'd ripped down from in front of hotels,
jumping on cars and stomping up and down. Two hundred were arrested and
hauled off to mainland jails for the night. A thousand more were arrested over
the next two days.

Meanwhile, as demonstrators chanted outside the Fontainebleau, where
most delegates were staying, many of those delegates were sailing by on yachts
where they sat in deck chairs in striped blazers and cocktail dresses, watching the rabble through binoculars while waitstaff handed them martinis. To
Thompson they looked like decadent ancient Romans watching blood sport
in the Colosseum. The ruckus could have been nothing more than a distant
rumble, however, from the *Miss Florida*, an opulent three-story yacht permanently docked at the Pelican Harbor on Seventy-Ninth Street, where California
governor Ronald Reagan and his wife, Nancy, were hosting a reception for
"three hundred close friends," including Vice President Spiro Agnew, the John
Ehrlichmans, the William F. Buckleys, and Frank Sinatra.

None of the old-money elite partying on the boats, nor the straw-hatted
conservative boosters filling the convention hall, seemed to notice the secondary
articles in the papers each day, just beneath the convention hoopla, regarding
that odd little break-in at Democratic headquarters in Washington. On Monday
there was DEMO BUGS HEARD BY NIXON MEN: *Time* magazine reporting that the
microphones planted in the Watergate were transmitting to the Committee for
the Re-election of the President (known to many as CREEP). On Tuesday, the
second page of the *Herald* carried NIXON FUND VIOLATIONS TO BE CITED: Bernstein

and Woodward reporting more on the campaign contributions being diverted to the "Plumbers," G. Gordon Liddy's "dirty tricks" team behind the Watergate break-in and other machinations. Right next to it was an *L.A. Times* report that CREEP had purchased thousands of dollars' worth of electronic security equipment in the months before the break-in, including walkie-talkies seized on the day of the arrests. A matching walkie-talkie was found in the desk of White House consultant E. Howard Hunt. This was all on page two. On the front page was Ronald Reagan addressing the cheering throngs inside the convention hall: "If the senator [McGovern] persists in these extravagant utopian promises [his tax and welfare proposals] then he is guilty of a deception on a scale never before known in our political history."

That night, as he watched leisurely from across the bay at his compound on Key Biscayne, Richard Nixon was nominated almost unanimously to seek reelection. It was the third Republican nomination in twelve years for a man they used to say couldn't win the big one.

· · ·

That Friday night the hoopla was gone, the campaign having rumbled off to battleground hot spots across the nation, and the convention hall was empty. The Orange Bowl, however, was packed to see the Dolphins collect another exhibition victory. Despite the win over Atlanta, Earl Morrall looked obsolescent again, going three for ten with just eighteen yards and an interception. "I'm just not doing the job," he said glumly at his locker afterward. "I better start, or I won't *have* a job." That wasn't too likely: Shula hadn't convinced Joe Robbie to pick up the $85,000 salary for Morrall, his old stalwart and a Super Bowl MVP, just to bench him for a kid out of the University of Tampa—no matter how old and decrepit Morrall looked so far. And that kid, Jim Del Gaizo, spent the game in the coaches' box helping with the charts. He'd cut a gash in his finger on a closet door and was on the injured-waiver list for two weeks, further cementing Morrall's role as the backup. Luckily, Griese was making it look easy, going eight for twelve with a nifty sixteen-yard touchdown pass to Warfield. Jim Kiick finally got some solid playing time instead of Morris, and the old partnership of Butch and Sundance split a hundred-yard game evenly; the defense was nearly perfect for three quarters, and the Dolphins rolled, 24–10.

Morrall was slightly improved the next week up in Washington as the Dolphins lost a close one to a team favored by many to make the Super Bowl. Last year the Redskins' new coach, George Allen, had turned around the least successful franchise of the past quarter century, and suddenly they were a playoff team. This year they had also staved off a challenge by human rights groups intent on changing the team name, which was in essence a racial slur. A slew of articles in the D.C. press over the past ten months had highlighted the growing controversy: Native American advocates compared the team name to such possibilities as the Washington Dagos or the New York Kikes. After meeting with a delegation representing a variety of Native American organizations in the off-season, however, team president and minority owner Edward Bennett Williams refused to make a change. The fans overwhelmingly wanted to keep the mascot, he said; what's more, a change would cost "thousands of dollars." "This is getting silly," Williams said. "Suppose blacks got together and demanded Cleveland's football team stopped calling itself the Browns, or ornithologists insisted that Baltimore was demeaning to birds because the name is the Orioles." And that was that for another half century.

In RFK Stadium, Morrall was only four for ten with an interception, but three of those were desperation heaves in the final minute, and he did make a couple nice long throws, one of which got the Dolphins downfield for a tying field goal late in the game. But Washington had a long drive in the fourth quarter and kicked the game-winning field goal in the final minute to win 27–24, replicating the score and manner of victory in Miami's Longest Game playoff win the year before. Nonetheless, pundits were starting to notice that Shula's squad was even better than they'd been in 1971. The only question mark seemed to be that backup quarterback spot. No matter, as one local sportswriter put it: "Within the next week Shula will pick Morrall or Del Gaizo as his backup quarterback and it will be forgotten, since the No. 2 man is rarely seen once the season starts. Let's face it—if Bob Griese goes down, there's trouble, no matter who the backup is."

On a Sunday afternoon, September 10, the Dolphins finished the long preseason schedule with a home game against another NFL heavyweight that would loom large in the upcoming season, the Minnesota Vikings. With the largest Orange Bowl crowd ever of 79,298, Shula played his first team most of the game even while giving a few promising subs such as Den Herder, Mandich, and Bob Matheson a chance to compete for starting spots. Griese went all the way, as did Minnesota's star, Fran Tarkenton—apparently Shula had seen enough of Morrall and named him the number two man anyway, sending Del Gaizo back to the taxi squad—and the final stats sheet looked like a regular-season game: Csonka, Morris, and Kiick running the ball, Warfield and Briscoe catching it. The preseason ended on an exciting note as Griese led the team to two long touchdown drives in the fourth quarter for a comeback victory, 21–19. With a minute left and a fourth down on the Minnesota six-yard line, the Vikings were surely expecting a pass, and Griese surprised them by handing off to Morris on a right-end sweep. Mercury followed Larry Little to the outside, then cut back in and fought his way across the goal line. The play won the game, giving the Dolphins an even 3–3 preseason record. More importantly, Griese's unusual call would stick in Minnesota's memory, and the quarterback filed that fact in the back of his mind. Miami would be going up to Minneapolis to play the Vikings for real in just three weeks.

Center Bob DeMarco wasn't there for the last preseason game. A week earlier, Shula, under constant pressure from Monte Clark to make Jim Langer the starting center, had finally told DeMarco that Langer had won the starting position. Insulted at the thought of being replaced by a sub who had never even played center before, DeMarco asked for a multiyear contract or to be traded, and very soon he was in Cleveland, where he'd be the starting center that year before retiring. His roommate and best friend on the Dolphins, Nick Buoniconti, was furious. "They're making a mistake," he ranted, throwing furniture around the locker room when he heard the news. Informed of that, Shula calmly instructed a reporter, "Be sure to tell Buoniconti this is not his week to run the club." A few weeks later Monte Clark said simply, "Langer's too good not to play. I'd like someone to show me a better center in all of football, but I don't know when everyone else will know it." Everyone else, it turned out, would know it very soon. Langer played every down that season, and Clark, reviewing films afterward, noted that he needed help blocking his man only three times out of five hundred. He would go on to play 128 straight games at center, was chosen by the NFL as the greatest center of the 1970s, and was elected to the Hall of Fame the first year he was eligible.

· · ·

Finally, training camp and the preseason were over. It was mid-September, eight months after the mortifying Super Bowl loss, and Shula and his team were ready to make good on their promise to themselves. In that final exhibition game, the way they played—and the way the overflow crowd rocked the Orange Bowl bleachers—"you would have thought another championship was on the line," according to one observer, and afterward Shula said with satisfaction, "We felt it was important to win." Mercury Morris agreed: "We needed this win psychologically. It brings us into the right frame of mind for Kansas City."

Most agreed that the squad that would travel back to the site of the breathtaking Christmas Day playoff was even better now. The Griese-Warfield combination was really flowering in its third year; both stars had been sensational throughout the preseason. Marlin Briscoe was a big addition at wide receiver. Kiick and Csonka looked stronger than ever, and now they were joined in the backfield by Morris, who, finally given the playing time, had made the most of it. A bit of friction was building from the overcrowded backfield—neither Kiick nor Morris could be happy sitting on the bench—but "they were trying harder than George McGovern to present a unified front."

"We're ahead of where we were at this time last year," said Norm Evans. "We've been together longer. . . . Now we can work on the fine details. . . . This is the winning edge Coach Shula talks about, that little bit of technique that makes you a fraction better than your opponent." There seemed to be a consensus that the only possible weakness in the offense would be if offensive tackle Doug Crusan's injury kept him out. As it turned out, though, his substitute, Wayne Moore, was just as good. Similarly, the only question mark on defense was injuries to the line: both Bob Heinz and Jim Riley had gone down wounded. But Heinz would come back strong, and the injuries allowed Vern Den Herder to shine; he would replace Riley and become a beloved mainstay of the line for ten seasons.

So, in fact, there was no weakness. What else was needed to get back to the Super Bowl and win it? A little luck, of course: you couldn't suffer too many injuries or "have things not break right for you," Shula conceded. "The other thing that I've found," he mused, "is that you have to get a hot streak. You need a streak in there where you win four, five, or six in a row. Last year we had an eight-game streak. The year before we had a six-game streak that got us in there." If anyone remembered his words on the first day of training camp, they'd know Don Shula was thinking about a little bit longer winning streak than that this year.

One and Oh

On September 16, the day before the 1972 NFL season began, the *Miami Herald* declared: U.S. INDICTS SEVEN IN BREAK-IN CAPER AT DEMOCRATS' HQ. There was also news of Israeli armed forces entering Lebanon on a search-and-destroy mission against Arab guerrillas, the latest in a series of reprisals after the murder of eleven Israeli athletes and coaches at the Munich Olympics ten days before. And of course a hijacking story: three Croatians holding fifty-one passengers hostage on a Swedish airliner. It seemed there was a hijacking story every week. (And in fact, on average, from 1968 to 1972, there was.) But this Watergate narrative seemed to be gaining steam as the presidential election moved into its final two months. The indicted included Howard Hunt, Gordon Liddy, and James McCord, all three intimately connected to the White House. The other four were Miamians, known to the White House as the "Cubans." Their leader, Bernard Barker, the ex-CIA agent and Batista secret police, now a bifocaled notary public, was also arrested this day in Miami on a charge of fraudulent use of his notary public seal in cashing the now famous $25,000 check made out to the Committee for the Re-election of the President. A Miami judge freed Baker on bail and set the trial date for October 30—eight days before the presidential election.

In Vietnam, fighting remained fierce. That weekend South Vietnamese marines had taken back the Quang Tri Citadel and were turning their sights northward, but North Vietnam still held large swatches of territory south of the demilitarized zone. Henry Kissinger was back from Paris and reported little progress in his secret negotiations with Le Duc Tho.

It seemed unlikely, though, that either the war or recent legal events, however suspicious, would throw a wrench in the Nixon machine, powered by a full tank of foreign diplomacy successes and good economic news. In February he had made his historic visit to China, meeting with Premier Zhou and Chairman Mao. His single-minded warming of Sino-American relations also pushed Brezhnev and the Soviet Union into a new era of détente, forged during Nixon's May 1972 visit to Moscow. And ever mindful of the fact that Eisenhower's refusal to stimulate the economy with federal spending prior to the 1960 election had consigned him, Nixon, to defeat against Kennedy—"Goddamned old fool," he'd fumed privately at the time—Nixon engineered a wage-and-price freeze, combined with massive government spending, which was in essence a fake economic fix. It would lead inexorably to enormous inflation and a major recession in 1973 and 1974, but as designed it ensured low prices and a strong economy through the '72 election. Nixon's tremendous downhill momentum over the summer had even softened the American public's disillusionment with the war. A new Harris poll indicated that a majority of voters supported the continued heavy bombing of North Vietnam, and an even larger portion, sixty-four percent, approved of the mining of North Vietnamese harbors—if only to hasten the end of the war. A whopping seventy-four percent agreed "it is important that South Vietnam not fall into the control of the Communists." And few if any experts were opining at this point that the investigation of the burglary at the Watergate Hotel would lead any higher than campaign strongmen Hunt and Liddy, who surely were acting on their own.

• • •

On Sunday, September 17, another campaign began: the Don Shula–Miami Dolphins march toward redemption. The team was in Kansas City for the season opener as a four-point underdog. Despite their Super Bowl appearance, made possible by their historic playoff game against the Chiefs followed by a sober dismantling of Baltimore, the Dolphins weren't even picked by most to win their division. Around the country, virtually every sportswriter was picking Baltimore to take the AFC East. Miami had been very lucky to get past K.C. in the playoffs, they said (true); the great Johnny Unitas still had the edge over the nerdy Bob Griese (false); and the Dolphins were going to be handicapped by a daunting schedule in the early part of the season. This last point belied the

many naysayers who would later point to the Dolphins' 1972 schedule as one
of the easiest in the league. It sure didn't look that way at the time. Three of
their first four games were against Kansas City, Minnesota, and Joe Namath's
New York Jets, all three of which were considered Super Bowl contenders. Bill
Braucher and Jimmy the Greek were two of the only ones to point out that
after that rough stretch things got easier and the Dolphins might be able to
put together a nice winning streak.

But first, Kansas City. The game would be the regular-season debut of
$51 million Arrowhead Stadium. Just nine months earlier the Dolphins had
retired the old Municipal Stadium in style with the NFL's Longest Game. It
was Christmas, and like other moms across South Florida mine had a special
meal prepared to be eaten a little late, after the four p.m. playoff game. (Though
Jewish, we traditionally had a turkey dinner on Christmas.) The Dolphins had
never beaten the Chiefs in six previous tries, but finally their fans had reason to be
hopeful. We flipped on the black-and-white tube in the family room and watched.
And watched, and watched. . . . Christmas Day turned into Christmas night as
the two teams slugged it out for hours on a surprisingly thawed, muddy field.

The Dolphins came from behind to tie the game just before halftime, again
at the end of the third quarter, and again in the fourth: Kansas City went up
24–17, but Bob Griese, his injured left shoulder throbbing with pain, led the
Dolphins down the field as the clock ran down, finding Marv Fleming in the
end zone for the five-yard touchdown that would send the game into overtime.
Or would it? Ed Podolak, who had his best day ever with an extraordinary 350
yards running, receiving, and kick returning, took the ensuing kickoff, broke
through the wave of Dolphins coming downfield, and streaked out near midfield. It looked like only a little boy was left to stop him: #1, the kicker, Garo
Yepremian. Garo was not known for bringing down runners; he was more likely
to run away from them. On this occasion, however, he managed to get in the
way of Podolak, who lost a couple steps, allowing cornerback Curtis Johnson
to run him out of bounds at the Miami twenty-two-yard line. Three plays later,
Jan Stenerud came out to wrap it up.

Stenerud, a Norwegian who had come to the U.S. on a ski-jumping scholarship at Montana State, had been the best kicker in the AFL before the merger,
and this year had been chosen as the NFL's All-Pro kicker—a fact which rankled
Yepremian, the league's high scorer. In this game, Stenerud had already been

charged with a missed twenty-nine-yard field goal when an attempted fake went awry. Now, though, he would erase that snafu from history by knocking through this thirty-two-yard game winner. "It's all over," said Kiick to Csonka on the sideline. But somehow the All-Pro kicker missed the easy one, pushing it wide. "I guess it ain't over," said Kiick. The game went to overtime.

Podolak had another near-game-winning kick return in overtime, leading to another Stenerud attempt to end it all, but this time Buoniconti broke through the line and blocked a forty-two-yard attempt. Yepremian got his own chance to win the game but was short on a fifty-two-yarder. Then, well into the sixth quarter of play, Griese remembered a favorite play of Csonka's, the "roll right, trap left," also known as the "misdirection" play. Throughout the game, Griese said, "I kept hearing the Chiefs yelling, 'Watch out for the misdirection!' So I didn't run it. And I almost forgot about it." On the snap, three offensive linemen move to the right for what looks like a sweep, but Larry Little and Norm Evans pull from the right side to the left, and when Csonka gets the handoff he cuts left behind them, moving against the grain of both teams. Csonka was almost completely drained by this point. He'd lost eighteen pounds bulling for precious yards in the dank winter air. But when Griese called the play in the huddle, he looked over at Csonka and saw his eyes light up. "I took the ball," said Csonka, "and boy I was a happy cat 'cause they all got fooled, and I was following Little down the field. . . ." He ran almost untouched down into Kansas City territory, a twenty-nine-yard gallop that might finally break the game.

A minute later, on came little Garo Yepremian to try again, from thirty-seven yards out. Griese couldn't bear to watch the kick, just kept his eyes on Karl Noonan, the holder. "The ball felt very good off my foot," said Yepremian. He turned and ran toward the sideline without even watching the flight of the ball. Then he stopped. "I thought, 'It's so quiet. Maybe I missed.'" It was quiet because he had *not* missed. Csonka, blocking on the field goal unit, screamed, "It's good!" And then all the Dolphins were screaming. Griese saw Noonan leap upward, arms stretched up toward the sky, and he just laughed out loud.

In Miami, it was 7:35 p.m. Most games in that era were over in two and a half hours; this one had gone an extra hour. (Today, with all the extra commercial time-outs and instant-replay reviews, that much play would take at least four and a half hours.) All over South Florida, ovens were turned back on, dinners were warmed up, and we all sat down to a happy Christmas meal. Hours later, just before midnight, when their plane came to a stop at Miami International and the hatch opened up, the team could hear a roar of cheers come floating in. Fifteen thousand fans were inundating Concourse 5 to welcome the team back. At Gate 77, police led Shula and his players through a narrow opening in the sea of handkerchief-waving fans. For hours the traffic leaving the parking lots was creeping a few inches at a time. When the Yepremians finally got home, the neighborhood was asleep, but the neighbors had decorated their house and the whole street with signs: WE'RE NO. 1! and THANKS GARO! Don Shula was even longer getting home. When he and his twelve-year-old son, David, finally got to their car, they found it wouldn't start. Rather than wait for a mechanic at that hour or wake Dorothy with a phone call, they hitched a ride with a carful of fans. ("Which way are you heading?" "Coach, we'll take you anywhere you want to go!") He needn't have worried about waking his wife. When they got home, the house was lit up, the neighbors helping Dorothy celebrate while they waited for Don.

• • •

Jan Stenerud never really got over his failures that day, particularly the missed chip shot at the end of regulation. Even forty years later he would hang his head when asked about it and try to express his grief at having let down his team. "Do you want to talk about my mother's funeral, too?" he said to one reporter, and hung up the phone. So one can imagine how raw it was nine months after the event, when the Dolphins came back to town and it was all the press wanted to ask him about. The Chiefs wouldn't even allow reporters to interview him in the week before the game. The press was given a tape of him answering softball questions from the team staff. Len Dawson, the quarterback, shrugged off allusions to the heartbreaking loss and got in a dig of his own: "People are always going to remember the last game that you've played. I'm sure Miami's heard about the Super Bowl, too."

You might say that. They'd heard little else from their boss all summer. In recent days, however, Shula had been talking to his guys more about the Christmas game. He was always looking for some way to fire his men up for the game at hand, and this week it was easy: for one thing, Kansas City coach Hank Stram had been telling the press that this '72 Chiefs team was the best he'd ever had. Not only that, Shula said, but they were going to be gunning for vengeance. Marv Fleming agreed, though he had his own take on it: "Stealing their money the way we did, I know they're going to be feeling revenge. They're going to be hitting hard. I hate a thief, especially when he's stealing my money." Fleming, who had stockbroker and real estate licenses and considered himself more of a businessman than a football player, was perhaps projecting his mercenary motivation onto the opponent. He liked to point out how, between his championship years as a Packer and his two playoff years in Miami, he'd earned $75,000 in postseason bonuses alone.

That past Christmas, Kansas City was unseasonably warm. This September weekend, temperatures were also far above normal. Unlike many NFL coaches, when on the road, Shula always insisted on a Saturday practice in the stadium they were visiting. This week it was especially important, for his men were playing in a new stadium. As they warmed up and ran some plays, they were not impressed. For one thing, it had a god-awful artificial turf similar to their own in the Orange Bowl. Also, as Warfield told Griese after catching a pass behind the goalpost and having to stop short before hitting a concrete wall, "The guy who designed this stadium didn't give much thought to the end zone." Csonka pointed to the stone steps coming down from the wall. "You think I couldn't break an ankle on those things? Or my neck?" The sun was beating down, hot as hell. Buoniconti was telling a reporter how he hated these Saturday practices on the road. But he respected Shula's method and talked about how hard they'd been training in the Miami cauldron. "If it's this hot tomorrow," he said, "we're ahead already."

Some players—Csonka and Kiick, among others—would have liked to sample the nightlife in the various cities they visited. But Shula would have none of that. "As far as I'm concerned," he said, "from the time a team arrives in town they're only there for one reason and everything they do should be directed toward one objective—sixty minutes of football on Sunday." With that in mind, Saturday nights were well scripted: at nine thirty all players and coaches were together in the hotel for a "snack." "That breaks up your evening pretty good," said Kiick. The topic of conversation was the next day's game. Beer was provided, but not too much. Eleven p.m. was curfew, with bed check.

Curfew for players and coaches, perhaps, but not for the owner, and certainly not for the traveling band of sportswriters. Joe Robbie was holding court long past midnight at the rooftop bar of the Hilton with Bill Braucher and a couple other newspapermen from New York and Dallas. The Dolphins were even better than last year, he opined. Kansas City would pose no problem this time, and Miami was sure to return to the Super Bowl behind its peerless coach. "Gentlemen," said Robbie in a wavering voice, probably not for the first time that night, "let us drink to a very good year."

· · ·

Chiefs fans packed the new stadium on Sunday to celebrate the opening of Arrowhead. The Dolphins came running out of the tunnel in their white visitors' uniforms and lined up on the sideline. Nick Buoniconti felt the hot sun on his face and smiled: it was a scorcher. He looked around at his teammates and nodded. Cornerback Tim Foley felt the adrenaline tingling: "You get that thrill nowhere else. . . . When they introduce you and you run out and all the people boo and the people are yelling, and screaming . . . You look around at the guys in white jerseys—it's those forty guys against eighty thousand. You feel like, Here come the lions; it forges you into a group."

The Chiefs swore they weren't thinking about the Longest Game. But whatever the reason, from the opening kickoff, they seemed still hung over from that long winter night. On the third play of the game, Ed Podolak fumbled at midfield, and Dick Anderson recovered at the Miami forty-three. A few plays later, Griese passed twice to his new wide receiver, Marlin Briscoe. First a fifteen-yarder down to the nine-yard line, and then, after a loss on a running play, a pretty fourteen-yard pass that found Briscoe slashing across to the right sideline, leaping and folding his body to gather the ball as if being handed a baby in midair, just inside the pylon marking the goal line. The newest Dolphin had scored the first touchdown of the 1972 season.

· · ·

The word going around my friends was that the new guy, Briscoe, wasn't just a top wide receiver; he used to play quarterback! If Griese got hurt, we told each other, he could replace him. We certainly weren't going to use that old guy, Morrall, who looked so bad in preseason. I had a vague idea that Briscoe himself was an experienced veteran who had played quarterback back in college. In fact, he was twenty-six years old, and just four years earlier he had been runner-up for AFL Rookie of the Year as a quarterback for the Denver Broncos.

Growing up in Omaha, Nebraska, Briscoe had been a quarterback ever since peewee league. He had a fine career quarterbacking for Omaha University and was drafted in 1968 by the AFL's Broncos—but as a defensive back. And it wasn't just because five foot ten and 170 pounds were cornerback, not quarterback, dimensions. Professional football simply did not have Black quarterbacks. Just as most women interested in medicine still became nurses, Black football players became receivers, runners, defensive backs—pretty much any position except those of leadership: middle linebacker, center, and quarterback. Before signing with Denver, Briscoe insisted on a clause in his contract that he be given a three-day tryout at quarterback during training camp. He got the clause, and the tryout, and then made the team as a cornerback. But when the quarterback broke a collarbone and the backup struggled, Coach Lou Saban put Briscoe in near the end of a home game against Boston. He completed his first pass for twenty-two yards and led an eighty-yard touchdown drive, running it in himself from twelve yards out. The rest of the year he split time with the other two quarterbacks but started five games, played in eleven, and finished with 1,589 yards passing, 308 rushing, and 14 touchdown passes—a league rookie record. In one game he outplayed second-year man Bob Griese, passing well and running for two touchdowns himself to beat the Dolphins.

It seemed like a fairy tale come true for the rookie. "The thing I remember," he said, "is the support I got from my teammates and fans. . . . That was amazing. Fans came up to me after the game. They were great. Back in those days, the fear was that white players wouldn't follow a Black quarterback and fans would be pissed off. That didn't happen." Saban apparently was not as enlightened. He never considered Briscoe a potential quarterback for 1969 and informed him he would be back at cornerback. Briscoe asked to be traded, was told no one wanted him, and ended up making the Buffalo Bills as a free agent. The Bills, however, had perennial all-star quarterback Jack Kemp and two strong backups (including James Harris, who five years later would become the first Black quarterback to start and win an NFL playoff game, for the Rams). So Briscoe accepted a move to another new position, wide receiver, and promptly became expert at that too. He was a starter his first year and then made the Pro Bowl in 1970 with fifty-seven catches for over a thousand yards. After another good year in 1971, though, a new coach arrived in Buffalo: Lou Saban. Before he even played a down for him, Briscoe was traded to Miami.

He couldn't have been happier. He knew he still wouldn't be playing quarterback, as Griese was the team stalwart and they had also just added Morrall.

But aside from his differences with Saban, he was going from 1–13 to a Super Bowl team. It also happened to be Paul Warfield's team. When Briscoe had suddenly to learn a new position in 1969, his model was Warfield, the NFL's preeminent wide receiver. He'd study films of Warfield and spend long hours after practice trying to re-create his every move: "By the time I got to Miami," he recalled, "I had him down." The contrast between his old team and his new one was glaring, from the first day of training camp to the winning drive of the last preseason game, when, as Marlin put it, "In Buffalo we would have been throwing on every down. Griese was throwing—but when *he* wanted to throw." Even when the Dolphins played that playoff game in Kansas City last Christmas, before he knew he would be a Dolphin, he said, "I suffered with Miami all the way. I'm always for the underdog—because I've been an underdog all my life."

• • •

On this day, Kansas City was hotter than Miami. It felt worse than Miami on the worst day of summer training camp. It was ninety-one degrees at kickoff, but a thermometer on the field, where the enormous stadium corralled the heat and reflected it off the hard carpet, registered a hundred and twenty. After a long career in Miami, Shula said that this game was the hottest he'd ever coached in. When he came running out of the tunnel with his team, he was wearing a light blue blazer—a cooler, more casual look than the jacket and tie he'd worn in last year's playoffs. The blazer quickly disappeared. His white shirt had a pocket with notes he had written down for the game, but at some point he reached for them and they were useless: the ink had run into his shirt. (Shula never wore a jacket or tie on the sideline again. Stram kept both on throughout this steamfest, and it couldn't have helped his mood.)

"I've never played in a more miserable, hot, sweltering, rotten game," said Doug Swift. The antiwar liberal from Amherst never had much use for displays of military force, but today, he said, as a formation of fighter jets thundered overhead and cannons were fired in celebration of the opening of Arrowhead, "it delayed the kickoff another twenty-five minutes while we were all out there on the sidelines . . . it was just killing me."

It was probably hurting the home team more. They gave up four turnovers; Miami never had to drive more than fifty-seven yards for their scores. The game was close for most of the first half, but then Griese led a quick drive to the Kansas

City forty, and Yepremian nailed a forty-seven-yard field goal with a minute left. Jake Scott intercepted the next Len Dawson pass, and the Dolphins had the ball at the other forty again. A crisp thirty-yard throw to Warfield, slanting in to the middle, put the ball at the ten-yard line, and a Morris eight-yard run set up Larry Csonka for a two-yard blast to give Miami a 17–0 lead at the half.

. . .

The Dolphins had a somewhat new look with Briscoe and Morris shining on offense, but one thing was very familiar: Larry Csonka powering through the middle like a hussar on a rampage. For Dolphin fans, he was Old Faithful in pads. Griese would hand to Csonka, and approximately one million of us would be screaming "Go, Zonk!" at our television sets as number thirty-nine, a horse of a man as big as his linemen, would go barreling into the fray, carrying defensive backs on his shoulders for an almost guaranteed three or four yards. Each week at an offensive meeting Shula liked to ask his players what plays they thought would work best against that week's opponent, considering the films they had been watching of that team's defense, analyzing its strengths and weaknesses. Someone might note a susceptibility to sweeps; someone else might think a play-action pass might work well against overzealous linebackers. Week after week, Csonka gave the same answer: P-10. The simplest, cleanest running play imaginable: Griese takes the snap, turns, and there's Csonka to take it from him. The linemen thrust straight ahead, no fancy switches or pulls, and Zonk pounds right through. If asked to elaborate, he would explain: "No need for the fancy stuff."

He was the spitting image of his great-grandfather, a six-foot-five, 250-pound marshal in nineteenth-century Missouri. Larry grew up on an eighteen-acre farm in Ohio, and when he wasn't in school or playing football he was digging holes, baling hay, and shoveling manure: "I used to hoe beans until I wanted to hit my father with the hoe." But he wasn't about to do that. If anyone thought Larry Csonka was tough, they had to look only one generation back to see why. Joe Csonka had once been a bouncer and famous brawler. "If my father liked you, he hit you on the arm," said Larry. "If he didn't like you, he hit you too. And believe me, he can hit you quicker than you can think about it." Larry grew up thinking all women woke up their husbands the way his mom did—tapping them with the end of a long broom handle.

Not surprisingly, Larry grew up hardy. He slept in an attic with no heat. When he got hurt, he was expected not to cry or complain. For a six-one, 215-pound fifteen-year-old, football was the natural game. He went to Syracuse as a linebacker but switched to fullback his sophomore year, and by the time he was done there he'd broken every Syracuse rushing record—and his predecessors included Ernie Davis, Jim Nance, and the immortal Jim Brown.

He loved the football at Syracuse, but he hated the weather. He got home to Ohio by hitchhiking, and it seemed it was always snowing. One winter weekend his sophomore year, he hitchhiked home, borrowed a car, and eloped with his high school sweetheart, Pam. She came back to Syracuse with him, and he moved out of the dorm and got a job as a night watchman in a parking lot. It wasn't an easy life, despite the fun of college football. So when he got the phone call that the Miami Dolphins had drafted him, he was glad, though he knew nothing of that two-year-old AFL team. He'd known the Bills were interested in him, and the last thing he wanted to do was to stay in upstate New York.

South Florida in 1968 was about as far from small-town Ohio and upstate New York as you could get without a passport. Larry and Pam drove around Miami Beach looking for a place to live, but that was not their style. They lived briefly in North Miami Beach but then found a house down south near Homestead, a less developed area that seemed like a good place to raise a family. "Out west it was wide-open back then," he said. There were bean fields and swamps all over, even deer hunting, though the deer were smaller than he was used to. "But there was a wildness, and once I found that out and the fishing in some of those canals, I thought I could adapt fairly quickly."

He was the starting fullback from the beginning, but in his first couple of years Csonka was more famous for his broken nose than for any achievements as a runner. He'd broken it for the first time as a kid when a startled steer whacked him with its head. Ever a Csonka, he just pinched the nose back into place, ignored the blood, and continued his work. He broke it four more times in high school and college, and its crooked outline became his distinctive look. Then, in his first couple of pro seasons—in addition to other physical calamities, such as a cracked eardrum that filled with blood, broken blood vessel in his eye, and painful bone chips in his elbow—he broke the nose four more times. But it wasn't the nose that was so worrisome as what was behind the nose. In the fifth game his rookie year he took a shot to the head on a pass over the middle and was unconscious for five minutes. He had no memory of going back to the huddle and running for eleven yards on the next play, or of being carried off the field after that. He woke up when they were trying to get him on a stretcher, and he insisted on getting up and walking off on his own. "That's just the Hunky [Hungarian] in me. I wasn't about to get carted out of there like a dead man in front of thirty thousand people."

Then he got knocked out of a game in Denver with another concussion. The next week, in San Diego, he had to be helped to the bench in the second quarter and didn't recall a thing after that until the fourth quarter. "If this keeps up," said a Miami neurosurgeon, "Csonka will have to reevaluate his occupation. Or he may become like a punch-drunk fighter." However, not all doctors in the sixties and seventies took concussions as seriously. Another doctor the team consulted said not to worry: "Most concussions last no longer than twenty minutes and are seldom accompanied by brain cell damage. It just takes a little while to recover." Players liked to joke about getting their "bell rung," and sportswriters had a ball with head injuries. After Jake Scott got knocked out of an exhibition game, one wrote, "Jake exited with a dreamy smile, back on the snowy slopes in a world of his own." In another game, "Mumphord dashed in when Tim Foley heard chapel bells in the third quarter." HUFF DOESN'T REMEMBER TOO MUCH OF GAME, ran one whimsical headline in the *Miami Herald* about a college game.

After Csonka passed out at home and Pam had to call an ambulance, the team ordered him a special helmet with water in it to cushion the blows, but he said it only slowed him down. In 1969, when he suffered another broken nose in an exhibition game, the speculation began that his career was over after just one full year. X-rays showed "a questionable abnormality" in his skull, and he was ruled out of action indefinitely. A month later he was back, though, without much of an explanation from anyone, and he played the rest of the season, almost catching Jim Kiick for the team rushing lead.

The cure for Csonka's cranial woes came in 1970, and it turned out it wasn't a water-cushioned helmet that did the trick, or the horseshoe-shaped fiberglass nose guard that became a fixture on his helmet in 1971. It was the arrival of Don Shula and offensive line coach Monte Clark. As the offensive line evolved into the league's best, Csonka got jackhammered into the ground less often, and he started giving out the punishment rather than taking it. The concussions became just some good stories from his past, and he was able to develop into the league's top fullback. Not that he didn't still get the occasional nosebleed. After one jarring tackle in Buffalo in 1971, Csonka came back to the huddle with the nose out of joint again. "It was really bleeding bad," he said, "making bubbly noises and coming out in a steady stream. I leaned over to hear the call and bled all over Marv Fleming's pants and shoes. I noticed Marv's eyes getting bigger and bigger, like he was going to upchuck. So I turned the other way and bled on Kiick's shoes. He likes it. It makes him think he's really in the game."

In Shula's first year, 1970, Csonka and Kiick shouldered the rushing load almost completely. They carried the ball 193 and 191 times, respectively, with Morris next in line with only 60 carries (though for an astonishing 6.8-yards-per-carry average). Csonka was the more productive runner of the duo, with 874 yards, but Kiick was still the top total-yardage man, as his team-leading 42 catches gave him 1,155 total yards running and receiving. In 1971, Kiick's and Morris's numbers remained about the same. Morris, despite his high average, would be relegated to kick returns in the playoffs; his time would come in 1972. Csonka, though, reached the upper echelon of NFL runners in 1971, notching his first thousand-yard season and averaging 5.4 yards a carry—remarkable for a big man who ran mostly up the middle, and more than any runner who got at least a hundred chances. His 1,051 yards were third most in the entire league.

The value of Csonka, though, went far beyond his numbers. "Zonk was the blood and guts of our team," Larry Little said. "He was like another lineman in the backfield. We knew if we did our job, he would get the needed yardage. He would run over anything in his way, including teammates if they didn't get out of the way. And when you saw him on one side of the huddle and his nose on the other side, it made your own pain hurt a little less." The effect began even before kickoff. "If you weren't excited before the game," said Tim Foley, "all you had to do was look at Csonka rocking back and forth in front of his locker."

Little wasn't kidding about getting out of his way. "I'm afraid if I don't block enough, he'll hit me and break my back," said Norm Evans. But defensive backs had much more to fear. After all, they might only be 190 pounds of pure muscle. And Larry Csonka didn't try to cut around you. If you were lucky, he would just try to run right through you. But as often as not, he would throw his forearm at you like a bludgeon. Shula and assistant coach Carl Taseff had taught him that trick from their face mask–less days playing for the Browns. "My collision with Csonka went from the top of my head out my ankle," remembered Dallas linebacker Thomas Henderson, who weighed 220 pounds. He was out of action for five weeks. One time up in Buffalo, Csonka delivered his famous forearm to the jaw of safety Pete Richardson. "It folded him up," said Csonka. "He was down on the ground, doing 'the twitch.'" It happened at the sideline, right in front of Shula, who shouted, "Great hit!" But then the referee's yellow flag flew, and he began marking off fifteen yards against the Dolphins. "What are you doing?" cried Shula, as a penalty after a hit is always against the defense. "It's against your number thirty-nine," shouted the ref. "Look what he did to that defensive back." Most seem to agree that it's the only time a runner was called for unnecessary roughness for hurting a defensive player.

Csonka was quick to point out, though, that his impetus in delivering such blows had nothing to do with meanness. "I'm driven by common sense," he said. "If a guy hits me from the side, I smack the ground first and he piles onto me. If I take him on, head up, it's the other way around and he cushions *my* fall." In fact, despite his reputation for toughness, Csonka was one of the more sensitive and intelligent players in professional football. Howard Cosell, that connoisseur of rhetoric, called him "one of the most articulate athletes I have ever known." He was, and remains, one of the most copious sources of witty and insightful commentary on his old team. He didn't accumulate quite enough credits to graduate Syracuse, what with football, gainful employment, and starting a family, but he took four years of English literature courses by choice and enjoyed them. "I resent being called a bulldozer or a battering ram," he said. "It's dehumanizing. Anybody who uses his head for a battering ram has nothing better to do with it. I don't like being thought of that way."

Even his teammates, though, had cause to remark on his physical anomaly. "The meanest looking of the man-mountain people in camp," wrote Mercury Morris in his rookie-year diary. "I thought I had big thighs till I saw his," said Kiick. "And he never lifts weights." Csonka had a painful case of turf toe from battling his primary foe—the artificial Poly-Turf in the Orange Bowl. His feet had become gnarly, bruised appendages that caused him to shuffle tenderly, pigeon-toed, when off the field. Tim Foley was astonished to see Csonka purposefully jumping up and down on the bad toe before games. Turns out he was trying to make it hurt so bad that it would go numb and he wouldn't have to think about it during the game. Larry Csonka refused to take pain-killing drugs.

"I like to run where there are holes," said Kiick. "Larry likes to run where there are people." Every old Dolphins fan has an image in his mind of Larry Csonka fighting through the body-strewn center of the field, carrying one or two opponents on his back or legs as he strains forward for one extra yard. After watching one such scene on the 1971 highlight reel—Zonk taking two hits and fighting his way over the goal line, then looking up, his helmet askew, sweat and mud dripping off his nose guard, showing no emotion as he flips the ball to the ref—Shula called it "the very image of manhood."

• • •

Csonka's touchdown just before the half accounted for two of the 118 yards he would accumulate on opening day in Kansas City. With a seventeen-point lead, the Dolphins in the second half would fall back on their still-nascent MO of ball control: run, run, run, and watch the clock unwind while the other offense desperately waits for its turn. The heat that day made it an almost sadistic strategy. Sixty fans collapsed in the stands and had to be treated in Arrowhead's two pristine first aid facilities. The artificial carpet they were playing on became a frying pan. "On that rug," said Foley, "every time you cut you could feel the heat in your feet." Blisters bloomed. On the sideline, players soaked their feet in buckets of cool water. When they returned to the field, said one player, "you could hear the feet squishing away." But as painful as it was for the Dolphins, it was worse for the Chiefs, who had not undergone quite the same infernal training camp. The home team sat on their bench like a chain gang on break, too tired to wipe the sweat off their faces, spraying water on their faces, holding oxygen masks to their faces.

A field goal put Miami up 20–0. As time ran out in the third quarter, they had the ball deep in their own end. Both teams turned wearily to walk to the other end of the field. With disbelief they looked up: Miami's number sixty-six, Larry Little, the man who hated the twelve-minute run so much he faked fainting to get out of it, was sprinting across the tartan-patterned turf from one end of the stadium to the other like a mad dog in the midday sun. His teammates looked at each other, laughed, and ran after him. The Chiefs walked. "We almost had to call a timeout after that," said Norm Evans. But no one on either team now doubted that the game was over. Miami controlled the ball, and Yepremian's two missed field goals, from fifty and forty-three yards, were barely noticed.

Kansas City scored a touchdown in the final minute after a long pointless drive, and the final score was 20–10, Miami's first season-opening win since 1967.

The Dolphin defense was supreme when it mattered, forcing those four turnovers and never allowing Dawson, Podolak, or All-Pro receiver Otis Taylor to get going. With Jim Riley still out, Vern Den Herder played his first big game and shone. And defensive coordinator Bill Arnsparger unveiled a new scheme he had cooked up, in which number fifty-three, linebacker Bob Matheson, morphed into a lineman and back again at will. "Nothing we haven't seen before," said Hank Stram, but others would disagree, and the "53 defense" would gain some fame before the year was through. On offense, a trend of the Shula era continued. In the Wilson years the Dolphins ran the ball slightly less than half the time. (To be fair, they were usually trying to come from behind.) In Shula's first year, the team ran the ball sixty-two percent of the time, and in 1971 they repeated that. In 1972 it would be over seventy percent.

A ground-dominated offense was not, as many in Miami assumed, a Shula trademark. In Baltimore, with the arm of Johnny U, his offense threw almost as much as it ran. (And when he had Dan Marino in the 1980s, the Dolphins were in the air as much as sixty-five percent of the time.) Perhaps it was the input of Howard Schnellenberger, a friend from their days as assistant coaches at the University of Kentucky, whom he brought with him to Miami as offensive coordinator. With his ever-present pipe and his witty, soft-spoken manner, Schnellenberger seemed more like a tenured philosopher than a football coach. Although he was also the receivers coach, he may have learned the running-game creed when he was offensive coordinator for Bear Bryant at Alabama: even with Joe Namath at quarterback, Alabama ran the ball about seventy-five percent of the time. And before coming to Miami, Schnellenberger was an assistant to another infantry general, George Allen of the Los Angeles Rams.

But it may have been simply that as Monte Clark built a nearly perfect offensive line, the Miami running game became so good that there was little reason to risk passing the ball. Fans started to get the idea right off the bat in the Kansas City game, as Griese handed the ball off forty-two times and threw it only fifteen. Like no other team in history to that point, Shula's Dolphins became an instrument of domination on the ground. Long, slow, time-consuming drives became the norm. They "controlled the clock," a phrase suggesting godliness, and it sometimes seemed that way. If the other team couldn't get the ball, how could they win?

Two and Oh

Once the season began, players had Mondays off. So there was at least one day to let the bruises begin to heal, let the muscles recover. It was worse after a game played on the thin artificial turfs of the early 1970s. In the Kansas City locker room Larry Csonka had complained to a reporter, "I'd like to take you out there and bounce you off that stuff twenty-one times—that's asphalt under there, you know—and see if you could walk tomorrow." Larry Little would get home from games and collapse in bed, "maybe watching the second game on TV, thankful it's somebody else out there instead of me. . . . I don't like to get out of bed on Mondays, either, unless I need treatment. I'm pretty beat up on Mondays."

The only time off for Don Shula was Sunday evenings, after a game, when he would relax with Dorothy and the kids at home or, more frequently, take his coaching staff and their wives out to dinner. Other nights were spent studying opponents. "From July until the end of the draft [in February]," said Joe Robbie, "that man devotes every waking moment to football." The rest of the year it was merely a full-time job. On Monday morning after returning from Kansas City, Shula woke at six thirty a.m. as always and was in the Biscayne College chapel at seven for Mass. After a quick breakfast he was in his office at seven thirty, a half hour before the other coaches showed up.

Coaches didn't have strained, bruised muscles to rest, and Mondays were film day. Every few hours they would emerge from the film room bleary-eyed to refill their mugs with coffee. Their notepads filled up with little insights into opponents' blocking habits and coverages, their own team's mistakes, opportunities for improvement. Tuesdays the players arrived and were treated to a curated version of the film festival, showing them just what they needed to see. After a light practice—no pads, no hitting—the coaches would reconvene long into the night, drawing up game plans for Sunday. Wednesday and Thursday were long days, with full practices, including full contact in pads. Friday was a bit lighter, the exertion waning into the weekend in preparation for game time.

Already the Dolphins, like other teams, were getting banged up. The most troubling two casualties at this point were defensive end Jim Riley and offensive tackle Doug Crusan, both lost since the preseason. However, their substitutes, Vern Den Herder and Wayne Moore, had performed so well since then, including in the Kansas City game, that fears were allayed. It was a good thing that Den Herder turned out to be so good, because a few days later Riley, the starter since 1968, was declared out for the season. In fact, he would never play again. And although Crusan had been declared ready to go, Shula was happy to keep Moore in there for the time being.

Having two excellent players for one spot was a good problem to have, and he had the same dilemma with Jim Kiick and Mercury Morris. All during the exhibition season, as Morris drew comparisons to everyone from Gale Sayers to O. J. Simpson, Shula was asked daily who would be the regular, and he would just smile. He'd named Morris the starter in Kansas City and been rewarded with a fine performance. But Kiick was in the dumps. He was a team man and had only good things to say about Morris, but he couldn't disguise his disappointment after four years as the backfield costar. Reporters saw him sitting dejectedly on the bench and in the locker room and descended on him, and like Morris after the Super Bowl—when he complained publicly that he hadn't touched the ball—Kiick couldn't help but let out some of his frustration. "I don't want to take anything away from Merc," he said, "who I like as a friend and admire as an athlete. Yet I wouldn't have any honesty or guts if I didn't say I feel very disappointed. It hurt my pride not to start in Kansas City. What have I done to not deserve it?"

He was right: he looked as good as ever in preseason, but Morris was too talented to keep on the bench. Still, Kiick felt he was at the peak of his career, and it was frustrating. Csonka tried to avoid the subject when prodded by a TV reporter: "Well, Jane, this is a touchy subject and I don't want to get into it very much. It's tough for me to say anything because I'm best friends with Jim and of course I'm friends with Merc. . . ." But everyone knew, and could tell from Csonka's downturned face, that he rued the busting of Butch and Sundance.

Shula was more concerned with a letdown after the big opening victory over one of the league's best teams. This week they were two-touchdown favorites at home against the struggling Houston Oilers, who after being two-time AFL champions in the 1960s were now at the nadir of a four-year wallow through the NFL. Shula didn't like it from a psychological perspective. With a trip to Minnesota to play another Super Bowl contender the following week, there was plenty of opportunity for a mental week off. As always, though, Shula would find a bone of motivation to throw to his pack. He talked up inexperienced quarterback Dan Pastorini and receivers Ken Burrough and Charlie Joiner like they were Pro Bowlers (which in fact they would become). "We have to establish the ground game," he told his men as though for the first time. And, more to the point: "The thing this ball club must realize is that a poor performance cancels out the good effort against Kansas City." This game, he told them, will count just as much in the final record.

Alone in the college cafeteria early each morning after Mass, Shula would read the *Miami Herald* over his breakfast of sliced grapefruit and coffee. It would be hard for a football coach not to glance at the sports section first. See what grief Braucher was giving him over the Kiick situation. Then the front page. Israeli forces were withdrawing from their invasion of Lebanon provoked by the Munich Olympics massacre. Claiming to have killed sixty terrorists, they retreated triumphantly back to Israel in time for the beginning of Yom Kippur. Below, that elongated double byline of Bernstein and Woodward was there again: Jeb Magruder and another top Nixon campaign official had each withdrawn more than $50,000 from a fund for secret intelligence-gathering activities against the Democrats. Politicians. Meanwhile, Gordon Liddy, Howard Hunt, Bernard Barker, and the other Watergate burglars pleaded not guilty in Washington and were released on bail.

Another story in the paper that morning sported a byline that had also been appearing frequently. Edna Buchanan was a New Jersey transplant who had joined the *Herald* a couple years earlier. In the 1980s Calvin Trillin would write, "In Miami, a few figures are regularly discussed by first name among people they have never actually met. One of them is Fidel. Another is Edna." She wouldn't officially go on the police beat until 1973, but already she seemed to have a nose for the bizarre and the macabre—as well as for a good lead, as she showed this morning: "A man wandering along a Miami Beach street in his undershorts and carrying a blood-stained knife Sunday morning led police to the scene of a murder." Don Shula must have just shook his head and smiled: you're not in Painesville anymore. Miami. Funny place for a football team.

• • •

There had only *been* a Miami for seventy-six years. Before that—even for some years after its founding, to be honest—there had been nothing more than swampland, mosquitoes, and a few hardy humans. The Tequesta tribe had a settlement there at least as far back as 700 BC, but they did not long survive the arrival of Europeans that began with Ponce de León in 1513. For almost four centuries after Ponce de León, though, South Florida stubbornly resisted civilization. Florida passed from Spain to Britain, back to Spain when the American colonies won their independence, and then finally to the United States in 1821. General Andrew Jackson and his successors waged an inhumane and illegal war of genocide against the Seminole peoples between 1818 and 1858 and finally succeeded in removing them, but for fifty years after that the southern part of the state remained inaccessible and undeveloped. When Julia Tuttle arrived by mail boat in 1875 to see the land her father had purchased, the nearest railroad station was four hundred miles to the north. Her father, Ephraim Sturtevant, was a former college professor who had settled in the South Florida wilderness in 1870 and become a fruit grower, county judge, and state senator.

Tuttle returned in 1891, now a forty-two-year-old widow left with few resources other than some mosquito-infested swampland in Florida. Her father had died as well; she sold his land and bought 640 acres on the north bank of the Miami River. For some mad reason she had envisioned a city growing there. After the winter of 1895 brought freezing temperatures all the way down to West Palm Beach and ruined crops throughout much of the state, she finally convinced Henry Flagler, who'd cofounded Standard Oil with John D. Rockefeller and was now leading capitalism into Florida with a pioneering railway, to extend his tracks all the way to Miami. He took her idea and ran with it, erecting the Royal Palm Hotel to complement his Palm Beach Inn (which later became the

Breakers). In 1896 the few hundred residents voted to incorporate the city of Miami. The entire wooden town burned down that Christmas, and they rebuilt it with brick and stucco. Two years later Tuttle died of meningitis, and her name was soon largely forgotten compared to that of her neighbor, William Brickell, and the developers to come. Carl Fisher and John Collins arrived and, as T. D. Allman wrote, "together they transformed a slender, low-lying offshore strip of shifting sand, roach-infested palmetto groves and slimy mangrove swamp into one of the most bizarre, most illuminating wonderlands this nation has ever seen." They called it Ocean Beach and finally incorporated it in 1915 as Miami Beach. An army of mostly Black laborers dug up the mangroves, dredged the water channels and the bay, scooping up tons of muck and almost doubling the land mass of the island. Andrew Carnegie came, William Jennings Bryan came, President Harding came. Al Capone came. And in the 1920s Miami and Miami Beach became America's Caribbean paradise.

For some people, anyway. Not only were Blacks barred from entering Miami Beach (except to work menial labor), but as long as Carl Fisher had his way, Jews too were unwelcome. Miami Beach was a "restricted" paradise at least until Fisher died in 1939, having lost most of his fortune. The hurricane of 1926 had ravaged the area and rendered the real estate all but worthless. But the dream of Miami would not die, and the area "rose from the ashes" again as the Depression waned. In the post–World War II era, as Fisher rolled in his grave, Miami Beach became a haven for Jews who had escaped the shtetl long ago and now were escaping the northern cold. And Miami, served by Pan Am's "flying boats" operating out of the marine airport at Dinner Key, became the gateway between North and South America.

By the 1960s, though, Miami's colors were fading. The California lifestyle was all over television, and Miami, as Allman put it, "was a dowdy refuge of retirees and other people of the past." The Cuban refugee airlift program, also known as the "Freedom Flights," between 1965 and 1972 brought a new Cuban injection into the population, but it was nothing compared to what would come in the 1980s. Jackie Gleason pumped some life into Miami Beach when he taped his hit television show at the Miami Beach Auditorium from 1966 to 1970, but Jackie Gleason wasn't exactly the Beach Boys. As the 1970s began, Miami as a vacation destination was mainly for an older, middle-class crowd. And Miami itself, the city, was a run-down cityscape that emptied after dark. The only time I remember going downtown, other than a school event at Miami-Dade Community College, was to get my first passport.

Miami in 1972 was still inchoate. Pre–*Miami Blues*, pre–*Miami Vice*, eight years before the Mariel boatlift. (In 1980, Castro suddenly allowed over a hundred thousand political prisoners and one or two thousand other "undesirables"—such as criminals and mental patients—to leave Cuba; between April and October, they made it to South Florida via every kind of small boat you could imagine, forever changing the local culture. The Orange Bowl was the site of one of several makeshift processing centers.) There had already been a Latin American presence, particularly since Castro came to power, but the Latino population was mostly in the Little Havana area. Still largely segregated by tradition and economic circumstance if no longer by law, the Greater Miami area was a quiet, relatively uncrowded sprawl of communities almost unrecognizable from a vantage point twenty years later, when outsiders began to think South Beach, a Miami Beach neighborhood packed with models and drug kingpins and flashy young entrepreneurs, was a city unto itself. South Beach in the early 1970s was where families like mine went for an actual day at the beach. The grassy area between the sand and Ocean Drive had never hosted bikinied models, spring break hedonists, or Rollerbladers. All you saw between parking on the street and walking to the water was a community of retirees sitting in woven beach chairs on the grass, whiling away their final years. To the west of Miami, where housing developments and shopping malls now smother the landscape and increasingly encroach on the vital Everglades, there was still farmland, still wetlands. Where we lived, in Kendall, you could gather your own tomatoes and pole beans at U-pick farms. Coconut Grove was a quiet area with a few galleries and restaurants, still some affordable housing left for bohemians, easy to drive in and park for lunch, maybe hit some tennis balls in the park.

Larry Csonka wasn't the only Dolphin to enjoy the good hunting back then. Manny Fernandez remembered good deer, duck, turkey, and hog hunting before the government flooded large areas of the Glades in the 1990s to create filter marshes to remove farm pollution from the water. He and fellow defensive lineman Bill Stanfill, his best friend on the team, would drive Manny's swamp buggy out into the Everglades on Friday mornings before dawn. Fridays were light practices, and they didn't have to report until the first meeting at eleven.

Time to get in some good hunting or fishing. They'd have fun with gators too. Catch them by hand, get a rope around the snout, and drag them out. Rub their bellies, put them to sleep. Lots of folks ate them, illegally, but Manny and Bill had nothing to say about that.

Miami had never been much of a sports town. When baseball legends Johnny Evers, Christy Mathewson, and Walter Johnson came to play exhibitions, they couldn't fill even the five-hundred-seat bleachers in the old Royal Palm Park (downtown, near where the Dupont Plaza Hotel would be). The same indifference greeted Red Grange and Notre Dame's Four Horsemen in the 1920s when they played all-star football games in a makeshift stadium in Coral Gables. The University of Miami had a football team beginning in 1926, and some pretty good ones in the 1960s, but they could never come close to filling the Orange Bowl and by the 1970s were drawing only paltry audiences. The one attempt at professional football, the Seahawks, drowned quickly in that series of downpours.

Joe Robbie's big gamble on the Dolphins didn't pay off until he brought in Shula, Shula brought in his crack coaching staff, and the team finally began to win. Players who had suffered through the early years witnessed the sea change. "When Kiick and I got there [in 1968]," said Csonka, "we weren't the new thing anymore and we also weren't winning, so we weren't exactly the talk of the town. We had some core fans, but just maybe ten to twenty thousand people." Everybody in Miami was from somewhere else, he noted, and that was true. My family was typical of South Florida: my siblings and I were born in New York State, and we moved to Miami when I, the youngest, was three. I didn't know any kids whose parents were actually from South Florida. "Most football fans down there were fans of another team," Csonka pointed out. It wasn't just football. The *Herald* reported that in 1971 undertakers had shipped 4,854 bodies "home" for burial.

Around the country, Miami was not thought of as a place for tough, disciplined football players to thrive. It was a place for swimming pools and beaches, snowbirds and retirees playing golf and mah-jongg, catching the Early Bird at Franklin's Prime Steak House ($2.95 Sirloin). More high-rolling visitors might take in the show at the Eden Roc. As one reporter wrote, "Who thinks of apple-cheeked American youth playing a fast game of touch on Jackie Gleason Drive or Arthur Godfrey Road? Who would expect hoarse cries of "Dee-fense!

Dee-fense!" from a bathing suit salesman dressed in a robin's-egg-blue sports jacket and ocher slacks?"

Of course, that highly stylized view was primarily of Miami Beach, a separate city, and ignored the swift expansion of Greater Miami in the 1950s and 1960s to include suburbs all the way out to ours. Every year more schools, playgrounds, churches, and shopping malls were being built to accommodate the families flocking down, and these families rarely included "vermilion-trousered gents and leopard-leotarded ladies" such as that reporter observed out on the Beach. Still, even the locals never expected a championship team. "People had no confidence in Miami as a major metropolitan area," said Joe Robbie. "No confidence that they were big league." Their first season, the Dolphins barely averaged twenty-five thousand fans in the cavernous Orange Bowl, and their popularity rose no quicker than their record, climbing to just over thirty-two thousand in 1969. One Dolphin Doll (the teenaged cheerleading group) remembered, "the Dolphins used to give tickets to our parents. They would give tickets to anybody to try to fill the stands." Robbie did everything he could to get the bandwagon rolling, to no avail.

It was nothing a winning season—or even the prospect of it—couldn't fix. Almost from the beginning of the Shula era in 1970, excitement began to build throughout the community. Grocery stores no longer gave away Dolphins tickets to customers who bought enough produce. I AM A DOL-FAN bumper stickers spread from Datsuns to Thunderbirds to Lincoln Mark IVs. The Orange Bowl saw its first Dolphins sellouts, and thousands of fans started greeting the team at Miami International every time they flew back home. The players could feel the change in the electric charge shooting around the Orange Bowl, eighty thousand fans madly waving white handkerchiefs. The hankies were something still new in '72: when they were playing the Colts the previous November, WIOD's Rick Weaver was curious just how many in the stands were listening to the broadcast on transistor radios, so he asked them to wave handkerchiefs. After that, fans made sure to bring a white hankie to the game to wave at every celebratory opportunity.

"Oh, what that team did for that city," said Larry King. In 1957, when he was twenty-four and his name was still Larry Zeiger, he had come down from Brooklyn on a tip that Miami would be a good place to break into radio. That he did, moving quickly from sweeping up at little station WAHR on Miami Beach to flipping disks and then interviewing local celebrities. Soon he had his own interview show on WIOD, broadcasting right out of Pumpernik's deli on Miami Beach, where he would get the likes of Bobby Darin, Frank Sinatra, and Jackie Gleason to sit down with him. Live interviews became his bread and butter for sixty years and more, but King was also made part of WIOD's broadcast team for Dolphin games, and his career blossomed along with the team. "It was never a unified city," he said. "It was a city of Chicagoans, of New Yorkers. We used to look strangely upon native Miamians. But that team brought the town together and created a mini metropolis, more than just a beach for people to come to in the winter. And I give a lot of credit to that Dolphin team and the way that city adopted them."

By the time the 1972 Dolphin express got on track, the players were South Florida celebrities, a far cry from 1966. The newspapers were full of ads featuring players: Csonka, Kiick, and Warfield were regulars for Surreys menswear, Warfield in his "White Is Beautiful Too" suit, Csonka wearing nothing but mesh underwear. Everyone was familiar with Bob Griese strolling through an empty Orange Bowl in a Sears suit, and he was soon to appear in national TV commercials for a children's laxative—with his mother. Lesser stars were paid to pose in full uniform sitting on and around a luxury car. Even fishing equipment got hawked: "Ask a Tough Guy About a Tough Reel. Ask the 'Zonk.'"

As many as eight players had their own radio show at some point during those years. "Anything with that Dolphin on it will sell," said a clerk at a store in Dadeland, the ten-year-old mall that, over three miles from us, had been the closest when we'd moved to Miami. (It would soon be unthinkable to have to drive that far to a mall.) It wasn't enclosed and air-conditioned until 1969. The clerk showed a lamp with the leaping dolphin insignia on the shade, going for $49.50. The store printed up hundreds of bumper stickers—GO DOLPHINS with the insignia—for a penny apiece and sold them for a dollar. Thirty South Florida companies had applied to NFL Properties for the right to sell white handkerchiefs with the official insignia. Car emblems, posters, medallions on chains, infant onesies, watches—anything sellable was more sellable with the helmeted dolphin. Even, oddly enough in Miami, stocking caps. Some businesses, however, were suffering. A letter from the Florida Barbers' Association complained that the players' fashionably long hair was cutting down on their business.

On Sunday afternoons during the season, golf courses and tennis courts emptied. At the Kendalltown Tennis Club, it was usually difficult for us kids to get a court on the weekend. The tennis boom was in full swing, and our whole family had jumped on board the year before. Families were crowding the clubs and the public courts with their wood rackets (along with metal T2000s), white tennis dresses, and men's mesh shirts. Clubs like ours had crowded clinics and social events like team tennis on Saturday nights, when we'd run around with friends and watch our parents cavort in friendly competition, beer bottles collecting by the net posts, dragonflies buzzing up in the mercury vapor lights. We spent our whole summers there, unchaperoned, running from the tennis courts to the swimming pool to the clubhouse Ping-Pong room. The courts were packed all year on weekends; there was one court designated the Junior Court, with a long waiting list. But we could have had our pick of courts on autumn Sunday afternoons—or would have, if we'd been willing to miss the Dolphins game. Even the traffic was noticeably lighter from one to four P.M.—and this was also true when the game was only on the radio. In 1972, home games were still blacked out in the local viewing area even if the game sold out. (The next year a new federal law would require the blackout to be lifted if the game sold out seventy-two hours in advance.) About twenty bars in Dade and Broward Counties acquired long-range antennas that could pull in the broadcast from WBBH-TV in Fort Myers, and they packed in the Dolfans. Some ham radio enthusiasts, like the father of one friend of mine, installed towering antennas on their roofs that could get the signal. But most fans spent the afternoon positioned around a radio. My brother and I would kneel or lie on the shag carpeting in the living room in front of the hi-fi, the voice of Rick Weaver imprinting itself permanently on our temporal lobes. At halftime, we'd run into the front yard with our football for fifteen minutes and try to re-create the heroics we'd heard him describe.

For their first four years, the Dolphins were happy to fill half the Orange Bowl; forty thousand was a particularly good showing. In 1970, with the advent of the Shula era, attendance rose dramatically, and the last two games of the season, with the Dolphins knocking on the playoff door, were sellouts. The next year, home games were close to full but didn't quite sell out until the final three games. In 1972, though, every game in the Orange Bowl featured the screaming, feet stomping, and hankie waving of 80,010 souls, with the exception of the first home game, September 24 against Houston. Because of monsoon-like weather—half as much rain fell that day as had the entire month so far—only 77,821 people showed up.

Bad weather can be an equalizer in football, but on this day the rain served only to tip the scale. Two Houston fumbles in the first five minutes led to quick Miami touchdowns. Even Csonka fumbled—one of only two times all year—or the score could have been even more lopsided. Worse than the slippery ball, though, was the slippery field. Players on both teams were sailing around like my friends and me on our backyard Slip 'N Slide. Every cut, every pivot, was an adventure. The culprit: Poly-Turf II.

Poly-Turf I was bad enough. When the city of Miami announced plans in early 1970 to lure the Super Bowl back with the promise of a trendy new artificial field, Joe Robbie and Don Shula assumed it would be either Astroturf (by Monsanto) or the 3M Tartan turf used in Dallas and Pittsburgh. Both companies put in bids at about $350,000. But the city, perhaps channeling Robbie's frugal instincts, instead went with the American Biltrite Rubber Company of Massachusetts. A newcomer to the artificial-turf business, it was offering a bargain price of $205,933, with another fifty grand off if the Orange Bowl scoreboard would display the product's name. The turf went down that summer, POLY-TURF SYNTHETIC GRASS BY AMERICAN BILTRITE went up on the scoreboard, and the derision began. "If they don't do something about these damn rugs, I don't know how long I can take the punishment," said Csonka. They were basically playing football on a thin carpet laid over concrete. But aside from the pain it inflicted, the Poly-Turf apparently wasn't made to survive in the Miami heat. By the second year it began to decompose in the subtropical weather. It actually played better in the rain, but it couldn't take the heat. "The stuff is falling apart," said Howard Twilley. "It's getting slippery, and it's coming off on my shoes."

American Biltrite had guaranteed the product for five years, and they agreed to replace it with a new, improved version for 1972. Poly-Turf II got tentative good reviews in the preseason, but then in September Houston came to town, and so did the rain. The original turf was so much better when wet that the team would sometimes sprinkle water on it for better traction. Now, as the rain fell all day long, the water accumulated on top of the new turf, forming puddles. They tried squeegees, but the water just kept coming. The team had ordered new shoes from Canada, with rubber bumps on the soles instead of spikes, but they did little good. Receivers went down trying to make cuts. Csonka came around end on a sweep and, instead of launching himself forward into the defense, found himself flat on the ground. He got up and spiked the ball angrily into the wet plastic. Poly-Turf I could take no sun; Poly-Turf II could take no rain.

"Our greatest opponent was the field," said Csonka in disgust after the game. Garo Yepremian suggested using a helicopter to evaporate the water, "or maybe the other guys could bring their hairdryers out on the field." (Garo was bald.) Larry Little felt "ashamed" of their home field, and Marv Fleming said, "It's the worst, the most awful, most terrible, the baddest—did I leave anything out? And besides that, I hate the field."

Jim Kiick got the start at running back, and after Houston's opening fumble at their own fourteen, he took it into the end zone on two carries. The next series, Houston's punter, Dan Pastorini (who was also their quarterback), fumbled the long snap, and this time Mercury Morris carried three out of four plays for twenty-two yards to score again. Csonka scored on a short run in the second quarter—Miami's new three-back running attack had run the table—and it was 20–0 at halftime. Another fumble, by Morris in the third quarter at his own twenty-five, let the Oilers get within a couple touchdowns, but then Griese led a classic Dolphin drive, ninety-three yards in fourteen plays, killing the first half of the fourth quarter, and when he finished it off with a six-yard touchdown pass to Kiick, wide-open in the left flat, it was 34–13, and the Dolphins were two and oh.

Shula gave Earl Morrall a little work at the end, to sharpen him up just in case something should happen to Griese. Morrall took over with six minutes and thirty-three seconds left, with Charlie Leigh and Hubert Ginn in the backfield, and you couldn't have told the difference. Morrall took the team right down the field, chewing up the clock until time expired with the Dolphins on the Houston four-yard line. He completed the one pass he threw. "We have to establish the ground game," Shula had said, and they appeared to have done so. They ran for 274 yards on a Slip 'N Slide and amassed 435 total yards to Houston's 167. Houston did not have the league's most feared defense, but it would turn out that it wouldn't matter too much that year whom Miami was playing. "We are going to drive the ball on the ground even if King Kong is on the other side," offensive line coach Monte Clark had said at the end of the pre-season. And Monte Clark was not someone known for hyperbole. An amateur poet, musician, historian, and psychologist, Clark was a sensitive soul who had excelled as an NFL offensive lineman for eleven seasons and joined Don Shula in Miami in 1970.

The offensive line is the fundamental building block of the offense. Clark's undertaking, under Shula's vision, was to create the basis of a ball control offense that would make a great defense even greater by virtue of so much rest during the game and that would turn one of the league's best passing combos into luxurious gravy. He did so with the most unlikely candidates imaginable. They were castoffs from other teams, long shots who'd never been given a chance before. They called themselves the Expendables. Larry Little, the only one who was already an All-Pro by 1972, had been far from it when Clark and Shula arrived in 1970. An undrafted free agent out of college, he'd been traded to Miami from San Diego in 1969 after starting only three games in two years there. Norm Evans, who shouldered Little on the right side of the line, was an original Dolphin, left unprotected by Houston in the 1966 expansion draft. When Shula arrived, he said, "It doesn't look like Evans can play in the NFL, but we can't be sure. We don't know what he's been *told* to do." On the left side, Doug Crusan was the only lineman who'd been a number one draft choice, out of Indiana in 1968, and he'd been solid. But now he was injured. His replacement, Wayne Moore, was another undrafted free agent who had failed to make the team in San Francisco in 1969 and was taken off waivers by Miami the next year. Bob Kuechenberg, the left guard, had come to the Dolphins from semipro ball in 1970, been cut, reclaimed off waivers, put on the taxi squad, and finally somehow became a starter in 1971. And Jim Langer had only become a center this year, replacing the veteran DeMarco in preseason.

The Expendables were starting to look more and more like the Dependables. Okay, the Oilers were hardly a true test, but the Miami line had already proven themselves superior up in Kansas City against a first-class defense. And it's not like every team was plowing through Houston for 435 yards. The Miami backfield and receivers were feeling very confident about their men up front. The defense was equally appreciative, especially in the heat. "That's a hell of a feeling," drawled defensive end Bill Stanfill, "just sitting and watching the big hoss [Csonka] go for what, eleven minutes at a stretch, then come back with a seven- or eight-minute drive, and we might only play eleven or twelve plays in the first half."

The running backs concurred. Kiick had to be feeling a little better, after getting the start, a couple touchdowns, and a solid share of the running with fifty-five yards. Zonk got his seventy-five, but Morris had nothing to complain about either. He and Kiick shared time evenly, taking turns coming in for entire series, and he was the team leader with ninety-four yards. It was clear by now that Eugene "Mercury" Morris was finally going to have his chance in 1972.

• • •

Morris had the rare distinction of being able to remember when his father got his first car. His parents conceived him when they were fifteen and were sixteen when Gene was born. Luckily, his mother's parents were solid people with a solid if modest income, and Gene and his four siblings—along with his parents, who were really still kids—were raised by their grandparents. Gene's grandfather, a truck driver, had built his own small trucking business in a working-class suburb of Pittsburgh, and Gene (like his father) worked for "Smitty" when he wasn't in school. Unlike some of his Dolphin teammates, Morris never experienced segregation or even much outright racism—or maybe it was just, as he himself intuited, that his athletic talent formed an "invisible shield" around him. From Pop Warner through high school, his best friend and he were always the only two Black players on the team, but Morris was so good, he wasn't taunted—or maybe he was just so fast, he was gone before he could hear it. As he put it, simply, "I could always run faster than anybody else."

A star all through school in football, baseball, and basketball, he shone most when running with a football. Although most of the major college football conferences were still only taking white players, Morris got scholarship offers from all-Black Florida A&M and integrated West Texas State, and he headed straight for the Texas panhandle. He'd never played on a segregated team before, and he wasn't about to start now.

In Canyon, Texas, a small town near Amarillo, he got his first taste of Jim Crow. Although the football team was integrated, the Black players were pretty much the only African Americans around. And it was made clear to them that they should stay away from the white girls, no matter how small that made the dating pool. Well, Gene Morris had exhibited a strong anti-authoritarian streak since childhood, and he didn't take kindly to the advice. It wasn't long before he was secretly dating a coed who had been Miss Amarillo and would later be runner-up for Miss Texas. "They told us, 'Now we don't want you dating any white girls,'" he remembered. "Okay, tell you what, let me go get the baddest one, then tell me that. And I was eighteen years old!" The girl's father had married a Mexican woman himself, but this was beyond the pale. He sent word that he was going to come to a game with his shotgun and shoot Morris in the end zone. Gene never took that too seriously, but his teammates told him they would be celebrating his touchdown runs on the sideline.

Freshmen weren't allowed to play varsity, but Morris did more than make a name for himself in his last three years. His junior year he led the nation in rushing until the final week, when USC's O. J. Simpson overtook him. Senior year, Morris set national records with 340 yards in a single game, 1,571 yards in a single season, and 3,561 yards in a three-year career. None lasted too many years, but the season record was good for only one week: Simpson stole another one from Morris on his way to the Heisman Trophy. Playing for the famous Southern Cal team in the prestigious Pac-8 Conference, Simpson always seemed to overshadow Morris and his little independent team in Canyon. It was a friendly rivalry. When West Texas was in Pasadena for the Junior Rose Bowl game and USC was playing the Rose Bowl, Simpson sent Morris his autograph, unsolicited. In later years, when they met, Morris was sure to bring up the topic of Super Bowls.

Even out in Canyon, though, Morris did get noticed. The nickname "Mercury" took hold, and when a photo spread appeared in *Life* magazine showing him with cardboard wings attached to his helmet and feet, he became a household name. He was drafted by Miami (after Buffalo took Simpson; sometimes you were better off being second best) and arranged for his new silver Corvette to be delivered at training camp. He had something else he hadn't planned on: a pregnant wife. In Miami for the 1968 College All-Star Game, Christmas of his senior year, Morris had met and hit it off with an Eastern Airlines stewardess named Kay. The second time he saw her was when she came to visit him in Texas in February. The third time was in a Columbus, Ohio, church that summer: she had written him in the spring saying she was pregnant, and he agreed to get married.

He worked hard at training camp, but for the first time in his life he was not the star. George Wilson was content with his backfield of Csonka and Kiick, and Morris did little to endear himself with the coach with his "Coach says it's okay to lose seven games?" statement and his *Miami News* diary. (In the rookie show that summer, he portrayed his new rival Kiick by donning bell-bottoms and a striped jersey and coming onstage holding hands with a Csonka impersonator, but it didn't seem to bother Kiick or Csonka too much.) He did get to return kicks in '69 but alienated Wilson even more when he got caught for a safety on that punt return. It was a difficult season, made worse by his ill-considered marriage. He and Kay had very little in common, and after Eugene Jr. was born in November, she and the baby moved back to Columbus.

Morris was ready for a new beginning in 1970, and he was happier than any player for Shula to take over. But on the very first day of practice after the strike, in the final gloaming session on that memorable first day of four practices, he collided with a rookie linebacker in the dark, hobbled off the field, ended up having knee surgery, and didn't practice again for six weeks. He didn't get in a game until October and ended up with only sixty carries all year (for a superb 409 yards). In 1971 Shula was finally ready to try the three-back system he'd been contemplating since he inherited Csonka, Kiick, and Morris, but first Csonka and Kiick missed two weeks with their contract holdout, and then Morris got injured again in preseason, this time with a sprained ankle. Although he recovered completely, Shula said the time off had cost them the chance to incorporate him into the backfield in a big way. A frustrated Morris saw it differently: "As long as Csonka and Kiick are around, there can never be a three-back offense. Three won't go into two." True to his forecast, he had only two games that year with more than five carries and only one carry all through the playoffs. It was still all Butch and Sundance. (Morris did make the Pro Bowl as a kick returner.)

In later years Morris was able to rationalize Shula's motives in underutilizing a runner with his obvious talents, a man who came to Miami as the leading rusher in NCAA history. "For one thing, I didn't fit into his prototype of the big-back duo that he liked—like [Paul] Hornung and [Jim] Taylor in Green Bay, or like Kiick and Csonka." But in fact that illustrious Packer team had had a swift-footed number twenty-two of their own, Elijah Pitts, and Shula had been itching to add the speed of Mercury to his mix since he arrived in Miami. Why he didn't was not due to a little missed time in preseason. The real reason lay in what Morris said next: "Shula didn't have enough confidence in me the first couple of years. I had to play a certain way to earn that confidence. One thing you can't do is make mistakes, and I made some mistakes. . . ." He fumbled six times in 1970, for instance—as much as Kiick and Csonka combined with but a fraction of the number of carries.

Such a calm-headed appraisal, however, was missing after Morris watched from the bench as his offense was stifled by the Cowboys in the Super Bowl. It didn't help that his backup at West Texas, Duane Thomas, had had a big game for Dallas, with ninety-five yards and a touchdown. Morris stewed on the sidelines, aching for a chance to get in there, but he never got the call. In the somber locker room afterward, as his teammates undressed and showered, he sat in front of his locker in full uniform and headband, arms crossed, obviously displeased. A reporter stopped by, and Merc let loose: Why hadn't he been used? Part of the offensive game plan was to run the ball outside, and in practice they'd been drilling sweeps over and over, with Morris the ball carrier. But in the game his number was never called. A few more reporters congregated around him as he went on and finally erupted: "The only time I got off the bench was for kick returns and the national anthem!" When Shula found out, he was livid. He marched over to where the Mercury press conference was and confronted him: "If you have something to say, you say it to me first." He summoned Morris to a meeting in his hotel room the following morning, at which he took a more measured tone. After Mercury apologized for his locker room tirade, Shula explained that he still had big plans for him. "But I need to find out whether or not you are capable of being a play-in, play-out, full-time player." Shula explained that because of training camp injuries the first two years they were together, he had never had a chance to properly evaluate him.

"Coach, just give me the opportunity because I know I can do it," said Morris.

"I promise you you'll get that chance when training camp opens," said Shula. "So be ready for it."

Things were looking up, personally as well as professionally. Shortly after Kay had left, he'd met another stewardess, Dorothy, at their apartment complex pool. They never married, but they had a son together in February 1971. In the middle of the 1971 season, however, Dorothy left for California with an offer to become a Playboy Bunny. Thinking a baby might hamper the life of a bunny, she left little Maceo with his dad, but childcare wasn't so easy either for a single NFL player. Morris hired a neighbor to take care of the boy during practices and games for the rest of the year, but life was difficult. Fortunately for him, if not her career, Dorothy was back before the 1972 season, and the three of them moved into a four-bedroom house in South Miami, purchased with his recent Super Bowl payout.

For the moment, his personal life was stable, and Mercury Morris was ready to take Don Shula up on his promise. He showed up at camp in July "with anticipation burning in his eyes." He'd always been in astounding physical shape, the strongest guy on the team, no problem doing 150 straight push-ups or bench-pressing 360 pounds. But now he put more time into learning how to block: "I'm five-ten, one-ninety, but I learned how to bring down those six-six, two-seventy-pound guys, and as I became more efficient in blocking, that helped keep me in the game too." Blocking and pass receiving were the areas where Kiick clearly had his number, so he worked on his pass receiving, too, and showed marked improvement.

He also got the most out of every carry in practice and in exhibition games. It didn't take a three-time Coach of the Year to see what Mercury could add to the Dolphin offense—or any offense. He was one of those rare running backs who had every fan leaning forward or even jumping up in anticipation the moment he touched the ball. Every handoff or pitchout had touchdown potential. His distinctive style—swinging the ball, gripped between hand and forearm, far out from his body, on the edge of control, daring fate—thrilled fans to the point of angina. He would glide out toward the sideline or break through a hole in the middle of the line, and then as he appraised the next line of defenders he would stop for just a moment and dance, throwing his weight back and forth from foot to foot before darting into daylight. He was both mercurial—changeable from speed to power, animated, sprightly, quick-witted, volatile—and Mercurial: faster than anybody he knew. In his newest form he was not only exhilarating but dependable too. By the end of the preseason—after leading the team with 346 yards in fifty carries, an astounding-for-anyone-not-Merc 6.9 yards per rush—those Gale Sayers comparisons were coming. His performance in one game, wrote Bill Braucher, "would have been astonishing if not for the fact he has been consistently astonishing, to the point where the spectacular is expected." With Sayers just retired (and Simpson yet to distinguish himself after three years with the ineffectual Bills), he said, "Morris off his summertime exploits appears to be in a class by himself as a runner. There seems no way he can be restrained from functioning at least on an equal footing with Csonka and Kiick." At the end of the summer, the substitute running back whose career high season was 409 yards and who hadn't played a down in the Super Bowl eight months earlier was featured in a full-page newspaper ad, strutting along in a white suit from Cruise Casuals: "Mercury Morris just bought a double knit suit direct from the factory for $49." He was pushing in next to Csonka and Kiick in more ways than one.

In addition to his uniquely heart-stirring running style on a team used to a duller power-running game, Morris had a distinctive response to scoring touchdowns, and he was finally getting more of a chance to show it. After only two rushing touchdowns in his first three seasons (plus three more on kick returns), he had five in the preseason and would run for twelve more this year. And when he crossed the goal line, he spiked the ball like no one else in town. The spike itself, as a celebration, was barely older than this team. Homer Jones of the Giants invented it in 1965; he tried throwing the ball into the stands in jubilation, but that was outlawed. So he started throwing it right into the ground. The gesture quickly caught on among the more demonstrative players, but no one spiked the ball quite like Merc. "It wasn't a spike," he said, "it was a bust. It was an attempt to bust the ball, and I would try to make it bounce as high as I possibly could, so they'd have to go like this"—tilting his neck up—"and look up at the ball knowing full well I'm finished with it."

Perhaps the folks back in Canyon, Texas, did mean "mercurial" after all, for now that Morris was the center of preseason attention, Dolphin fans were learning just how animated, lively, and quick-witted he was. "He's like a time bomb," said Braucher, "set for various explosions. A writer has to follow him around twenty-four hours a day or have no peace. You never know when you're going to pick up the opposition paper and see a headline about Mercury."

His teammates were familiar by now with the personality. "He's a real character," said Doug Swift. "A delightful character, very interesting, very articulate. It's just not always clear what he's articulating. But he's flamboyant, and you know he's sort of dippin' on the thin edge of whatever." He loved music and even hosted his own jazz radio show Sunday nights from nine to midnight on

WCKO-FM. But he knew what kind of sound was needed in a football locker room. The morning after leading the team in rushing against Houston, he entered the training room early, in a tank top, beret, and round shades. Only Csonka was there, soothing his Poly-Turf bruises in the whirlpool and chatting with a reporter. Danny Dowe, the equipment manager, had the stereo on low: an FM station playing Andre Kostelanetz's new Cole Porter LP. Morris punctured the atmosphere like he was breaking through the line—"This will never do, Danny!"—and turned the needle to a hard-rock station, possibly 103.5, the brand-new WSHE ("She's Only Rock 'n Roll"). It might have been "Smoke on the Water," or "Ziggy Stardust," or "Tumbling Dice" from *Exile on Main St.* He turned the volume up. Csonka and Dowe just looked at each other.

Other times, said Morris, "it was a locker-room battle between the country-and-western of Howard Twilley and Power Jam 99 by me. He'd put on country, I'd switch to Power Jam, he'd switch it to country, I'd put it back to Power Jam, until finally . . . we listened to Power 99."

"Merc was living on his own planet," said Eddie Jenkins. "He was a cultivated man, a jazz aficionado. But he just liked to mix things up. He'd go in the locker-room shower and yell, 'Black is beautiful! White is the beast!' Zonk and Kiick would just be shaking their heads: that's just freakin' Merc."

Morris had earned his place in the backfield, but he was very aware that he was "going to upset that balance of Butch and Sundance," as he put it, and that he would need to be thick-skinned and also supportive of his teammates to make it work. Still, he said, "sometimes in the beginning I would sit right in between them on the bench, just to let them know that this is how we're gonna roll here." It was a tense situation sometimes, and Csonka was not pleased with a photo in the paper after the Houston game of the three of them on the bench that he felt appeared to show him "grinning at [Morris] like he's the number-two man now." Throughout the season, though, the three of them were always sitting there together on the sideline, and the image was one of togetherness, not dissent. Morris had seized his place on that bench, but Kiick and Csonka knew he belonged there.

Three and Oh

Before the season, many experts had predicted a Super Bowl between Kansas City and Minnesota. The Dolphins beat the Chiefs on the road, and now they faced another trial in Minneapolis. In this case, though, the burden of a long flight was offset by the chance to leave the Poly-Turf far behind and finally get a chance to play on real grass. And as they stepped off their Eastern Airlines charter plane at Minneapolis–St. Paul International on a late-September Friday afternoon, the bracing fifty-five-degree air felt like a sweet vacation after a summer in Miami. Dick Anderson took a deep breath: "Football weather."

The Vikings had some of the most passionate fans in the country, but only about forty-five thousand of them could fit into Metropolitan Stadium, the NFL's smallest arena. The rest would have to listen on radio or travel outside the blackout area. At the stadium, some of the lucky ticket holders arrived en masse: one group of eighteen men showed up in a Viking-purple bus—at eleven in the morning on Saturday. "We're going to eat, drink, and celebrate right up until game time Sunday," said one of them. "That's a twenty-eight-hour tailgater." Their wives had traveled with them but were in a hotel.

Sunday, October 1, the weather was sunny and crisp, the field genuine midwestern grass, a perfect setting. And the Dolphins couldn't move. The first eight times they had the ball, they produced zero points. These two teams, among the cream of the league, had similar dispositions. They both liked to run the ball and control the clock, but they both also had superstar quarterbacks—Griese and Fran Tarkenton—known for their creative scrambling as well as their arms. And while the Dolphin defense was little known but fast gaining in stature, the Vikings were already there. Their defense had allowed the fewest points in the league in 1971, and their defensive line, featuring Carl Eller, Alan Page, Jim Marshall, and Gary Larsen, were the feared Purple People Eaters. In 1971 Eller was the NFL Defensive Player of the Year, and Page was even better: he was the first defensive player to be named league MVP. So it was no shock that even the Dolphins found themselves punting series after series. Luckily, Larry Seiple was responding to the challenge, averaging forty-four yards a punt in length and just as impressive in height, allowing no runbacks of note. The only points of the first half for either team came when Tarkenton executed a nifty play action on third and three from his own forty-four-yard line. Tim Foley and Jake Scott, overeager and expecting the run, bit on the fake, and Tarkenton was amazed to see wide receiver John Gilliam completely on his own streaking downfield. He hit him with an easy lob for a fifty-six-yard touchdown. Gilliam had burned the Dolphins for a long touchdown in the final exhibition game as well, and this would not be the only afterimage from that game.

The rest of the first half continued to be dominated by defense. Dick Anderson recovered a fumble at the Minnesota seventeen-yard line, but on the next play Griese, looking for a quick strike to Warfield, was intercepted. Shortly thereafter Doug Swift dealt Tarkenton his first interception of the season, but the Purple People Eaters stopped Miami flat. The Dolphin defense, recently endowed with its own moniker, the "No-Name Defense"—a reference to its lack of stars—was similarly unmovable. It was a treat for old-fashioned fans, who loved a tough defensive battle on the grass. Even for professional football, this was a brutal bar fight of a game: "The fiercest game I was ever in," Csonka recalled. He had good reason to remember it. In the first quarter, Griese sent him up the sideline for a short pass. As he reached up for the ball, linebacker Roy Winston delivered a clean, perfectly timed shoulder to his lower back. Csonka's head snapped back as if he'd had a car accident, which is what it felt like: "It was the hardest hit I ever received in all the years that I played football. The fans got their seven dollars worth on that one." Indeed, it was the kind of sanctioned violence that has always been at the heart of the game, as much as critics might decry it and devotees repress it. The ball went flying out of bounds, and Csonka was left agonizing on the ground. "He hit me in the kidney and it scared me bad," he said afterward. "I could hear my teammates gasp on the sideline right there. I couldn't feel my feet. I thought I'd broken my back. Then the feeling came back in my legs but they were on fire."

The hit was near midfield, right in front of the Dolphin bench. "Get up!" Csonka could hear Shula yelling at him. "They're going to think you're hurt!" "I *am* hurt," he murmured, as if anyone could hear him. He managed to get to the bench, or near it, where he lay back on the ground. Shula came over to assess the situation: "You can't get hurt, Csonka! You've got to go." ("That was Shula," Larry Little laughed later. "He believed certain people couldn't get hurt: 'You gotta go, you've got to go!'") Csonka looked up at him: "I think my goddamn back is broken. Screw the game." But Shula had made him so mad that he forced himself back up in anger, and when Miami got the ball back there was Csonka in the backfield. Winston could hardly believe it: "I've been in this league eleven years, and I can't remember getting a better shot at a guy. Csonka is something." When he heard that later, Csonka said, "They ought to know you can't kill a Hunky by hitting him in the back. You've got to hit him where his brains are, and I won't tell you where that is."

It wasn't the only bloodcurdling hit of the game. Jim Kiick took a similar shot from another linebacker, Wally Hilgenberg, on a similar play. As Kiick went up to catch a pass, Hilgenberg nailed him with a shoulder, just flattened him on the ground. This was the game in which cornerback Tim Foley staggered off the field at one point "hearing chapel bells," but as was the case so often for the Dolphins that year, his backup, Lloyd Mumphord, was just as good. Overall, it was a day for two of the greatest defenses in NFL history to shine. At the end of the first half, it was still 7–0 Minnesota.

In the third quarter, Miami got on the board, as Garo Yepremian trotted on for field goals of thirty-eight and forty-two yards. In this ferocious battle of muscular behemoths, it was a diminutive Cypriot immigrant who proved most valuable, keeping Miami within striking distance until the end.

• • •

Yepremian's grandfather came to Detroit from Armenia in 1913 and saved up money from a factory job before returning home, only to be murdered by Turks of the Ottoman Empire during the Armenian Genocide in 1916. His parents were living in Cyprus as British subjects when Garabed Sarkis Yepremian was born in 1944. They fled ethnic strife there and moved to London, and in 1965 Garo was playing some semi-pro soccer and working in a clothing store. His older brother Krikor had gotten a soccer scholarship to Indiana University and was now studying law there. When he was unable to get Garo a soccer scholarship because he had played semi-pro in England, Krikor decided Garo should become a professional football kicker. He had watched some football on television and was sure Garo could kick field goals better than Detroit's Wayne Walker, who was primarily a linebacker. Straight ahead with the toe was no way to kick a ball, thought Krikor, and he was right: Walker was eight for twenty-two that year and only made one from more than forty yards. Pete Gogolak, now with the Giants, had become the first full-time soccer-style kicker in professional football just two years earlier. Krikor shipped a football to London and told Garo to practice. He finally got him a tryout with the Lions in October 1966 and negotiated his contract for him.

A few days later, Garo Yepremian was the kicker in the first football game he ever attended. In the locker room, he carefully watched his new teammates to see how to put on the pads and uniform. When he kicked off and saw a mass of enormous men running at him, Garo, at 142 pounds with a twenty-eight-inch waist, fled for the sidelines. He did improve Detroit's kicking game, though, making thirteen of twenty-two field goals, including a record six in one game (although, like Walker, he was only one for eight over forty yards). And the antics of a European immigrant playing a new game among much larger men made for good anecdotes. The stories got passed around so much between players, journalists, and fans that it's difficult now to ascertain what is true. Alex Karras, Detroit's star defensive tackle (and later an actor; he played Mongo in the film *Blazing Saddles*), got the most out of it, telling Johnny Carson on *The Tonight Show* that when Yepremian made an extra point late in a game they were losing badly, he ran off the field jumping with his arms in triumph. "What the hell are you doing?" Karras said he asked him. "I keek a touchdown!" yelled Garo. Or maybe he said that after he kicked those six field goals against Minnesota. Karras changed his story frequently.

Despite Yepremian's solid performance, the next season the Lions couldn't seem to decide between him and Walker, using them on an alternating basis throughout the season. They each made a third of their field goals, but after the season Yepremian was released. He kicked for the Michigan Arrows of the short-lived Continental Football League for part of their only season, then went into the Army National Guard as a cook for a year. In 1969 he was out of the Army, out of football, and out of work. Desperate, he and his brother began making ties and selling them to department stores. Then, in 1970, when Don Shula went to Miami, personnel director Joe Thomas showed him a letter he had picked out of several hundred from luckless football players trying to get a shot. Shula remembered the little Armenian who had done all right with Detroit, and he invited Yepremian to training camp. Garo arrived with $10 in his pocket and needed Krikor to wire him $30 more to survive the players' strike.

Yepremian impressed Shula early in camp, but Karl Kremser, Miami's rookie kicker in 1969, had been very accurate from short distances. Shula put Yepremian on the taxi squad at the beginning of the season, but when Kremser missed a short one in the embarrassing opener against Boston, he changed his mind and activated Yepremian for the Houston game, and the grateful immigrant responded with two solid mid-range field goals. "I want to thank you very much," he said to reporters afterward. The next week against Oakland he hit two field goals over forty yards, and he was the newest Dolphin sensation. (Kremser was soon teaching German and coaching soccer. He led the team at Killian, my high school, to the state championship in 1977. Yepremian's little brother Berj was the placekicker at Killian in 1972 and 1973.) In 1971, Yepremian missed three field goals in a disappointing tie with Denver in the season opener, but he held on to his job by making five of five the next week. "I want to thank you very much," he told the press. He went on to win the league scoring total that year and topped that off by ending the Longest Game with aplomb. By then he was already a favorite among fans and also among his teammates. They made fun of him as the Lions had—it was hard for hulking football players not to rib a 140-pound teammate—calling him "Keebler" because of the cookie company's elfin mascot. But they also recognized a positive energy coming off Garo, a cockiness despite his self-deprecating humor, a confidence that he would make the tough kick in the big moment. "A beautiful little guy to have around," as Norm Evans put it.

He never minded the teasing, because no one made more fun of Garo than Garo. "He believes he is funny, to a fault," wrote one reporter. He showed up at training camp in '72 with a bushy mustache worthy of Cheech Marin of Cheech and Chong. "A lot of people want me to shave it," he said, "but this is my pride and joy. It's the only hair I can grow." (He was hoping a razor blade company might pay him to shave it off in an ad, but when no offers came he shaved it himself before the season opener. He kept the muttonchop sideburns, which looked like they weighed more than the rest of him.) His bald head and peripatetic history gave him the air of an older man, but he was still only twenty-eight.

He had a shaky preseason and in the first two games made only two of five field goals. But up in Minnesota "Keebler" delivered the goods. His two medium-range strikes were hardly "gimmes" on natural grass in an era when only about sixty percent of all field goals were made, and thirty-nine percent of those in the forty-to-forty-nine-yard range—and that's on all surfaces. While most players hated the hard pounding on artificial turf, kickers then and now love it. It's much easier to kick off a hard surface than soft sod. So Yepremian's thirty-eight- and forty-two-yarders with a loss looming in a tough-fought game were clutch performances yet again. Midway through the third quarter, the score was only 7–6 for Minnesota.

The Vikings then managed their first productive drive since that bomb to Gilliam early in the game. Fran Tarkenton looked like Bob Griese, mostly handing off during a grinding fourteen-play, eighty-yard drive, and as the clock ran out on the third quarter, Minnesota had fourth down only six inches from the goal line. When play resumed, longtime Vikings fullback Bill Brown got those six inches right over the middle, and Minnesota led 14–6. Miami had almost a quarter to play, but they needed two scores—there were no two-point extra points in the NFL then—and the Viking defense had given little ground so far. The oddsmakers, who had picked Minnesota at home, were nodding their heads sagely.

The Dolphins saw it differently. Marlin Briscoe had reason to note, just as he had in the last exhibition game against Minnesota, how far he had come from Buffalo: "If this was Buffalo, the first thing we'd do is panic. We'd immediately try to throw the bomb. Our quarterback would get sacked and the game would be over. But things are different here in Miami. We knew, deep in our hearts, we'd win."

This fortitude began to seem quixotic when the Dolphins were forced to punt on their next possession and the Vikings started moving again. But the defense then pushed them back with consecutive losses, Minnesota punted, and Miami took over on its own twenty. An eighty-yard, ten-minute Dolphin special would have been perfect if they were down by five or six. But they were down by eight with eleven minutes to play.

And after three runs they were looking at a fourth down, with one yard to go, from their own twenty-nine. The clock was running. Even so, with about nine minutes to play, the normal thing would be to punt. It was still likely the offense would get two more chances. But Shula jutted out his jaw and motioned Griese to stay out there. "The guys looked like they were coming back," he said cavalierly after the game, "and I wanted to give them the chance. If I got to get beat, I'd just as soon get beat by two or three touchdowns." He breathed again when Morris took it three yards over the middle—lots of room to spare. Griese followed that with an eighteen-yard pass to Morris up the sideline, and things were looking much more optimistic until a rare fifteen-yard penalty on Larry Little for holding had them facing a hopeless third-and-twenty-five from their own thirty-four-yard line. That's when Briscoe, the new starting wide receiver, got the call to do something different.

He wasn't surprised when Griese made the call in the huddle: a flanker-reverse pass, with Briscoe throwing. Buffalo had let him throw twice last year off the reverse to good effect. "We've had this play ready since the season opened," he said, "and Griese just thought this might be when it could go." Might as well: they'd be looking for a long pass from Griese, which made a first down that way unlikely. Maybe if he handed it off to Kiick, they'd assume he was just trying to get a few yards to set up a better punt. Kiick took the ball heading for a sweep out right but then handed it in turn to Briscoe coming over from the right end. Problem was, big number seventy, the great Jim Marshall—experienced enough at age thirty-five to have seen these tricks before, and still agile enough to be the starting right end for seven more years after this—was right in Briscoe's face. He'd seen the reverse coming and was too far in for Griese to block him. He lunged at Briscoe as the receiver ran backward to elude him, and ended up sprawled on the grass empty-handed. But as Briscoe spun around to face forward, now way back at his twenty-one-yard line, another Purple People Eater, Alan Page, smack in the middle of eight straight Pro Bowl seasons, had faked out Bob Kuechenberg and was ready to plow Briscoe back to his own goalpost. Marlin calmly set his feet and launched a pass downfield just before getting hit. And there was Jim Mandich, the young tight end, in for Fleming precisely because of his pass-catching abilities, coming back for the ball at the Minnesota forty-six. He twisted around one defender and was brought down by two others at the forty-four.

It was an almost miraculous play, with Briscoe having to single-handedly elude two all-time-great defensive ends, spin around, and throw back across the field to a receiver who had been covered but came back to the open spot. But maybe not for Marlin the Magician, as he was known at Omaha. "For me that play was more or less routine," Briscoe said later, "'cause that was my style of play. I had been doing that all my life."

As extraordinary a play as it in fact was, it gained only twenty-two yards, leaving Shula with another tough decision. It was fourth down again, with three yards to go for a first down. A field goal attempt would be from fifty-one yards. (The placeholder set up seven yards back, and the goalposts were right on the goal line, not to be moved to the back of the end zone until 1974.) Yepremian had never made a field goal over fifty yards in a game that mattered and in fact had only tried it five times in his career—the last time a couple hours ago, in the first quarter, when Page had stretched up to block a fifty-two-yard attempt. He'd been short on a fifty-two-yarder in the Longest Game and short on a forty-nine-yarder in the Super Bowl loss. He stood on the sideline now, certain his team was about to punt or—more likely, he figured—go for the first down. Long field goals had to be kicked at a lower trajectory and thus were more likely to be blocked, as had just happened to him this game. Coach would never ask him to make his first fifty-yarder now, with the game on the line. Then he heard Shula's voice: "Field goal! Field goal!" "I was so shook up," he remembered. "But I said to myself, if he's got that much confidence in me, I should have confidence." There wasn't much time to think about such things, though. He got set, Morrall laid down the ball, Garo swung his left foot, and the ball swung end over end, just barely clearing the crossbar: 14–9, Minnesota. (A couple days later, at practice, Shula asked him what the longest field goal he'd ever made was. "That was it!" Garo told him, stunned.)

Now he was expecting Shula to call for an onside kick, to make sure they got another chance to score. But with just over four minutes left, Shula trusted his defense and told Garo to kick deep. Up to the task, the No-Names clogged the line, pushing the Vikings back two yards in two running plays, and then swarmed all over Tarkenton, ruining his third-down pass attempt. After the punt, Miami took over at its own forty-one-yard line. The clock showed two minutes and eleven seconds left and one time-out remaining.

Once again Briscoe had an opportunity to observe his new coach and quarterback's cool confidence under fire. Rather than come out throwing desperately, Griese handed off to Morris. Despite the surprising call, though, the Minnesota line stopped him after only two yards, and the two-minute warning sounded. Now, after the break, Griese really did have to throw, and he faded back, looking for Warfield, but was thrown to the ground as his pass fell incomplete. Dolfans' hopes dropped a notch lower until they saw a yellow flag sailing toward the prostrate quarterback. The referee said Bob Lurtsema, a reserve lineman, had made a late hit on Griese. Roughing the quarterback: fifteen yards. Lurtsema protested the call on the field, he complained about it in the locker room, and almost fifty years later he was still harping on it. "Six years and this has never happened to me," he said after the game. "I had my arm around him and he fell. I could have given him a shot but I didn't do it. Isn't that terrible?" He weakened his case, though, a few minutes later when he told another reporter, "My momentum carried me into Griese, who had fallen down." Forty-six years later it was "I turned around to watch the ball and Griese made a fake fall. I never touched him. He had brushed into me." Lurtsema can be forgiven for not wanting to be the first player ever to admit using unnecessary roughness. Whether a good call or a bad call, however, it was a big play. Miami now had a first down at the Minnesota forty-two.

At this point Minnesota had no idea what Griese would call. They showed pass coverage, Griese gave it back to Morris on a sweep to the sideline, and Mercury scampered for fourteen yards, down to the twenty-eight. Then Shula made another surprise call. Marlin Briscoe seemed to have secured the starting wide receiver position over Howard Twilley; he'd caught three passes against Kansas City and three more today, and had made that critical pass in the previous possession. Twilley was standing on the sideline, a good sport as always, cheering for his teammates, when: "Shula says 'Howard, you're in for Briscoe.' And I thought, 'What??' I didn't say a word, I just went in."

· · ·

Too small, too slow, too injury-prone. It seemed that Howard Twilley, one of the original Dolphins, was always on the brink of being traded, or cut, or just benched. Growing up in the Houston suburb of Galena Park, he never dreamed he'd make it in the NFL. Even now, people seemed to forget that at Tulsa he had set the all-time NCAA record for pass receptions and was runner-up for the Heisman Trophy. He hadn't played much as a rookie for the brand-new Dolphins, but he'd started almost every game since (aside from 1969, when he joined the injury parade). With his high forehead and chiseled jaw, he was a ringer for Willem Dafoe, except that Dafoe was still in high school. So instead writers compared him to, say, "a student manager pressed into uniform." Indeed he was a college graduate with honors in electrical engineering, and only five-foot-ten. But he had the hands of a pickpocket and a workingman's attitude. "Twilley's relentless blocking and able hands overcome a slowness, [which is] why nobody can beat him out of a job," wrote Braucher. "Shula admires him, but would trade him in an instant. . . ." In 1970 Shula had brought in his leading receiver from Baltimore, Willie Richardson, to join Warfield, but Twilley beat Richardson out. In 1971 Miami's top draft pick, Otto Stowe, was supposed to take over the number two wide receiver position, but Howard hung on to it. It became something of a joke every training camp: Shula would say to a pool of reporters, "I wonder who we'll get to replace Twilley this year." In 1972, apparently, it was Marlin Briscoe. A Pro Bowl receiver who could also offer the occasional throw as he'd just done to keep them alive in Minnesota? Briscoe's athleticism made Twilley look like he should be in grad school. But Howard just took it all in stride. At training camp, Shula announced that Twilley's wife, Julie, had had a baby, and when a reporter there asked the name, Twilley said, "We were going to name him Don, but that was before he traded for Briscoe." Later he conceded, "You don't trade a number-one draft pick unless you expect the [new] guy to start. But I plan to compete. I guess I'll just have to work harder on my blocking. That's the only thing that keeps me in this league."

It wasn't just his blocking. It was his hands and his precise patterns. "You'd look at him," said Eddie Jenkins, "see how slow he was, but Howard's moves were so deliberate. He'd turn you around. He'd make a cut with a head fake, and you'd be heading to the sidelines while he's going the other way." He had something else going for him too: Bob Griese. Twilley and Griese were close friends who, along with their wives, socialized often. "They called him Bob's son," joked Yepremian, "because Howard would follow him everywhere. He would be his shadow on and off the field." (Howard was a year older than Bob.) But friendship had nothing to do with why Griese wanted him in the huddle in key situations. Twilley got open, and Twilley caught the ball.

An injured leg had kept him out of most of the preseason, making it even easier to install Briscoe as the starter. But he was healthy again, and he should not have been so surprised when Shula called his name with two minutes left against Minnesota, down by five, in the middle of what had to be their final drive. Griese knew what he wanted.

They were already down to the twenty-eight-yard line and had plenty of time. Minnesota probably figured Griese would use his bread-and-butter running game a bit. So Griese threw to Twilley, a crisp down-and-out to the twenty-yard line. Now surely he'd let Csonka or Kiick get the first down, or maybe look for Warfield deep. In fact, he *was* looking for Warfield, but Warfield was covered. Then he saw Twilley running the secondary pattern, a slant down the middle of the field, wide-open and screaming, "Bob! Bob!" Twilley took the perfect pass in the numbers and cut through the infield dirt—baseball's Twins still had three games left—before being brought down at the three-yard line. He'd been in for two plays all game and had taken his team within three yards of an unlikely comeback victory.

First and goal at the three, over a minute left. Bob Griese had so many options. During the week, he would work with Shula and offensive coordinator Howard Schnellenberger to come up with a game plan, including an arsenal of plays. But during the game, except for during time-outs when he could consult with Shula, Griese chose the plays. Perhaps now he remembered the end of the final exhibition game, when Minnesota was in the Orange Bowl. They'd expected a pass on fourth and goal at the six, and Griese had given them Merc running a sweep for the winning touchdown. Coach Bud Grant had said publicly that he'd been watching the film of that play over and over. Surely now Grant would be expecting a run, with first down from the three-yard line, after two straight passes. Even Jim Mandich was surprised to be in the game now, as Marv Fleming was an unrivaled blocker in such situations. "I thought we'd just pound the ball to Csonka," he said. But one of the ways Shula had been determined to improve his team this year, since back in July, was to be able to throw to the tight end over the middle. They'd been criticized for their inability to do just that in the Super Bowl, and Shula made it a priority in training camp.

No one admired Griese's masterful play calling as much as Csonka. Griese liked to rush his team into their huddle so he could then stand back and think of a play. "You'll see him looking over at the other team," said Csonka, "just thinking of what play he's going to call. He runs the show like nobody I've ever seen." Now Griese looked up and saw the Vikings had put in a goal line defense to try to stuff the Miami running game: five linemen and only three defensive backs. He smiled, leaned back into the huddle, and barked, "I-19 split delay on two!" His teammates were surprised but kept their poker faces as they lined up in tight formation, and the Vikings hunkered down for the smash. Griese took one last look at the defensive alignment and knew it was duck soup. He took the snap, made a perfunctory fake handoff to Csonka up the middle, and looked up. Mandich had pretended to block for just a moment and then darted into the end zone, uncovered. Just as Roy Winston came charging in at Griese, hoping to do to him what he'd done to Csonka, Griese lobbed the ball across the line to Mandich as easy as playing catch in the backyard.

The Dolphins rarely celebrated touchdowns. Morris liked to spike it, Twilley would sometimes toss it up in the air with two hands, but the others would usually just get up and jog back to the sideline with their teammates, calmly satisfied. But this had been a striking comeback against one of the league's best, and several linemen swarmed Mandich, hugging him. Even Griese ran into the end zone and tried to get in the act, although no one seemed to notice him.

The Dolphins had overcome their tough early-season schedule and were three and oh, having beaten two Super Bowl contenders along the way. The No-Name Defense had sacked the infamous scrambler Tarkenton five times and handed him his first three interceptions of the season. After that missed assignment on Gilliam in the first quarter, they only allowed fifty yards passing the rest of the game. And the offense, tangled up in purple most of the game, came through with two clutch drives at the end. A reporter noted the "strangely businesslike atmosphere" in the locker room afterward. This team of Shula's had developed a group intelligence and maturity, particularly after the Super Bowl loss—a single-mindedness that didn't include whooping it up. It wouldn't be the first time a visitor was surprised by the calm of the Dolphins locker room after a fabulous victory.

Or maybe they were just recovering after a street fight of a football game. A lot of bruises were starting to be felt, now that the adrenaline and painkillers were wearing off. Larry Csonka sat hunched over on a bench by his locker, feeling that hit he'd taken from Roy Winston in the first half. Forty years afterward, waking on cold spring mornings in Alaska, he would slowly sit up in bed and think about Winston. Now he looked up at reporters and said, "Nothing serious, just a broken back and a ruptured kidney."

Nearby, Bob Griese was displaying a bit of uncharacteristic jocularity: "Zonk should never have dropped that ball. He should have shaken off that guy and gone ten, fifteen yards downfield." Csonka just shook his hanging head. Finally he managed to stand up and make his slow, pigeon-toed shuffle out of the locker room.

Four and Oh

No one exemplified the sharp collected mindset and assiduous nature of this Dolphin team like Bob Griese. He intellectualized football like perhaps no one else but his battery-mate Paul Warfield. "Almost every minute of every day [during the season] I devote to the study of football," he said. When he wasn't in meetings or out on the practice field, he was scrutinizing films, examining every defensive tendency of that week's opponent. The way backs lined up in certain situations, the way they reacted to various pass patterns. How individual linemen drove off the snap of the ball. He watched those films like Bobby Fischer studying old games, squeezing every drop of information out of them. And in the heat of battle, that preparation would result in calling the perfect play at the perfect time. "In a game," he said, "I think of myself as looking down on a situation from above, like a chess player. I can see moves coming and I'm ready to make them." He concentrated so hard during games that he would be unaware of the crowd, the players on the sideline, even teammates on the field. Sometimes one would say something to him before the huddle, and he wouldn't even hear.

This cerebral player was somewhat undersized for the NFL. His arm was relatively weak. Journalists persisted in contending he was not physically gifted, that he succeeded mainly with intelligence and preparation. He even said it himself, joining in with the team charade that they weren't the most natural athletes: "I don't think I had any great assets, I wasn't big strong, fast. . . ." But as with the others, it was absurd for Griese to pretend he wasn't a superb athlete. Growing up in Evansville, Indiana, he was a three-sport star in high school. He made All-State in basketball, and after going undefeated as a starting pitcher in high school and American Legion ball his senior year, he was approached by major-league baseball scouts, but he had already accepted a football scholarship at Purdue. At first he played all three sports there, too, but by his junior year it was strictly football. Still, some years later, when Cazzie Russell, an NBA all-star for the Knicks and Lakers, was asked to name the best defensive player he ever faced, pro or college, he didn't hesitate: it was Bob Griese.

In football, it took him a while to rise to the top of the quarterback depth chart. In addition to his slight stature, he had a sidearm delivery that often produced a wobbly throw. But his coach recognized his understanding of the game and pressure-proof accuracy, and before long he was the four-year starter. He was also the placekicker, and in his very first game he scored all the points in a 17–0 victory over Ohio. He only got better from there, and in his junior year he turned in a historic performance in a dramatic upset over top-ranked Notre Dame. As a senior, he led Purdue to its first-ever Rose Bowl, where they beat O. J. Simpson's USC team 14–13.

Dolphins personnel director Joe Thomas knew he wanted Griese in the 1967 draft—"The kind you really need," he said, "is the one that can pick a defense apart in the short-to-medium range. How many times does a quarterback have to throw the ball sixty yards?"—but there was a lot of pressure on him to take Steve Spurrier. Spurrier had won the Heisman over Griese, and he had done it at the University of Florida. He'd even been born right in Miami Beach. The fledgling AFL team could use a hometown hero. Thomas had the fourth pick in the draft, and he sweated out the first three. Baltimore took Bubba Smith, and Minnesota took running back Clinton Jones. Now Thomas was really nervous, because San Francisco had the third pick, and they were well stocked at quarterback. He was taking Griese no matter what, but he feared for his job if he brought the wrath of South Florida on himself. Finally, though, San Francisco announced its choice: they were going with the Heisman winner. Thomas took a breath of relief and selected Bob Griese.

It was a generally accepted axiom back then that it took four years, either watching from the bench or taking knocks out on the field, to become an effective NFL quarterback. So it was not surprising that the star rookie, the fourth pick in the entire draft, was sitting on the bench when the 1967 Dolphins season began, watching John Stofa, who had only been second-string the year before for the Dolphins' inaugural year. It looked as if the burly Stofa, a former star at

the University of Buffalo, was finally ready to excel in the pros. He completed
his first two passes and ran in the touchdown himself to make the Dolphins
look more like the Packers on their first drive. But the next offensive play
ended with Stofa writhing on the ground, his ankle snapped in half. "Griese,
you ready?" George Wilson asked. He was. He went an eye-opening twelve for
nineteen with two touchdown passes as the Dolphins beat the Broncos, and the
Dolphins were set at quarterback for the next thirteen years. Although the team
would suffer more than its share of lumps in its second season, Griese learned
from each defeat and began his practice of studying game films, figuring out
just how defensive backs tipped off their coverages by lining up to the inside of
a receiver or behind a linebacker. If you'd done your homework, you could see
just what was about to unfold. He ended up throwing for two thousand yards
that year for a struggling team and made the AFL All-Star Game as a rookie.
He continued his rise his second year, improving in every department. But
then came a tough period, as if that old adage had come back to collect some
unpaid dues.

First there was George Wilson's dismal final season in 1969. Crippled
by injuries, the team slid to a 1–6–1 record before Griese joined the casualties
with a sprained knee that ended his season. He had completed fewer than half
his passes and had spent much of his time showing off his spectacular running
ability as he fled defensive linemen on the rampage. When Don Shula arrived
the next year, he told Griese he wanted him to give up his scrambling and stay
in the pocket. "Make me a pocket," said the quarterback, "and I'll stay in it."
That's just what Shula and Monte Clark did, almost immediately, and Griese
became a run-oriented pocket quarterback as the Dolphins shot out to a 4–1
record. But then came the inexplicable 0–87 score over three games and the
calls for Stofa to replace him. Next to a *Miami News* column that repeatedly
asked, "Is this the quarterback to lead us to a championship?" the sports editor
Jeffrey Denberg wrote a little piece consisting of a hundred names, including
George Wilson Jr. and John Stofa but also George Plimpton, Ronald Reagan,
Charlton Heston, and fifty-six-year-old Sammy Baugh. One hundred names
followed by: "All these are better than the Dolphins' No. 1 quarterback. Now."
But Shula stuck with his man and was rewarded the next week, as Griese went
fifteen for nineteen before a half-full Orange Bowl and the Dolphins began
another winning streak against New Orleans. They put Baltimore back in its

place at home and then sealed a *Monday Night Football* win against Atlanta with what would soon become a Miami Special: the eighty-yard clock-killing drive. The 0–87 shipwreck was now a fading nightmare, and Griese was the fans' quarterback again as the Dolphins wrapped up their season with six straight wins, an impressive 10–4 record, and their first playoff appearance.

The death of his father when he was ten was the defining moment of Griese's childhood; it drove him into himself, forging a withdrawn but determined personality. During the darkest moments of that 1970 season, he said he wasn't depressed. "I'd rather work it out by myself. I don't talk about it too much and don't analyze it in public. I prefer to turn to other things, like my wife and family. I prayed some, too." What we fans saw was the all-American handsome quarterback, with the Redford blond hair, the cool mastery on the field. What we didn't realize was what a wall the boy in Indiana had built around him. Or maybe it was just his natural personality. "Sure, I'm quiet and introverted," he said. "I know that. I don't always get a kick out of sitting around and talking with a couple of teammates or sportswriters. I'm often as happy being by myself."

Even after throwing a big touchdown pass, he would remain apparently cool, emotionless. Csonka would say, "Helluva pass!" and he might wink and say, "Thanks, Zonk." Usually he'd just turn and trot to the sidelines, perhaps clapping his hands slowly together, as more than one writer put it, as though he were applauding at the opera. But he bristled at the aspersion "emotionless": "I'm not emotionless, it's just that when we make a touchdown, I'm immediately thinking about how to score the next touchdown. And when we win a game, I'm thinking about the next game, because it's not all over yet—until we win the Super Bowl." And when they lost that ultimate game to Dallas, and his teammates were slumped at their lockers, devastated, Griese finally exploded in profanity: "This is a damn disappointing way to end the year."

Some sportswriters resented him for his aloofness and would even revel in Schadenfreude when he failed. "What's the matter with that guy?" visitors would ask Braucher in the press box. His answer: Griese takes some knowing. For their first four years together, Griese was a mystery to Csonka: "I had no idea what was going through Bob's mind. He doesn't make friends easily or quickly. Until he knows you, he keeps a no man's land between you and him." Other teammates, even later, would call him "kind of a strange person, aloof." Morris recalled him as "the kind of a guy who wouldn't even talk about himself in the first person. He'd say, 'The quarterback doesn't have time,' or 'The quarterback is only concerned with . . .' That was the kind of dry toast Bob was at that time."

It's not that he didn't have friends on the team; he was close with Twilley and also good friends with Dick Anderson, Tim Foley, a few others. It's just that it wasn't important to him to be the Namath or Sonny Jurgenson type who partied with his teammates all night. He knew he had their respect on the field. "I've never seen any quarterback like him anywhere," said Nick Buoniconti. "In a game he is distant. He's like a real general in a real war. He doesn't talk to anybody on the sidelines. I don't think anybody would dream of talking to him or patting him on the back or anything." Players knew better than to disturb him when he was contemplating which play to call, and the huddle was sacrosanct. Morris would get a "laser look" to kill when he so much as blew a bubble with his gum while Griese was calling a play.

By 1972, with four seasons of pro experience, Griese had become the consummate quarterback. "Bob is so in command at all times that it's remarkable," said Shula. "He's got everything; I just don't see any weaknesses." In particular, said the coach, his quarterback was a master of play calling. "I might send in five or six plays a game from the sideline, but the rest of the time Bob's on his own. He gets a kick out of calling the right play." He also got a kick out of "pulling" the defense offsides. For in addition to everything else, he had become the king of the "cadence call"—or as one reporter called it, "Griese's hut-hut trickery." In addition to whatever audible (change of plays) a quarterback might call at the line of scrimmage, he always ended with the "huts," "hut" being short for "hike": the command for the center to snap the ball back to the quarterback. A quarterback keeps the defensive line off guard, unable to tee off on the snap, by varying which "hut" the ball is snapped on. So calling in the huddle, "I-19 on three," means no one must budge until the third "hut." No matter the tone of the quarterback's voice. Shula, while with Baltimore, had noticed Deacon Jones, the great defensive lineman for the Rams, get fooled repeatedly by another quarterback's "non-rhythmic cadence," by which he meant the quarterback would bark louder on the wrong "hut" and vary the timing in between. Johnny Unitas wasn't interested, but when Shula came to Miami, Griese took to the ploy like Don Rickles to celebrity roasts. Of all Griese's attributes—from his sangfroid to his play calling to his perfect tosses—my brother and I loved his cadence calls most. We (and thousands of other young Dolfans, no doubt) tried it out all the time in touch football games. And a five-yard penalty in a Dolphins game could be as satisfying to some of us as a Csonka charge up the middle.

Far more important, though, was the play selection, and indeed Griese had made a science of it, spending the week before a game calculating just the right succession of plays that would break down a particular defense. His fellow professor of offensive strategic studies, the equally reserved and intellectual Paul Warfield, said that Griese "wanted to call the best play on every down to have the greatest chance of success on that play. He was an unselfish player who wanted the team to win. He enjoyed throwing and I enjoyed catching as much as anyone else. But he even turned down incentives in his contract for touchdown passes because he wanted to be free to call the best play in every situation." Yes, Griese studied every film, analyzed every defense. But sometimes, he conceded, it all came down to intuition: "It's a feeling. You get to a certain part of the field, a situation in the game, and you just *feel* that something will work. Sometimes you're right."

Other times, maybe it was just coming across the right reading material at the right time. On October 8 the team was in New York City to play the Jets, and Griese was relaxing before the game in the locker room, flipping through *Pro!*, the NFL's official magazine. Csonka was joking to reporters about his and Kiick's big Saturday night in New York City: "Well, Jim went to see his buddy Joe Namath. I spent some time with a reporter from *Time*. Then we had our regular meeting at nine-thirty for hot dogs and Cokes. Coach Shula made only one announcement at the meeting: he told us the time for Sunday chapel services. I'll guarantee you we had a full house for the services. And I didn't even bother to count."

Griese flipped the pages. For all he knew, Namath was sipping some hangover tonic or chatting up the Gotham reporters. Joe Willie Namath, Broadway Joe, bigger and stronger than Griese, with the jaw-dropping arm and the personality to go with it. Usually seen in white Gucci loafers, a full-length mink coat, and a blonde on each arm, while Griese was home with the wife and kids. "I know people expect a quarterback to be flamboyant," Bob said, "but I'm just not." Namath also had a Super Bowl championship: four years earlier, he'd commandeered that shocking Super Bowl III victory against Shula and Earl Morrall's Colts. The Jets were great in '68 and '69, then had two disappointing seasons, but were looking strong again in '72. Well, Bob hoped Joe Willie had

had a particularly late night out on the town last night. He flipped idly through the program. Then stopped on one page, eyes widening.

There was an interview with the Jets' third-year defensive back Steve Tannen. Tannen was one of the few Jews in the NFL, and Griese might have remembered his name from the *Miami Herald* sports pages when Tannen was a standout for Southwest High. (He later was an All-American for the University of Florida.) In the interview, Tannen was asked who were the toughest receivers he'd ever had to cover. His top two were the Chiefs' Otis Taylor (no surprise) and Howard Twilley. *Howard?* Griese couldn't believe it. Had Tannen forgotten about a certain future Hall of Famer on the other side of our line? Well, okay. Briscoe was the second starter now, but he had come up lame with a thigh injury in the pregame warm-ups. Just as well; sounded like Tannen had Howard in his head. "After I read that," Griese said, "I figured I'd give Tannen another opportunity."

• • •

First he'd have to watch Namath a little, as New York won the coin toss. And Joe Willie looked as though he'd been in bed with his teddy bear at ten p.m., as he drove the Jets right down the field in twelve plays for a touchdown. On the one-yard touchdown run, Cliff McClain fumbled into the end zone, where the Jets recovered it for the score, a lucky break the Dolphins would see happen again that year. It didn't bother Griese. "I knew the worst they could do was score seven points," he said. "I was just waiting for our turn."

Griese drove his team into Jets territory and then wasted no time testing Tannen. He went for Twilley on third down, but Tannen made a good play and swatted the ball away. Yepremian pulled a thirty-eight-yard field goal attempt wide, so they got nothing out of it, but Griese wasn't about to let Tannen off the hook. Next possession, Miami drove back down the field, to the New York sixteen. And this time Griese again went for Twilley, calling one of their favorite patterns: the post, in which the receiver slants in toward the goalpost. Tannen actually had Twilley covered pretty tight, but the pass was perfect, and Tannen couldn't quite touch it and ended up flat on his back as Twilley caught it and rolled through the baseball infield dirt into the end zone, bouncing right back up with a two-handed flip of the ball to the referee. He caught three more passes and might have had another for a touchdown, but Tannen interfered with him (and got called for it) at the three-yard line in the fourth quarter. "Shoot," said

Twilley in a faint Texas drawl. "I'm lucky I was even in there. I only heard I was starting just before the kickoff."

Jim Kiick got the start in his return to his home area and scored twice, as well as running for 53 yards to complement Csonka's 102. In the second quarter he put Miami ahead with the consummate Kiick touchdown: six tough yards up the middle between Little and Evans and his trademark dive just over the goal line. Kiick had a bunch of friends from Jersey in the stands, and as he stood up in the end zone, there in front of him was a banner some of them had hung over the railing: RUN KIICK OR TRADE SHULA. Kiick came trotting back to the sideline with a grin on his face: "That's my boys, all right."

Miami was in front to stay as the defense completely stymied Namath after the opening drive; he completed only nine of twenty-one passes the rest of the game. The Dolphin defense had become good with the arrival of Shula in 1970 and done nothing but improve since then. Now they had become dominant. They had a reputation for bending but not breaking, but in '72 they bent about as much as a steel rail. They were tops in the NFL in both points and yards allowed. "Our defense in 1972 was so good that they spent little time on the field," said Csonka. The reason had much to do with a balding, soft-spoken Kentuckian with a distracted air and a sedulous attention to detail.

Bill Arnsparger grew up in Paris, Kentucky, in the 1930s, barely got into World War II as a young marine, came home and graduated from Miami University in Ohio, where he played football under coach Woody Hayes. He stayed there and began his coaching career right under Hayes, before following him to Ohio State. By 1959 he'd been coaching the defensive line at Kentucky several years when a young guy named Shula arrived to handle the defensive backs. (Schnellenberger showed up to coach the receivers the same year.) Five years later, when Shula took over the Baltimore Colts, he brought Arnsparger in as the defensive line coach, and they would work together for the next ten years, half in Baltimore and half in Miami. Arnsparger resigned after the 1969 season in Baltimore, as his wife urged him to seek a career that was a bit less consuming (or so he said), but apparently moving to sunny Miami was enough for her, and the Arnspargers came south with the Shulas.

Often kidded for his mismatched clothes and distracted air, at forty-five he was yet another pedagogical figure on this Dolphin team. The coaching staff would have looked at home in the faculty lounge at an ivy-covered liberal arts school. There was Schnellenberger, "a pipe and slippers kind of guy," as Marlin Briscoe put it, quietly offering sage advice only when needed. Monte Clark's ex-lineman physique belied his sensitive artistic nature. Arnsparger was more the absent-minded professor, although on the sideline, with his large glasses, baseball cap, and cigarette dangling from a plastic holder in his mouth, he looked a lot like gonzo journalist Hunter S. Thompson. He was not, however, known for lost weekends and overindulgent drug use. A reticent, diligent worker, Arnsparger fit in perfectly with the Shula ethos. He would watch game films—and would make players watch plays that had gone wrong—over and over until he was satisfied. "One More Reel" Arnsparger, they called him, but that moniker could have been latched on to Shula or any of his assistants, not to mention Griese, Warfield, or Buoniconti. Buoniconti, the thirty-year-old veteran, called Arnsparger "a genius of defensive coaches. The man knows more defense than anyone I've ever known. Working with him has been a revelation." Arnsparger surrounded himself with players who loved his systematic approach to the game. "I was a technician and awful compulsive, as my wife could tell you," said Doug Swift. "Our players had an intense desire to play the game right. . . . There was a certain compulsive kind of spirit on our defense: Buoniconti, Foley, Johnson, others. . . . There's a lot of perfectionism in that group of people." The young new defense Arnsparger assembled in 1970 featured five first-year players, and Miami allowed a hundred fewer points than the year before. And they just kept improving until they were the best, even if no one knew their names.

Legend has it that Dallas coach Tom Landry unwittingly christened the "No-Name Defense" when he remarked in training camp, "I know it's only four months after the Super Bowl, but I can't remember the names of the Miami front four." But in fact the press had been employing the soubriquet throughout the 1971 season as this band of castoffs and low-draft picks—similar to the offensive line—began to shine as a group.

Their leader, middle linebacker and future Hall of Famer Nick Buoniconti, had a name even his wife sometimes misspelled and was deemed too small for the NFL; he toiled seven seasons for the Boston Patriots before being unloaded to another AFL team, the Dolphins. Tim Foley was another who was too small and slow à la Twilley. Some said he couldn't have played for any other NFL team. Manny Fernandez went undrafted and came to Miami as a free agent. Doug Swift was unnoticed coming out of little Amherst College and was cut by Montreal of the Canadian Football League before getting a shot in Miami. Lloyd Mumphord, an invaluable defensive back, was drafted in the sixteenth round out of Texas Southern. Den Herder was another low-round pick who barely made the team in 1971. Although the Dolphins made the Super Bowl that year, they had no defensive starters in the Pro Bowl and only two defenders on the team at all: Jake Scott and Bill Stanfill. But their anonymity didn't bother them; in fact, it became a badge of honor. "We love that 'No-Name' business, honest," crowed Buoniconti after the New York game. "Don't you think that makes you feel pretty darned good when you go out and stop Joe Namath and an offensive line like the Jets have?"

Arnsparger and Buoniconti kept Namath off guard by confronting him with a plethora of different formations. As one quarterback put it that year, "Most defenses show me two basic looks. The Dolphins showed me twenty-two." Sometimes they'd have the traditional front four rushing the quarterback; sometimes they'd have only three linemen and an extra defensive back. And those defensive backs were never in the same place: "The way we kept moving around," said Mumphord, "[Namath] had to make his decision at the last second. I could see he was having trouble recognizing the different looks he was getting." Jake Scott made things worse by continually tricking Namath. He figured out that Namath had figured out that Scott tipped off certain coverages by his initial position and steps, so he began altering them, starting one way then going another. Namath got so frustrated that he began screaming obscenities across the line of scrimmage at Scott. After the game, he was more composed: "They used a lot of zone variations . . . and with that Matheson defense you've got eight bad guys running around back there. And that means you've got a helluva problem."

He was referring to the new defensive alignment Arnsparger had unveiled on opening day in Kansas City, and which he went to today after showing a traditional defense on the first drive. Namath called it the "Matheson defense," but in Miami it was known by Bob Matheson's number: the 53 defense.

It was an innovation inspired by misfortune. Back in August, when Miami lost defensive linemen Bob Heinz and Jim Riley in the same week, Arnsparger found himself down to five linemen. And one of those, number one draft pick Mike Kadish, was something of a disappointment to Shula, stressing the coach's pet peeve by showing up twenty pounds overweight and several tenths of a second slow. Someone tried to excuse him by pointing out he'd gotten married after graduation. "Who'd he marry," Shula asked, "a refrigerator?" (Kadish ended up spending the year on the taxi squad before being traded to Buffalo, where he had a solid career.) Arnsparger found himself doodling in his notebook late after practice, moving X's and O's around, tic-tac-toe with twenty-two squares. The next morning he walked into Shula's office and asked, "What do you think of this?"

They'd always known Matheson was not your typical linebacker. Six-foot-four but only 235 pounds and a fast runner, he was something of a Proteus. He'd run the hundred on the track team at Duke but also was a shot-putter and threw the discus. He played running back two years, then linebacker. He was drafted by Cleveland as a linebacker but after a couple years was asked to gain some weight and play mostly defensive end. That made him feel slow, ineffective, and miserable. After four years he was, in his words, "in the twilight of a mediocre career" when he was traded to Miami in 1971.

His first year he mainly spelled Buoniconti at middle linebacker. But Arnsparger's plan, drawn up in his notebook that summer of 1972, was to make better use of his versatility. Shula liked what he saw, and they began practicing it. But he wasn't about to let on publicly what they were up to. Reporters asked why Matheson was playing the line, and Shula told them, "The easiest thing [with the injuries] is for us to put Matheson at end. He's been able to go in there and do a pretty good job on the pass rush. We certainly didn't want to do it, but we were forced to." He was doing a lot more than playing end, but Shula didn't want to talk about it. And in the last two exhibition games, they just used the same old system of four linemen and three linebackers like every team. Players wondered if that new crazy stuff had been abandoned.

Then, on opening day in Kansas City, Shula unveiled the 53. They lined Matheson up as a defensive end, either down in a three-point stance or crouched in a two-point. Then Buoniconti would call out a coverage or revise what he had called in the huddle. Matheson was a terrific pass rusher, so often he did just that. But other times he would fade back into a linebacker position and play zone defense. Sometimes when he did that either Buoniconti or Swift would blitz from the other side. Arnsparger, who wasn't a fan of risky blitzing, called it "safe pressure." That way they'd get the full four-man pressure on the quarterback but with the element of surprise. In addition, they could do all this with the normal four defensive backs, or sometimes they would take out linebacker Mike Kolen, move cornerback Tim Foley up to that area, and bring in Lloyd Mumphord and so have five DBs to cover receivers.

Chiefs coach Hank Stram had insisted it was nothing new. And in fact many colleges used the three-man line with a blitzing linebacker, and Shula was quick to point out that some pro teams did that too. The difference was that Matheson, with his experience and size, often acted just like a defensive end. And occasionally they could keep him at end and still blitz other linebackers. Later, Arnsparger would be given credit for inventing the scheme, featuring the dual-purpose man hovering on the end of the line, that evolved into the ubiquitous "zone blitz" defenses of the 1990s and later.

The new alignment was particularly effective in passing scenarios—but then Dolphin opponents usually found themselves in a passing scenario. The 53 ended up being used about two-thirds of the time that year. "We put people in catch-up situations," said Matheson, "and then we'd go to this stuff and give them fits. Offenses just didn't have the sophistication to handle it that first year."

The Jets did no better than others. After passing for about five hundred and three hundred yards the previous two weeks, Namath had only 152 against Miami. A bunch of that came in the third quarter, when he threw a perfect bomb to Jerome Barkum at the Miami ten. But Dick Anderson dragged Barkum down inside the one-yard line, and the Miami defense showed another facet they would become famous for: the goal line defense. They plugged the line to stop three straight runs and then, when an offsides penalty gave New York another shot, Jake Scott deflected a third-down pass, and all the Jets got was a short field goal. "That Dunaway really stopped up the middle," sighed Namath. He hadn't seemed to notice that Jim Dunaway, a ten-year veteran lineman with Buffalo who had been traded to Miami that year, had failed to get on the field in time for the goal line stand, and the Dolphins had stuffed the Jets on first down with only ten men.

The new defense humbled Namath, and the offense wasn't too shabby either. Griese threw for an uncharacteristic 220 yards, almost all of it to his wide receivers, on a 400-yard day for the offense. It was a rare occasion when the Dolphins passed for more yards than they ran. A fumbled punt deep in their own end by Charlie Leigh in the fourth quarter led to a short touchdown run a few plays later, giving Jets fans brief hope, but a forty-three-yard field goal by Yepremian iced the fourth victory, 27–17. In the locker room, wearily peeling tape off the braces protecting his million-dollar knees, Namath admitted, "Miami's tough. With that kind of defense and that offense, you've got a hell of a problem. You've got to score every time you've got the ball."

The Dolphins didn't get a big night on the town in Manhattan, but they got what they wanted. They flew home that night, and six thousand fans were there to greet them at the airport, yelling as if they'd just won the Super Bowl. It was becoming a tradition after away games. Many people held up homemade banners: NO NAMES MEAN NO NAMATH, CSONKA IS A BEAUTIFUL PERSON, and BOB GRIESE FOR PRESIDENT. Well, maybe congressman, if he had any interest. At least they weren't calling for John Stofa anymore. The kid from Indiana was the most popular introvert in Florida.

Five and Oh

October fifteenth was sunny and hot. My dad drove our Chevy Impala downtown, my brother Ron and me in back. It was a twenty-minute drive from Kendale Boulevard to the Orange Bowl, in a neighborhood completely foreign to us. We found a free parking spot up on Fifteenth or Sixteenth Street and walked the mile or so down Seventeenth Avenue, over the Miami River, to the stadium. Although we had moved to Miami the same month the Dolphins played their first game ever, we had never been to a game. But I remember the excitement of Garo's winning field goal in the Longest Game, and also the disappointment of the Super Bowl loss, so somewhere between the arrival of Shula and Christmas in Kansas City, my father had replaced his childhood Eagles with the Dolphins and convinced his two boys to hop on the wagon. He was never a fan of large, noisy crowds, however, preferring to watch on TV or even listen to the radio, which may have sparked memories of listening to Eagles games before his father bought the first television in their neighborhood in 1947. But either at our urging or out of the instinct of an American dad, he had decided to take us to see this exhilarating young team in person.

Living in South Florida, the very fact of a long walk was a memorable anomaly. This unfamiliar ramble, between Overtown and Little Havana, would have felt dangerous at night and probably uncomfortable even on a weekday. But as we neared and crossed the river, people wearing aqua and orange, shorts, T-shirts, halter tops, and polyester slacks of unlikely hue emerged from the side streets and joined the growing southward current, and there was safety in fandom. We kept merging with other rivulets of humanity and only slowed when we reached the boisterous throng flowing around the stadium.

Many of the fans walking near us carried transistor radios to listen to the radio broadcast as they watched the game. Some had the WIOD pregame show on, but it would not have been surprising if one of those radios carried the voice of Helen Reddy singing, "I am woman, hear me roar . . ." The pop feminist anthem had been on and off the charts since its release in May, but now it was back for a long strong ride to December, when it would displace the Temptations' "Papa Was a Rolling Stone" at number one. The song seemed to be rising synergistically with the women's movement that had found new life in the 1960s with the publication of Betty Friedan's *The Feminine Mystique* in 1963 and the founding of the National Organization for Women in 1966. The first full issue of *Ms.* magazine, featuring a giant-sized Wonder Woman on the cover ("Wonder Woman for President"), was out at the Democratic Convention in July, when its cofounder Gloria Steinem and NOW took over the third floor of the Betsy Ross Hotel, a run-down relic of the forties on Ocean Drive in South Beach. Shirley Chisholm, the first Black woman in the United States Congress, was running for the presidential nomination, and NOW was busy support-ing her, but the women were also fighting for the Equal Rights Amendment, which had passed Congress earlier in the year and been signed by President Nixon (but which would fall just short of receiving the necessary three-fourths of states' approval). The Betsy Ross "was a power center," wrote Theodore H. White. "Mimeograph and Xerox machines spewed out leaflets in thousands of pink, yellow, green, blue sheets; the switchboard at the hotel jammed; fuses blew; and each night, after dark, couriers boarded the buses to travel north on Collins Avenue and . . . stuff mailboxes or slip leaflets under delegates' doors." Even as the landmark *Roe v. Wade* case was being considered by the Supreme Court—it would be argued for the second time in October and the Court's historic decision delivered in January 1973—the women's groups were fight-ing an uphill battle, lobbying for an abortion rights plank in the Democratic campaign platform. The McGovern campaign, though sympathetic, felt it was political suicide and secretly influenced enough delegates to vote against it. Already sadly diluted ("freedom of choice . . . should be fully respected, consis-tent with relevant Supreme Court decisions"), the plank died on the floor in a close vote. As the convention ended and Miami Beach emptied out, "*WOMEN POWER 1972* remained stained on the Betsy Ross's third-floor carpet, in faded red paint."

Despite the abortion setback, women's rights were on the rise. Popular culture, though, tends to lag behind social movements, and any visitor leafing through the *Miami Herald* knew that women in America still had a long way to go. It was one thing that, in a world with no internet, the entertainment pages were packed with ads for porn movies, at cinemas from the euphemistically named 79th St. Art Theatre to the Strand Stag Theater on Seventh Avenue ("Stag-O-Rama Continuous from 9 a.m."). The "legit" theaters weren't much better, carrying all sorts of mainstream soft porn, including a startling number of sexy-doctor-and-nurse movies like *Tell Me Where It Hurts* ("It's the nurses who are contagious!"). It was often hard to tell where the comedy ended and the porn began, as the ad for *Carry On Doctor* (rated PG) was right next to that for *Oh! Doctor!* (rated X). The most famous porn film yet, *Deep Throat*, which inspired the nickname for Woodward and Bernstein's Watergate informant, had been filmed mostly in Coconut Grove and North Miami in early 1972 and would soon replace *Fiddler on the Roof* at the Sheridan on Miami Beach.

Then there were the live sex shows, not just the typical "Girls Girls Girls" at the Burlesk on Collins but also the more upscale "The Love Machines" at the Eden Roc ("The most provocative show in town . . . the next step after 'Oh Calcutta!'") or "Vie Parisienne" at the Americana, with a *Herald* ad that looked like a *Playboy* cover. The leading newspaper in South Florida, a family paper, was practically pornography: any kid leafing through to get to the Dolphins reportage could learn that "Geisha Girls" were available morning to night for ten dollars "total price." "Grecian Girls," too, for that matter. Even much of the mainstream advertising in other sections objectified women with little self-awareness. St. Pauli Girl beer implored readers to "Enjoy a cold girl." National Airlines, based in Miami, ran constant ads featuring attractive stewardesses imploring, "I'm Laura [or Cheryl, or Jo]. Fly me." (At least Laura didn't have to wear miniskirts or hot pants and leather boots, like the stewardesses on Pacific Southwest.)

The front page wasn't always much better, often featuring "general interest" photos and captions that were shamelessly objectifying. "Rack 'em up!" showed a buxom blonde leaning over a pool table and explained that this enticing "scenery" was actually Sandra Peters at the U.S. Open Billiards Championships. Another front page this year featured a photo, right next to a story headlined S. VIETS REPULSE 9 ATTACKS, of a young woman in a bikini strolling by some attentive construction workers at Lion Country Safari, with the header "A Fringe Benefit." All this in a city founded by a woman.

Seventy years after Julia Tuttle died, Jane Chastain moved from Atlanta to Miami and began working for WTVJ Channel 4. In Atlanta she'd been the nation's first local woman sportscaster, but Chastain was no feminist; in fact, she was a conservative Christian who would deride feminism in her later books and political commentary. But even a conservative woman, especially one who looks like a model in an airline ad, has to fight sexism every inch of the way. Interviewing athletes twice her size on camera, Chastain would implore them to answer to the camera, and they'd say, "But, honey, I'd much rather look at you." When she first went to Dolphins training camp in 1969 to get some on-camera interviews, George Wilson refused to acknowledge her presence. He eventually relented, though, and even invited Chastain to come interview him. When it was over, several Dolphins lifted her up in triumph and deposited her in a nearby dumpster, an act she accepted cheerfully as her initiation into the boys' club.

Gender, however, meant about as much to Don Shula as race: all he cared about was whether you could do the job. He admitted that when his players first told him about Chastain, "I figured they were impressed because here was a good-looker talking about football, but Jane sure surprised me with her knowledge of the game. It only takes me two or three questions to see when a reporter's been doing their homework. Jane is a girl who conducts intelligent, competent interviews. She's not past throwing a controversial question at you either. There's no way you can talk your way around her. She'll just come right back at you until she's satisfied you answered the question." Shula quickly accepted her as one of the local media—and one of the best. But after noticing that her attire at training camp—a miniskirt and leather go-go boots—was of more interest to his players than the tackling dummies, he quietly asked her to wear less distracting outfits.

Despite her success in Atlanta, in Miami she was at first limited to three feature stories a week and, as she put it, "no hard sports, nothing live, no anchoring." Three years later, as the 1972 season began, she was anchoring the sports segment of Channel 4's *News at Noon* and also had her own national radio show, *Girls Rules*, heard in every state, on over two hundred stations. Still, a

Herald profile of her that year got her "delicately flowing shoulder-length hair and 35–22–35 figure" into the lead paragraph. Yet even while fighting her way up in the masculine environment of sports journalism, she wanted no part of Women's Lib. Her Christian conservative beliefs outweighed any feeling of solidarity with her gender. She wasn't alone, as an even greater majority of women than men were planning to vote for Nixon in November.

NASA had just announced that it was considering female astronauts for the future—but only because, according to an agency medical expert, "the lack of normal sex relationships could cause a significant buildup of tension during missions lasting a year or more." The U.S. Senate had one woman but was about to become all-male once again. When considering mortgage loans, banks often still refused to consider the salaries of women "of child-bearing age." And sexist hiring practices were freely admitted. "Nobody has a better chance at a job [here] than a good-looking woman," said the Palm Beach assistant tax assessor in a public interview.

Edna Buchanan was familiar with the biases working women had to put up with. Moving from New Jersey to Miami on a whim in 1965, she got a job at the *Miami Beach Daily Sun* and found her calling in the journalistic life. Five years later she moved to the *Herald* and had to fight to get the sort of assignments her editor considered fit for a man. Rather than cheerfully negotiate the obstacles like Chastain, she fought them head-on: at one point she threatened to purchase the one qualification she was missing from a sex toy store and display it on her desk in a flowerpot. Finally now, at age thirty-three, she was starting to get the beefy, sordid crime assignments that would make her career. POLICE NAB 18 AT HEROIN 'SHOOTING GALLERY' was her story on the day of the Dolphins-Chargers game. Just in the past couple of weeks there had been the 'POLITE' SOUTH DADE KILLER who abducted couples on dates, raped the woman, and then allowed her to dress before shooting both; the suicidal man whose wife accidentally shot him dead, and the lonely elderly man who announced his suicide and then made good on it (both of those stories the same day); and the latest in a series of bombings targeting Cuban Miamian businessmen—this one a hand grenade thrown from a car into the yard of Enrique DeLeon's Southwest Thirteenth Street ranch house. (He blamed pro-Castro Communists.)

Hers were the sort of stories that delighted the writer Charles Willeford. In the mid-1970s, when Willeford and his wife, Betsy, became good friends with my parents, he was a somewhat forgotten author of dime novels and quirky gems like *Cockfighter* and *The Burnt Orange Heresy*, now teaching writing at Dade South, as we called the community college branch right near our house. But all through the 1970s and early 1980s he was assimilating material that percolated into his four smash Hoke Moseley detective novels, beginning with *Miami Blues* in 1984. As he chronicled the transformation of Miami from a sleepy vacationland to a crossroads of cocaine-fueled abandon, he struggled to convince fact-checkers that, as his wife Betsy put it, "anything you can say about Miami is true." A decade after he died in 1988, Betsy told me, "Miami was the perfect place for Charles to live. When I see a headline like DEAD BODIES IN CAR CAUSE RUBBERNECKING DELAY, I really miss him."

In 1972, Miami was just beginning that metamorphosis. Thomas McGuane was already writing of "the world of American bad actors who, when the chips are down, go to Florida with all the gothics and grotesqueries of chrome and poured-to-form concrete that that implies." The links between the "Cubans"—the bungling burglars of Democratic headquarters—and the Watergate scandal were one early manifestation of such Miami madness. In mid-October the story was slowly gaining steam. Bernstein and Woodward reported on October 10 that the FBI had established that the bugging of the DNC was part of a "massive campaign of political spying and sabotage conducted on behalf of President Nixon's reelection and directed by officials of the White House and the Committee for the Reelection of the President."

The extensive network of chicanery and outright crimes linked to Nixon were having little effect, so far, on his political health. Neither was the ongoing violence in Vietnam. Since the reescalation of aerial attacks by the U.S. in late 1971, about two hundred American servicemen had either been killed or taken prisoner or were missing in action. The rate of loss was the highest by far since Nixon had taken office in 1969. And yet Nixon announced in October that there would be no letup in the bombing. Meanwhile, Henry Kissinger dangled the possibility of peace, allowing himself to be quoted that his secret talks with Le Duc Tho were "at a critical and decisive stage."

McGovern, the same day, announced that on the first day of his presidency he would immediately order the cessation of all bombing and other military actions in Vietnam, terminate all shipments of military supplies, and begin the "orderly withdrawal of all American forces from Vietnam, from Laos, and

Cambodia." As if to underscore his point, U.S. bombing of Hanoi that same day badly damaged the French diplomatic mission and wounded its chief diplomat, evoking protests from Paris.

None of this seemed to have any effect on the polls. And this same week the *Miami Herald* gave Nixon its endorsement, despite his "somewhat arrogant campaign apparatus, guilty of such collegiate antics as the Watergate affair," his "dark cult[ist]" vice president, his "nomination of two unqualified candidates for the Supreme Court," and the fact that "the Nixon administration has struck out on five of the six 'great goals' of the 1971 State of the Union address." Some endorsement. Still, the paper insisted that Nixon had shown a "capacity to govern," and it hoped that "the people will speak overwhelmingly for Richard Nixon on the first Tuesday in November." McGovern, in other words, was even worse. The Democrat's campaign was "an unmitigated disaster," he was a poor judge of men, and he himself "can't even charm a garter snake." The electorate apparently agreed: McGovern trailed Nixon by twenty-eight to thirty-nine percentage points, depending on the poll. For the first and last time, my parents volunteered for a political cause. For decades my father would lament the conversations he'd had while making phone calls for McGovern. Four times out of five, the person who picked up the phone would inform him of their intention to vote for Nixon. Dad would lose his calm demeanor: "Don't you read the papers? The man is a crook!" But they would just brush that off: the economy was strong.

. . .

The fans milling around the Orange Bowl on October 15 were similarly unconcerned with Washington subterfuge. "Mild: sunny, high near 85," the paper had said, and so it was. A solid blue dome baked a patchwork of South Florida humanity—hot pants, floppy racetrack hats, muscle shirts, polyester dresses and miniskirts, loafers and flip-flops—growing by the minute, wandering around looking for companions, looking for the right gate, looking for tickets and selling them. The game had sold out sometime over the weekend, and we had arrived with no tickets. The scalpers standing around or walking the perimeter, holding up two, four, twelve tickets in the air, were our only hope. Finally Dad found one who wasn't trying to gouge us for $16 a ticket—twice the original price—and we were in.

We had previously been to the Orange Bowl only to see the fireworks on the Fourth of July. Trudging in a crowd up endless ovoid spiral ramps and then suddenly that first glimpse of the interior: that wondrous view again, a new strange universe. The unimaginably vast curve of the stadium, the pristine green field so far below, the same achingly pure blue sky above but ever more stunning for its extraction from the whole. And there, down below on that unreal plastic surface, stretching, running, tossing the ball around, were the players we had only read about, heard described on the radio, or watched on our television screen: Griese, Csonka, Warfield, the rest of those magical names. The fifth game of the season was only the second home game, and it would be the first in the typical Miami weather that favored the Dolphins. It was a classic Dolphin game in the Orange Bowl.

The stadium was old even then. It had been built in 1937 as Burdine Stadium, an early example of corporate naming rights—Roddy Burdine was a Miami pioneer who founded the department store of the same name—before being renamed in 1959 for the Orange Bowl college football game, which it had hosted since 1939. It originally held twenty-four thousand people, and new end zone seats in the 1940s and a second deck in the 1950s tripled the capacity. In the summer of 1972 Joe Robbie, who was continually finding new ways to squeeze more seating into the old horseshoe, added permanent bleachers in the east end zone (where Flipper used to flip) at team expense, almost five thousand new seats that brought the total to the glory-era eighty thousand and ten.

The Orange Bowl lent the Dolphins an undisputed home advantage. First of all, there was the climate. The oppressive training in Miami summers led to that "camel-like" superiority in autumn, when they'd see the opposition bent over on the other sideline—the north sideline, of course, which had no shade—flirting with heat exhaustion. Flying home from a Miami game in 1973, the San Francisco 49ers had to make an unscheduled stop in Denver to treat a dozen players suffering from dehydration. The seats were closer to the field than in most stadiums, allowing the crowd to become part of the game. "When the offense would drive down to the closed end of the stadium," said Csonka, "we could *feel* the fans screaming—the place vibrated. It felt like a giant heartbeat." On a number of occasions, the opposing quarterback had to stop his cadence call and tell the officials that no one could hear him. But eventually he would have to go ahead and run a play whether they could hear him or not. More so than anywhere else at that time, in the Orange Bowl the crowd "became something of a weapon," as Csonka put it.

They were bartenders from Hollywood, retired schoolteachers from the Keys, even bathing-suit salesmen from the Beach. There was dentist Bob Depuy of Fort Lauderdale, clearly audible from row twenty of the upper deck as he blasted his trailer-truck air horn powered by a portable oxygen tank from his office. Halfway up from the thirty-yard line, someone was screaming, "Kill them! Kill them!": Mrs. Flo Quigley, a warranty clerk for Fincher Oldsmobile, right on Second Avenue in old downtown Miami. There were celebrities like Flip Wilson and Mickey Rooney, both season-ticket holders. All together they were a guaranteed eighty thousand and ten fans at every game, waving those hankies, screaming, "We're Number One!" and singing the ubiquitous song, "Miami Dolphins Number One."

At the San Diego game, they weren't singing it quite yet. Lee Ofman, a struggling musician in Louisiana who was a Dolphin fan, wrote it during the week after the squeaker up in Minnesota. It was released in November, became an AM radio hit, and sold more than a hundred thousand copies by the end of the playoffs. We even sang it in music class at Kendale Elementary. (In 1978, when we heard a Houston Oiler version being played at the Astrodome on television, we all thought the Oilers had stolen it. In fact Ofman, angered at being cheated out of his royalties, had recorded a new version for Houston. He finally made a little money off of that one but eventually gave up the songwriting and became a lawyer.) In October 1972, some fans in the stands were erupting into a precursor, "We Love You Dolphins," which cast Shula as a Clausian figure ("There's joy all around, / Since Shula came to town") and whimsically hinted at destiny ("Go go Dolphins, / You can win them all!").

· · ·

Despite all the advantages of being home, the Dolphins were a little edgy before the Chargers game. For one thing, as much as they loved the atmosphere of the Orange Bowl, the horrid playing surface lent some ambivalence to their mood. At least in Minnesota and New York they were playing on good old grass. American Biltrite had held a press conference on Friday to admit the problems with Poly-Turf II: its new nylon base held water like a vase. They promised to take ameliorative steps immediately: in addition to enlarging the protective tarpaulin covering the field, they would research ways of quickly removing water before and during games, and they were establishing a new shoe bank of more than two hundred pairs featuring short conical rubber cleats for the use of both home and visiting teams. (There was already a shoe bank for Poly-Turf I, but "it's a completely different problem now, almost the reverse.") Don Shula was unimpressed. "I'm tired of the buckpassing," he said Sunday upon discovering that the tarp had not been on overnight and the field was wet for pregame warm-ups. "If any water is on the field during the game, it's a fiasco and nothing can be done."

Larry Csonka didn't even feel like talking about the hated turf. His back was still bruised and aching from the game two weeks ago in Minnesota, and he didn't want to think about the wounds he'd get from the turf today. Marlin Briscoe was still hobbling with his thigh injury. And Manny Fernandez showed up in the locker room miserably sick, straining to suck air into his lungs. San Diego had had the top offense in the AFC the year before; the Dolphins could ill afford to lose Manny for this one. The team physician, Dr. Herbert Virgin, examined him and x-rayed his lungs. "Okay," he patted Manny on the back. "Go get 'em." Just a little pneumonia; he'd get him to the hospital after the game.

After disappearing into the locker room, the players came running back out through a cheering gauntlet of Dolphin Dolls: the junior high and high school girls who served as the team's cheerleaders and baton-twirling halftime entertainment. This was the year the Dallas Cowboy Cheerleaders replaced their own high schoolers with adult women in provocative uniforms, the birth of a national sensation. But the Dolphins stuck with their schoolgirls (whom Joe Robbie didn't have to pay a dime). In 1978 the Dolls finally disbanded. "It's no longer a wholesome thing," said their director, Bill Allen, "and we have a wholesome group." (The Dolls were also enduring verbal abuse from fans in the front rows, whose view was blocked by the girls. There is no record of such objections to the Dolls' sexy successors, the grown-up Dolphin Starbrites.)

Out on the field, the hot sun was evaporating the overnight rain. Conditions were perfect as Bob Griese got things going on his first possession with a nice pass to Warfield on an out pattern to the sideline for a nineteen-yard gain. Ron and I jumped out of our seats: Warfield! Two plays later, however, Griese was sacked hard by Deacon Jones, the massive seven-time Pro Bowl defensive end for the Rams, who had moved down the coast to San Diego this year. Jones hit him so hard, the ball came popping out, but Larry Little fell on it. Griese got up slowly and trotted off. "Norm Evans is having a tough time with Deacon," said color commentator Henry Barrow on someone's radio. "He must be talking to himself, saying I've got to do better than that." Perhaps Jones wasn't pleased to have heard that he was the inspiration for Griese's famous cadence counts.

The No-Names had stopped the fine San Diego offense flat the first time, and they did it again, Miami taking over at midfield after a botched punt that went off the side of the foot. Morris swept to the left for nine yards, then carried again for the first down, and it looked like Griese's offense was going to begin its inexorable digestion of real estate. On first down, Griese faked to Morris to the left and faded back, looking for Kiick, who was open deep on the right side. As he fired the ball, Deacon was charging at him from the left, and defensive tackle Ron East was flying low, Superman-style, right at Griese's ankles.

Everyone's attention—ours in the stands, television viewers', even the radio announcers'—was downfield where the underthrown ball was almost intercepted. Just an incomplete pass. Then came the words from Rick Weaver: ". . . And shaken up on the play is Griese." East had engulfed his ankles just before Jones hit him high. Griese "felt a riot of pain" and sat up grabbing his ankle. Norm Evans saw he'd let Deacon clobber Bob again, and his first chest-emptying thought was that he'd just blown the whole season. On television, in view of millions, Don Shula surveyed the scene and let his gaze drop to the ground for just a moment before the jutting jaw rose again and he confronted the future. In the upper deck we stood watching as they strapped Griese onto a stretcher and wheeled him off to cheers and waving hankies. Griese was oblivious; his lower leg was numb now and he was sure it was broken. He was thinking about how his career began on opening day five years before, with John Stofa writhing on the ground with a leg broken in almost the same spot. On the sideline, Bill Stanfill turned to Manny Fernandez: "Cuz, we're in deep shit now." Shula said later, "I wanted to throw up."

The coach looked at his old soldier Earl Morrall, who'd been a lifesaver off the bench for him in '68, and whom he'd brought in just that summer to be Griese's backup. "Better loosen up, Earl," he said. "You're going in." Morrall made a little throwing motion with his arm and said he was ready. "Don't you want to throw a few balls?" "No, I'm fine." And in he went. Csonka, Morris, and Twilley just looked at him for a moment. Morrall had played for Pittsburgh in 1956, when Morris was a nine-year-old Steelers fan. Twilley had owned an Earl Morrall football card in the seventh grade, when Morrall played for San Francisco. "Our fathers had talked about this guy when we were kids," said Csonka. Morrall arrived at the huddle, looked at Csonka, and said, "What do you think?" "I just looked at him and said, 'Earl, it doesn't matter what *I* think. It's what *you* think!'" There was a current of unease running through the eleven Dolphins out there on the Poly-Turf, not to mention the eighty thousand watching them. "Okay everybody," said Morrall in his plainspoken way, "stay calm, we're gonna be all right." A couple guys smiled. "All right now, let's keep it going." He called a handoff to Zonk—safe bet—and the big man gained six yards. Then he ran what he called "an old faithful play": a short pass to tight end Marv Fleming on a delay. Fleming, with a defender wrapped around his ankles, may have been thinking of Griese on his way to Mercy Hospital, because he looked around frantically to see if anyone was about to take a potshot at him, and as a defensive tackle was about to do just that he dropped to the ground without bothering to stretch the half yard he needed for a first down. No matter: Garo Yepremian came out and kicked a thirty-seven-yarder for a 3–0 lead with five minutes left in the first quarter.

Morrall, who had held the ball for Yepremian, came trotting off the field and was greeted by Stanfill, the towering young defensive end from Cairo, Georgia. They were next-door neighbors, part of a pod of Dolphins inhabiting the Greenbriar motel and apartment building up in Hallandale Beach. "Old man," cried Stanfill, who, unlike Den Herder and Swift, was not considering a future in medicine, "get those cataracts in motion and turn up your hearing aid. Let's go!"

Morrall was the same age as the offensive coordinator, Howard Schnellenberger, and three years older than Monte Clark, the offensive line coach. He was only four years younger than Shula. The next oldest player on the team was seven years younger than him. He'd been an NFL quarterback since 1956, and he looked it. On a team decorated with long hair, drooping mustaches, and muttonchop sideburns, Earl Morrall sported the same close shave and crew cut he'd had as a rookie sixteen years earlier.

No one doubted his credentials. After leading his high school team to the Michigan state championship and Michigan State to the Rose Bowl crown—and turning down professional baseball offers—Morrall had been a valuable quarterback for five NFL teams before Miami, but mostly coming off the bench. Remarkably, the former Pro Bowler, first-team All-Pro, and league MVP had only been the starting quarterback for four of his sixteen seasons so far—and one of those was 1968, when Johnny Unitas was injured in the final preseason game and Morrall replaced him all year. That was the year he led Shula's Colts to a 15–1 season and the NFL championship only to fall to Namath and the Jets in Super Bowl III. (The Super Bowl then was still the AFL versus the NFL.) Then, in 1970, Unitas was injured much of the time, and Morrall started nine games before Unitas returned in the playoffs to lead Baltimore back to the Super Bowl. And in that one, when Dallas knocked Unitas out of the game in the second quarter, Morrall replaced him again and this time led the Colts to victory. But even in that triumph he was far from masterful, blowing a first-and-goal opportunity in the first half and throwing an interception near the goal line in the second half before a cascade of Cowboy blunders led to a winning field goal for Baltimore in the closing seconds. So even Earl Morrall's greatest achievements had been imbued with human imperfection.

The man could play NFL football, though. No one was too worried (so they said) about his dismal performances in the exhibition season. "I knew he could handle the quarterbacking," said Csonka, "but I didn't know if he could handle it physically. What I was afraid of was that he was going to be on the next stretcher. I didn't know how tough that old bulldog was until he got in the fight." On the sideline, fiery Nick Buoniconti was passing the word around to the defense: "We've got to shut the bastards out!" However, as Bob Griese, who'd been frustrated on his ambulance ride that there was no radio for him to follow the game on, now sent hospital orderlies scrambling for a transistor radio, the proficient San Diego offense moved straight down the field and tied the game with a short field goal. Just before the field goal, Henry Barrow broke into the radio broadcast to report that Dr. Virgin had told him a dislocated ankle would keep Griese out six to eight weeks. "Holy smokes," lamented Rick Weaver softly, abandoning his radio voice for a moment.

The game almost went further south when Morris fumbled the ensuing kickoff, but luckily it bounced straight forward and he was able to dive onto it. And then, after a Miami punt, Charger running back Mike Garrett wasn't so lucky. He dropped a handoff, bounced it off the Poly-Turf like a basketball, and then batted it up into the air, where Dick Anderson grabbed it in full stride and went into his idiosyncratic sprint—bent forward, head and shoulders down, legs pumping—thirty-six yards for an easy touchdown. Just a few plays later, Lloyd Mumphord, in as a fifth defensive back, intercepted a John Hadl pass over the middle of the field, giving Miami the ball at the San Diego thirty-four. A few minutes after that, Bob Griese's wife, Judi, entered his hospital room along with Julie Twilley. Julie had left the stadium in sympathy with her friend as soon as Griese had exited on the stretcher. "Hey, what are you doing here Julie," Bob shouted at her, holding up his radio. "Your husband just scored a touchdown!" Earl Morrall, after backpedaling facing straight ahead in his old-fashioned style, had just found Twilley all alone in the right corner of the end zone for an eighteen-yard score. Twilley did his signature leap and two-handed toss of the football high in the air, and Miami had a safe 17–3 lead at halftime.

With that, the pressure was off the old man. Although San Diego had more yards, it felt as though Miami was dominating the game. In the second half, Morrall mainly just had to hand the ball off as the Dolphins put on their clock-killing running-game choke hold. And his buddy Stanfill seemed to be living in the Chargers' backfield, sacking the quarterback and decking running backs barely after they received the ball. Morrall did make a couple memorable passes, one for a big gain to Twilley over the middle and then a gorgeous touchdown pass to Warfield. This came after Csonka, who'd missed most of the week's practice with his bruised back, returned to his normal business of bruising the defense. After the long pass to Twilley in the third quarter, Csonka chose to run through cornerback Lenny Dunlap rather than around him. Dunlap tried to go low on him, and Csonka just bent down and delivered what was basically an uppercut with his right forearm, removing him from his path for an eight-yard gain. Dunlap had to be helped to the sideline, but he staggered back onto the field a few plays later, only to be beaten badly by Paul Warfield on an in-and-out pattern to the corner of the end zone. First Zonked, then Warfed, poor Dunlap left the field again with the game all but over. We got one more thrill when Jake Scott made an outrageously athletic interception to stop another long drive, staying just in bounds and then dancing about thirty yards worth to gain seven. He looked like my brother cutting this way and that like a moth in lamplight, preventing me from touching him in our narrow front yard. Otherwise it was mainly ball control. San Diego got a touchdown after a Charlie Leigh fumble, but the Dolphins had their fifth win, 24–10.

The joy of another victory on such a gorgeous day suffused the crowd as we filed down the ramps, dispersed to the streets, and walked back over the river to our cars. As Dad pulled into traffic, though, WIOD was doing its postgame locker room show. Almost fifty years later I can still remember the calm, measured, but foreboding tenor of the players' voices as they discussed the game. Underlying it all was the injury to Griese. Although they all professed faith in the skill and experience of Morrall, you could tell that they were wondering if their championship season was in peril. Or maybe they were just feeling bad for Bob; after all, Earl had completed eight of ten passes with two touchdowns, and they'd won easily.

Dr. Virgin found Manny Fernandez, congratulated him on a good game, and said he was admitting him to the hospital. No need to reexamine him; he'd seen the X-rays before the game. "You've got pneumonia," he said. Fernandez and Jim Dunaway, whose back was hurting more and more each week, were told to get over to Mercy to join their fallen quarterback. When they got there Griese was holding court up in room 478, his right leg elevated in a cast below the knee. "A lot worse things could happen, like I told my wife," he said. "I might have been killed in an accident going home from the Orange Bowl."

Once we got out of the local traffic from the game, the ride home was quick. The 836 expressway, still only three years old, whisked us over to the Palmetto, and we were back on Kendale Boulevard in fifteen minutes. A long, curving spine of similar stucco ranch houses, suburban lawns, kids out throwing a ball or biking on the sidewalks. It was just after five, and on the hour the news had come on the radio: more about Watergate and the Nixon campaign. Although no one was directly implicating the president yet, his campaign had clearly been up to all sorts of unlawful capers. Dad parked the Impala, with its lonely McGovern sticker—the only political bumper sticker we ever had—in the driveway, and we jumped out the back, no seat belts to bother with. We'd been to our first Dolphin game ever, and despite the loss of Griese we were still undefeated. Nine more regular-season games to go, four weeks until the election. The Dolphins, like Nixon, looked unstoppable.

Six and Oh

The Tuesday after the San Diego game, just as twilight was darkening the Atlantic Ocean off Hallandale Beach, a couple of Miami Dolphins were walking along the sand with their kids after a long day of practice. Doug Crusan could just make out a figure in the water, paddling a long surfboard southward. He pointed it out to Terry Cole, a running back on injured reserve all that year. "Hey!" shouted Cole, "you the guy that's paddling from Boston?" "Yeah!" A voice came back from the waves. "Know where I can get a room cheap?" Larry Capune was almost through his mission to paddle his seventeen-foot board from Boston to Miami. He was close but would need one more day. Crusan and Cole took him back to their place, the Greenbriar, a plain two-story white building with green trim right on the beach, which they, along with six other Dolphins families—the Stanfills, Morralls, Rileys, Mathesons, Dunaways, and Kindigs—took over for the football season. The families were excited about helping this seafarer. Turned out he was a famous long-distance paddler from California. In the first week of his odyssey, back in August, he washed up on a Hyannis beach and ended up spending two days with the Kennedys. Now he was with Dolphins. "The reason he's doing it," said Crusan's wife, Diane, "is to show young people that there's more than one kind of trip. His surfboard's parked right outside our front door, and in the morning Jill Cole's going to fix his breakfast and he's going to start paddling again at nine a.m."

Eight players—a fifth of the team—were living at the Greenbriar, enjoying the off-season rate of $250 a month until December 15. They filled the front building, facing the beach. Every morning, two cars would fill up with eight football players to drive the twelve miles down to Biscayne College for practice. "The Stanfills and their kids lived right above us," said Crusan. "Bill and I would get in the car each morning, go to practice, hit the heck out of each other sixty, seventy times a day: I was left offensive tackle, he was right defensive end. Then we'd shower, get in the car, and head home. You round the bend of this baby-L-shaped hotel, and your whole mindset changed. There's the kids running around: 'Daddy's home!' The doggone ocean thirty yards away. You'd sit on the beach at night, and it was pitch-dark. There wasn't much around when we were there. The phones didn't work after five p.m. when the switchboard closed, so when we were away at road games the wives would bang a broom handle on the ceiling or wall to signal: We're okay, everybody's locked in. It got a little lonely out there at night, with little kids. Well, the Greenbriar's torn down now. High-rises and bright lights everywhere."

Earl Morrall was one of the Greenbriar bunch, although most of the time he had his apartment to himself. His wife, Jane, and their four kids stayed home in Michigan so their school life wouldn't be interrupted—Earl was the only player with kids in high school. The family visited him every other weekend, turning the little two-bedroom apartment into "wall to wall beds." As Jane was expecting a fifth child in January—on Super Bowl Sunday—this might be the only year in the Greenbriar for the Morralls. Earl had been famous in Detroit and Baltimore, but life as a permanent backup down here had been pretty quiet. Practice, practice, early to bed. Fishing with the family when they were down. A practicing Catholic like Shula and Griese, he attended Mass every Sunday. Now, though, as he replaced Griese for what looked like at least the rest of the regular season, all eyes were on him.

At times, when he appeared among his hirsute, bell-bottomed teammates, Morrall looked like Spiro Agnew at a rock concert. (In fact, that very week the vice president was campaigning in Chicago and made an appearance, along with Frank Sinatra, at a performance by the Osmond Brothers. Onstage, he promised Donny he'd make sure David Cassidy got drafted.) But Earl Morrall knew how to win football games, and despite his age he was a rock. Six-foot-two and a trim 205 pounds, all muscle. He was far from the only conservative member of the team, but he was the only one who dressed and wore his hair like an Eisenhower Republican. He swore he wasn't making a statement with the crew cut: "I wear it this way because it's comfortable. It's funny, but the long

hair business began as a symbol of individualism. Doing their own thing, as
they say. Not any more. It seems long hair means you are part of a group. I'm
the individual now." "Earl was just like Bob," said Mercury Morris. "They both
acted like old men. The difference was, Earl *was* an old man." Others saw him
differently. "He was a homespun kind of guy," said Briscoe. "Earl was just the
opposite of Griese—gregarious and very personable around the other players,
joking around and loose. 'Maaaaarlin come over here,' he'd say to me." Morrall,
unlike Griese, would jump around after a touchdown and pat guys on the back.
In practice he'd sometimes get mad at himself for throwing a bad pass and lose
his temper, screaming, "Cheesy weezy," or "Dagnabit," or even "Horse manure!"

His career had seemed to be winding down before Shula grabbed him
in '68 to back up Johnny Unitas, and the same was true this past off-season
when Shula signed him. When he was performing so poorly in the preseason,
and many were calling for Del Gaizo to be Griese's backup, Shula stood behind
Morrall, later as much as admitting that it was only his "fond memories" of the
brilliant campaign Morrall gave him in '68—and probably also the winning
performance in Super Bowl V after Shula was gone—that led him to keep the
struggling Morrall and send Del Gaizo to the taxi squad. "Shula would say Earl
couldn't hit the side of a barn in practice," recalled Morris, "but when the time
came for him to throw in the game, he could throw. And he came through."

Now, suddenly, Morrall's career was back in full swing just when it looked
as if Unitas's might be over. The week after Morrall came to the rescue against
San Diego, he was named the AP Offensive Player of the Week, while the Colts
announced they were benching the thirty-nine-year-old Unitas and building
for the future with young quarterback Marty Domres. On Friday, Dolphin
equipment manager Danny Dowe brought an old wooden rocking chair from
home, wrote Morrall's name and number on it, and placed it in front of the
quarterback's locker instead of the usual folding metal chair. Earl sat down
and tried it out. "There he is, crew cut and all, right out of Queen Victoria,"
noted a historically confused teammate. Larry Csonka was thinking more of art
history: "Whistler's Mother," he said, shaking his head. "We ought to get Earl
a shawl," laughed Griese, who had come over in his cast and crutches to have
a look. Someone threw a towel and Morrall obliged, wrapping it around him.
"Outta sight," said Briscoe, and Marv Fleming couldn't stop laughing. They
should have given him a horse, not a rocking chair, because ol' Earl was riding

into town to save the day one more time. Shula had surely reminded his team that week, as he did the press, that Morrall had won fifteen games for him in '68—more than any NFL team had ever won in one season.

When Morrall came into the San Diego game, Miami suddenly had no backup quarterback. Carl Taseff huddled with Marlin Briscoe on the sideline, giving him a crash course in case Csonka's fears materialized and Morrall went down too. Briscoe had shown in the Minnesota game that he still had a quarterback's arm and moxie. But Shula wanted Briscoe at wide receiver when his leg healed, so before the next game he activated Jim Del Gaizo from the taxi squad. Del Gaizo had long since healed his cut finger and had been practicing every week. He was ready to go, and maybe with a weak Buffalo team coming to town that week Shula could give him some valuable playing time.

October 22, however, brought one of the nuttiest games, a deluge of bloopers that hearkened back to the days of Wahoo McDaniel and Joe Auer, and Shula never had the luxury of resting Morrall. It began normally enough, with a Dolphin eighty-yard touchdown drive that killed the first half of the first quarter. Morris swept five yards behind the masterful Little and the Dolphins were up 7–0. The defense stopped Buffalo cold, and Morrall led another easy-as-ice-cream drive all the way down the field until they had first and goal at the seven. On third down from about a foot away, Kiick looked as if he pushed across the goal line but was ruled down just inches short. In Super Bowl V, less than two years earlier, Morrall had the Colts down to Dallas's two-yard line, and he sent Norm Bulaich (another future Dolphin) up the middle three straight times in vain. Then, on fourth down, he went to the air and threw an incomplete pass. Perhaps remembering this, Morrall now called for Kiick to run again on fourth down. He tried to leap over the top but was repulsed for no gain.

There was still little cause for concern, as Miami had completely dominated both lines of scrimmage so far. They stopped Buffalo again, and the first quarter ended with Miami having outgained Buffalo, 133 yards to 14. But the goal line failure turned out to be just the first nip of a snakebit game. Maybe it was the Bills showing up at the stadium with the wrong uniforms that threw everything off. They'd somehow brought their white home outfits, so the Dolphins had no choice but to wear their dark away jerseys. In any case, on Miami's next possession, the normally dependable Kiick fumbled on his own twenty-five, and Buffalo got a field goal without earning a single first down.

Then, when Miami got the ball back, Csonka was called for holding, one of the few times in his career, canceling an eleven-yard Kiick run. Then another holding penalty, on Larry Little, killed a beautiful fifty-seven-yard pass play to Twilley. The Dolphins under Shula were used to being the least penalized team; even holding penalties were a rarity for them. Now it was first and thirty-four at their own ten-yard line, and it was Morris's turn to step on the banana peel. He lost two yards on a run, and then on second and thirty-six he came out of the backfield and put up his hands to grab a short, easy pass from Morrall. But the ball bounced out of his hands and right into those of linebacker Ken Lee, who ran untouched into the end zone. Buffalo still didn't have a first down, but they were winning 10–7.

Miami got the ball back and began moving right down the field, run after run. But despite the gains—Zonk for five, Kiick for seven, Zonk for five, Kiick for four—restless boos were sprinkling down out of the stands. Dolfans were apparently not yet indoctrinated into the relentless marches of the Shula running game that would become famous in the next couple of years. They wanted to see more passing! As if to substantiate their complaints, Morrall was slow to spin around on a handoff to Kiick, and the ball popped loose, truncating another strong drive. The defense was having no such problems, and Miami got the ball back again, but yet another promising drive was cut short after some solid gains, on a play that would draw national attention at the end of the season. Morrall faded back, turned, and threw a screen pass across the field toward Morris. But a blitzing linebacker tipped the ball as Morrall threw it and it fell to the ground. Neither Morrall nor Morris even tried to recover what they thought was an incomplete pass, but another Buffalo player fell on it, and the refs called it a recovered lateral. One question was whether the ball was thrown forward or not, a matter impossible to tell later from the films. Don Shula was less equivocal, screaming at the line judge nearest him that it was obviously a forward pass and even losing his composure enough to grab the official's arm. The yellow flag flew high, and Buffalo was given another fifteen yards, down to the Miami twenty-one. No one noticed the clear error the statistician up in the press box made in his notebook: he recorded the play as a fumble by Morris and attributed the nine-yard loss was to him.

"Eighty thousand rude people waving handkerchiefs," as *Sports Illustrated* referred to them, tended to side with Shula. A thundercloud of boos descended on the stadium, and it didn't lift for more than five minutes. Six times in a row Buffalo quarterback Dennis Shaw came to the line, began to call his signals, and then had to stop and call his team back to the huddle. The crowd "made an ass of itself," wrote Edwin Pope. Finally, Shaw got the play off and handed to O. J. Simpson, who was immediately flattened by Manny Fernandez for a loss. And on the play after that, Fernandez broke through the line again, as though the offensive line weren't there, charging Shaw like a mad buffalo himself and sacking him, with help from Den Herder and Stanfill, for a fifteen-yard loss. "Had to get back Shula's fifteen," he cracked after the game. Buffalo still managed a field goal, but disaster was averted. After a week in the hospital, Manny was playing like a marauder sprung loose from the stockade.

A week earlier, after playing the San Diego game with pneumonia, Fernandez had been ordered to the hospital. He complied, but not immediately. "I told them 'Screw you,'" he remembered, "'I'm going to get drunk, and then I'll go to the hospital.'" He and some teammates went to the Score, Nick Buoniconti's restaurant on the top of a downtown condominium building, and partied on the rooftop terrace with a gorgeous view of the city. At about one in the morning he got dropped off at Mercy Hospital and checked in—Dr. Virgin's orders, after all. He stayed all week, getting rest, antibiotics, and respiratory therapy, was released for the Buffalo game, and checked right back in afterward. "I don't know, I guess I was well rested," he said. "They had me on two IV's at halftime. Put a couple of pints of fluid back in me."

Manuel José Fernandez might have been the greatest of Joe Thomas's bargain deals. He had gone unpicked in the 1968 draft, largely a result of his college coach ("a backstabbing lying no-good son of a bitch," according to Fernandez, and that was in a good mood, fifty years later) telling all the scouts that Manny was "a sorehead who can't be coached." After the draft, though, Thomas remembered watching Fernandez play: "the quick reactions, his use of forearms the size of hams, and that certain quality sought more than all the others—instinct for the target, no matter who stands in the way." He brought him down for a tryout and mollified critics by saying that it would be a boon to the struggling Miami club to have a player with Latin American heritage. In fact, Fernandez's grandparents all came from Spain, and his parents were both born in Hawaii. He grew up in San Lorenzo, California, a small town south of Oakland. When he appeared on *The Tonight Show* after winning two

Super Bowls, and guest host Don Rickles asked him about that connection with Miami's Latino fans, Fernandez admitted, "I can't even say 'adios' in Spanish."

Although only six-foot-two, Fernandez was one of the first Dolphins to train with weights, and as Howard Cosell put it, he "developed his upper body to astonishing proportions." "He's always got two people blocking him—a guard and the center," said Coach Mo Scarry, "and lots of times a back stays in to pick him up if he splits the double block." Against Buffalo, with his lungs full of fluid, Fernandez made an outrageous twenty tackles, saving a day of bloopers and mix-ups with his indomitable play. Two of those twenty tackles were the crucial ones following the fiasco of the blocked screen pass and Shula penalty. He kept the game close there. And then, on the second play of the second half, he made the play of the game.

It was a simple running play. O. J. Simpson had gone nowhere on first down, so on second down from the twenty Simpson moved right as a decoy, and Shaw was to hand off to Jim Braxton with the right guard pulling over to lead the way. But as Rick Weaver called it, "Fernandez comes in and almost steals the ball . . . he does! Fernandez steals the ball and the Dolphins have it at the ten-yard line! That's right, let's get those white handkerchiefs out!" When the guard turned to pull, Fernandez, expecting a pass on second and long, had shot in before the center could come over to slow him down. He actually beat Braxton to the quarterback, and when Shaw spun around and held out the football, Manny simply took the handoff. He headed for the end zone, but Shaw slowed him down and Braxton came back to tackle him at the ten-yard line. Csonka scored on the next play, and the Dolphins had taken back the lead for good.

Some wondered whether Manny had taken the ball on purpose. With 20/200 vision, he was almost legally blind and wore his glasses everywhere, even into the shower—but not on the football field. "I would have scored," he joked, "but I was afraid I'd run into the goal post." Csonka liked to say that Fernandez played by "frisking everybody within reach, and the one with the football he keeps." However, as Fernandez explained later, "I'm not *that* blind. The football's a pretty good sized object. I shot the gap, the quarterback turned around and was just holding the ball out, so I grabbed it and kept on running. Somebody had to take it, didn't they?"

It happened so soon after kickoff that we almost missed it. A week after our trip to the Orange Bowl, we were back to our routine of listening to home games on our hi-fi and playing touch football in the front yard at halftime. As soon as the final first-half seconds ticked off, Ron and I would grab the football and run outside, followed by Dad, to get the most out of the fifteen-minute intermission. This was one-on-one touch football, with Dad playing a position that, to my nine-year-old ears, sounded like an old and hallowed tradition: the "quarterback for both teams." Our front-yard gridiron was maybe forty feet by twenty feet, turfed with the thick-bladed St. Augustine grass ubiquitous in those South Florida subsections. When you fell on it, you felt a gentle prickly cushioning as your body crushed the semi-rigid blades.

Jim Kiick remembered a similar scene from his childhood in New Jersey. He was a huge fan of Frank Gifford and the New York Giants in the late 1950s, and occasionally he'd get to go to a game at Yankee Stadium. "But mostly I'd watch the road games on TV and listen to the home games on radio. Just from the excitement of it, at half time me and my brother would go outside into the backyard to play football. He was five years younger than I was, and that made me think I was a good football player. In our games, he was always the underdog."

I was the underdog too. My brother was the fastest kid in our elementary school and loved nothing better than to play "get away," dancing around the yard with stutter steps and sharp cuts, just as Jake Scott had done on his interception the week before, never letting me quite touch him. He idolized Paul Warfield and would mimic his precise pass patterns and intense concentration on catching the ball. I was two and a half years younger and a markedly low achiever when it came to foot speed. It is possible that through our entire childhood I never once caught my brother while he was holding a football. But when I was on offense he'd let me score a touchdown now and then to keep me interested. I must have known that intuitively, but it didn't take anything from my pleasure in running a little curl into the end zone like Jim Kiick, in the corner formed by sidewalk and driveway, and taking in the pass from Dad for the score.

It may have been Kiick's secondary status in the Dolphin backfield beginning that year, his slowness compared to Mercury, that I identified with. But for whatever reason, however scenarios work their way into the minds of nine-year-olds, during that season's halftime touch-football games I "was" Jim Kiick, just as my brother "was" Warfield. (Perhaps our dad, who had just turned forty, identified with old Earl Morrall, coming in to toss the pigskin for any team that would still take him.) I may have been particularly inspired that

Sunday in October, for with Morris nursing a sore ankle Kiick got more carries than anyone against Buffalo. For one week at least, he was Butch Cassidy again.

"A lot of my game was heart," he said later and then repeated the refrain that seems almost like a badge of honor to the 1972 Dolphins: "I wasn't physically gifted." As with the other players, the modesty seems misplaced: he was the best athlete in his high school in Lincoln Park, New Jersey, a working-class town thirty miles west of Manhattan. His father, "Big George" Kiick, who worked in the Rheingold beer plant in Orange, had played for the Pittsburgh Steelers in the 1940s for a couple hundred dollars a game, before and after his years as an Army lieutenant fighting Nazis in Italy in World War II.

Despite his local success, Jim Kiick was almost overlooked for a college scholarship. As he admitted, his grades may have been a factor. However, the coach at Wyoming happened to notice his play while watching films of another New Jersey player. Kiick went out west and starred for the Cowboys, despite feeling out of place. In the small western city of Laramie, where all the guys were wearing T-shirts and boot-cut jeans, Kiick "walked around in Italian knit shirts with black silk pants and alpaca sweaters and sharp pointed shoes. Everybody thought I was a gangster." By his own admission, he spent more time playing pool than going to class. He also met Alice, a local high school cheerleader, and like Csonka he got married his junior year of college (after Alice had graduated, and despite considerable opposition from both mothers). His football stats in college were solid but not eye-popping, somewhat similar to how he'd do in the pros. A respectable four yards a carry, about five hundred yards a year, and plenty of catches coming out of the backfield. It was far from certain he'd be drafted, with those numbers coming out of Wyoming—the word going around was that he was too fat and too slow—but Joe Thomas worked his magic once again. He'd spent a couple days at practice in Laramie the previous summer: "As far as I was concerned Kiick was a winner." Thomas wasn't looking for another running back after having scored Csonka in the first round, but when he noticed Kiick was still available in the fifth round, he couldn't resist. "And if I knew then what I know now, we'd have grabbed him sooner."

Kiick met Csonka at the college All-Star game, when they were both sneaking out past curfew. Their sartorial disparity might have prevented an immediate bonding: mod clothes and long hair for Kiick, a more conservative look for Csonka. But when they got to Dolphins training camp, their names were on the same dorm room, and that was that. They played together, partied together, became best friends despite their obvious differences. "Larry likes to fish," said Kiick. "I hate the outdoors. But I could enjoy it with him. I like to play basketball or shoot pool. He doesn't give a damn, but he'll come watch." Whereas Csonka's father had instilled a powerful work ethic in him on the farm, "Big George" Kiick may have failed in that endeavor, if he had even tried. His son spoke of the "forty-year-old kids" in his hometown "who have found a way to do nothing in life. Just hang around, play some basketball, drink some beer, relax. That's the way I'll be."

If the norm on the Dolphins was a studious, intellectual approach to football, Kiick was an anomaly: "I'm not a student of anything. I stopped growing mentally at seventeen. I know absolutely nothing about football. I don't know how to read a defense. I'm always afraid they'll quiz me on something I'm supposed to know." He relied on instinct and a natural athleticism he shrugged off. It didn't mean, however, that he had any less motivation or desire than his teammates who frequented the film room. He prided himself on being the starting running back for four years, and when he suddenly had to share playing time with Morris, no matter how much he professed the "whatever's good for the team" ethos, it hurt.

"Oh, I hated it, I hated it, certainly," he admitted later. He'd always liked to play his way into a game, getting into the rhythm of running, blocking, catching, play after play. "It's a momentum thing," he said at the time. "There's no time to get that momentum when you're in and out." He'd gained over a thousand yards running and receiving combined each of his first four years. After the 1968 and 1969 seasons it was he and not Csonka who played in the final two AFL All-Star games. Remember, he was Butch and Zonk was Sundance, the sidekick. Now he was just a supporting character. "It's a shock after starting four years," he'd said after the opener in Kansas City. "I'm just very disappointed." Later it became clear that Shula intended to start them in alternating games, and play them in alternating series, and see how that went. Against New York and San Diego, Kiick got the ball more than Morris, and today against Buffalo Morrall just kept calling his number, and for the first time in a long time he got more carries than anyone. Csonka still was the leading rusher, with 107 yards on eighteen carries, but Kiick got the momentum he craved, crashing into the line or sprinting around end twenty-five times (for eighty-one yards), in addition to two pass receptions. In our front yard, "ol' Dad," the grizzled veteran, called my number every single play we had the ball, and I probably scored one or two touchdowns while my brother and father shared a knowing smile. One thing is statistically certain, though: I did not win the game.

When we came running in to listen to the second half, the Dolphins were ahead in yards gained, 198 to 30; in first downs, it was 12 to 1. And yet the Bills were winning, 13–7. In the locker room, Shula was too befuddled by his offense's smorgasbord of errors to even scream at his players. He tried to look at the bright side: "Well, we couldn't have played any worse, and we're still in the game." Of course the defense had been almost perfect, and Fernandez started the second half by stuffing O.J. and then stealing that handoff. Csonka scored on the very next play on a ten-yard sweep, and Miami was finally ahead again, 14–13. Then they stopped the Bills again, and this time cornerback Curtis Johnson broke right through the middle of the line and blocked the punt, giving Miami the ball on the Buffalo twenty-six. On the first play Kiick ran half the distance, down to the thirteen. Finally, it seemed, the Dolphins were taking over.

But the gremlins were not done with the Dolphin offense. Morrall saw Morris going in motion the wrong way, tried to wave him back, and incurred a delay-of-game penalty. Then Warfield slipped on the Poly-Turf and was unable to catch a short pass. On third down, they once again failed to get the play off in time, and the second delay-of-game penalty made it third down and twenty-one yards to go. Morrall threw an incomplete pass, but Csonka was called again for holding—his second of the game and as far as anyone remembered the second of his career—which put the ball back at the thirty-nine-yard line. Morrall sent Csonka up the middle for seven, just trying to get better field goal position, but this time the refs called a personal foul on Norm Evans. It's hard to overstate how uncharacteristic this torrent of penalties was for Shula's Dolphins. It had only been two and a half seasons, but already we took it for granted that it would be the other team, not ours, that made the mental errors. These transgressions simply didn't happen. But a personal foul on Norm Evans? On "Pope Norm," as his teammates called the mild-mannered born-again Christian? This was historic.

He didn't like the nickname when it was bestowed during the Dolphins' inaugural training camp, but it was better than "Big Filthy," the moniker assigned to defensive lineman Ray Jacobs, and he grew to accept it. A small-town Texas boy, Evans had been drafted out of Texas Christian by both Minnesota of the NFL and Houston of the AFL and chose the Oilers, for less money, to be closer to home. He was stunned a year later to be offered up in the expansion draft and taken by the new team in Miami. (During the 1965 season in Houston, with the expansion draft looming, anytime someone missed a tackle or dropped a ball, someone would start singing "Moon Over Miami.") He was a starter on the first Dolphin squad ever and ended up starting almost every game for eleven seasons and making two Pro Bowls. More importantly, for him, it was during the Dolphins' very first training camp, one night in that dumpy motel in St. Petersburg, that he found Jesus on the television, in the person of preacher Bob Harrington. The "Chaplain of Bourbon Street" had made his name "preaching from the stages of saloons and strip joints, storming the gates of hell for the souls within." The next night, while most of the team was getting drunk at Dad's Rendezvous out on Gulf Boulevard, Evans and his wife, Bobbie, went to Harrington's crusade at the Open Bible Tabernacle in St. Pete and, as he wrote in his memoir, *On God's Squad*, "I thank God for that night when I prayed and asked Jesus Christ to take control of my life, because He did."

Six years later, on a team whose coach and quarterback attended Mass every morning and that "travel[ed] with enough clergy, mostly Roman Catholic priests, to field a second specialty team," Evans was the religious leader. He arranged for chapel services before every game, including a guest speaker—or he would do the honors himself. But he wasn't evangelical about it. "There was a very relaxed attitude about religion on the team," said Eddie Jenkins. "No one was sticking it to anybody." Morris remembered how Evans would come knocking on hotel room doors—"You coming to chapel, Merc?"—and he'd roll over in bed, rub his eyes: "Sure Norm, I'm coming." "I roomed six or seven years with Norm," said Larry Seiple, "and I was a smoker and not religious, but we had a great relationship. Some weeks I went to chapel, sometimes I couldn't get my rear end out of bed."

Evans would walk around the locker room before games, shaking each man's hand seriously and offering a few words of encouragement. He'd often offer solace on the sideline to a player who'd made a big mistake on the field. He was clean-cut on and off the field. He'd pull players away from potential brawls. But here was the ref, after making NFL history by calling Csonka for holding—*twice*; after two straight delay-of-game penalties; throwing his yellow flag and calling personal foul, unsportsmanlike conduct on . . . number seventy-three. Pope Norm. Evans explained later that he had taken a cheap shot under the chin from safety Maurice Tyler. "The first rule in such a situation," he opined, "is not to hit back, because the officials always catch the guy striking the second blow. But I never even struck back." No one else seemed to see the retaliation, either; maybe the ref just assumed any red-blooded football player would fight back. In any case, it was now fourth and forty-four yards to go for a first down, from the Buffalo forty-seven. The fans were stunned: What was this, 1967? In came Garo Yepremian to try to salvage the fiasco with the longest field goal of his career and the longest in Dolphins history. With the wind behind him, his fifty-four-yarder easily cleared the crossbar, and the foibles were forgotten. "Old Garo really came in and did it to them," said Evans. "When he made that kick, it just showed what faith can do."

Buffalo kept it close with another field goal, but after Morrall led another classic eleven-play, eighty-yard drive for a touchdown, it was all over. The game, that is, not the oddities. When Morris finished off the drive with a fifteen-yard power sweep, fans and teammates couldn't believe what they were seeing: Paul Warfield running right up to cornerback Alvin Wyatt and jawing at him.

Norm Evans would have had to share the team's "Least Likely to Trash Talk" award with the great receiver, but on this zany day even Warfield lost his cool. Wyatt had been in his face, yakking at him all day. So when Wyatt was late getting to Morris on the touchdown run, Warfield had to pose the question, "Hey man, where were you? You've been talking all day. What happened this time?" In the locker room, he cooled off a little: "That's true, I did say that. But I don't think that's blowing my cool. I just thought it was an appropriate thing to say at that moment in the game."

Morris's touchdown made it 24–16 with just a few minutes left. Buffalo did manage to move down the field, succeeded on a desperation draw-play run on fourth and nine, and scored on a short pass with sixty-seven seconds left, but without the two-point option in those days they could only draw within one point. In a final head-scratcher, they kicked off deep instead of trying an onside kick; all Morrall had to do was put his knee to the ground twice. The crowd, disgruntled earlier, now cheered loudly and counted down the final seconds. The Dolphins were 6–0 with a 24–23 victory.

In the locker room, words like "weird," "crazy," and "bizarre" were being tossed toward the microphones. Buffalo coach Lou Saban called it "the strangest game I've seen in all my years." "The most ridiculous game I've ever played in," sneered Buoniconti. "We used to have a lot of games like this," said Evans, remembering the sixties. "The only difference was, we used to lose 'em." Earl Morrall called across the room, "Hey Manny, go on back to the hospital! We'll call you in time for the next game." (Fernandez did just that: spent another week at Mercy getting respiratory therapy before taking on the Colts.)

That night Don Shula, normally a sound sleeper, was wide-awake at three a.m., unable to wind down. His ten-year-old daughter, Sharon, heard him shuffling around and got up, and they sat together in the kitchen for a glass of milk. The afternoon's near shipwreck had frazzled his nerves, but he was relieved that they had managed to win again even while making so many blunders. Many years later it would be almost forgotten that, in the middle of the greatest season ever, the perfect team played a ludicrous game, dribbling the ball around and committing mental gaffes like the Bad News Bears. And that the main reason they won was Manny Fernandez coming through with twenty tackles, crashing through the line twice in a row after a seemingly disastrous miscue, and then later taking a handoff from a flabbergasted quarterback to turn the game in the proper direction. And he did it all only halfway through a hospital stay with pneumonia.

Seven and Oh

Don Shula made sure Manny Fernandez was out of the hospital in time to fly up to Baltimore the next weekend. The Colts had lost five of their first six games, but that wasn't going to fool their old coach into complacency. For one thing, during the preseason Baltimore had been picked by many to make a third Super Bowl trip this year; their dismal record so far had to be an early aberration. And Miami had never won a game in Baltimore. In fact, Shula's two trips back since his acrimonious departure had both been humiliating losses: 35–0 and 14–3. How Carroll Rosenbloom, who'd publicly derided both Shula and Robbie for the "theft" of Shula, must have reveled in those results. Shula finally got revenge in the 1971 AFC championship game, and now Rosenbloom was gone as well. After publicly complaining about how spoiled Colts fans were, he made a swap with new Los Angeles Rams owner Robert Irsay: Irsay got the Colts, and Rosenbloom headed out west to claim the Rams. At his first press conference, Irsay, an air-conditioning executive from Chicago, called his new team the Baltimore Unitas Colts: "I intend to keep Unitas with this team and with this town and this state. I pledge to you I will not move the Baltimore Colts." (Unitas was gone in six months; twelve years later Irsay broke a million hearts when he absconded in the middle of the night, moving the franchise to Indianapolis.)

Although Rosenbloom wasn't there anymore in 1972 to taunt Shula in the press, the Baltimore fans were still sore that he had left them for Miami. Even worse, he had trampled their hopes in the playoffs the year before. They and their team would be looking for revenge as well as a fulcrum on which to turn their season around. Shula had no shortage of motivational points with which to get his team fired up to play a 1–5 team.

. . .

The week was a spinning weather vane of war announcements. On Monday, the papers and TV news were trumpeting reports from Saigon, where Kissinger had been having daily meetings with President Thieu, that a ceasefire was imminent. But those who read deeper had to wonder, for none of the main sticking points had been resolved. In fact, the very next day Thieu declared, "We have not agreed to any ceasefire."

On October 26, Kissinger announced, "Peace is at hand," a phrase eerily similar to Chamberlain's "Peace in Our Time," pronounced in Munich thirty-four years earlier. In fact a true treaty between North and South was no closer than ever. What was closer was an American agreement to leave South Vietnam to its fate and get out of Dodge. Privately, Nixon and Kissinger discussed the unfeasibility of an independent South Vietnam, with or without American support. All they were angling for was a way to convince Thieu—long enough to get the treaty signed—that the U.S. would have his back. "If a year or two years from now," Kissinger confided in the president, "North Vietnam gobbles up South Vietnam, we can have a viable foreign policy if it looks as if it's the result of South Vietnamese incompetence." But that artifice could not be revealed— not ever, hopefully, but certainly not before November 7. Instead, the Nixon administration kept dangling the perception that the peace they had promised was all but assured. Just a couple weeks to go, to keep that niggling Watergate investigation from ruining things too. Those *Post* reporters had revealed that Bob Haldeman, Nixon's chief of staff and widely considered the man closest to the president in the White House, was one of those authorized to approve payments from the secret cash fund designated for "dirty tricks," including the Watergate break-in. But the Haldeman bombshell and others were quickly buried under the headlines PEACE IS AT HAND, PEACE AT TIP OF PEN, etc. McGovern had been trying to get America out of Vietnam for almost a decade while Kennedy, Johnson, and then Nixon escalated U.S. involvement. But that would matter little if it appeared Nixon had finally done it.

In the meantime, in South Asia, both sides intensified their attacks to try to gain as much territory as possible before the ceasefire. North Vietnamese troops captured twelve hamlets within forty miles of Saigon, and the South Vietnamese recaptured two of them, with plenty of casualties on both sides. Six more Americans were wounded from rockets and mortar rounds, but protests at home were lessening. Attention was turning back to politics and culture. Ira Levin's *The Stepford Wives* presented a terrifying vision of suburban men countering women's liberation by murdering and replacing their wives with submissive robots, and Marlon Brando was enjoying the resuscitation of his career with the success of *The Godfather*, released six months earlier. Nixon still looked like a lock, and football fans were wondering when the Miami Dolphins' luck would run out.

. . .

Maybe this was the week when the law of averages would catch up with both the Dolphins and the Colts. The fans in Baltimore had to feel stunned by the unexpected futility of their season so far. Even worse, the new general manager was trying to force out franchise hero Johnny Unitas, despite the new owner's promises. Most everyone agreed that their record was not an accurate indicator of this team's quality. It was surely about time for a Colts victory and a Miami misstep. "After all," wrote Bill Braucher, "the 6–0 Dolphins cannot win them all, and the 1–5 Colts are long overdue."

The new Colts GM was none other than Joe Thomas, the scouting genius who had provided Robbie and Shula with the haystack needles that no one else could find. Another Ohio boy, son of immigrants like Shula (Yugoslav in this case), Thomas played college football at Ohio Northern in the early 1940s and worked his way up from coaching high school to college to finally joining the Colts as an assistant in 1954. In 1960 he became the personnel director for the new expansion team in Minnesota, a position that he seemed born for. "With me they didn't have to waste money," he said. "I was single. I was a loner." From Chicago to Pocatello to Natchitoches, he was the paradigmatic scout, sleeping in cheap motels, hanging around practice fields, practically living in film rooms, running to catch the last Ozark Air Lines flight of the night from Indianapolis to Boston. Operating with a meager expense account, he saved money by parking in an empty field a long walk from the Minneapolis airport. One frigid night he returned to find that his engine had been stolen.

But he was good. His first spring with Minnesota, he visited ninety-two colleges, and he built the Vikings from an expansion club to a contender with elements such as Tarkenton, Eller, and Marshall. When Joe Robbie, the Vikings fan from Dakota, finagled his way to a pro football team in Miami, his first hire was Thomas. Their shared devotion to thriftiness made it seem like a perfect partnership, but it hampered even Thomas's work. The first couple years, before he insisted otherwise, he wasn't allowed to recruit west of the Mississippi because the air fares were too high. Still, it was with Miami that he really made his name. While the Dolphins were struggling for a foothold in South Florida, Thomas was living out of a suitcase, scouring America's playing fields for talent. He drafted Griese over Steve Spurrier, he drafted Csonka over MacArthur Lane. He saw an All-Pro guard inside Larry Little, whom others could see only as a part-time lineman in San Diego. He found Kiick out in Wyoming, he followed Jake Scott from Georgia up to Canada, he found free agents Kuechenberg and Fernandez and so many more. His crowning stroke, however, was the acquisition of Paul Warfield.

Nineteen seventy wasn't a bumper crop for wide receivers coming out of college, and Thomas felt Miami, which was making do with Twilley and Noonan, needed someone with breakaway speed who could go all the way at any moment: "But I wasn't interested in just a deep threat. I wanted the best deep threat." He had the third pick in the draft and let it be known he was willing to trade it for a big-time receiver. The Browns needed a new quarterback and wanted that draft pick. "There's only one player I'm interested in," Thomas told owner Art Modell. "Who, Warfield?" "Yeah." Modell just laughed. Warfield wasn't just the greatest receiver in the league; he was an Ohio boy, a lifetime Brown in his heart, a local hero. But Thomas kept working on Modell, explaining that this was the only way he could hope to get Terry Bradshaw or Mike Phipps, the two top quarterback prospects of the year. Pittsburgh was surely going to take one of them in the first round, but Green Bay, with the second pick, was by all indications going for a lineman. Miami's pick was as good as a franchise quarterback. The day before the draft, Modell finally relented. "I put the phone down very gently," Thomas said, "and held it a long time. I wanted to capture the moment." Paul Warfield received the shocking news that he was moving to Florida, and Cleveland got Mike Phipps, who never lived up to his promise. (He did lead them to the playoffs in 1972, but each year he threw more interceptions than touchdowns and eventually was traded to Chicago.)

From original Dolphins Norm Evans and Howard Twilley through Matheson and Den Herder in 1971, Joe Thomas almost single-handedly constructed the perfect team. Yet his relationship with Robbie was always rocky, both men having brusque, prickly personalities. Thomas was an odd duck, a genius at personnel but inept at personal relations. In later years, with other teams, he would hire and then fire as head coaches two of the Dolphins' integral 1972 assistant coaches, Howard Schnellenberger and Monte Clark. "A lot of bad things were said about him over the years," said Clark, "but not nearly enough." When Robbie refused to promote him to general manager after the 1971 season, Thomas resigned. Then, in July 1972, came the announcement that he was the new vice president and general manager of the Baltimore Colts. Turns out Thomas had engineered the whole Irsay-Rosenbloom Baltimore-LA swap, with his own career advancement as part of the deal. When it was announced, he and his wife, Judi, grabbed a flight from Miami to Baltimore for the press conference. (The loner had finally married at the age of forty-seven.) They were supposed to change planes in Philadelphia, but there was yet another hijacking going on there, so they landed in Wilmington and took a long cab ride. In Baltimore, Thomas, echoing Irsay, said he had no plans to shake up the Colt roster that year: "We should be right up there winning [with the current lineup]."

But by late October, after the Colts' horrendous start, Thomas was bent on jettisoning old lumber, no matter how beloved, and building a new championship team much as he had in Miami. After a shutout at the hands of the Cowboys put the Colts' record at 1–4, Thomas insisted that Coach Don McCafferty bench the immortal Unitas and start the young Thomas project Marty Domres. When McCafferty refused, Thomas simply fired him and replaced him with assistant coach John Sandusky (an old Browns teammate of Shula, his assistant in Baltimore, and later his longtime assistant in Miami). Domres responded with a big game as the Colts all but beat the Jets until a tipped ball became a long Namath touchdown bomb. So, in spite of all the drama and upheaval, the Colts were waiting for the Dolphins with some hope of a turnaround. And the undefeated visitors were only slight favorites.

Colts fans, however, not only would have to watch their beloved Unitas pace the sideline that day, they'd have to watch their other Super Bowl quarterback play in aqua and orange. Earl Morrall was returning to face the team for whom he'd been the league MVP in 1968 and the winning Super Bowl quarterback two years later. Asked about the pressure of returning to Baltimore, he just said, "I've had pretty good success in here as a visiting quarterback, too," reflecting upon his travels with the Lions and Giants.

On game day, October 29, Earl met an old buddy at midfield while their teams were loosening up. It was fifty-nine degrees and drizzling, the infield dirt at Memorial Stadium quickly turning to mud. "Aren't you getting a little too old for this?" asked Johnny Unitas. "Well, John, you're a pretty old buck yourself," said Morrall in his unaffected twang. Unitas was in fact thirty-nine, a year older, and they had been opponents and teammates in this league for seventeen years. They were friends and drinking buddies, but they each had their pride. When Morrall replaced the injured Unitas in '68 and led Baltimore to the Super Bowl, someone asked Unitas if he'd be able to win his job back next year. "Hey," he shot back, "I'm still the quarterback of this team." And he was. Two years later, when Morrall replaced him again in Super Bowl V and won the game, another enterprising journalist asked Unitas if a star like him might feel some resentment. "Yeah," he said, "if you're a horse's ass you would."

Being benched for Marty Domres, though, was another matter. He surely would have loved another chance to take on Earl, show him who was still Mr. Colt. But instead of a battle of ancients, it was old versus new. Domres started the game with his best drive of the day only to see Jim O'Brien miss a forty-two-yard field goal. (O'Brien was the somewhat shaky wide receiver/kicker who had won the Colts' error-strewn Super Bowl with a thirty-two-yarder.) Now, after the miss, Morrall showed Domres how it was done. He commandeered another quintessential drive: eighty yards in ten plays (eight of them runs) for the touchdown. And that was about the end of the suspense in this one, as Baltimore never got close to scoring again. In the second quarter Curtis Johnson blocked a punt and recovered it on the Baltimore twenty-two. Morrall let Briscoe have some fun, tossing an overhand lateral to him over on the left, from where Briscoe threw a bullet to Warfield down near the goal line. (It appeared he got over the line, but in any case Csonka bulled the final inches on the next play for another touchdown.) Then, late in the first half, Sandusky brought in a new kicker, a soccer styler named Shlapak, but Lloyd Mumphord blocked his long attempt, and Garo Yepremian made a short field goal for a 16–0 halftime lead. (One extra point had been blocked.) And early in the third quarter, Johnson made another great play, nailing the punt returner deep in his own end, causing another fumble, which Charlie Leigh recovered at the twenty. A few plays later, Morris swept left behind Kuechenberg for another easy touchdown, and the final score of 23–0 was set.

Though some might have found it a boring game, Dolfans didn't, and of course Shula was thrilled—particularly since it was the special teams that had dominated this one. Like many fringe players fighting to stay in the league, Shula had been a mainstay of the Cleveland and Baltimore special teams in his playing days and had a fondness for those "suicide squads," as they were sometimes called. Whether you were tearing down the length of the field looking to launch your body into someone, or waiting at the other end to deflect such human missiles, it was a dangerous business. "I used to run downfield with my head on a swivel," looking out for ambushes, Shula said. But those six different units—either kicking or defending kickoffs, field goals, and punts—were often the key to victory, Shula realized. "He was the first I knew of who felt that special teams were a third of the game," said punter Larry Seiple. "Nobody realizes what got the Dolphins to the Super Bowl last year was their specialty teams," said Deacon Jones about an hour before he knocked Bob Griese out of the regular season. "They're the best in football. And that's Shula's doings." At Baltimore, he was the first NFL coach to name a captain of special teams, which meant a suicide squadder was among the group at midfield for the coin toss to start each game. He was so into it in Miami that although Carl Taseff was officially the special-teams coach, Shula personally helped plan and watch over the practices, even running downfield with the kick coverage, his swiveling head now tuned to pick out men who could give the Dolphins that extra winning edge.

Players like Maulty Moore, Charlie Babb, Larry Ball, Eddie Jenkins, and Jesse Powell made the team because of their value crashing down the field on special teams. Another was Charlie Leigh, who was the only NFL player ever signed right out of high school. (He wrote to Commissioner Pete Rozelle, explaining that he was married with a child on the way and needed to support them, and Rozelle made an exception for him.) After a taxi squad stint with Pittsburgh, Leigh had bounced around ten teams in the Continental and Canadian leagues (and also played some for the Browns) before latching on with the Dolphins in 1971. He was the fourth or fifth running back but took over most of the punt returning from Jake Scott in 1972 and ended up third in the league while also excelling in punt and kickoff coverage. Other special teamers were starters or part-time starters who shone on special teams as well.

But it was two outstanding cornerbacks, Curtis Johnson and Lloyd Mumphord, who were the superstars of the suicides. Johnson was Miami's starting right cornerback his entire nine-year career, and Mumphord, who had been the starter on the left before losing his spot to Tim Foley, still played a lot in the 53 and nickel-back defensive lineups. In fact, his four interceptions that year were second only to Jake Scott. He also blocked two field goals, and Johnson blocked a field goal and two punts.

Aside from being cornerbacks with special-team prowess, Johnson and Mumphord were both known for their calm, quiet intelligence. While Johnson was a solid 195 pounds, his six-foot-one height augmented half a foot by a fashionable afro, Mumphord was slight even by cornerback standards—five-ten, and it was often said his listed weight of 176 must be with pads on. He'd made it in the NFL on speed and skill. He was strikingly handsome, with trimly cut receding hair and a full beard. Briscoe the chess fiend called him "Mr. Wizard" for his enthusiasm for acquiring knowledge and experience in all areas of life. Mumphord had lost his starting position in '71 but got his playing time when he could and was named captain of special teams. The Colts remembered him well from the 1971 AFC championship game when he blocked an O'Brien field goal to maintain the shutout. Mumphord and his coach would rub each other the wrong way in 1974, but in '72 Shula was all admiration: "You have to admire Lloyd. He's been a number-one who's been knocked down. Yet instead of brooding or complaining, he's given life to our specialty teams. Look at the weight he gives away. If the quickest, fastest guy on earth didn't have this (he thumped his chest indicating heart), he wouldn't get it done."

Curtis Johnson was perhaps the quietest member of the team. "I loved that guy," said Briscoe, "but I never heard more than five words from him." Reserved, introspective, but also notably articulate, Johnson was also a remarkably talented and clutch football player. "Johnson gets beat five or six times every practice," said Curt Gowdy, "but when they play the game it's another matter." And talk about being grounded: Johnson grew up in Toledo, starred for the University of Toledo—where he led the team to an undefeated season his senior year—and later retired there, becoming a firefighter in the Toledo Fire Department for many years.

Johnson and Mumphord led a special-teams unit that was critical to the Dolphins' success. "You might not realize it," said Shula to a reporter, "but our special teams may have given us the edge at Minnesota in field position when we had to have it. We really shut down their returns." In the Baltimore game, the special-teams role was self-evident: three of the four scores resulted directly from Mumphord and Johnson heroics. Morrall only threw fifteen passes, letting Csonka, Morris, and Kiick carry the offensive load fairly evenly as Miami rushed for nearly three hundred yards.

Of course, there was also that big zero on the scoreboard for Baltimore, and the No-Name Defense was rewarded by being named, as a unit, the AP Defensive Player of the Week. It was another confirmation of how this group subordinated individual glory for team play. Manny came out of the hospital again and had merely an excellent game for a human. Buoniconti, who was such a team leader that he rarely was singled out for his own individual accomplishments, contributed six tackles and three assists to complement Den Herder's seven and two. Most importantly, the defense had done a heroic job over the first half of the season overcoming potentially disastrous injuries. When Bob Heinz went down with a fractured vertebra in the preseason, there was Jim Dunaway, the nine-year starter and Pro Bowler from Buffalo just arrived in a late-career trade, to step right in. And now Dunaway's bad back had finally laid him low; he was to have season-ending—and, as it turned out, career-ending—surgery that week. But Heinz was back ready to play after six weeks and had a good game in Baltimore. "Big Bart," as Stanfill called him, comparing his body shape to a famous pear, had been drafted right behind Stanfill in '69. He became a starter in '71 and remained one, a powerful presence in the center of the line next to Fernandez, through the glory years of '71–'74. Then there was Jim Riley, the Oklahoman who had been drafted by Miami in '67 and was the starting defensive end since '68, blowing out his knee in training camp: another thriving NFL career at an end. But here came Vern Den Herder, a hardly noticed rookie last year, to fill another gap. "Den Herder is playing spectacular football," crowed Buoniconti after the Colts game, "and I don't know whether people really realize it."

Doug Swift was perhaps the least likely Dolphin of all (after his roommate, Yepremian). The son of two doctors in Syracuse, New York, Swift had played his college football at little Amherst College in western Massachusetts, an elite liberal arts school known more for Rhodes Scholars than linebackers. Or, as he put it, the college "wants everybody to know the football players would rather be playing the flute." But Amherst football coach James Ostendarp told Swift he had the potential to play pro football, and according to Swift, who was majoring in art rather than follow his parents' footsteps, "it was that or a teaching job at some private high school." When he got no NFL offers, he tried out for the Montreal Alouettes of the CFL but was cut by the end of training camp. ("The coach up there was some kind of a Nazi," said Swift's girlfriend, Julie. "He didn't like Doug's long hair or some of his ideas about life.") It was time to teach art, but Ostendarp said wait a minute. The NFL was enduring the 1970 players' strike, and training camps were like ghost towns. Ostendarp asked his friend George Young, who had been an assistant in Baltimore under Don Shula, to call the coach and suggest he give Swift a look. Shula, trying to start his first Dolphin training camp, needed bodies, and he also had no idea who his outside linebackers were going to be, and so Swift found himself at Biscayne College, working and sweating harder than he'd ever imagined. He was smarter than the other rookies and free agents, learned the formations fast, was big enough—six-four, 225—and hit hard. When the veterans returned, Swift was anxious, but after only a few days he had a revelation: "Hey I can really play against these guys. In fact, I can play as well as them."

His teammates must have been bemused by the new arrival. Swift was hardly the typical pro football player. He flopped around camp in his beach shoes, long blond hair, and "granny glasses"—Foley called him "pink-glasses Swift"—looking as if he'd be more comfortable at an antiwar demonstration. (A "freaky guy" and "a free thinker," Csonka called him.) When the veterans made the rookies sing their college fight songs during training camp, Swift notified them that Amherst didn't have a fight song. "I could give you a few bars of 'Lord Jeffrey Amherst,'" he offered. "One of the all-time great characters," as Buoniconti called him, he had a juicer in his dorm room at camp and made carrot juice every day, along with the homemade yogurt. "We had orange peels everywhere," said Garo Yepremian, "and next thing you know our room was full of fruit flies. When I woke up, I saw a roach here, a roach there, and a dozen fruit flies." Swift took to the offbeat Yepremian, whom he called "more mature" than most football players. "I don't dig athletes or athlete types or coaching types," he said. That first year, before Swift got married, the linebacker and the kicker were roommates during the season in bohemian Coconut Grove. The furnished apartment had two rooms, one with twin beds and the other a king-sized bed.

They flipped a coin: Swift won and chose the twin beds. "I couldn't believe my luck," Yepremian remembered. He was feeling less fortunate when their pad turned into a real-life production of *The Odd Couple*: the kicker was meticulous, while Swift's area was overflowing with plants, fruit, flora and fauna of all sorts. But one day Garo came home to find his roommate soaking his feet in hot water and Epsom salts while kneading dough for black bread, and he knew everything was all right. "That is a beautiful picture," he said.

Shula didn't care about a player's politics or hair or what kind of bread he baked. He saw in Swift a combination of on-field intelligence and the ability to put a ball carrier on his back. He'd been wondering who he was going to come up with for his outside linebackers to flank Buoniconti. He liked another rookie, Mike "Captain Crunch" Kolen, on the weak side (usually the side without the tight end). And now on the other side he had another surprising freshman. "Inside of Swift," said Shula, "inside that liberal exterior, there is an animal struggling to get out." When the dust settled, the Amherst art major was a starting linebacker in the NFL—and remained a starter for his entire six-year career.

Swift was happy with the company he'd earned. When he began training camp, he wasn't even sure "if football was his thing." In 1972, well into his third year as the starting strong-side linebacker, he felt "comfortable with just about everyone on the team . . . a nice, pleasant bunch of people who [take] an interest in each other. There aren't any real sociopaths . . . and that's unusual for a pro team, 'cause there's a bunch of maniacs out there." Buoniconti had good reason to be feeling cocky about his defense as well: they were leading the league, allowing only eighty-seven points in seven games. "And those points weren't all against the defense," the feisty captain went on. "Buffalo got twenty-three last week, but only ten against the defense." Braucher, who was listening and enjoyed pushing back a little, pointed out that the Dolphins offense helped the defense quite a bit by keeping them off the field with those long clock-killing drives. Even if Miami didn't score, the opponent was usually starting from deep in its own end. "Okay, okay," said Buoniconti, turning back to his locker. "We're leading the league the way it is, so what the hell does it matter?"

Eight and Oh

With half the season gone, seven games and seven wins, Don Shula had a new preoccupation: squelching any talk from players or press of a potential undefeated season. Like a manager in the dugout as a perfect game moves into the late innings, he didn't want to hear a word about it. He may have had reason to think that it was more than superstition: the only two NFL teams ever to finish the regular season undefeated and untied, the 1934 and 1942 Chicago Bears, both lost the NFL championship game. He himself had overseen a sterling 13–1 season in Baltimore but then lost the Super Bowl. All that mattered to him was walking off the final game of the year a winner. "Undefeated" was to be unspoken.

"We don't even talk about that," he told Bill Braucher when the reporter, who had been toying with the forbidden word for weeks now, brought it up. "We still haven't won anything." Pushed a little, he went on: "The players have to be continually reminded that every ball game is a step along the way. An undefeated season is meaningful only in a year that you win the Super Bowl." He seemed to be getting more prickly with each victory, more wary that musing on history could be his team's downfall. When a reporter mentioned that two more wins would make him the ninth, and youngest, coach to win a hundred NFL games, he shot back, "What difference does that make? The only thing that matters is getting back to the Super Bowl—and, more important, winning it."

It was impossible to keep the press from asking about the record, though, and some players were a bit more comfortable with it. "It's nice to think about going undefeated," said Stanfill. "But realistically, it's extremely hard to do in a league so well balanced and with luck playing such a big part every week. My own thoughts concern getting into the playoffs." Others, like Buoniconti, were less laid-back: "People waiting for us to have a letdown? Letdowns are for los-ers! Besides, how can you have a letdown the way this guy keeps you working on an even keel?" Shula was masterful at getting his team up for each and every game. Before the first game, he made sure they knew how Kansas City would be out for revenge after the playoff loss in the Longest Game. Last week he had assured them that the Colts would be out to prove their record a fluke. This week it was easy: they had let their guard, and their poise, down against the Bills at home and had very nearly suffered an embarrassing loss. Now they were going up to Buffalo to face their frenzied fans and the cold weather. All Shula had to do to iron out any complacency was show the films from two weeks ago.

• • •

By the time November arrived, most every player on the Dolphins—and around the league—was feeling his share of pain. Despite all the strategizing, the intri-cate plays drawn up on paper, the speed and elegance of receivers and runners, the precision of a perfectly thrown spiral, the game was inherently savage. The lines charged each other like medieval armies; linebackers crashed into full-backs like wrecking balls. And Don Shula's Dolphins, for all their intelligence and belief in classroom and film room preparation, were as tough as any team, and by some accounts a lot tougher. "Most people are never that committed to anything," Jim Langer told journalist Dave Hyde. "I went to Minnesota to finish up my career, and if they had a hangnail guys didn't play. Our bunch of guys would crawl across broken glass with no clothes on to get to the field. That doesn't make us heroes. That just made that team what it was." In that 2001 article, Hyde sounded like a Civil War historian as he chronicled the wounds and medical travails that hounded the '72 Dolphins. Late in his Miami career, Langer was so intent on playing that he allowed Dr. Virgin to place a block of wood on his knee and hammer it to reset the screws in his knee. Unfortunately, the procedure failed, as it also ripped open his sutures, causing more than one teammate to retch. Kuechenberg played the end of the 1973 season with a quarter-inch-thick steel-alloy rod inserted into his broken arm. Bill Stanfill lumbered out there with broken bones, a repeatedly bruised liver, slipped discs. Others played with broken arms, broken wrists, throbbing knees and ankles. Virgin concocted a "Xylocaine cocktail"—basically, a mixture of that local anes-thetic with the powerful anti-inflammatory cortisone—that got the players on the field for games, and he would often check Stanfill out of the hospital just for a game, then check him back in as he did for Fernandez. Virgin's actions appear a bit dubious from today's vantage point, but he also might have been the team's hidden MVP.

In Virgin's defense, the deleterious effects of cortisone overuse were not well-known at the time. It was considered something of a miracle drug, with few or no side effects. So before every game Virgin would perambulate the locker room with his needle and bag as the players called out, "Over here, Doc!" They took it in the ankles, the knees, the shoulders; Larry Little once took it in his chest and Mandich once in his neck. (They did not repeat those harrowing injections.) Stanfill, who would pay a higher price than any for his gridiron fortitude, took the Xylocaine cocktail in virtually every part of his body. But each player, to a man, later contended it was his own choice. "My attitude was pure and simple: I'm going to play today," said Kuechenberg years later. "That was it. Whatever it takes, I'll do it. Tape me. Shoot me up, Doc. Whatever it takes."

Doug Swift, the Amherst art major and son of physicians, was more philosophical: "It's a pretty brutal game, I guess. You get conditioned to it . . . mentally conditioned. If you *can* play, you play. The only time I get scared is when I'm groggy. You get hit in the head, you know. . . . You stumble around and you don't know where you are. People are yelling and screaming, and there you are just weaving around. You're trying to understand what everyone is so excited about." Of course, just as frequent use of cortisone was considered harmless, very little was known in 1972 of the long-term effect of repeated concussions. Football players threw themselves against each other with carefree reckless-ness, readily accepting the broken bones, the torn ligaments, the necessity of painkillers and surgeries, but with no inkling of the damage all those hits were inflicting on their brains. That reckoning would come later.

For now, all that concerned Shula's warriors was being ready to play up in Buffalo on Sunday. Buoniconti had his dislocated left shoulder wrapped all week. Morris was constantly icing his right ankle, a preseason injury that would hamper him all year. He didn't like to take the needle, but at this point it was either numb the ankle or watch Kiick take back the playing time he'd worked so hard for. He began taking the Xylocaine cocktail, too, along with his weekly little green pill.

"Greenies," they called them. Dexamyl was a commonly prescribed amphetamine in the fifties and sixties for obesity and depression. It was also used by
millions of bored housewives, wayward youths, and professional athletes in
what some doctors later called "America's first amphetamine epidemic." As with
cortisone, little was known of the adverse effects—in this case, addiction—and
doctors prescribed Dexamyl freely. In the early seventies, bottles of it were
ubiquitous in NFL locker rooms, displayed openly. Bob Griese said they were
"as common as pregame taping." (Maybe not quite, as he didn't take them.)
Morris's rookie year, the Dolphins' trainer had given him Seconal to help with
his insomnia before games, and Dr. Virgin gave him Dexamyl to get him up
for the game after the Seconal. But he didn't use it regularly until the 1972
season. He'd take one greenie at ten a.m. on game day and then find himself
wide-awake at three a.m. that night, manically chewing the same gum he'd had
in his mouth all day. He soon came to realize that he didn't need or want the
pills, but each time he considered stopping, he'd think how the team hadn't lost
a game all year, and he didn't want to jinx it. He finally quit the greenies in '73
and had just as good a season.

• • •

Whether they would talk about it or not, and despite the usual aches and
pains, the Dolphins were clearly on a roll. Seven and oh, and no one left in the
regular season, aside from the Jets and Giants, who seemed likely to disrupt
their charge. But theirs was not the only express train unable to be derailed
this autumn of 1972. Despite the war in Vietnam and the unfolding scandal
of Watergate, Richard Nixon's campaign for reelection was all but assured of
victory. Decades later, political websites and every major newspaper would
have complex analytical programs with which to construct the probabilities of
a candidate being elected. In 1972 there was Jimmy the Greek. James George
Snyder (born Dimetrios Georgios Synodinos in 1918 in Steubenville, Ohio)
acquired his nickname, and fame, as a bookmaker in Las Vegas for NFL games
beginning in the late 1950s. By the late 1960s pretty much everyone knew the
name Jimmy the Greek, and in the 1970s and 1980s he was a familiar face
on CBS, calling the point spread for each week's games (despite the fact that
betting on NFL games was illegal). He would be fired in 1988 (for proclaiming that Blacks were better athletes due to breeding practices by American

slaveholders), but in 1972 he was an icon of American pop culture. And all the papers covered his announcement on November 4 that Nixon was an overwhelming one-hundred-to-one favorite to win reelection. He even declared, via some obscure calculus, that the president had a one-in-six chance of winning all fifty states.

Richard Nixon must have loved not only the odds but the way they were presented, as if for a major sporting contest. He was the first president to be a bona fide American sports fan. He had wanted to be an athlete, and had in fact played on his college football team, "but only because they needed bodies to fill out the squad," as one biographer put it. "I can remember Dick on the ground [at practice] most of the time," remembered a teammate, "but we'd pick him up and he'd be ready for the next play. That's what we admired about him. He never got into a ball game, but he was there and took it every week." At Duke Law School in the 1930s, he was at every football game "cheering himself hoarse." As Eisenhower's running mate in 1952, Nixon embarrassed those around him with his unrestrained screaming at a Yankees-Dodgers World Series game. Years later, when he was a committed Redskins fan, his wife, Pat, sent their daughter Julie to fetch the president for dinner. The ubiquitous White House tape machine caught Julie finding him screaming at the television during a tense Redskins-Cowboys game: "Hit him, hit him, goddamnit! Son of a bitch!" Julie's response: "Uh-oh."

The First Fan was as annoyed as the rest of us at being unable to watch home games on television. It's hard to believe he couldn't have a long-range antenna installed on the White House roof, though, so maybe it was a fourth-quarter reelection play when he publicly implored Congress in October 1972 to pass a bill forcing the NFL to lift the blackout on home games that sold out forty-eight hours in advance. He also couldn't help himself from getting involved from time to time in Redskins affairs. He called Coach George Allen often, had him over to the White House, and when the team was in a bit of a slump in 1971 he visited them before a big game and gave a pep talk, which some players credited with charging them up and getting them into the playoffs. Quarterback Billy Kilmer, though, after a few drinks one afternoon, felt it was a bit much: "[Nixon]'s something else. He calls all the time. He even called the coach on election night to talk about the game. But he's really hurting us. He [said] that Cleveland had . . . quarterback problems. Then Cleveland gets all psyched up and they're much harder to beat. I think I'm going to ask George Allen to tell the president not to talk about a game until after we've played it."

Considering Washington was 11–1 at the time, Nixon couldn't have been hurting them too much. And George Allen wasn't the only coach to receive Nixon's attention. The year before, after the Dolphins had won the AFC championship game, Don Shula received a phone call at one thirty a.m. (Fortunately, he was not asleep, as he was watching a network rebroadcast of the game.) He was stunned to hear it was the White House and that he should please hold for the president. Then came the singular Nixon voice over the line: "Coach Shula, I want to personally congratulate you on the great effort that your team displayed today in winning the championship." They talked for a few minutes about the game and about the challenge of taking on the Cowboys in the Super Bowl. Then, after a thoughtful pause:

"Coach, I think it would be a good idea for you to use a pass that you throw to Warfield."

"What pass, sir?"

"You know, that slant-in pattern where Warfield starts down and then breaks into the middle of the field." This play was one Griese and Warfield used often and to great effect; as Mike Freeman later wrote, this was like suggesting to Mick Jagger that he sing "Satisfaction" at the next Stones concert.

"Yes, Mr. President, we do plan on using that slant-in pass to Warfield against the Cowboys."

"I think it can work for a big gain."

"Yes, sir, it can." (Miami did in fact use the play against Dallas, four times, and each time the Cowboys saw it as if they'd been in the huddle. Twice the announcers noted that that was the play President Nixon had suggested; Shula had mentioned the phone call in a press conference. The next week, an august organization called the Dallas Bonehead Club awarded the president their "Bonehead of the Year" trophy for his armchair quarterbacking.)

"Well, again my congratulations on a fine victory."

Shula wrapped up the late-night chat with his characteristic poise: "Thank you for taking the time to call and for your interest in professional football, Mr. President."

It was not the first contact between the two men. In January of 1969, when Shula suffered that embarrassing loss to the Jets in Super Bowl III, Nixon was the president-elect, a man basking in the ultimate redemption after having lost a presidential election and a gubernatorial one and famously declaring himself out of the game. ("You don't have Nixon to kick around anymore.") While preparing for his own inauguration, Nixon took the time to write a letter to Shula. "He said that he knew how disappointed I was in not winning the game," said Shula, "but he had been a loser who had just turned a winner. He felt that if I continued to work and believe in myself that I would be able to turn it around."

Nixon eventually came to feel he and Shula were friends, and although some close to Shula implied that the affection was unidirectional, Nixon had reason to feel an affinity for the football coach. Like Shula, he had grown up in modest circumstances in a small town, in his case Whittier, California. Shula went to a nearby college and lived at home because his scholarship was tuition only. Nixon was a star student and might have gone off to Harvard or Yale but for the expense; instead he enrolled at local Whittier College and lived at home. (Shula, however, did not develop Nixon's lifelong resentment and distrust of the elite.) Each found his calling early and combined natural ability with prodigious hard work to rise quickly to the top of his profession. (Second-youngest vice president ever; youngest coach to win a hundred games). And whether due to envy or bad luck, each was saddled with the censure "Can't win the big one." Perhaps it was this albatross that provoked each to develop an almost Ahabian determination, an overwhelming work ethic focused on winning that big one—and, having won it, to win it again. "His absorption [was] almost frightening," Nixon's daughter Julie remembered. "[As a senator] he spent nights in his office," wrote biographer John Farrell, "dozing on the couch or catching a few winks of sleep and a shower in a Capitol Hill hotel. . . . Pat and the girls didn't see him . . ." In thirty-three years of head coaching, Shula missed a day and a half of work: one day when his wife had an operation, and a half day when *he* had one. He planned every minute of every day of practice, down to exactly where each player would stand for warm-up exercises. Nixon fired off micromanagerial memos to family and staff about state dinner menus, the proper amount to tip waiters, the height of Washington's portrait, and the type of art to be displayed at American embassies around the world.

When Shula arrived in Miami, he immediately directed a desegregation of the team, from the locker room to the training camp dorm rooms. As Eisenhower's vice president, Nixon was—surprisingly, considering the racist diatribes running through the White House tapes in later years—a prominent and relatively liberal force for civil rights. He pushed hard for a civil rights bill, against skeptics in both parties, and was instrumental in getting it through the House with bipartisan approval. (Working against the bill were John F. Kennedy and Lyndon Johnson, both trying to shore up Southern support for the 1960 presidential election.) Shula's insistence on integration was probably less a dedication to racial equality than yet another instance of orchestrating every detail in search of victory. Not that he wasn't for equal opportunity—by all accounts he was—but the motive behind every move he made with the Dolphins, however slight, was to gain the winning edge. Martin Luther King Jr. was hopeful about Nixon's civil rights work—"I am coming to believe that Nixon is absolutely sincere about his views on this issue"—but he seemed wary of a similarly utilitarian motivation: "There is a danger in such a [magnetic] personality, and that is that it will be turned on merely for political expedience when at bottom the real man has insincere motives. I hope this is not the case with Nixon. He has a genius for winning people . . . If Richard Nixon is not sincere, he is the most dangerous man in America."

Shula and Nixon also shared a winning humor that was not always associated with their public image. Farrell writes of Nixon "prowling a hotel hallway in his bathrobe one night during the 1968 campaign [and coming] upon an aide who was escorting a young lady to his room. 'Mike, we don't have to get those votes one at a time, you know,' he said." When Marv Fleming—one of the first football players to wear an earring—joined the Dolphins, he figured he'd get a rise out of Shula. Turning the side with the earring to him, he said, "Hey Coach, notice anything?" "Sure, Marv," said Shula. "You lost one earring."

After Nixon's suggested pass pattern to Warfield had failed miserably, along with the rest of Miami's strategies, in Super Bowl VI, Nixon sat down to write another letter to Shula. He could empathize with the coach. Not only had he lost some big ones in '60 and '62, but even after finally winning the presidency he had found himself deep in the doldrums in June 1971. His approval ratings were at a nadir, as he seemed powerless to bring the war to a conclusion, and he faced raucous disapproval from both left and right. He would come roaring back in a matter of months—by the next summer his reelection was all but guaranteed—with foreign-policy triumphs abroad and ruthless subterfuge at home. But he may have felt that Shula, after the embarrassing loss to Dallas, was in a place similar to the one Nixon had been in. "Dear Don," he began. "I know how disappointing it must be to you and members of your fine team to have this season end on such a disappointing note. You can take a great deal of pride, however, in the fact that you brought the young Dolphin team to the very heights of pro football competition." Then, perhaps ruminating on his own all-consuming drive to bring down his opponents and secure reelection, he concluded: "And I would not want to be on that other team the next time your young Miami players have another shot at the Super Bowl. Regards, Richard."

On Thursday, November 2, five days before the 1972 election, the *Miami Herald* expressed its "pleasure" in reiterating its endorsement a month earlier of Richard Nixon for reelection. (The *Miami News*, the *Fort Lauderdale Sun-Sentinel*, and every other South Florida paper with the exception of the *Daytona Beach Morning Journal* and the *Daytona Beach Evening News* had also endorsed Nixon.) Nixon, they said, had presided over a strong economy at home and had made bold strides in thawing the Cold War with his historic trip to China and his détente with the Soviet Union. This was what the people cared about: with an overwhelming majority on November 7, he would be able to "bring a needed sense of unity and purpose to the United States."

It had been "a dismal campaign in every particular way," wrote James Kilpatrick. The Nixon administration, "tarnished by scandal . . . leads not by ardent choice but by dispirited default." Even Republicans who abhorred Nixon and his shady tactics—like Bob Woodward, who was working day and night to expose that corruption—couldn't bring themselves to vote for McGovern. Bernstein, a Democrat, voted for him "unenthusiastically."

Nixon himself had made no campaign appearances at all until late September, isolating himself in the White House from the slowly accumulating Watergate stories and the disingenuous peace negotiations. When he finally hit the trail, it was with amiable confidence, playing the piano and singing "Happy Birthday" to Democratic representative Kika de la Garza after a West Texas campaign speech. The next day he visited his former treasury secretary John Connally, a Democrat, who was hosting a dinner at his San Antonio ranch for 350 Democrats who were supporting Nixon, including two sons of Franklin Delano Roosevelt and a bunch of old Lyndon Johnson aides and pals. Connally headed the national "Democrats for Nixon" campaign; thirty-two percent of Dems said they preferred Nixon that year, and that was down from forty percent in the summer. McGovern was simply too liberal for many centrist Democrats, and too plodding for the left-wingers. Many powerful Democratic entities, including the AFL-CIO and mayors like Chicago's Richard J. Daley, were sitting this one out.

Woodward and Bernstein led a small cadre of investigative journalists who were keeping Watergate in the news throughout the fall campaign, but the Nixon campaign succeeded in shielding their man from the scandal; it wasn't until long after the election that the president would be personally tied to the burglary. "It is difficult for us to believe," wrote the *Herald*, "that the President sat in on any planning to infiltrate the headquarters of the Dem Party and place wiretaps." Moreover, they pointed out, "people don't care about the bugging because 'it's just politics.'" This was certainly confirmed by my father's campaign calls around Miami. He was flabbergasted at the apathy, echoed by a letter to the editor: "Much ado about nothing. It made good copy and still may make more. The whole incident was ill-conceived and the planning was childish. However, nobody was hurt as far as I can see. Watergate will probably soon be forgotten."

All those headlines suggesting a tantalizing truce to end the Vietnam War were suddenly gone; Kissinger had failed to keep the promise alive until after the election. He had kept stalling as Saigon and Hanoi refused to budge on their demands, and finally the U.S. had no choice but to miss Hanoi's deadline for signing a pact. In the meantime, B-52 bombers based in Guam and Thailand continued to drop "probably the most massive amount of bombs in the history of aerial warfare." On Election Day, voters read that Viet Cong forces had downed three U.S. aircraft near Da Nang, killing four U.S. airmen: the worst American casualties in months. But by now nothing could slow the Nixon reelection juggernaut.

· · ·

Despite Nixon's runaway lead, the nation remained deeply divided by the war and by economic and social crevasses. The two sides of the country had been on display in microcosm at the Democratic and Republican conventions on Miami Beach, and the battles played out on those streets might have worried Don Shula that his team would be riven by the politics and social forces of the day. Marv Fleming and Larry Little had campaigned for McGovern in the off-season, Paul

Warfield was a good friend of Marv's and a fellow Democrat, and Marlin Briscoe was politically minded and an admirer of Angela Davis. Rookie Eddie Jenkins had been involved in political protests at Holy Cross and, with his gregarious personality, might stir up political talk in the locker room. On the other side, Howard Twilley, Nick Buoniconti (a "Democrat for Nixon"), and a few other Dolphins had appeared at the Republican National Convention, introduced by Ronald Reagan: "I know you Oklahoma delegates are going to recognize this fellow: *Harold* Twilley!" Jenkins remembered Mercury Morris and others good-naturedly "taunting Twilley all day long" for his support of Nixon. Doug Swift was the team player representative in the NFL Players Association, and he and Twilley were forever arguing about the union.

But neither Watergate nor Vietnam nor players' union dues were going to sabotage the Dolphins' campaign in 1972. "Nobody was going to let that get in the way of what the team was about, that we were going to win no matter what," said Twilley. "We really never noticed [political upheaval] much other than the headlines," said Vern Den Herder. "We had a job to do, and it was pretty much all football." Manny Fernandez later became a staunch right-wing Republican, but he said that at the time "we weren't very politically minded. Didn't have any hippies on the team. Not even Doug Swift, though he was about as close as you could get." To a man they maintained that Shula kept them so intensely focused on winning that there was no time for politics. "Shula would never go for that kind of crap [political bickering]," said Morris. "We were unified because of Shula," said Twilley. "Vietnam was an unfortunate involvement," remembered Paul Warfield, "and there was a divisiveness in the country, to be sure. But I've never been associated in my career with a team that was so focused as that 1972 team."

Two days before the election, the Dolphins were more concerned with avoiding a November surprise up in Buffalo. Buffalo would be primed to score an upset at home after coming so close in the Orange Bowl, naturally over-looking the uncharacteristic circus of errors performed by the Dolphins that day. Mercury Morris was charged up for the game, as he always was against Buffalo. He would never let go of his semi-cordial grudge against O. J. Simpson. Two weeks before, neither running back had shone, as Simpson was held to fifty-four yards by a No-Name Defense keying on him, and Morris mostly sat it out with a sore ankle. (He actually did quite well when he was in there, gaining thirty-five yards and scoring two touchdowns on only five carries.) But, feeling better today, he wanted a big game against O.J.

Shula was wise enough to start Morris against his rival and saw it pay off on the very first drive, as Merc escaped for a thirty-three-yard jitterbugging scamper that set up a thirty-three-yard Yepremian field goal. Then, later in the first quarter, he outdid that run with a spectacular twenty-two-yard sweep that put the Dolphins ahead 10–6. He took the pitchout from Morrall, made a 360-degree spin after being hit, eluded another tackler, and bounced off two more as he dove into the end zone. It was a good thing the running game was going strong, because Morrall completed only two of ten passes in the first half, and one of those ten was intercepted for a touchdown with two minutes left in the half. That made it 16–13 Miami—Yepremian had kicked a couple more short field goals—and it looked to be another fiasco and a tie game at the half when Buffalo drove into Miami territory in the final seconds. But a Tim Foley interception at the ten-yard line preserved the lead, and in the second half Miami took over with their ground game and defense. On the opening drive of the third quarter, the Dolphins ran the ball ten straight times, from their twenty to the Buffalo seven. Finally, on the eleventh play of the drive, Morrall faded back to pass and found Marv Fleming in the end zone.

It was gratifying to Fleming anytime he caught a pass at all, much less a touchdown. The starting tight end for the Packers when they won the first two Super Bowls, he was known more as an invaluable blocker than a pass catcher. And he took pride in that. "You and me, baby, you and me," he'd say to tackle Norm Evans as they broke from the huddle and lined up shoulder to shoulder. "We're gonna clear out this side." Watching him at his first Dolphin camp in 1970, Shula just shook his head and smiled: "What a winner." "Marv fires out like a coiled-up rattler," said Evans, "and he comes down on that strong-side linebacker like an avalanche. Just a devastating blocker. When he came here in '70, I would just stand around and watch him scrimmage. Seeing him throw a block was like appreciating a Van Gogh original. He made knocking people down into an art." "Marv relished his role," recalled Paul Warfield. "He was one of the most unselfish players and was crucial to our running game. You could not run off tackle or outside without a great blocking end like Marv, one of the most highly efficient and dedicated players, who time after time had the thankless job of putting his head into someone's gut." But as much as he may have relished the role, everyone loves to catch touchdown passes, and Fleming was clutch. He'd caught only thirty-one passes in his first two seasons in Miami, but he pulled in four in the Kansas City playoff game, including the touchdown that sent it into overtime.

Now he squeezed the ball in the end zone to put the Dolphins up by ten in Buffalo and then flipped it to the ref, began to trot back to the sideline, and stopped. There, in the end zone grass, was one of Marv's favorite sights: a green-back. (A wheeler and dealer who reveled in making business contacts wherever he went, the thirty-year-old had been very successful already in investing his pro football earnings, and when giving interviews he loved to accentuate the financial side of playing football.) He bent over and grabbed the $10 bill as a little touchdown bonus.

Buffalo had scored only one touchdown on offense, and in the second half the Dolphin defense got serious. As usual, they held the ascendant star O.J., who had gained 189 yards against Pittsburgh's "Steel Curtain" the previous week, to minimal yardage: forty-five yards, after fifty-four in the first game in Miami. (In his unprecedented 2,003-yard season the next year, his worst game was a 55-yard effort in Miami. He did get 120 against them at home, but even that was below his average that year.) The No-Name Defense was becoming very well-known. In the middle, as always, was Buoniconti, the fiery compact Italian American from Springfield, Massachusetts. As an offense broke its huddle and approached the line of scrimmage, it would see number eighty-five, 220 pounds packed into a frame an inch shy of six feet, resolute in the middle of his team-mates (who dwarfed him), standing in his peculiar way, legs twisted toward each other, right foot crossed over the left. He looked a little odd, a little small, with the wrong number for a linebacker. (The NFL had let him keep his old AFL number.) But no one took him lightly. He reminded one reporter of "an extra in one of those inscrutable Sophia Loren movies." More likely a Scorsese film set in Little Italy. When O.J. had that 120-yard day against Miami in '73, it was because Buffalo kept running the ball to get him yardage even though they were way behind. After each run Buoniconti would scream at them, "You assholes!"

"Nick was a little guy," said Doug Swift. ("That fuzzy little wop, about that damn high," said the six-foot-five Stanfill in such an affable drawl that nobody could be offended.) "Everybody would hunch over in the huddle," continued Swift, "and Nick would still stand up. And he'd be in there carrying on and cussing and, you know, he looked truly like a gladiator. Nick drives himself like a nut. He's a hard-working character. I think he's also crazy."

Like Twilley and Foley, Buoniconti had always been told he was too small and too slow to make it in the NFL. "But the thing you can't measure with a computer is heart," said Don Shula, "and that's what Buoniconti had. Plus he had this tremendous leadership ability. He wouldn't tolerate mistakes from his teammates, and he never made any mistakes himself." He grew up in a tough Italian neighborhood on the South Side of Springfield, but looking back he said the entire neighborhood felt like one big family. Next door was his grandfather, who had emigrated from Naples in 1918 and started a bakery. Nick grew up working in the bakery, which his brother would eventually take over, and developed his toughness playing sandlot football. "He was the best athlete in the South End," recalled his brother, "he was the toughest kid in the South End, and he was one of the smartest kids in the South End." When he graduated Notre Dame, though, his own coach felt he couldn't recommend him to the NFL—"He'll run through a wall. But the hole will be small," he told scouts—and so Buoniconti was drafted only by Boston of the AFL, and in the thirteenth round. He was an immediate starter there, though, and all-AFL from his second year on. (He was later named the AFL's all-time best middle linebacker.) He also earned his law degree, taking night classes at Suffolk University. He was sure he'd finish his football career in Boston and settle there with a law practice. He was shocked to be told after seven excellent seasons that he'd been traded to Miami for a backup quarterback, Kim Hammond (who'd be out of football in another year), and a linebacker, John Bramlett, who weighed even less than Buoniconti. Even Joe Thomas couldn't believe the deal he'd got: whenever it came up, he'd just shake his head and smile. Buoniconti seriously considered retiring rather than moving his family to Florida, but in the end he used his reluctance and his prowess at negotiation to finagle a three-year contract out of Robbie, with a big raise into the $50,000 level.

His first year in Miami was George Wilson's tumultuous final year, but Buoniconti liked Wilson and was disappointed when Shula's takeover was announced. It didn't help that Shula and Arnsparger instituted a completely new defensive scheme, with Buoniconti expected to be the equivalent of a defensive quarterback. "I was terribly discouraged," he said. "The responsibilities of the middle linebacker under Shula are massive." About halfway through the 1970 season, Buoniconti was feeling completely dejected, afraid that he wasn't able to make the transition. Shula called him into his office and told him he knew how he felt. "It takes maybe eight or ten games to learn this defense," he said. "You're doing a real good job. Just quit worrying. You're going to make it." From that point on, Buoniconti's star did nothing but rise. He learned to trust Shula, even when the coach replaced his best friend on the team, center Bob DeMarco, with the young Jim Langer. And by 1972, when the No-Name Defense was being recognized as the league's best, Buoniconti was its undisputed leader. "Nick sort of kept an uncle's hand on most of the defense," said Swift, "and I felt pretty close to him for it. I admired him." Tim Foley went even further, evoking a questionable paternal model: "Nick was the Daddy. If we made a mistake he'd scream and holler and yell and spank us."

Avuncular. Paternal. "Intense" was the first word his wife Terry came up with when asked to describe him. The linebacker was now also a partner in the South Miami corporate law firm of Greenberg & Bodne, and although he could put in only a few hours a week during the season, he was full-time the rest of the year. At the moment, most of his off-field working time was occupied by the running of the business he started shortly after the Super Bowl loss, All-Pro Graphics. He recruited more than a hundred NFL colleagues and sold their images for printing on posters, calendars, schoolbook covers, drinking cups, and more. In 1972 he was able to send each player a check for $300 and expected that number to be over $2,000 the next year. Buoniconti himself earned about $100,000 from All-Pro Graphics in 1972, double his football salary. He was quite glad he hadn't retired in Boston three years earlier, and he certainly had no plans for hanging up his cleats now: "The sun shines every day down here, and Shula has that happy smirk." He had made a very different life in Miami for his kids—Gina Marie, nine, Nick Anthony, eight, and Marc Anthony, six—than he'd had growing up in Springfield next door to his grandparents and a plethora of aunts and uncles. (His grandmother had somehow given birth to thirteen daughters.) But some things remained the same. "I made up my mind we'd name all our boys Anthony in the middle. My aunt Carmela likes it."

• • •

From July to January, Nick Buoniconti's agile mind found plenty to occupy itself with away from law and business. The Shula-Arnsparger defense "relied on intelligence," he said. It had to, for the squad lacked the big muscle or Olympic-level speed that characterized most great defenses. Tim Foley liked to say that with him and Johnson at cornerback—normally a speed position—it was more like having four safeties. They rarely used man-to-man coverage—only occasionally when they were blitzing. Mostly it was zone defense, relying on discipline. "It was synchronized, a thinking man's defense," said Buoniconti. "You had to adapt because you might change your signals two or three times before the ball was snapped. All of it was dictated by what the other team was doing." And Buoniconti always seemed to know what the other team was doing. He studied films of opposing offenses so hard that a lineman lining up just a few inches wider than usual would tip him off to the play. Griese got an inkling in practice of what other quarterbacks had to face; time after time, he'd bring the offense up to the line of scrimmage and hear Buoniconti yelling out just what they were about to do. "I'd think: How'd he know that?" O. J. Simpson gave Buoniconti the credit for how the Dolphins consistently held him far below his average. He became so used to Buoniconti filling up the hole he was supposed to run through that he would find himself running to the wrong place on purpose, hoping to elude the linebacker. Or he'd be in his stance, see Buoniconti shifting his players around, and scream for his quarterback to call an audible.

Usually, though, the Dolphins were able to hide their foreknowledge. Buoniconti would just yell out code for what he wanted his men to do. For instance, they had one play called a "ram charge," which meant the defensive ends would fire hard against the inside shoulders of the offensive tackles instead of their outside shoulders. In concert with that, two linebackers would loop around and cover the outside. If anyone blew their assignment, it would result in a gaping hole. "Nick was the general," said Den Herder. "And if he called a stunt, he knew it was going to be carried out. He'd shout out, 'Ram!' and we all knew it would happen." In later years Buoniconti liked to say, with pride, that his defense made only seven mental errors that season in close to a thousand plays.

Of course, they weren't all No-Names. Scott and Anderson were Pro Bowl safeties, and Buoniconti was a well-recognized veteran headed to the Hall of Fame. They also weren't all lightweights who relied on smarts and craftiness to get the upper hand. Bill Stanfill was a powerful, lanky six-foot-five and had been the nation's highest rated defensive lineman coming out of the University of Georgia in 1969. The Dolphins took him with their number one pick, and he became a career starter and five-time Pro Bowler. He'd grown up on a farm in Cairo, a little town in the southwest corner of Georgia. As he explained to Dave Hyde, milking cows each morning before school strengthened his hands and wrists, maneuvering two-hundred-pound cotton sheets got him ready to handle running backs, and getting knocked down by steers "taught me how to get back up" and keep going after the quarterback. Sitting in the locker room after practice, spitting tobacco juice into a beer can, his thick Southern inflection was full of good humor. "It sure is fun to hit the quarterback," he told a reporter. "Especially when they have the ball. But if you get to hit them anyway, that's a lot of fun too." He had his pickup truck outfitted with two gas tanks and a plastic urinal with a hose going right down through the floorboards. That way he could drive from Miami all the way back to Cairo, a case of beer on the seat next to him, without stopping. Or so he said. As well as being one of the most physically gifted, Stanfill was one of the team's big jokers.

Still, despite the imposing physiques of Stanfill and Fernandez and the bone-crushing hits of Swift and Kolen, it was brilliant strategizing—devised by Arnsparger, commandeered by Buoniconti, and carried out nearly flawlessly by all eleven men on the field—that made the No-Name Defense the best in the league. "Nobody knew what we were doing," said Tim Foley, referring to the last-second adjustments the defense would make just before a play to disguise their intentions. He was correct. Joe Namath would go on and on about how they kept flummoxing him. "The Dolphins give you the impression they know what you do and what you're going to do," sighed a scout from the Giants, in the Orange Bowl press box to help prepare for a game later in the season. "They seem to have complete knowledge of the exact situation. The defense acts like it has control of the opposing offense."

• • •

With the defense holding Buffalo to 172 total yards (compared to 327 for Miami, 254 of it running), Fleming's touchdown catch early in the third quarter all but sealed the game. In the fourth quarter Mercury came back in after getting poked in the eye—nothing was going to keep him from showing up O.J.—to make a spectacular one-handed catch with a defender right on him for a twenty-six-yard gain down to the three-yard line. Then he ran it in himself from there for the final winning margin, 30–16.

In the locker room afterward, Morris sat with a contented weariness, holding the game ball. "I wanted to give it to the offensive line," he said, "but Shoes [Shula] told me to keep it." He'd finished with 106 yards on only eleven carries—his second century game ever—to show up O.J.'s forty-five in front of the Bills' crowd. Not far away, a group was discussing how Marv Fleming had found that $10 bill in the end zone. "I could have landed with my face mask right on top of it and never seen it," said Manny Fernandez. "In fact, only Marv would find money on the field." It wasn't clear whether he was referring to Fleming's financial prowess. Marv was also known by his teammates as something of a mystic, an amateur philosopher who had even written an as-yet-unpublished treatise entitled *The Mind Garden.* "I've been concentrating hard in practice," he was saying now. "If you keep it up, it will come to you." Larry Csonka was sitting nearby. "That's a case where virtue was its own reward—and then some," he piped up. "I'd like to find something in the end zone one of these days, besides lumps. Hey, how about splitting the sawbuck with me?" Fleming just smiled and walked away.

In another corner of the room, original Dolphins Norm Evans and Howard Twilley were reminiscing with Cookie Gilchrist, the All-Star runner for the Bills in the 1960s, whom Robbie had brought to Miami midway through the first Dolphin season. By the time he got to Miami in 1966, Cookie was over thirty and out of shape, and he ended up playing only that half season before retiring. But Nick Buoniconti well remembered playing against him for five years and described him as a predecessor to Csonka: "Cookie was absolutely brutal. He was one of the few runners I've ever seen who could totally terrorize smaller defensive backs." Now, in the locker room in Buffalo, Gilchrist reminisced a bit about that first Dolphin season, the highlight of which was his late-night carousing with Wahoo McDaniel. "It's like a hundred years ago," he sighed, comparing that group to this year's team, with a perfect eight-and-oh record. "These guys are a bunch of terrors."

Nine and Oh

On November 7, 1962, Richard Nixon, at a press conference after losing the California gubernatorial election—two years after losing the presidential election to John F. Kennedy—spat out his famous valedictory. He rambled on for fifteen minutes. It had been a sleepless night, the election not decided for certain until morning, and he railed against the various circumstances that had worked against him, in particular a hostile press, before finishing: "I leave you gentlemen now. And you will now write it. You will interpret it. That's your right. But as I leave you, I want you to know: just think how much you're going to be missing. You don't have Nixon to kick around anymore. Because, gentlemen, this is my last press conference."

Ten years later to the day, Nixon joked to a group of supporters, "I have never known a national election when I would be able to go to bed earlier than tonight." When he woke in the morning he had won a second term as president in one of the most impressive landslides in history. His 60.7 percent share of the popular vote was the third greatest since the early nineteenth century, and his 520–17 tally in the Electoral College was second best since 1820. (Only Massachusetts and the District of Columbia went for McGovern.) He had barely had to campaign. The economy was strong (partly due to his duplicitous wage and price freeze); a nuclear confrontation with the Soviet Union or China seemed less likely than ever, thanks to Nixon's diplomatic coups; and McGovern had failed to command the large moderate swath of his party. Although he really didn't need to, Nixon appeared on national TV the night before the election: "I urge you to send a message to those with whom we are negotiating. . . . I would urge you have in mind . . . one overriding issue, that is the issue of peace. . . . We have made a breakthrough in the negotiations which will lead to peace in Vietnam."

Despite this clearly not being the case, despite the news stories on Election Day of fresh fighting and fresh deaths, Mr. John Doe, as someone put it, voted according to his paycheck. It wasn't that the people loved Nixon. Adulation had never been within his grasp. The electorate found him uncharismatic, lukewarm personally, but competent. They trusted him to keep the ship floating while they pursued their happiness. The landslide was clearly not a bellwether of conservatism, for the voters maintained a Democratic majority in both houses of Congress. The Republicans picked up twelve seats in the House but were still a 242–192 minority. And in the Senate, the Democrats actually gained two seats. One of those winners was a young New Castle County, Delaware, councilman named Joe Biden. Still underage for a senator—he attained the required age of thirty a few weeks after the election—Biden came back from a thirty-point deficit in the summer polls to defeat the two-time incumbent J. Caleb Boggs by just three thousand votes. He was no doubt helped by the Twenty-Sixth Amendment, which only a year earlier had lowered the voting age to eighteen. For Richard Nixon, though, the election was still a triumph, a moment of personal fulfillment. In 1968 he had barely won, but now the apotheosis was complete, from the depths a decade before to a two-time winner of the political Super Bowl.

Wednesday afternoon the president and his family, along with Henry Kissinger and several other key aides, flew on Air Force One to Homestead Air Force Base, twenty-five miles south of Miami. After greeting a cheering crowd of military families there, they climbed aboard a helicopter for the short hop up to Key Biscayne, the seal-shaped island that looks as though it's swimming southward from the Seaquarium, a few miles off the coast of Coconut Grove. Key Biscayne later became the site of high-rise hotels and the fifth biggest tennis tournament in the world. But in the early seventies it boasted just a couple large hotels, a small residential community, and Crandon Park. Crandon had Miami's other major beach: no surf, but a scattered grove of coconut trees, a wide expanse of soft white sand, and warm placid water deepening so gradually, it seemed like perpetual low tide. The park also had Miami's only zoo, a modest affair embellished by a white Bengal tiger and a miniature scenic railroad. The future site of the Miami Open was just a few public tennis courts across the road from the beach. After my family joined the tennis boom in 1971, we sometimes hit balls there after a day at the beach.

Richard Nixon was a young senator when he began vacationing on Key Biscayne in 1951. In 1968, just after being elected president, he purchased two typical South Florida ranch houses next door to the home of his closest friend, Charles "Bebe" Rebozo, the owner of Key Biscayne Bank. "One of the few people in the world with whom Nixon felt comfortable," perhaps because, as Nixon put it, "he never brings up unpleasant subjects," Rebozo was a self-made man, much like the president. His family had left Cuba for Miami in 1920, when he was eight. After graduating Miami High (voted "best-looking"), he worked as a Pan Am steward, owned a gas station, fixed tires, and—most presciently—began buying up undeveloped land around Miami. By the time he met Nixon on Key Biscayne when they both were thirty-eight, Rebozo had made a bundle in real estate; he would start the Key Biscayne Bank a decade later and also become Nixon's investment advisor and real estate broker.

Nixon had his new Key Biscayne property, along with Rebozo's, enclosed by an eleven-foot-high hibiscus hedge, and this compound became known as the Winter White House. The U.S. Department of Defense later built a helipad with $400,000 of taxpayer money, and it was on that half-acre platform constructed on concrete pylons in the water off the Nixons' lawn that they landed just after eight p.m. the day after the president's reelection. Several hundred neighbors and other supporters greeted them, airing out their campaign signs one more time.

In the morning, Nixon walked out back in the warm morning air, the sun just splashing on his glorious view of Biscayne Bay and, off in the distance, Coconut Grove. After breakfast he and his aides began putting together his second administration, which would involve a significant cabinet shake-up. Kissinger, though, would remain as national security advisor (becoming secretary of state the following fall) and was on Key Biscayne to discuss the final stages of American involvement in Vietnam. He had failed to get a truce signed in time for the election, but it hadn't mattered. Now there were no more elections for Nixon, and the objective was to get out of South Asia as quickly as possible so the president could enjoy the credit for peace; by the time that peace—and South Vietnam—crumbled, American culpability for that would be forgotten. And to get out of there "with honor" meant heavy bombing until the North could be brought to sign a truce. A few days later the U.S. doubled the number of air strikes, flying more than seven hundred sorties over North Vietnam, Laos, and Cambodia in a twenty-four-hour period. Nixon and his family went "houseboating" that day on Rebozo's *Cocolobo II*, which looked like a 1940s Miami Beach bungalow stuck on top of a dinghy. They sailed down to Key Largo, and the Nixons returned that evening via helicopter, as was their custom.

Another arrival on Election Day at Miami International was Meyer Lansky. The seventy-year-old gangster had fled to Israel in 1970 and been seeking asylum ever since. Now, forced out of Israel, he had flown from Tel Aviv to Zurich, then to Rio, Buenos Aires, Asunción, La Paz, Lima, Panama, and finally, having failed to be granted asylum anywhere, Miami. He was woken up in his Braniff International seat by federal agents, arrested, and taken to FBI headquarters downtown. (Like Capone, he would be indicted on tax-evasion charges, although Lansky was eventually acquitted. Also like his old colleague, he'd spend his final years on Miami Beach, dying in 1983 with little money to his name.) Free on $250,000 bail, Lansky took a cab to the Sunny Isles oceanfront motel, where his son worked. Chatting with FBI agents about the decline of morality among young folks, the presumably Republican mobster smiled: "Looks like [the election's] going to be a landslide."

• • •

Richard Nixon wasn't taking anything for granted on Election Eve when he made his televised appeal to the voters. Don Shula was also concerned about overconfidence that week. His team had gone through half the season already without a loss and now were waiting at home for the 2–6 New England Patriots (renamed in 1971). Jimmy the Greek had the Dolphins as two-touchdown favorites, but Shula was wary. The Patriots had been a vexation ever since he'd come to Miami. His very first game as Dolphins coach had been that embarrassing loss up at Harvard Stadium that had him screaming at his team in the locker room. Then in 1971 the Dolphins had gone up to brand-new Schaefer Stadium in Foxborough, Massachusetts, with a 9–1–1 record and been embarrassed again in a three-touchdown loss. This week's game was in Miami, but no one who knew Shula thought he might take the Patriots lightly. "That was no fluke last year," he told his players and the press alike, and he meant it. In fact, the Patriots were not a bad team. With Heisman Trophy winner Jim Plunkett and his former Stanford teammate, quick little receiver Randy Vataha, they had a sharp offense and a promising outlook. They'd had a respectable 6–8 record the previous year, and if it wasn't for them the Washington Redskins would also be 8–0 right now, for the Pats beat them, barely, in the second game of the season.

Shula didn't need to prod his guys too much; they remembered last December very well. "They killed us, 34–13," said Jim Kiick on Wednesday after practice. "No fluke. They just outplayed us all the way. And that was the day I fumbled"—his only fumble of the entire season. Kiick was nursing a sore knee now, which had had to be drained after the game in Buffalo, but he wasn't talking about that. He was eager for playing time. This time last year, at the season's halfway point, he had over five hundred yards rushing and was on the way to his fourth consecutive year with over a thousand yards combined rushing and receiving. Csonka had overtaken him as top dog, but he was still Zonk's undisputed backfield sidekick. Butch and Sundance. This year it was more like Sundance, Merc, and Butch. "Realistically," he said, "I realize this could help me [injury-wise] in the long run. But I can't convince myself. It's the same with me as it is with Unitas. Pride. And Merc wouldn't be the player he is if he didn't feel the same way. No, we don't discuss this particular situation. We just try to help each other. But I know that inside he must feel about like I do." Outside, too: Morris's right ankle wasn't getting any better, and he would need the Xylocaine cocktail to keep him playing for the rest of the season.

At game time on Sunday, November 12, it was eighty-four degrees and humid. The Miami weather helped soothe the joints a bit, but more importantly it was a huge advantage to the team that was used to it, that ran gassers in it. As they stretched and warmed up on the steamy Poly-Turf, the Miami players felt their confidence expand. It was as though they were already up a touchdown. After only four plays, they *were* up a touchdown. Dick Anderson picked off the first Plunkett pass at the sideline and took off with his unique, hunched-over running style, from the New England twenty-six-yard line all the way down to the four. Improbably, the sharp-minded Anderson said he thought the five-yard line was the goal line, which explained why he dove exuberantly across it. No matter: on the next play, Morris took the ball on a sweep left and followed Bob Kuechenberg right into the end zone. A few minutes later Morris duplicated the feat with another four-yard touchdown sweep left, this time behind Csonka, who punished cornerback Honor Jackson even worse than if he'd been carrying the ball himself. This was all in just the first twelve minutes. By halftime an eighty-eight-yard drive, a shorter one sparked by another Curtis Johnson field goal block, and another long drive to a short field goal had produced a 31–0 lead. Morris already had three touchdowns and would lead the runners today with ninety yards. A Jake Scott interception in the third quarter led to a sixteen-yard touchdown pass from Morrall to Briscoe, and after that the most interesting development was the debut of Jim Del Gaizo.

He had grown up in the working-class beach town of Revere, on Boston's North Shore, only a few miles but worlds away from blue-blooded Beacon Hill and the ivory towers of Cambridge. The AFL's Patriots were born when Del Gaizo was thirteen, and he "used to go to all their games" while he was playing for Revere High. He took a scholarship to Syracuse, where he was Larry Csonka's teammate for a couple years, but then transferred to the University of Tampa, where he could be a starter, and led them to an 8–2 record his senior year. "I wasn't drafted, though," he said, "and I begged the Patriots for a chance. I phoned them. I had my Tampa coach call them. I even had my high school coach call them. They said no, they didn't like left-handers, and besides I wasn't a pro prospect." A year later, though, he convinced Shula to give him a tryout at camp, and the Dolphins signed him as a free agent. Since then he'd been mostly on the taxi squad, even after a strong preseason this year. He'd outperformed Morrall in the exhibition games, but of course when the season began Shula kept the Super Bowl MVP as the backup and relegated the free agent to the taxi squad again. But when Griese went down, Del Gaizo became Morrall's backup, and he knew his history too: "This is a great break for me," he told the press. "What the hell, didn't Griese get into the lineup [his rookie year] because another guy broke a leg? Well, I'm twenty-five years old and I've never played an NFL down. Maybe Morrall will fall down some stairs."

Now, four games later, with a 38–0 lead, there he was, the focus of eighty thousand pairs of eyes, trotting onto the Orange Bowl field to face his childhood team. Early in the fourth quarter he faded back at midfield and hit Marlin Briscoe on the right sideline; the Patriots cornerback went for the interception and was too late, leaving Briscoe to sprint the rest of the way down the sideline for a forty-eight-yard touchdown. On the next series, Shula told Del Gaizo to keep the ball on the ground and run time off the clock. But after mostly running the ball to the New England thirty-nine, Del Gaizo called for Jim Mandich to slant deep over the middle, and there he was, several steps ahead of two defenders. Del Gaizo hit him in the numbers, and Mandich easily ran it in. Shula was a bit embarrassed, as he never wanted to run the score up on anyone, and he screamed out at Del Gaizo, "Goddamnit, I told you to keep it on the ground!" But when the young quarterback came running off with a sheepish grin, Shula couldn't help but give him a pat on the helmet. "It was good for Jim to get his feet wet," he said afterward.

Del Gaizo completed four of six passes for 146 yards, an astonishing statistic for a first-timer. He wasn't the only one to benefit from the mismatch. Marlin Briscoe was back catching his first passes in six weeks, after being out first with a pulled hamstring and then due to "Twilley's annual demonstration that he belongs in there somewhere." He hauled in four for 128 yards and two touchdowns, his biggest day as a Dolphin. And Otto Stowe, the speedy, elegant wide receiver in the Warfield mold, who'd been Miami's second draft pick the year before but found himself stuck behind Warfield, Briscoe, and Twilley, got in there against the Patriots and hauled in a forty-nine-yarder from Del Gaizo, his first catch since game three. "Otto Stowe, Marlin Briscoe and Jim Mandich: they'd be regulars on most other teams in the NFL," said Del Gaizo, and he was right.

• • •

A couple weeks earlier Shula hadn't wanted to discuss the prospect of winning his hundredth game as an NFL coach. After beating the Patriots, though, there was no getting out of it. It was all the press wanted to talk about: he was the ninth coach to accomplish it, but by far the youngest and the quickest, only halfway through his tenth season as head coach. That milestone, along with the now nine-game winning streak, was focusing enormous attention on Shula. If he wasn't already the country's premier football coach when he signed with the Dolphins, he definitely was now. With a salary, stock options, and advertising opportunities that would soon make him a millionaire, living in a subtropical paradise, coaching a team that didn't exist when he got into football. It was a life the young man from small-town Ohio couldn't have imagined.

He was now 100–30–5 as a head coach, 29–7–1 in Miami, and 9–0 in 1972. How did he do it? everyone wanted to know. "I'm just a guy who rolls up his sleeves and goes to work," he said. "I'm about as subtle as a punch in the mouth. I don't have peace of mind until I know I've given the game everything I can."

The final score against New England was 52–0. The Dolphins players overlooked the kid from Revere and awarded the game ball to the coach.

When they had tried to give him one after beating Baltimore the year before, he declined: "No, thanks, the only game ball I want is for the Super Bowl." This time he politely accepted but made sure they hadn't forgotten: "The game ball I really want is at the end of the season. I'm proud of my hundredth, but it won't be nearly as meaningful if it doesn't fit into a championship." What about the pressure of the perfect season so far? a reporter asked, and Shula predictably spat back: "There's no pressure on that. The pressure is to win the world championship."

On the other side of the locker room, where Jim Del Gaizo usually dressed in peace, he was gabbing to a gaggle of microphones about how the Patriots had refused to give him a tryout. "My touchdowns didn't really mean anything in the game, but they meant a lot to me. . . . I was almost on welfare in Tampa [last year]. There was no other way I could make a buck. I can't do anything else. I tried selling insurance. I tried selling clothes. But I can't sell nothing." Bob Griese came limping by in his cast. "Hey, Big-Time!" he yelled with a laugh. "Yeah," Del Gaizo replied, turning away from the reporters. "Ain't this a gas?"

Now that the Dolphins were past the halfway point, fans and the press were starting to talk about the possibility of going all the way without a loss—whether Shula and his players wanted to discuss it or not. Bill Braucher had been enjoying the speculation as early as the fourth week, when he tried to get Shula to admit that 1972 was looking like a season made in heaven. "You got Briscoe for a draft pick. Then you have Mercury healthy and you finally get the three-man backfield. Even bad news turns out to be good: Heinz and Riley get hurt, which brings on Den Herder and makes you remember Matheson used to be a defensive end, which brings on a whole new defense. Then Langer, a guy off the specialty teams, turns out to be one of the best centers in the league. It's even reached the point where you go for it on fourth down at your own twenty-nine, make it, and beat the Vikings. Let's face it, this year you can do no wrong."

"You guys have the easiest jobs in the world," Shula needled him right back. "You always get to celebrate everything before it happens. We're going good, sure, but say the same to me after it's all over." At the time, the Dolphins were only four and oh. But that was after the toughest part of the schedule. Would Shula have been satisfied to be three and one? Braucher wanted to know. Don, just this once, let down his guard and smiled at Bill: "I tend to think in terms of winning 'em all."

The Orange Bowl in 1969, with downtown Miami, Biscayne Bay, and Miami Beach in the distance. "When the offense would drive down to the closed end of the stadium," said Csonka, "we could *feel* the fans screaming—the place vibrated. It felt like a giant heartbeat." (State Archives of Florida)

The same year, the author finds his brother downfield in their new suburban Miami subdivision.

Jane Chastain (L), the nation's first female sportscaster, moved to Miami in 1969. Coach George Wilson, in his last year in Miami, was less amenable than Don Shula would be to a woman sports reporter. But by 1972 Chastain was an accepted and respected presence. She and Anita Bryant (R) were prominent Miami women in the early '70s who would later espouse right-wing values. (Tel-Air Interests, Inc.; *Billboard* magazine)

But in 1972, Gloria Steinem (L) and the National Organization for Women came to town for the Democratic National Convention. And Shirley Chisholm (R), the first Black woman in the U.S. Congress and the first woman to run for the Democratic Party's nomination for president, addressed the Convention in Miami Beach. (Library of Congress; Thomas J. O'Halloran/Library of Congress)

South Beach in the 1970s was a far cry from the hip, hedonistic saturnalia it would become. This Andy Sweet photo of old South Beach perfectly illustrates the author's memory of retirees whiling away their days between Ocean Drive and the beach. (Andy Sweet Photo Archive)

South Beach at the beginning of the '70s: a small, eroded beach for families to enjoy. The beach ended at the historic, but even then run-down, White House Hotel. ("Coffee Shop: Bathers Welcome.") The building and pier are long gone now.

Butch (Jim Kiick, L) and Sundance (Larry Csonka, R) were everywhere in South Florida in '72: out on the town, at charity events, and of course in the Dolphin backfield, where they were inseparable since 1968. Until 1972, that is. (Roy Erickson, State Archives of Florida)

Mercurial: Morris thrilled like no other runner. In 1972 he finally took his place in the backfield alongside Kiick and Csonka. (Vernon Biever/AP)

The three-back offense (L to R): Kiick, Csonka, and Morris. "Sometimes," said Morris, "I would sit right in between them on the bench, just to let them know that this is how we're gonna roll here." In fact, the three got along well, and Kiick and Morris put aside their personal ambitions to "make one great running back together" and complement future Hall of Famer Csonka. (Tony Tomsic/AP)

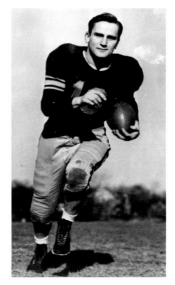

ABOVE LEFT: Richard Nixon warming the bench for Whittier College, 1933. (Rue des Archives/GRANGER)

ABOVE RIGHT: Don Shula starring for John Carroll U, 1950. As president, Nixon saw something of himself in Shula and several times wrote or called him. (John Carroll University)

President Nixon and best friend Bebe Rebozo, a Miami businessman, at a Dolphins game. Nixon was the first president who was a bona fide sports fan, and he screamed at the TV as much as any other Redskins fan. (HistoryMiami Museum)

Vietnam Vets Against the War, including Ron Kovic (with flag), march to Republican National Convention headquarters at the Fontainebleau Hotel in August 1972. At the hotel, Kovic read a letter to President Nixon pleading for an end to the "insanity" of the war. (Tony Schweikle, State Archives of Florida)

A team of opposites: introvert Bob Griese (L) clowning around with extrovert Nick Buoniconti. The Italian American from Massachusetts led his defense as brilliantly as the midwesterner Griese ran the offense. (AP)

Foreground, L to R: Dick Anderson, Curtis Johnson, and Tim Foley present a variety of styles on the first day of Don Shula's "boot camp." All three were pillars of the No-Name Defense. (Jim Kerlin/AP)

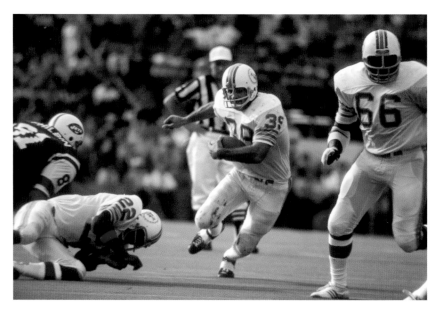

Csonka, "like a hussar on a rampage," with the great Larry Little leading the way. As usual, blood has dripped from Csonka's broken nose to his uniform. (Tony Tomsic – USA TODAY NETWORK)

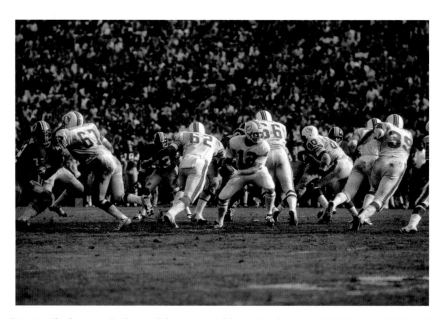

"Best in the business": three of the Expendables—Kuechenberg (67), Langer (62), and Little (66)—plus Marv Fleming (80) form an incomparable escort for an incomparable running attack. (Dick Raphael – USA TODAY NETWORK)

A sideline symposium: professors of strategic football Griese and Warfield confer. Laconic, systematic, and assiduous, the two All-Pros were a brilliant passing combination on a team that ran the ball 70 percent of the time. (Malcolm Emmons – USA TODAY NETWORK)

One of the most elegant athletes ever, in any sport, Paul Warfield combined world-class speed with a gymnast's body control and an artist's hands. "He personifies class," said one teammate. "He's like satin," said another. "He was such a force for us. When he was on that field, everyone was afraid of him." Warfield leaps above Jack Tatum to put the scare into the Oakland crowd in the 1974 playoffs. (Walter Iooss)

Howard Twilley—tough, clutch, invaluable—does his best Willem
Dafoe while waiting for his moment. (Malcolm Emmons – USA
TODAY NETWORK)

Garo Yepremian, an Armenian immigrant from Cyprus, was the most unlikely
Dolphin hero, but he was the best kicker in football. (David Durochik/AP)

"Sock it to me!" Connecting with the times on the '72 campaign trail: while Spiro Agnew is off stumping at an Osmond Brothers concert, President Nixon clowns around with Sammy Davis Jr. at a "Young Voters Rally" at the Miami Marine Stadium. (AP)

ABOVE LEFT: Nixon was less popular with protesters at the Republican National Convention. (John Charles Buckley, State Archives of Florida)

ABOVE RIGHT: After he took over for the injured Griese, thirty-eight-year-old Earl Morrall was given a rocking chair for his locker. Over the next couple years various other old-folks items were added. (AP/*Miami Herald*)

In the play that turned around the AFC championship game, punter Larry Seiple took off on a fake punt and found himself chasing the Steelers downfield. "I think Coach Shula had told me at some point, 'You can do it—as long as you make it.'" (*Miami Herald*/McClatchy)

Shula went into Super Bowl VII with the enviable task of having to choose between two great quarterbacks. (Mark Foley/AP)

More No-Names (L to R): Swift, Buoniconti, and Fernandez. The Miami defense stopped Washington cold in the Super Bowl, and Manny Fernandez had a masterful performance. (Dick Raphael – USA TODAY NETWORK)

The MVP award however, went to Jake Scott for his two interceptions. Smart, brilliantly athletic, mutton-chopped, and "dead eyes": Scott in '72. (AP)

In the Super Bowl, Yepremian had had visions of throwing a glorious pass, but it didn't quite work out that way, as Morrall tried desperately to block. The fiasco following a blocked field goal precluded a perfect 17–0 score. (AP)

Final redemption: Shula about to be hoisted by Buoniconti and Al Jenkins (Morrall on left, Joe Robbie on right). (AP)

Bedlam in the Coliseum, and "THE DOLPHINS ARE 'SUPER'" on the scoreboard. (Long Photography – USA TODAY NETWORK)

The scene awaiting the Dolphins at the Eastern Airlines parking lot: 17–0 says it all. (AP)

ABOVE LEFT: The author (R) and his brother celebrated 17–0 the next weekend with some football at Fairchild Tropical Garden.

ABOVE RIGHT: In 2010 the Dolphins memorialized Shula's greatest moment with a statue outside the team's new stadium. (NT1952/Wikimedia Commons/Public Domain)

Forty years after 17–0, the Perfect Team finally made it to the White House. In front with President Obama, in their yellow Hall of Fame jackets: Buoniconti, Little, Griese, Warfield, Csonka, and Shula. Obama is gesturing at Shula after joking how it was Shula's '85 team that handed Obama's favorite team, the Bears, their only loss. (Official White House Photo by Pete Souza)

Ten and Oh

The day after the New England game, Joe Robbie threw a press luncheon for Shula at the Miami Lakes Country Club to celebrate win number one hundred. He presented his coach with a garish trophy he'd had made, featuring the game ball on a stand with a golden "100" on top, and he read to the press a telegram Shula had received from just over the bay:

> Heartiest congratulations for victory No. 100. You have done something no other coach in professional football has ever accomplished—100 victories in your first 10 years—and the Dolphins' record this season is nothing less than sensational. This new milestone is convincing proof of your superior coaching ability, and, therefore, I will do my very best to resist suggesting any more plays should you get through the playoffs and into the Super Bowl again.
>
> With kindest personal regards,
> Richard Nixon

As the chairman of the Dade County Democratic Committee and a friend of fellow South Dakotan George McGovern, Robbie might have had mixed feelings reading Nixon's congratulations. But he, like his team, "[didn't] let politics mix with business," as he said in his introduction. As for Shula, who admitted privately that he had voted for Nixon, he was clearly pleased with the recognition and the telegram.

Nixon was certainly enjoying following his two favorite coaches, Shula and George Allen, who were 9–0 and 8–1, as they led their own juggernaut campaigns. As he relaxed on Key Biscayne, though, even while basking in the afterglow of his landslide reelection, he remained occupied with more consequential matters. This Watergate thing, although it had failed to gain enough traction to throw his campaign off course, showed no sign of going away. And the breakdown in talks with North Vietnam meant he wasn't out of that morass yet either. Resolved to continue bombing the hell out of Hanoi until they came to an agreement, he ordered some of the most intensive air attacks of the war.

At home, with the election over and most American troops either home or on their way, public rage against the onslaught seemed to subside. People, at least in Miami, were talking more about hijackings. In the latest escapade, three desperados armed with rifles, handguns, and grenades had apprehended a Southern Airways DC-9 on Friday en route from Birmingham to Miami. A thirty-hour odyssey took them all over North America; finally, after circling over the Florida Keys and demanding to speak with President Nixon, they landed in Havana, where they were arrested by Cuban police. The public was used to stories like this by now. Throughout Dolphins training camp that summer, fans would skim through the hijacking stories on their way to the sports page.

As the demoralized Patriots flew out of Miami International Airport on Sunday night, landing there were the thirty-one survivors of the Southern Airways hijacking after their terrifying three-day international odyssey. Editorials railed against the lack of a coordinated screening system in the nation's airports. Many airports had none at all, and in others the security varied greatly from terminal to terminal. In Houston recently, three men had simply walked up to the gate without tickets, shot an Eastern Airlines attendant, and boarded the plane. In Miami that week, Pan Am installed MIA's first baggage X-ray machine to check for weapons in carry-on bags. The onus was on individual airlines, with the FAA and airport operators "urging" the carriers to screen passengers and inspect luggage. And MIA announced that for the first time badges would be required to restrict access to ramps and other operational areas.

A couple hundred miles north, at Cape Kennedy—the former and future Cape Canaveral, to which the Florida Legislature would restore its old name the next year—the three astronauts of the *Apollo 17* mission began their three-week medical isolation before their scheduled December 5 launch. Theirs would be the final Apollo flight, the last time humans would walk on the moon for at least fifty years. On Miami Beach, a longtime favorite, Jackie Gleason, made his return to the public eye as cohost of *The Mike Douglas Show*, taping a few special episodes down south. Gleason had not been seen on screen or film since *The Jackie Gleason Show* taped its last show in 1970, and he got a rise out of the sold-out crowd at the Miami Beach Auditorium with his old trademark sign-off: "Miami Beach audiences are the greatest in the world!"

A younger crowd was over at Pirates World, the theme park and concert venue in Dania, between Miami and Fort Lauderdale, where rising star David Bowie appeared on his Ziggy Stardust Tour Friday night. More conventional rock fans were relieved to read that they had at least four more years to see the Rolling Stones. Twenty-nine-year-old Mick Jagger announced in an interview that although he would "definitely retire at thirty-three," the band would be busy until then.

The more immediate concern in South Florida was playoff tickets. A win over the Jets that Sunday would clinch the division title, and it was by now a virtual certainty that the Dolphins would be hosting at least one playoff game. Last year, fans desperate to attend the team's first-ever home playoff game—the AFC championship game against the Colts—had waited in line for hours in the oppressive sun, some even camping out overnight. This year there might be no opportunity for tickets at all. With seventy thousand season-ticket holders now, and the remaining ten thousand seats earmarked for the opponent's fans, along with officials, players' families, and the press, there might be nothing left.

Sunday, November 19, Namath and the Jets were in town for what some fans were overexuberantly calling the "game of the century." By noon, an hour before the game, the grassy parking lots around the stadium were full, and thousands of people were milling about in the eighty-degree sunshine, eating their tailgate lunches, listening to WIOD's pregame show on the radio, looking for tickets. On an adjacent field the Miami Carol City High School marching band was practicing for their halftime show. Many people were circling the area, holding up banners and signs. Some of them were members of the United Farm Workers, the national union headed by Cesar Chavez. Chavez was in town that week to organize a strike by migrant sugarcane workers, and he'd spoken at a rally the day before at Bayfront Park. Southern Dade County was filled with tomato fields stretching from North Kendall Drive, just past where we lived, all the way down to Homestead, where Chavez was planning to open a UFW office to serve the more than eight thousand farmworkers in the area. The tomato workers were threatening to strike, as local farmers, who had promised a rise in wages per bucket from twenty to twenty-five cents, had reneged. The farmers claimed that a drop in market prices threatened them with heavy losses. The striking workers at the Orange Bowl that day were handing out printed team lineups for the game asking for support: "Think It's Tough Down on *That* Turf?"

Most of the other signs bouncing around the perimeter of the stadium were concerned with getting inside: NEED THREE TICKETS BADLY and the like. One man carried on his shoulders his little boy, dressed as a hobo, with a sign imploring PLEASE SELL MY DADDY TWO TICKETS. Two young women in hot pants took turns holding their sign: GET US TWO TICKETS AND YOU WON'T BE SORRY. But with Namath in town, no one was giving up their tickets. Even the scalpers had scant offerings. Over at gate ten, a group of thirty young men stormed the turnstiles, but the metal mesh screens had been pulled down low enough to make even paying patrons bend over to get through. A security guard just smiled: "Anyone that tries to jump over is going to bust his damn head."

Things were no more peaceful inside the Orange Bowl as one p.m. arrived. Even as a local minister delivered the usual invocation, asking blessings on both teams, one Jets fan down from New York vocalized the thoughts of many: "What is this, a religious service? Let's go!" ("The Dolphin hierarchy alone among the twenty-six NFL teams," wrote Braucher, "is so dedicated to pregame evangelism." Doug Swift, down on the sideline, was thinking how "the bullshit before the game is ridiculous. You're ready to go, and then you have to go through that bullshit. There's no need for those prayers, those invocations. It depresses me." If it had to be, he said, "I'd rather have a rabbi any day. They get to the point. 'God, bless this field, amen.' That's enough.") Various pockets of Jets fans, either snowbirds or transplanted New Yorkers, began chanting, "Go, go, Broadway Joe!" and were of course drowned out by the home crowd.

Finally the game began, one of the most ferocious of the year. The *Herald*'s Jay Maeder must have had *Death in the Afternoon* sticking out of his back pocket as he tapped on his portable Olivetti: "It was a fine murderous Sunday afternoon in the Orange Bowl and the crowd was feeling good and it was doing a lot of Zum-Zums and applauding many things." There were no bulls to slaughter, but there was Larry Csonka knocking Steve Tannen out of the game with his typical battle-ax forearm. "Hah!" shouted a security guard in the stands. "When Csonka hits 'em they stay hit!" The crowd roared as two teammates helped Tannen off the field. He returned later, but by the end of the game Csonka had removed three more Jets from the field: he bludgeoned safety Gus Hollomon unconscious, he bruised safety Chris Farasopoulos's kidney, and he gave linebacker Bill Zapalac a thigh contusion. "I weigh two thirty-five," Csonka explained matter-of-factly. "A defensive back weighs one ninety-five or two hundred. I'm building my momentum, and when he tackles me he's going to get it." Not that he enjoyed that: "I don't like getting hurt, and I don't like to hurt anyone else, either. The thought of it, in fact, makes me a little sick."

The animosity began even before kickoff, as the team captains met at midfield. Each shook the hands of the opponents—except for Joe Namath, who refused to even look at Earl Morrall. Earlier in the week, Morrall had been answering questions about Namath and let on that he was not an admirer of Broadway Joe's playboy lifestyle: "I wouldn't want my son to grow up to be like Namath." But Namath may have incited the ill will a few years earlier, in the run-up to Super Bowl III. When asked how he felt about going up against the NFL's MVP quarterback, Namath had smugly replied that the AFL had three or four quarterbacks better than Morrall. Today, snubbed at midfield, Morrall just laughed it off.

The defense had a lot more respect for Namath, still considered one of the best quarterbacks in the game despite ailing knees. They felt that against him they couldn't play receivers loosely at all. "Not against Joe," said Nick Buoniconti. "You're looking at him and you're maybe a couple yards off your man. Then wham! The ball is there before you can get to it." Today, though, Dick Anderson got the best of Namath on his very first pass of the day, stepping in front of the receiver to intercept and give Miami the ball on the Jets thirty-three. A few plays later, there was Howard Twilley once again beating poor Steve Tannen on a post to the middle—it seemed he was always just a bit ahead of Tannen—taking Morrall's pass as he knifed through the end zone, bobbling it, and covering it up as he fell to the turf. Namath came back strong, though, leading a Dolphin-like eighty-yard drive covering fifteen plays and eight minutes, finishing with a John Riggins one-yard plunge for the touchdown. Then, after Mercury Morris's second fumble of the day—the first, on a kickoff return, had been retained by Jim Mandich—New York got the ball in Miami territory, and Namath promptly threw a twenty-nine-yard bullet for a 14–7 lead.

This one wasn't going to be easy. Men were slamming into each other like bighorn rams, the trainers and doctors were busier than anyone, and the score would sweep back and forth until early in the fourth quarter. The teams had already swapped turnovers in the first quarter, and it happened again in the second. The Jets were down to the Miami fifteen-yard line, eighty thousand fans (minus the New York contingent) screaming "Defense!" to try to forestall what threatened to be an ominous deficit, and twice Namath came to the line and then backed away, pleading to the officials that he couldn't be heard. As always, this only made them scream louder. The third time the teams came to the line, Buoniconti stood a little closer to the line, crossed his ankles in his quirky way, glared at Namath, and did some screaming of his own: "Run the fucking play!" *That* Namath could hear. He ran the play. Buoniconti saw it develop, a pass pattern to Riggins over the middle, and cut inside just as the pass was thrown. His broken right wrist had a cast on it, but he threw both arms up like it was a stickup and managed to bobble and then cradle the ball at the Miami six and run it back to the sixteen. A few minutes later, though, Morrall was intercepted himself at midfield, and the safety ran it all the way down to the Miami nine. The defense stopped the Jets cold there, and a field goal made it 17–7 New York. The Dolphins hadn't been down ten points since the Minnesota game, and they wouldn't be again all year.

It didn't last long. Morrall promptly led them on an eighty-yard drive of their own, featuring a beautiful forty-four-yard bomb to Twilley, who got open deep down the sideline and caught it before being pushed out of bounds at the one-yard line. A couple plays later, just before halftime, Morris followed Norm Evans across the goal line, and it was 17–14. Twilley always seemed to shine against the Jets—and Tannen—and it was necessary today, as Warfield was sitting out with a sprained ankle he'd suffered against New England.

When the players came back out onto the hot turf, as the crowd settled back into their seats and the marching band filed off to their spot behind the end zone, the Dolphins to a man had some new determination. Larry Csonka and Dick Anderson were riling up the fans closest to them with their usual routine: jumping up and down and then ramming into each other, slamming their shoulder pads together to get psyched up and prepare each other for the maelstrom they were about to reenter. Mercury Morris did some stutter steps, testing his ankle, vowing to improve on his first half. With Kiick nursing his swollen left knee, Morris had a rare chance to play every down. "At halftime, I just felt I had things to do," he said. "I had dropped a couple, and if a disaster happened—you know, if we lost—well, you can imagine how I'd feel."

On Miami's first possession, they moved thirty-four yards in five plays, and then, from the New York thirty-one-yard line, Earl Morrall provided an unexpected highlight. Fading back to pass, he saw his receivers all covered and a swatch of open green to his left. So he did the last thing he wanted to do, and certainly the last thing Don Shula or any of the million watching Dolfans wanted: he took off running. Morris was down near the goal line on a pass pattern, and all he could think was: *Please don't get hurt, old man.* "That run must have taken thirty-five or forty seconds," he said. "I felt like I was watching it forever." Viewing the film that week, Morrall's teammates laughed and pointed out (falsely) a cheerleader running down the sideline faster than him. "Old Crazy-Legs Earl," Kuechenberg called him. In fact, though, for thirty-eight Morrall looked pretty good chugging it all the way down to the left corner, where he put a little fake on the cornerback and rolled into the end zone, popped up, and flipped a nonchalant underhand spiral to the ref. No biggie. "I think I ran about twenty-five yards for Detroit against Minnesota about ten years ago," he said afterward. Then he got in the spirit of the jiving: "Was it planned? Are you kidding? I'm a ten-second man in the forty-yard dash. I'm so slow the coaches are embarrassed to tell me my time." No matter: his thirty-one-yard run was the longest touchdown run for the Dolphins all year, in distance as well as time elapsed.

It put Miami ahead again at last, 21–17, and a familiar atmosphere of inevitable victory settled over the Orange Bowl. But there came Namath again, reviving his glory days, leading an eighty-yard drive featuring a perfect forty-one-yard bomb to Maynard, a seventeen-yarder to Riggins, and a nifty three-yard pass to put the Jets back on top, 24–21, with four minutes left in the third quarter. So much for the inevitable. However, the defense decided that was enough for Broadway Joe today. Buoniconti crossed his feet and screamed and began to anticipate every move, and Manny Fernandez performed his usual zombie act. Once again unable to practice all week, with a painfully aching back and a pulled hamstring from the New England game, Fernandez rose from the half dead and pounded the line all day. The Jets offense was smothered the rest of the second half. They rushed for only twenty-nine yards, and Namath was ineffective. And after Yepremian missed a chance to tie the game, pushing a forty-two-yarder left, Dick Anderson was in the right place at the right time yet again. Running back Cliff McClain fumbled on his own twenty-seven, and Anderson managed to beat a mass of bodies to the ball and secure it. "I just happened to be there," he said later, but he seemed to be there so often, usually running with such fumbled balls like a halfback. Today he just fell on it, but it was enough. A few plays later, Morris took a handoff from the fourteen, leaped over a blitzing linebacker, and cut a switchback against the grain, working his stutter-step dance before putting his head down and shouldering right through the cornerback on the goal line. It was 28–24 Miami, and New York never got close to scoring again. Morris had matched his halftime resolve and finished with 107 yards and two touchdowns to lead the team. Miami, after only 57 yards rushing in the first half, finished with 220 as they dominated the second half.

The game ball, though, went to Dick Anderson, who not only had an interception and a critical fumble recovery but also stepped in as punter. When Larry Seiple came in to punt with three minutes left, it looked as if Namath would get one more chance with a reasonable amount of time. But two Jets rookies ran into Seiple after he kicked, giving Miami a first down and in the process tearing ligaments in Seiple's knee. He was wheeled off to the locker room, and when the Dolphins had to punt again three plays later, Anderson, who had been Colorado's regular punter as well as defensive back all through his college career, came in and calmly lobbed a perfect thirty-six-yarder down to the nine-yard line. Now Namath had too far to go with only a minute and a half left and no time-outs, and the clock ran out after three short plays.

The pinch-hit punt was the coup de théâtre today, but Dick Anderson, along with his battery mate Jake Scott, had been the brilliantly unbreakable backbone of the Miami defense since 1970. They were best friends off the field as well, often vacationing together, even though they appeared at first glance to be polar opposites. Scott was the wild man from Georgia, his thick mustache grown audaciously back into his bushy sideburns, prodigiously athletic and smart, but a partier, a bar brawler, a girl chaser. Anderson was clean-shaven in those days—he later always had a well-trimmed mustache—and liked to spend his free time making money rather than making time. Of all the intelligent and motivated Dolphins who would do as well in business as they had on the field, Anderson was the consummate businessman. While Scott sped between Miami's bars and nightclubs in a red Corvette, Anderson drove his yellow Maverick to business meetings.

He arrived at practice each day with a briefcase and could often be found at the locker room's pay phone. Even during the season, he was running a company that sold insurance to banks and financial institutions and was also licensed to sell stocks and real estate. When he got a hard time for using the pay phone too much, he had a cellular phone—one of the earliest available incarnations—installed in his car. At lunch, while his teammates were recovering in the cafeteria, Anderson went out to his Maverick and opened the trunk, where the phone was housed in a big box. He'd push a button and wait until a green light told him he had a signal, then he would dial his various customers or associates. "In those days you needed another job if you wanted to get ahead," he said (although his Dolphins salary was $38,000 that year, about $250,000 in today's currency). "Shula was always yelling at me to get off my phone."

Joe Thomas had drafted Anderson in the third round out of Colorado, his hometown school, where he was a football and academic all-American. Anderson was another of those Dolphins who were supposedly not fast enough, but Thomas liked what he heard from Anderson's college coach: "Do not bet with this kid at anything: not at golf, not at jacks, not at pitching pennies. He is a player." Of all the mentally tough Dolphins who could be counted on to make the big play in the clutch, none were better money players than Scott and Anderson, who are still the top two Dolphins ever in interceptions. Many years later Don Shula said, "I don't think there has been a better safety combination in football than Scott and Anderson."

Jake Scott grew up in Athens, Georgia, and eventually came back home to the University of Georgia after going to high school in Arlington, Virginia. (He'd moved there with his mother, a psychiatrist, after she and his father divorced.) He was a star player in high school and got mostly As until he skipped most of his senior-year classes to hang out in pool halls. This led him to win the Washington, D.C., junior championship in pool but also prevented him from graduating. So he spent a year at a U.S. Naval Academy prep school, applied himself, and did so well that he received a bushel of scholarship offers. He went back to Athens, and although he played only two years, he is still Georgia's all-time leader in interceptions and interception-return yards. Longtime Bulldogs coach Vince Dooley later claimed that Scott was the greatest athlete he had ever coached—this despite the fact that Scott was so incensed at Dooley for breaking some promises to both Scott and his team that, when he was offered a contract by British Columbia of the Canadian Football League after his junior year, he left college and drove a brand-new Corvette to Canada. A year later, Joe Thomas paid $10,000 to the Montreal Alouettes, where Scott had been traded, and Scott took a $10,000 pay cut to come to Miami and play in the NFL.

In Miami he rejoined his college teammate Bill Stanfill, who complained, "I would have had a peaceful college education if it ain't for Jake. He carried me around for insurance—in case he started trouble, I'd finish it." Scott certainly would have disputed this account; he needed no insurance. It didn't matter that he was only six feet tall and 188 pounds. "Dead man's eyes" is how one teammate described him in saloon confrontations. When it was time for rookie hazing in 1970, no one even dared ask this twenty-five-year-old "rookie" to sing his college fight song: "He's the one guy no one messed with," said Manny Fernandez. Scott played the entire Perfect Season, including his MVP Super Bowl performance, with his right arm in a cast, and he was known to have used it for good effect in at least one barroom skirmish.

He'd played Super Bowl VI against Dallas with both hands broken, though he didn't know it. The left one was already in a protective cast after he smashed it on a Chief's helmet early in the first playoff game. Then he broke the right wrist early in the Super Bowl and just ignored it. Back in Miami, a surgeon put five screws in his left hand but decided to see if the right wrist would heal on its own and just put it in a cast. With both hands encased for a couple months, he said, "Now I find out who my real friends are—when I go to the bathroom." Perhaps with that in mind, he flew off to Colorado to visit Anderson. They hit the slopes, Anderson a lifelong expert and Scott a newbie with socks over his casts, green baggies over the socks, and of course no poles. "As long as you don't fall down, it's not too bad," he said. The two friends also invested their Super Bowl runner-up money in some Colorado real estate, including a 130-acre ranch between Aspen and Vail where, when not skiing, they could hunt, fish, and ride horses. By the time training camp began, Scott was told he would need surgery on the right wrist, too, but it was too late if he wanted to play in '72. So he just kept the cast on and had another Pro Bowl season. Yes, Jake Scott was tough, maybe the toughest on the team. But Dick Anderson said Scott was also the smartest player he had ever played with, never mind the lawyer at middle linebacker, the future anesthesiologist on the outside, and the guy up front who passed up veterinary school to chase quarterbacks.

Like Buoniconti, Scott had a vocal rivalry going with Joe Namath—as when Scott would fake Namath out with positioning and elicit a blue-streaked tirade from the quarterback. But it was friendly enough: Namath would sometimes join Scott in the bars when their schedules put them in the same town, and he was as impressed with Jake there as on the field. On a wager, Scott had once downed forty-three beers in one sitting. (Turns out it was unwise to bet against *either* Dolphin safety.) Observing the adulation Scott was receiving at one Miami nightspot, Namath shook his head: "And I thought I had women in New York. . . ."

Although they worked together in the defensive backfield for five years like one ingenious mechanism, and they vacationed and invested together, Anderson and Scott led very different lives. After practice on a Friday, Anderson would head home to his wife and two young boys, one and three years old. Scott would go out on the town with Jim Mandich or Manny Fernandez or any of the other young, single guys with an itch for the nightlife. In the fall of '72 Scott often found himself beginning his evening at Flagler Dog Track, a greyhound-racing venue since 1938, just a few blocks south of the airport. Greyhound racing would be all but banned in the next century, as opponents derided the cruelty the dogs were subjected to. But the 1970s were right in the peak of the dog-racing era, when Americans bet billions of dollars a year on greyhounds, and the "sport of queens" was ranked the nation's sixth most popular sporting activity. Joe DiMaggio, Burt Reynolds, and other celebrities were often spotted at Florida tracks, and a climactic scene in the Frank Sinatra movie *A Hole in the Head* was filmed at Flagler. In 1972 Jake Scott was often there to watch and bet on his namesake, the hottest greyhound of the season. Jake Scott the dog had won three straight, and Jake Scott the Dolphin was at the cashier's gate after each one, collecting. "He win it on class with a great stretch run," he said after one victory, in his best Damon Runyon vernacular. "They tell me he's the best of his litter. He's faster than Mercury M., that's for sure," referring to another Dolphin-named greyhound just as his teammate Morris walked by.

Flagler's location was convenient. One Saturday, Jake had been able to shoot down from practice in his Corvette to watch dog Jake win him some cash and then scoot over to the airport to barely catch the team flight to Buffalo (where he intercept and cause a crucial fumble on class). And when Friday evening races were over he found himself two blocks from Mike's Lounge, where he'd go meet Jim and Manny. The bars near the airport were "fertile hunting grounds," recalled one player. "More damn stewardesses living around there than you could shake a stick at." Mike's, at Le Jeune and Sixth, was a favorite Dolphin hangout. A four-foot-high blow-up of the team logo, signed by a bunch of players, sat propped up permanently on a corner table. One wall sported a painted mural of Csonka and other players in action. The owner, original season-ticket holder Mike McCune, estimated that another 175 or so season-ticket holders called his bar home on Sunday afternoons when the team was away. Other Sunday nights they would often see their heroes drinking right down the bar from them. Sometimes, said Buoniconti, there might be thirty-five players, plus wives and girlfriends, packed in there.

This was probably an exaggeration, for it was mainly the white players who hung out at Mike's. The efforts of Shula (and Fleming and Morris) to integrate the team were applied in the locker room, in training camp, and on the road. But this was still the early 1970s in Miami, and when practice or the game was over, as Eddie Jenkins said, "the white guys would go to Lum's and have burgers and beer, the Black guys would go to Prince Bar-B-Que on Twenty-Seventh Avenue. And from there to the Jet-A-Way." In 1972 the Jet-A-Way was perhaps the biggest nightclub in Black Miami. From the forties through the sixties, Miami had been a major hotspot for Black musicians, especially of course in the winter. As Paula Park wrote, "Performers like Lionel Hampton, Count Basie, and Sammy Davis Jr., were welcome to play the grand ballrooms of Miami Beach's hotels, but they had to sleep in Overtown hotels like the Sir John and the Mary Elizabeth. After playing for whites in the evening, they'd jam into the wee hours at Overtown and Liberty City clubs that charged black patrons rock-bottom prices."

In 1956, Cab Calloway moved down from the Cotton Club in Harlem and became the featured attraction at Miami's own Cotton Club just over the Venetian Way on Miami Beach. Back on the mainland, a host of Black clubs opened up: the Bottlecap, the Galaxy, Rockland Palace, Soul Place—and the

Jet-A-Way on Thirty-Sixth Street, on the southwest corner of Liberty City. While campaigning during the primaries, Shirley Chisholm, after speaking at Miami-Dade Junior College, made sure to put in an appearance at the Jet-A-Way, "shimmying and shaking in what one of her advisors called the 'Shirley Chisholm Penguin,' a modified boogaloo, before sitting down with her aides for a meal of fried chicken and souse (pickled pig ears, feet, and head). The crowd of two hundred loved it."

Jenkins loved it too. At Holy Cross he'd covered his dorm room with album covers by jazz singer Nancy Wilson. At the Jet-A-Way he got his first look at Betty Wright. Wright grew up in Miami in a musical family and began recording at the age of twelve. She gained local fame in the 1960s for her records and her performances in the Black clubs, and she burst onto the national scene with her hit song "Clean Up Woman" in 1971, when she was eighteen. In 1972 she was still playing a lot at the Jet-A-Way, often with her brother Milton. Jenkins was often there in the company of Larry Little, who, as Jenkins put it, "would hold court" there.

"Yeah, I was the Jet-A-Way king," Little admitted. He'd grown up on Nineteenth Street in Overtown, the son of a maid and a custodian. Now he had a $255-a-month, two-bedroom bachelor pad at the newly built Country Club Gardens ("Florida Living at Its Best: wall-to-wall shag carpeting, drapes, dishwashers, garbage disposal, rec building, sauna, tennis courts, 3 pools, overlooking beautiful Doral Country Club"). Marlin Briscoe and several other players lived right next door, at the Leisure Lakes apartments. Briscoe, a tennis enthusiast, enjoyed the proximity to the courts at Doral, where he met honorary head pro Arthur Ashe and sometimes had a lesson with him. On weekend nights, though, Larry Little led the way back downtown to the Jet-A-Way. "I was there with Marlin most of the time," he remembered, "or by myself so nobody would be keeping me from what I wanted to do. Eddie [Jenkins] was a young pup, but I let him tag along sometimes." Certainly no one enjoyed—or consumed more of—the house specialty than "Chicken" Little. (He got the nickname while playing for San Diego when one night he ate an entire chicken. Even under Shula's enforced diet, the moniker stuck.)

The Jet-A-Way was only three miles but a world away from Mike's Lounge. Both were a stone's throw from the airport, but otherwise they might as well have been in different cities. Not all nightspots were segregated, of course.

Marv Fleming's favorite late-night hangout was the Forge, a Miami Beach restaurant featuring delicacies such as baked Belgian escargot and its own nightclub, Alfred's Lounge. Fleming had been the most prominently featured of *Ebony* magazine's "Eligible Bachelors for 1970" just before arriving in Miami. Six-foot-four, 235 pounds, he had a surprisingly soft tenor voice that belied the image of a brutal-blocking NFL tight end. "Because I don't come across as a manly stud, people assume I'm gay," said Fleming when asked in a 1993 interview. "I'm for gay rights. I have many gay friends. But, no, I'm not gay." "Ah, er, Fleming, interesting fellow," stammered Packers great Max McGee when asked about the trade sending Fleming to Miami. For his part, Fleming was one of the few who were thrilled to be traded to Miami. "I was very lonely in Green Bay," he said, "and Miami, with its influential people, is my kind of place to live." Fleming felt at home at the Forge, a mostly white restaurant that had served Shirley MacLaine, Hubert Humphrey, and Walter Cronkite during the Democratic Convention and John Wayne and Henry Cabot Lodge Jr. during the Republican. But for the most part, the Dolphins, as harmonious a racially mixed group as you could find in America, went their separate ways at night.

As they dispersed to salve their wounds from the warlike encounter with the New York Jets, the white players may have been heading to Mike's again. "Mandich and I would take off for Mike's Lounge before the reporters even got in the locker room," Jake Scott recalled. "Going through the parking lot everybody would be handing you a beer, especially when you won." Later they would drive a little farther west. After most games that year, Scott and Mandich rented out the entire Pine Tree Bar, a nondescript watering hole out on Southwest Sixty-Second Avenue and Eighth Street. "It was just a neighborhood shot bar," wrote Hyde, "but some Sundays it seemed like all Miami showed up, the party spilling into the street. At the end of the night, they'd give the owner $500, with other players chipping in a fair share, and everyone would stumble off into the morning. . . ." In nearby Miami Springs, on the north border of the airport, one of the many municipalities making up Greater Miami, the cops were used to coming upon waterlogged Dolphins in the predawn hours. "Not you again, Jim," they'd say to Mandich, before escorting him safely home. One night they pulled over Manny Fernandez and strongly advised him to go home. A bit later they stopped him coming out of another bar, confiscated his car keys, and simply instructed him to pick them up at the station the next day. In Wahoo McDaniel's day, players might have spent the night at the station themselves, but now, in the Super Bowl era, Dolphins were a protected species.

While Jake Scott and others were beginning their night at Mike's, Dick Anderson was in a casual blazer, signing autographs at the Miami Springs Villas. A group of Dolphins wives had organized a fundraising cocktail party, at $25 a head, to raise money for the Kidney Foundation of Dade County. Anderson smiled as he signed a football a twelve-year-old fan held up for him. Some other kids surrounded Norm Evans, who groaned loudly as he lowered his battered body into a chair to sign their scraps of paper. "Semi-murderous," the *New York Times* had called the game. "It was a war, a war," Steve Tannen had said in the locker room, his left arm in a sling. "The roughest game of the year."

Larry Csonka had knocked three Jets out of the game, but he was suffering too. He was holding a towel to his nose to stop the bleeding, trying to remember if it was his ninth or tenth broken nose. On one of his carries, the defender had hit him low and popped him up into the air. "I came straight down like a B-52 and hit right on the top of my helmet. The impact drove the helmet down on the bridge of my nose. It didn't hurt the headgear a bit." Earl Morrall stopped by: "Come on, Larry, you going to the party?" "I'm going home and put ice on my nose. Alcohol gives me a nose bleed." Shula came by and commiserated a bit, saying he had broken his own nose a few times in his playing days. "Well," said Csonka, "the next time I break it you might say something more sympathetic than 'Get back in there!'" Shula laughed with the rest of them. Everyone was feeling happy despite the bruises and breaks. The team was ten and oh and had just clinched the Eastern Division championship with four games left to play. "They'll go undefeated," said Weeb Ewbank in the other locker room. "Who can beat them? I don't see any team left on their schedule who can beat them."

They weren't the only ones feeling satisfied. Dorothy Shula had suffered through fifteen seasons with her husband, sharing both the excitement and the frustrations, while raising three girls and two boys, all between seven and thirteen years old this year. She knew from the very beginning she'd be sharing her husband with football. On their honeymoon, he had her backpedal for him like a quarterback to see what sort of football genes he was mixing his own with. When they first started dating, she'd asked the PE teacher at the school where she taught to explain play designs and terminology to her. Shula still didn't always take her advice, particularly regarding onside kicks. "Every time Garo comes running up to the ball, I scream for it, but Don never listens." She was his fiercest defender, though, both to his bosses—"How can Don get coaching experience if he's always off scouting on game day?" she complained to his head coach at Virginia—and to obnoxious fans. (She even took a swipe at one drunken harasser behind her at the Super Bowl.) It wasn't always easy living with an obsessive football coach. "If there's something you'd argue about," she advised other wives, "save it for after the season." And those heart-wrenching losses, particularly in those two Super Bowls, threw a pallor over the entire household.

That night at home, after Miami beat the Jets for victory number ten, Dorothy Shula took an old souvenir out of a drawer and displayed it prominently in the kitchen. It was an old pewter plate with the inscription, "New York vs. Baltimore, 1969 Super Bowl." Joe Namath's guarantee, his disparaging of Morrall, the humiliation of Shula's Colts. No, Dorothy said, she didn't put the plate there for her husband's benefit. It was for her. "I like to be reminded of a hurt," she told a visitor, "when I've got some of it back."

Eleven and Oh

With ten wins and no losses, the Dolphins entered a new territory, in which there was no way to avoid questions about a perfect season. It's what everyone wanted to talk about at Shula's Monday press session after practice. "It would be nice to have that [a perfect record] to go along with everything else," the coach admitted. "It would be nice later on to look back on a Super Bowl title and an unbeaten year as well. But it's not important enough for us to risk any of our players who need to rest an injury." Then he went on to tell his audience about 1967. Shula and his Colts were unbeaten, with eleven wins and two ties, going into the last game of the year against division rival Los Angeles. In the final game of the regular season, Shula took his soaring Colts out to L.A., where George Allen's Rams knocked them back to earth. Deacon Jones, who later helped break Griese's leg in '72, and his Fearsome Foursome did everything but break Unitas's leg, sacking and intercepting him twice on the way to a 34–10 victory. That put both teams at 11–1–2; Los Angeles went to the playoffs because they'd beaten Baltimore head-to-head, and Shula learned about complacency. "It taught me something about undefeated teams," he now told the Miami press. "We were undefeated right up to the last game, and we lost everything. An experience like that teaches you what is meaningful. Championships are meaningful."

Aside from the 1934 and 1942 Chicago Bears, who each lost their first game of the year in the NFL championship game, San Diego in 1961 and Los Angeles in 1969 had started their seasons 11–0 before losing in the regular season and failing to win a championship. So Shula had little patience at this point with "undefeated" talk. Doug Crusan mentioned to a reporter that his dad, who was in town visiting that week, had asked his son if they would be able to do it. "I tell him we'd like to go seventeen and oh," he said. But in the locker room, he said, everyone was maintaining dugout silence.

• • •

The weather in Miami that week had turned darker and cooler. Highs were only in the seventies, cooler than usual, and the sun barely peaked through the cloud cover; a wet smell was in the air. One sight at Dolphins practice, however, appeared as though in a cone of heavenly light: Bob Griese walking gingerly around the field, unimpeded. On Monday, the day after the Jets game, he finally got the cast off after five weeks. For most of that time he had been at practice every day, riding a golf cart around, parking fifteen yards behind the huddle when the offense was running plays. He still took game films home every night to study, taking notes on what might work the coming Sunday. He still helped form the game plan, and he was there on the sidelines to help call plays in crucial situations. At practice he'd throw from a seated or standing position to keep his arm strong, but that was about it. At the end of the day, he'd watch from his golf cart as the offense ran off one last play. "Everybody up!" Shula would shout, and as the players all huddled around the coach for his final exhortation of the day, Griese whirled the cart about and rumbled off to the locker room.

Now he was walking, but it would still be a few more weeks before he could consider playing football. The bone was fine, but the question was whether the torn ligaments would heal sufficiently. As always, Griese's voice was stoical, all but devoid of emotion when he discussed the situation. "I'm not down about it," he insisted. "It's frustrating, but I've accepted it." Only in a rare instance did his words, if not his expression, betray his feelings. "I've known since training camp where this team is going, and it's not a lot of fun missing out on it. Suppose you had broken both your hands in an accident," he said to his hunting buddy, sportswriter Bill Bondurant. "And you were in the hospital unable to type. While you were in the hospital, your newspaper went on to win an award as the best newspaper in the world. How would you feel?"

Now Griese's cast was gone, but someone else's leg had one. Larry Seiple, the Dolphins' punter since year two, had been roughed up by the Jets and damaged ligaments of his own. Although punter might seem to be the position where injury was least likely to cause panic, Seiple had been a valuable commodity for the team through the years. The distance of his kicks was not spectacular—a solid forty yards on average—but he was something of a master at lofting them high enough to prevent sizable returns. Only nine of his thirty-six punts this year had been returned at all, for an average of six yards. As he liked to point out, if they subtracted the return yardage from the kicking yardage, he'd rank a lot higher in the league. (Of course, a lot of that was due to Shula's special-teams emphasis.)

He also was more than a punter. He described himself, in characteristic Dolphin fashion, as "not a great athlete, never have been," but he had been the superstar running back of his high school team in Allentown, Pennsylvania, and had a solid college career at running back for Kentucky, also catching a lot of balls coming out of the backfield. Shula said of this mediocre athlete: "He's a tight end, running back, you can use him as a defensive back, and I wouldn't be afraid to throw him in at quarterback." His first two years in Miami he only punted, but when tight end Doug Moreau got hurt in 1969, Seiple stepped into a new position and led the team with forty-one catches. He also was a threat when he came in to punt; once or twice a year, when the moment seemed right, he would take off with the ball instead of kicking it, visions of his halfback past flooding his mind. A few times he'd thrown for the first down instead. "I can't stand to sit around and just punt on fourth down," he said during training camp this year. "If I thought I were just a specialist, I'd quit the game." He launched his renegade sneak attacks more under George Wilson—"He never told me to do it and he never told me not to do it"—than with the more autocratic Shula, but, he confided to a reporter, "I'm waiting for a chance to do it again one of these days."

Now it looked as though he may have lost his chance for 1972. He was out at least two weeks, and possibly for the rest of the season, depending on how those ligaments healed. The four remaining regular-season games were meaningless—before 1975, the home field in the playoffs was awarded on a rotating basis between divisions, not according to regular-season records—and Dick Anderson was a reasonable substitute. Back in 1969 he had punted five times for a respectable 37.6-yard average, and this week he had come in against the Jets and laid down a Seipelian unreturnable thirty-six-yarder to seal the game. Still, Shula was already looking around the league Sunday night for a replacement. If Seiple couldn't come back for the playoffs, he wasn't going to risk blowing

their Super Bowl run on a shanked punt. As defensive backs coach Tom Keane
half joked at practice: "Anderson has hit more foul balls than Luke Appling."

Shula found his substitute in Billy Lothridge. Lothridge had been second
in the Heisman Trophy voting in 1963, behind Roger Staubach, as a quarterback
and punter for Georgia Tech, and later was an original Atlanta Falcon, where
he was the NFL's number one punter in 1967 and 1968 and also played safety.
When Seiple got hurt, Lothridge was retired and watching on TV at home in
Marietta, Georgia; three days later he was in Miami, lofting sixty-yard punts
for Shula, admittedly with that cool humid wind behind him.

Seiple wasn't the only casualty of the Jets brawl. Buoniconti was back
in his shoulder wrap, Jake Scott had a sprained neck, and Csonka's nose was
a favorite subject at practice. "Langer and I had a standing bet," recalled Bob
Kuechenberg, "as to which side of Zonk's face his nose would be on at game's
end." This time, though, it wasn't clear who had won. "Did you see Zonk's nose?"
asked trainer Bob Lundy. "It looks like a U-turn." "That's my outstanding statistic, broken noses," said Csonka before doing his best Yogi Berra: "That's all
right, I'll just tape it up and go. A little hurt never hurt anybody." Tell it to Jim
Kiick, who was still limping around practice with his bad knee. He'd consoled
himself this year by figuring his reduced role would at least spare his body some
blows, maybe extend his career. But here he was, gimped up anyway, barely able
to play the last couple weeks.

• • •

Henry Kissinger was back in Paris to negotiate a ceasefire with North Vietnam's
Le Duc Tho. The B-52s continued to swarm over North Vietnamese positions,
raining down their fire, but it seemed to be having little effect on Hanoi's stance.
On Saturday, Kissinger declared a week's recess in negotiations and flew back
to New York to confer with Nixon. The president was in New York for the
weekend after having delivered a monumental announcement on Thursday:
he was following up his historic trip to China earlier in the year by lifting the
twenty-two-year-old ban on commercial travel from the United States to China.

At Cape Kennedy, the *Apollo 17* astronauts were going through their
final preparations before their December 6 launch. Still in quarantine, Gene
Cernan and Harrison "Jack" Schmitt rehearsed their descent to the moon in the
lunar landing module in concert with flight controllers at Mission Control in

Houston. In Miami, *Godspell*, the hit Broadway musical from the year before, based on the Gospel according to Matthew, had made it to the Miami-Dade County Auditorium for a one-week run. And Elton John was making his South Florida debut with a show at the Hollywood Sportatorium, a monstrous concrete block of a venue designed for sports, ice-skating exhibitions, and auto shows that became, for lack of competition, the primary venue for rock concerts in South Florida in the 1970s and 1980s. John lit up the place with impressive Broadway shtick, appearing in white coat and tails, doing his best Fred Astaire in a trench coat, and sporting a purple fluorescent shirt that he ripped off at one point to prance about the stage.

Earl Morrall certainly was not at either *Godspell* or the Elton John show. With his crew cut and conservative clothes, he'd have stood out like a narc. When he'd been signed, Mercury Morris had kidded him, "Where in the world is Earl going to get a flattop in Miami?" But now that Morrall had led the Dolphins to six straight wins in relief of Griese, even he was appearing in the men's fashion ads. A handful of teammates had done newspaper spots for Cruise Casuals, but where Morris appeared ready for *The Mod Squad* in a white suit and psychedelic tie, Kiick was bare-chested over wild bell-bottoms, and Csonka sported bikini underwear, Earl Morrall looked like the insurance salesman cornering you on a day cruise to Bimini in your nightmares. Two-tone shoes, white slacks, and a garishly printed blazer, a gritted smile that betrayed how much he wished he were at his fishing shack in Naples. You can almost hear the "Cheesy-wheesy!" coming off the newsprint. What he wasn't worrying about was whether Griese was coming to take back his job. "I don't even think about that," he said that week in his homey intonation. "That's the story of my life. I've spent seventeen years in the pros being ready for anything that might happen. I just do the best I can and try to keep outside influences to a minimum."

Griese was walking more comfortably each day and starting to throw the ball on the move a bit. He said he hoped to be ready to play by the last game of the season, or maybe even the week before that. As eager as Shula might have been for his starting quarterback to return, it was going to put him in an uncomfortable if familiar situation. In 1968 he'd had to decide whether to reinstate Johnny Unitas for the Super Bowl or stick with Morrall, who had won fifteen of sixteen games. He went with Morrall, and it didn't work out, as Earl had a poor game and the Colts were upset by the Jets. However, Shula was nothing if not stubborn, and the betting line in the press was that he'd go with Morrall unless things turned sour.

At least he had a few more weeks to think about it. That week the Dolphins were home to face the St. Louis Cardinals in their season's only appearance on ABC's groundbreaking national broadcast, *Monday Night Football*. After beating the Vikings and Colts early in the season and looking like a playoff team, the Cardinals had slumped badly, and coming in with a 2–7–1 record they looked unlikely to give the undefeated Dolphins much trouble. The storyline over the weekend, therefore, was all about Howard.

Howard Cosell, the lawyer turned sportscaster whose trademark nasal drawl and smug intellectualism became a nationally famous routine, was at the peak of his career in 1972. The grandson of a Polish rabbi, born Howard Cohen in 1918 in North Carolina, he grew up in Brooklyn and changed his name while at NYU Law School to a closer approximation of his grandparents' old Polish name. (Ironically, and helpfully, it also made him sound less Jewish.) He practiced law for a few years but became more interested in sportscasting when he was asked to host a radio show featuring participants from the Little League, which his firm represented. From there he talked his way into a weekly sports radio show, and by the 1960s he was a well-known figure, anchoring the sports for WABC-TV and taking controversial but ultimately popular stands such as defending Muhammad Ali at the height of the Vietnam War when he refused to be drafted into the military. In 1970, when ABC signed on to broadcast a weekly NFL game on Monday night, the network's own Cosell was the perfect choice to put on the marquee with color commentator Don Meredith, the former Dallas Cowboys quarterback. After one year with Keith Jackson doing play-by-play, ABC brought in Frank Gifford, the old New York Giants star halfback, and the famed trio of Cosell, Meredith, and Gifford was complete.

The show dominated Monday night television from its very first season and single-handedly raised ABC from last to first in the network wars. It was more than just a football broadcast: like some sort of thrilling crime drama, it began with a montage of clips behind the scenes as the crew prepared, a shot of the analog ABC clock reaching nine o'clock, and jazz-fusion theme music. And then there was Cosell, the most mocked, derided TV personality around, and the biggest draw. Cosell was the reason *Monday Night Football* was the top-rated show every Monday night, regardless of who was playing or how close the game was. As a result, he would earn more than $250,000 that year in salary plus appearances. Fans and hecklers hounded him wherever he went. In 1971 he had even had a prominent cameo role in Woody Allen's movie *Bananas*, calling the play-by-play for both a third-world assassination—"He turns . . . and down! It's over. It's all over for El Presidente!"—and the main characters' wedding night: "Mellish begins to make his moves . . . the two are working together closely, the action becoming more rigorous . . . and that's it! It's over!"

As the crew prepared for their broadcast from the Orange Bowl on November 27—only the second *MNF* broadcast from Miami ever—trouble was brewing. One of the features *Monday Night Football* was famous for was its halftime highlights segment, during which Cosell would narrate a selection of plays culled from the best games of the day before. In an era when, aside from the two or three games televised in your area, the only chance to see a couple of plays from other games was during the brief sports segment on the local news, this was a rare chance to see several minutes of NFL highlights. Limited time constrained the producers to select four or five of the twelve games played, but the popularity of the feature led fans to express outsized anger over what they perceived as the systematic exclusion of their teams. In Miami, where Dolfans felt that the meteoric rise in their team's fortunes over the past three years had not been well represented by the *MNF* halftime show, Cosell provided an appropriately obnoxious target for their ire. No matter that Cosell, as he was quick to point out, had nothing to do with the selection of games to be highlighted: as the game approached, the "vile mail," as Cosell put it, increased. What did Howard have against the Dolphins? people wanted to know. Some were threatening: "Better not come to Miami, Howie, you'll not make it home again." (The FBI determined this one was from a young woman who hadn't meant any harm, just wanted to see more Dolphin highlights.) Cosell even called up Edwin Pope and pleaded his case: "Would you *please* tell the people of South Florida that I am not responsible for which highlights are shown at halftime. . . . It's just . . . well, they're so *profane*. And the telegrams. You can't imagine!" Pope did print the entreaty, and Shula did his part, asking the fans to try to understand that it wasn't Howard's fault: "I'd hate for anything out of order to happen here, in front of a national audience."

After a mutually insulting and antagonistic interview Cosell had with sportscaster Joe Croghan on Channel 10, the local ABC affiliate, Cosell received threatening phone calls to his hotel room. On Monday night, he had a police escort into the Orange Bowl, and officers with German shepherds were stationed all around the field during the game. (Some fans braved the dogs and ran on the field anyway, "waving their arms idiotically" as they streaked across the Poly-Turf; ABC according to policy didn't show these scenes.) The fact, however, was that Howard Cosell had great admiration for Don Shula and his team. He particularly admired Csonka, as mentioned before, and Warfield, who he felt, like Ali, "carried himself with great personal dignity and was extremely articulate and thoughtful." And on that night, although he twice referred to the "rabid crowd" (not necessarily in a negative way), he also raved about the defense and the offensive line. Most Miami fans never heard it, because the ABC broadcast was blacked out locally. And off the air, before the game, he professed, "Right now I rate Miami and Washington the best two teams in pro football, one-two, either way. I also think Don Shula could be one of the best three coaches in the game since World War II, along with George Allen and Vince Lombardi. I don't believe Shula will be satisfied with just winning one Super Bowl. He's going to want to keep on and on winning them."

It was unlikely the coach's march into history would be hampered on this cool (mid-sixties) windy Monday night. Three years into the AFL-NFL merger, there were still some teams that had not yet played, and this was the first meeting ever of the Dolphins and Cardinals. The Chicago Cardinals had a couple NFL championships from way back in 1925 and 1947, but since relocating to St. Louis in 1960 they had been consistently mediocre. Although the 1972 squad had four future Hall of Famers on it, injuries had decimated the lineup, and Cosell, Meredith, and Gifford didn't try very hard to hype the competitiveness of the game. They had more fun with oddities such as the fact that the St. Louis starting quarterback, Gary Cuozzo, worked as a dentist in the off-season.

Perhaps Joe Robbie had heard of Doug Swift's complaints about the Christian invocations, because the Dolphins invited Rabbi Irving Lehrman of Temple Emanu-El to do his thing that night, but the rabbi's "Thanksgiving" offering of gratitude to the "Heavenly Father" apparently didn't do much to inspire either team. The first half was a cavalcade of miscues on both sides. Miami's first drive was stalled by a holding penalty, but St. Louis then fumbled, resulting in a short Dolphin drive finished by Jim Kiick pushing his way in for a touchdown. The Cardinals were able to move the ball on a couple of nice drives, but one ended with a missed twenty-seven-yard field goal and the other with a Dick Anderson interception. The most interesting play, historically speaking, was a missed field goal by Garo Yepremian.

He had already been short on a fifty-four-yarder, which cornerback Roger Wehrli had run back from the goal line to the eighteen. (Before 1974, missed field goals resulted in the other team getting the ball on their twenty, regardless of where the kick had been tried from, so it made sense to return short ones like punts.) Then, in the second quarter, Shula sent Yepremian back out to try from fifty-one yards out. This one was blocked, and the ball skittered off to the right, behind the line of scrimmage. Strong safety Larry Wilson was about to grab it, with 230-pound linebacker Larry Stallings ready to flatten anyone trying to get in his way. But the ball took a funny bounce, as footballs will, and Wilson ran right by without being able to touch it. And there it was, right in front of Garo. He should have just fallen down on it, but instead he picked it up and made a mysterious attempt to propel the ball with his right arm. You couldn't really call it a pass; maybe he was trying to shovel it out of bounds. The ball went nowhere, hit someone's back, and fell to the ground, where several Cardinals smothered it.

Kiick later laughed about what he called Garo's lame tryout as a running back. But there was no attempt to run, just to get rid of an object he clearly regretted finding. Yepremian boasted, "I took it easy on them. Why rub it in?"—though the score was only 7–0 at that point. "But, really, I've thought about this thing happening before, and I was trying to get enough room to punt, but I didn't have time." Yepremian in fact was Shula's third option as a punter. After this little fiasco, though, one would think that Shula, with his overwhelming attention to detail, would have Yepremian practicing falling on the ball every day for the next week or more. To his own chagrin, he would not do so until training camp the next year.

Yepremian had been kicking from his own territory. So even though St. Louis now failed to get a first down, they were close enough to try a long field goal of their own. And this time Jim Bakken, who had missed the short one, came right through it with his toe, old-style, and made a forty-nine-yarder, despite Charlie Leigh, positioned back at the goalpost, doing his best to swat it down. The score was 7–3 late in the second quarter, and as Bakken teed the ball up to kick off, Cosell noted, "The Miami crowd has become quiescent." "What?"

Dandy Don Meredith came back. "They're just being quiet, not saying a lot." "Okay," conceded Howard, "we'll put it that way, Danderoo."

Miami managed three more points on a picaresque drive that included a nice Kiick run for ten (Meredith: "Look at ol' Sundance go," referring to Butch); a flea-flicker pass from Briscoe to Stowe for twenty-six; a pass interference call that kept the drive alive; Morrall tripping over his own feet while dropping back ("Well, when you've been in this thing for seventeen seasons, you're bound to fall once in a while"); a sharp pass to Briscoe down to the fifteen; then a sack; and finally a twenty-five-yard Yepremian chip shot. Dandy Don got in some more bon mots on St. Louis's next impotent drive when Cuozzo—Shula's backup for Unitas before Morrall—tripped himself exactly as Morrall had ("Like father, like son, I guess") and then threw a sideline pass nowhere near the receiver ("Well, that wasn't very well thrown even for a dentist").

Quiescent got even quieter, though, when Jake Scott fumbled the ensuing punt inside his own ten-yard line. St. Louis had a chance to tie the unbeaten Dolphins at halftime. But on the very next play they fumbled a handoff, and Bill Stanfill was there to pick it up. So it remained 10–3 at the half, despite Miami having almost double St. Louis's yardage and more than double the time of possession. "Well," said Cosell, coming back from a commercial, "they don't allow signs in the Orange Bowl, but some would defy the edict, as you see before you: a greeting for the unholy triumvirate." HELLO FRANK HOWARD & DANDY FROM HANDY went the poem spray-painted on a bedsheet hung over the orange parapet. ABC chose not to show some other scofflaw banners: WILL ROGERS NEVER MET HOWARD COSELL; DOLFANS CAN'T BELIEVE ABC IS SHOWING THE WHOOOLE THING (after the ubiquitous Alka-Seltzer ad); and ROSES ARE BLUE, VIOLETS ARE RED, NOT ALL DOLFANS WANT TO SEE BAD HOWARD DEAD.

Dolphin players seemed to agree later that despite Shula's best efforts to keep them motivated and the stimulation of playing at night before a national audience, they had come into the game without their usual fire. "You know why we were flat?" said Dick Anderson, who himself had recovered a fumble and intercepted in the first half. "Because the game didn't mean anything." So much for caring about an undefeated season. However, whether it was Shula's halftime talk or simply the thought of flailing on national TV against a losing team, the Dolphins in the second half looked like the league's best team again. "In the second half the offensive line just tore them apart," said Csonka, and he was happy to follow them, piling up the great majority of his 114 yards after the break. He signaled the change of attitude on his first carry, an eighteen-yard wild-bronco charge through the middle, highlighted by his trademark forearm uppercut, on this occasion lifting poor Roger Wehrli a foot into the air and casting him aside like a pesky palm frond.

On the next play Morrall threw deep left, just deep enough for Otto Stowe, who had beat his man by five yards, to turn back to the ball and pull it in while falling on his back in the end zone. Stowe, the number one draft choice out of Iowa State a year earlier, had been watching and learning from Paul Warfield for a year and a half and finally, with Warfield still nursing his sore ankle, had his chance to shine. And he did, finishing the game with six catches for 140 yards and two long touchdowns. One ball had come from the arm of his fellow receiver Briscoe, off a lateral pass from Morrall. Briscoe also had a big night with four catches and was asked about the receiver cornucopia that left him and Stowe on the second team. "Don't ask me," he said, "I've never been on a team that had a *first* team."

The two Stowe touchdowns, sandwiching a nifty twenty-nine-yard dash on an interception return by Lloyd Mumphord, quickly turned a hesitant first half into a second-half affirmation. It was 31–10 halfway through the fourth, and there it stayed. Jim Del Gaizo came in to mop up, and it was mostly second-stringers in except for number thirty-nine. Larry Csonka had ninety-three yards and wanted another century game. Four weeks before, up in Baltimore, Csonka had made the same request, with the same ninety-three-yard total late in the game, and Shula had refused. He just looked at Zonk and said, "They'd cut my head off if I let you go back in now and you got hurt." But with eleven wins now and a division title, he was feeling magnanimous. He told Del Gaizo just why Zonk was in there, and the quarterback sent Csonka straight up the middle three straight times for good measure, even though the first one got him an even hundred. After Csonka finally had had enough, one of the "rabid" young fans Cosell referred to managed to elude the police and the dogs and sprint out onto the field, stole the ball, and did his best to deliver it to Csonka on the sidelines. A security man ran him down, though, and tackled him from behind before he could carry out his mission. Shula was less concerned with the adulator than with his power runner. "I wouldn't have been able to live with myself," he admitted, if Csonka had gotten hurt on one of those last carries.

For most of the second half, the better battle was that waged during the commercials, between Panasonic's "Quatrecolor" television and Zenith's "Super Chromacolor." Quatrecolor was named "to help you remember its four technological advances," including solid-state electronics ("the only tube is the picture tube") and "easy controls" for picture, tint, brightness, and contrast. But Zenith showed "a wide variety of Americans from all over the country" choosing their Super Chromacolor in a test conducted by the Opinion Research Corporation of Princeton, New Jersey. RCA had won the race against CBS to develop color TV in the early 1950s, but manufacturers were still scrambling to claim mastery of this relatively new innovation. The first season of all-color prime-time shows didn't occur until 1966, and this year, 1972, was the first year that most households with televisions had a color set. My family was right in tune with the times: we had watched the Longest Game last Christmas in black-and-white, but this year we got to see all the away games in color.

The St. Louis game, though, was only on radio for us. Channel 10 had no choice but to show an old movie, the Elizabeth Taylor–Montgomery Clift classic *Suddenly, Last Summer*. We had Rick Weaver on WIOD instead of Howard, Frank, and Dandy—and only the first half, for my brother and me. It was a school night, after all. So we didn't get to hear the Dolphins finally exert their superiority and roll to their eleventh win, and we were long asleep when the locker room interviews came over the air around midnight.

Otto Stowe was awarded the game ball and kept it securely under his seat, like a boy who'd brought his new football to school for recess, as he faced the unusual sight of reporters at his locker. Stowe, who according to Marlin Briscoe "looked like Sly Stone, dressed like Sly Stone, wanted to be like Sly Stone," was a first-class wide-receiver prospect on a team four-deep with such talent. That night was to be the highlight of his career. Back on the bench after Warfield returned, he asked after the season to be traded, and the next year he was playing for Dallas. He was having a terrific year there—twenty-three catches and 389 yards to lead the team—when he suffered a severe ankle break in the seventh game of the season. He was out for the year, and he never regained his former agility, catching only two more passes—for Denver—before retiring in 1975. But this breezy Monday night in the Orange Bowl must have felt to him like the beginning, his personal opening night, as he sprinted across the turf under the big lights, wide-open, the way it surely would always be.

Twelve and Oh

The Thanksgiving cold front had blown through, and temperatures were back in the high seventies each day—pushing eighty, even—as the Dolphins got back to work preparing for their final three regular-season games. Early in the season Bill Braucher had written, "The Dolphins can't win them all," not as an assessment of the team but simply as an accepted truism. Now no one was saying that, especially after looking at the schedule. First came New England, a team they had beaten 52–0 a few weeks earlier. The final game was at home against the Colts, who bore no resemblance to the preseason favorite of four months before. The only good candidate for spoiler was the New York Giants, a hardy 7–4 team, who'd be waiting at Yankee Stadium on December 10. Pretty much everyone now was talking about a possible undefeated season. Except for the Dolphins themselves. In public, anyway.

"Obviously, Jim, we're going to have to lose a game," Bob Kuechenberg said to Jim Langer one day as they were working out together in the Dolphins' weight room. Until the previous month the "weight room" was a converted women's bathroom off of the pool at Biscayne College, where the team practiced. Few players worked out with weights in those days. "When I arrived in 1970," recalled Jim Mandich, "nobody considered lifting weights. That was for sissies." Manny Fernandez, the six-two, 255-pounder who could full squat 855 pounds, was living disproof of that last bit—he'd been weight-training since high school—but he agreed with the first part. "When I got to Miami there was no weight program," he said. "There was just one of those Universal gyms and it sat in a shower room. I used it, and Langer and Kooch joined me, but there weren't a lot of weight lifters in those days." They also paid, as did Mercury Morris, to join local gyms to get access to better facilities. The room at the college was so cramped that to use the bench press they had to put their feet up on the wall. Shula saw the new Nautilus equipment at Arrowhead when they went up to Kansas City for the first game of the season, and he also heard that his rival George Allen had installed Nautilus machines at the Redskins facility. Not about to lose the winning edge, Shula convinced Joe Robbie to buy $10,000 worth of Nautilus equipment and had it installed at Biscayne College in early October. He took some reporters through the training room, which was "groaning with wounded after a recent practice," to see the setup, but noted that he wasn't going to put his team through any new workouts on the machines in the middle of a grueling season. "We'll go with the strength we have for the rest of the year."

Kuechenberg and Langer and Fernandez wasted no time breaking in the Nautilus room, though. And it was during these after-practice sessions that Kuechenberg posed to Langer his proposition about perfection. "We gotta lose one game," he recalled saying, "'cause sure as hell you don't want to go undefeated, because you'd jinx yourself, and you'll blow the first playoff game."

"I suppose so," said Langer.

"Okay, so when?"

"Well, not this week. No way we're losing to St. Louis."

After the Monday-night win, Kuechenberg posed the question again, a little differently: everyone knows you can't go undefeated in the NFL, so which one were they going to lose?

"Not this week. No way we're losing to New England."

And so it went each week in the weight room. Langer's answer was always the same: Not this week.

• • •

As fans were getting worked up themselves about the prospect of a perfect season, life in Miami went on. Edna Buchanan was zipping around everywhere from Hollywood to Homestead in her Triumph Spitfire to produce her almost-daily cataloguing of the macabre. This Friday her story was about a debt-ridden bigamist with several wives and a slew of girlfriends; he had killed his most recent bride and then himself, leaving a note in his Dupont Plaza office: "Don't pay my bills, my life is enough." Down near Key Largo the same day, customs agents moved in on a boat anchored two miles offshore and after a brief shootout captured four men and the three thousand pounds of marijuana they were bringing in from Jamaica. This was only two days after Consumers Union, about forty years ahead of its time, formally endorsed the legalization of marijuana. The announcement did little to cheer the four young men now sitting in the Dade County Jail.

South Florida prepared for the influx of more Cuban refugees, as the Castro government announced it would allow the Freedom Flights, which had flown a quarter million people to Miami between 1965 and early 1972, to continue. Havana had said earlier there were no more eligible candidates, but now it announced that some 3,400 more refugees would be allowed to leave.

President Nixon was flying to Miami that weekend, just as the Dolphins prepared to head north. On Thursday the White House announced it had told North Vietnam it would allow no delay in ending the war and moving on to "peace and reconstruction." Most saw this as a warning not to Hanoi but rather to Saigon not to allow their insistence on the North removing all its troops from South Vietnam to forestall a ceasefire. Kissinger and Nixon both met with South Vietnam's chief foreign policy advisor at the White House Thursday before heading to Key Biscayne on Friday. Nixon may have hoped that his perceived peacemaking momentum would divert attention from the slowly building Watergate investigation. His landslide victory certainly seemed to have taken folks' minds off the break-in. Also on Thursday, Donald Segretti, the Los Angeles lawyer linked to the Nixon campaign's mission of espionage against the Democrats, was subpoenaed by a Senate subcommittee chaired by Senator Edward Kennedy. But that wasn't so bad; Segretti was a small fish.

$$\cdot\ \cdot\ \cdot$$

At Dolphins practice, the weather was warm again, the team loose. Bob Griese had begun jogging around the practice field each day, but he was still favoring one foot and not taking any snaps. Don Shula was facing his weekly task of preventing his team from having a letdown. Eleven and oh, next three games meaningless, heading up to Boston to play the 2–9 Patriots, losers of eight straight. It wasn't difficult for Shula to motivate himself, as the Dolphins hadn't won up in New England since he'd become coach. The players remembered. But still it was hard to get too fired up just three weeks after the 52–0 laugher in the Orange Bowl. And voices around the football nation were already starting to murmur about Miami's easy schedule this year. No one thought so before the season, but it was starting to look that way, largely due to the disappointing records of the so recently powerful Jets and Colts, each of whom the Dolphins played twice. Howard Cosell had mentioned the issue and then buried it on Monday night's broadcast: "Some say the Dolphins have benefited from an easy schedule. Forget about it. Anyone can beat anyone in this league." That didn't stop a sportswriter in Washington from referring to Miami's schedule as "New England every Sunday." Mercury Morris had the best answer to that: "Well, isn't it a damn good thing Washington isn't playing New England every Sunday. They'd be oh-and-fourteen." The Redskins' only loss of the year had been to the Patriots, back in week three.

• • •

As the Nixon family and other snowbirds began migrating south, the Dolphins left eighty-degree weather and flew up to Boston on December 2, the day before the game. Actually, Shula had their charter flight booked to Providence, which was just as close to Schaefer Stadium in Foxborough; he wouldn't say if it was to break his little Patriot jinx. He must have been glad to hear the weather forecast: unseasonably warm on Sunday, and Sunday only. Highs in the fifties. Ten years later the Patriots would roll a snowplow out of the shed and clear a spot for their placekicker to win a game against a Super Bowl–bound Dolphins team, but there would be no such shenanigans possible this week.

Saturday night, Don Shula was edgy. Everyone was gathered at nine thirty p.m. in the buffet room at the Marriott in Foxborough, just a few miles from the stadium. As always, Shula scheduled this meeting, with plenty of burgers and beer, to keep the team focused and off the streets. But where were Csonka and Kiick? Just what he needed: for those two jokers to go out partying and screw up another Patriots game, not to mention setting a bad example for the team. He went ahead and gave his little speech without them: We can't let our guard down, remember the last two years, etc. The two running backs showed up a little later, and they weren't walking quite straight. Csonka went to pour himself a beer, and most of it made its way into the glass. Shula didn't say a word, just gave Zonk the "look." As it happened, they had not been out on the town, just happened to meet "some people" in the lobby and repaired to the bar for drinks, in Csonka's case "a few" shots of Jack Daniel's. Then they "couldn't find" the buffet room.

If Shula had known that these guys, along with Mercury Morris, would rush for over 300 yards the next afternoon while his team outgained New England 501 yards to 217, he might have been less grumpy. Despite the comfortable weather, Miami started slowly, with just a couple of short field goals in their first four possessions. But then a long eighty-nine-yard touchdown drive made it 13–0. Paul Warfield was back, and he set up the score with a pretty twenty-two-yard catch at the one, leading to a standard Jim Kiick plunge. Warfield played only about half the game but showed he was ready, with three catches for eighty-nine yards.

Poor Shula had a nervous halftime nonetheless. Just before the break, Morrall and Morris bungled a handoff and New England recovered on the Miami thirty-six. And with twenty-two seconds left, Jim Plunkett shocked the No-Names with a thirty-six-yard touchdown pass to a rookie receiver, Tom Reynolds, whom they might have been overlooking. Thirteen to seven is a lot different than 13–zip, and Shula must have been wondering if the Boston jinx was on. But Vern Den Herder set the record straight on the third play of the second half. With Stanfill and Fernandez charging at him, Plunkett lobbed a screen pass over them and the slightly deeper Den Herder, toward his running back. "I didn't realize that guy was so tall," Plunkett said later. The six-foot-six diverted veterinarian reached up and grabbed the ball: "He threw it right to me," he said. "Then I didn't know what to do with it." With Stanfill holding Plunkett down, Plunkett screaming "Holding!" and Fernandez leading the blocking, Den Herder took off for the goal line. He didn't quite get there, slowed down by Fernandez in front of him and caught from behind at the eleven—"I blame Manny for tackling me," he said later—prevented from scoring a touchdown on his only NFL interception. A couple plays later, Morrall found Mandich for a three-yard touchdown pass reminiscent of the one that beat the Vikings, and the score was comfortable again, 20–7. "We were still in the game and had a good screen set up," said Patriots coach Phil Bengtson, "until that big guy got his hands up." "I'm the ultimate No-Name," Den Herder liked to say, alluding to sportswriters calling him everything from Van Der Herder to Vern Deerharder. Or, as his comrade on the line Bill Stanfill liked to call him, Vern

Den Dockawaker, Vern don Swaggaldasha, a different variation every time, or finally "that do-goody Dutchman. Oh hell, Vern's just a hell of a nice fella."

Den Herder's high school team in Sioux Center, Iowa, didn't even have a football team until his junior year. He already looked like a defensive lineman, though, tall and strong from throwing hay bales from a wagon. "It's a total body workout: legs, torsos, arms, and keeping balance as this thing is going through a field. That was my weightlifting program." He didn't grow up on a farm as Csonka had but worked on farms all through high school. Then he majored in chemistry at tiny Central University of Iowa (now Central College) and was not only their top lineman but also the four-year starting center on the basketball team. Not expecting any interest from the NFL, Den Herder applied and was accepted to veterinary school at Iowa State. Joe Thomas, however, had his eyes everywhere in college football and had taken note of the Iowa Conference MVP who would someday be in the College Football Hall of Fame. Den Herder got the call that he'd been drafted by Miami in the ninth round. He told the veterinary school that he had to go down to Miami and give it a shot but that he would probably be there for the start of classes in September.

The culture shock began on the night flight to Miami when the pitch-darkness of the Everglades was finally broken by a sea of turquoise lights: suburban Miami's distinctive nocturnal welcome. He'd just gotten married, and the honeymoon was basically six weeks of training camp—Vern in his dorm room with Maulty Moore, and Diane in a motel. By the end of training camp, they'd found an apartment in a complex up in Hollywood with some other players—Heinz, Kuechenberg, Foley, Kolen—that Vern had "gravitated to because we had similar ideas, lifestyles, values from strong Christian backgrounds." They formed a young, married, conservative clique at the C'est La Vie apartments (of all places), a modest two-story building a couple miles from the beach, with a small kidney-shaped swimming pool and two shuffleboard courts.

With two weeks left in training camp, the dean at Iowa State called and said they needed a decision. "Well," Vern told him, "I've made it this far, and it certainly wouldn't prove anything if I left to go to school at this point, so I guess I'm going to stick it out." He made the team as a sub and special-teams player and figured he could go to veterinary school in another year or two. "I don't have real good upper-body strength, and I'm not too fast," he said with good midwestern humbleness a couple years later, echoing the team line. His well-combed blond hair and thin mustache seemed to fit his soft-spoken style. "I figured to have trouble just making the squad this year." And that was in 1972, his second year. Then, when Heinz and Riley went down in preseason, Den Herder got his shot, and he went in Shula's estimation from "improving" after the first exhibition game to "I have plans for him" in August to "By the end of training camp, I knew I had a starting end in Den Herder." What he had, it turns out, was that year's team leader in sacks, one of the league's best ends, a solid starter for the next ten years.

No one seemed to know his name, but Vern had set the tone for a one-sided second half. Morris led the way with 113 yards, Csonka added another 91, including a 45-yarder straight up the middle which put him over the thousand-yard mark for the second straight season. A thousand yards was a more noteworthy achievement at that time; to date only two backs—the immortal Jims, Brown and Taylor—had done it more than two seasons in a row. (Csonka would join them the next year.) On the big run, Csonka ran almost unchallenged through the middle before finally being run down at the nine. "I never thought to go more than four or five on that play," he said. "When nobody hit me I almost stopped to find out why." The ramble led to a little eighteen-yard pop from Yepremian; a Doug Swift interception leading to a beautiful fourteen-yard pass from Morrall to Marlin Briscoe streaking laterally along the back of the end zone made it 30–7 after three quarters. In the last period Del Gaizo and his subs came in and added another touchdown on a Hubert Ginn run. (For some reason either Csonka didn't ask for the chance to get nine more yards for another century game or Shula changed his attitude and refused.) The Patriots brought in Brian Dowling, the famous Yale quarterback who was the model for the character B.D. in *Doonesbury* and was a backup quarterback in four different professional leagues over ten seasons. Dowling, in his best NFL appearance ever, led the Pats to two late touchdowns to make the final score 37–21.

The story of the day was the 304 yards rushing by the Dolphins. Even the greatest rushing attack ever rarely hit the three-century mark. They came close a couple of times that year, but this was the only time they'd do it in 1972. (The next year they'd accomplish it twice.) What made it even more impressive was that no one runner had an unusually high total. After Morris and Csonka, the backups Ginn and Leigh had 47 and 30, and the limping Kiick just six carries for 23. Csonka made his big push over the thousand-yard mark, and Morris was getting close. He would need 193 yards in two games, certainly a possibility. No team had ever been close to having *two* thousand-yard runners, and reporters began to mull the prospect. "Of course, I'd love to get it," said Merc. "But who knows what's in store in the next two games?"

Of course, such rushing accomplishments had as much to do with the offensive line as with those running behind them. And the men doing the dirty work had another record in mind: the all-time team rushing record, held by the 1936 Detroit Lions. The Dolphins were only 308 yards away with two to go. "I don't know how the runners feel about it," said offensive line coach Monte Clark, "but to us it's damned important."

Monte Clark, the architect of one of the greatest offensive lines in history, had been a solid starting offensive tackle for eleven NFL seasons, mostly with the Cleveland Browns, before he finally had to retire with an eye injury before the 1970 season. He heard Don Shula, taking over the Dolphins, was looking for an offensive line coach, and with a strong recommendation from Browns coach Blanton Collier, Shula's old boss at Kentucky—the football world was a small one—he got the job. Taking a look at the Miami line of 1969, Clark saw potential. Yes, there were three former Houston Oilers—and the best of that trio was original Dolphin Norm Evans, who had been a fourteenth-round pick for Houston. But Larry Little had made it to the AFL All-Star Game despite being bigger and slower than he should be. And Doug Crusan, a number one draft pick from 1968, was doing fine, if he still had a lot to learn.

His first summer in Miami, Clark made three crucial discoveries. Watching films of preseason games, he saw a rookie lineman for his very recent employer, the Cleveland Browns, who struck him as particularly intense. He was surprised to see the Browns had placed Jim Langer on waivers, especially after he learned from a couple conversations with his former mates on the Cleveland line that this kid was smart, eager, and tough. Clark convinced Joe Thomas to claim Langer off the waiver list, and the poor newlywed was on his way south with a twenty-five-percent pay cut. Then, looking over another waiver list, this one of the San Francisco 49ers, Clark did a double-take at an oddly familiar name: Solomon Moore, defensive tackle. Clark was from California, had played for the 49ers the first few years of his career, and was pretty familiar with their team. He'd never heard the name Solomon Moore, but he had played some pickup basketball that off-season with a promising young *offensive* tackle named Wayne

Moore. A little research unearthed the fact that his full name was Solomon Wayne Moore and that San Francisco was trying to sneak him through the waiver process, much as Cleveland was with Langer. Clark had Thomas sign Moore off the list, and another reluctant young man was headed to Miami.

The final piece of the puzzle was Kuechenberg, who narrowly escaped a career as a human cannonball, and whose primary experience was playing for the Chicago Owls. He'd grown up one of nine kids in a family of tough, hardworking German Americans in northern Indiana. His father Rudy, "a Bunyanesque figure to his fellow iron workers," had also been a middleweight boxer, a rodeo clown, and the human cannonball in a circus. When Kuechenberg graduated high school and was offered a football scholarship at Notre Dame, he was thinking maybe he'd had enough of school. As he recalled, "My dad basically said, 'Either graduate from Notre Dame or get in the cannon.'" His uncle had filled in for his dad once as substitute fodder—after Rudy had missed the net and broken his neck—and ended up being launched into the side of the Ferris wheel, breaking a number of bones. Bob went to Notre Dame.

He graduated in 1969 with a degree in economics and was drafted by Philadelphia. But the Eagles training camp, filled with "older vets who felt threatened and didn't exactly welcome rookies," left him feeling miserable and defeatist, and he walked out. His father called him a "pussycat," and his brother Rudy Jr., a linebacker with the Bears, called him a gutless coward. So he went back to camp and was cut on the final day. He signed with Atlanta but was cut there too. "Then," he said, "I realized that as miserable as I'd been in camp, I was more miserable on the outside looking in." He got work in Chicago selling business forms and played for the semipro Owls of the Continental League. They practiced twice a week and played their games before about a hundred fans at Soldier Field, which at that time could hold over a hundred thousand. Players were paid $150 a game—until the team ran out of money after four games. They finished the ten-game season anyway. "It was fun," he said, "and it kept me playing." He began looking for NFL teams that might need an offensive guard, and he targeted the Dolphins because his old backup at Notre Dame, Ed Tuck, had made the team there. Possibly using the same logic, Shula and Clark gave him a tryout in 1970 and saw just enough to keep him on.

Just enough. They waived him with the intent to keep him on the taxi squad, as Langer and Moore's coaches had done in Cleveland and San Francisco, but in this case it worked. No one wanted the erstwhile Owl. Like half the Dolphins, it seemed, he was considered too small and too slow. But he impressed Shula with his special-teams work and Clark with his potential at guard. Late that season, injuries promoted him to a starting spot for the last five games, and Kuechenberg was in for good. Shula had something of a soft spot for this kid who had "come off the sandlots," as he put it, and made good in the NFL. He also enjoyed using him as a verbal punching bag in practice, riding him hard for the holding penalties Kuechenberg accumulated in his early tenure. "Kooch!" he would shout, bringing practice to a temporary halt. "You are challenging the record of the great Baltimore guard, John Williams, who personally cost the Colts one thousand yards!" Or "Kooch is going for the Hall of Shame, and he has youth on his side!"

By 1972 Kuechenberg was solidly ensconced in the left guard position, where he would remain for fourteen years. Shula had lost a whipping boy and gained a cornerstone. And Kuechenberg, like his fellow Expendables, couldn't have been more pleased to find himself on the league's preeminent offensive line: "It's getting to the point," he said, "where it's enjoyable each week to know it's very likely you're going to go out there and kick somebody's butt."

Kuechenberg excelled for fourteen years "in the trenches" with a pugilistic mentality: "I just fight [the other guy]," he said. "As long as he's beating on my head and not the quarterback's, it's all right with me." Monte Clark, however, mentored his pupils on the offensive line with a more intellectual, even mystical approach. On his first day as a coach, at the 1970 training camp, he lined his men up and had them assume their three-point stance. Then he went up and down the line like a drill sergeant, making slight corrections in their attitude. For the veteran Norm Evans it was like going back to peewee ball, and he bristled. But before long he had bought into the Clark method, and he asked the coach what else he could work on. "Work on your stance," said Monte. Then he gave each lineman a copy of a book, and it wasn't a playbook. It was a mass-market paperback edition of the bestselling self-help classic *Psycho-Cybernetics*, by cosmetic surgeon Maxwell Maltz. It was all about visualizing one's goals and regulating one's self-image to break through unconscious limitations. Clark had his players work on visualizing blocking assignments, including all the permutations that might ensue in the maelstrom of actual play. In that way they could practice effectively without brutalizing their bodies on the practice field. Crusan remembered visualizing plays on the long drive back up to the Greenbriar. Jim Langer could quote from Maltz's book long after he retired. Even Kooch, the gladiator, said the technique changed and prolonged his career.

Clark was an artist at heart. He enjoyed poetry and music; that year in training camp he kept a double bass in his room and practiced every evening. But he was also "a 250-pound bundle of nerves, humor, and theory." Norm Evans said that in Clark's final season playing for Cleveland, he let his man reach the quarterback only once all season. "And knowing him, he probably chewed himself out about that one play for the rest of the week." When the Dolphins lost to the Patriots in his—and Shula's—first game in 1970, largely because his offensive line let Griese get sacked eight times, he collapsed with chest pain and was hospitalized for a night. He was as consumed with the pursuit of excellence as was his boss. Among the visualizations he led his men to pursue was one in which each one of them was the very best at his position. "Best in the business!" was his own mantra, employed all through the long day of practice.

And that they were, just two years after Clark's arrival. The best offensive line in the business, on the best team. With Miami's blowout of New England, everyone was asking not just about the team rushing record and individual achievements but whether the ultimate achievement might be possible. "Sure, we hope to go all the way [unbeaten]," Csonka let out in a rare admission. "We go after every game the way we should. If you don't go all out, you might get in a rut and not be able to shake it when it counts." One poor scribe made the mistake of asking Mercury Morris whether he felt the first 14–0 season was finally within reach. "We're not 14–0, so ask me about 12–0," he said. "It feels good, great so far, but I really won't be happy until we're 17–0. That's what it's all about, man, not 1,000, not 14–0, but 17–0. The season will be meaningless unless we get that Super Bowl. If not . . ." He stopped himself and shook off the thought. Maybe he was thinking of what his blockers had been telling him about that book: Dwell only on the positive goal; picture it so vividly as to make it "real." But don't talk about it.

Thirteen and Oh

"When I came down here for my first training camp," said Mercury Morris, "it was the week they walked on the moon." That was 1969, the summer of Woodstock and Altamont, the Manson Family, John and Yoko's "Give Peace a Chance," and of course Neil Armstrong and *Apollo 11*. "I got a kick out of watching Armstrong bouncing around in his spacesuit," Morris had written in his *Miami News* diary that week. "You know something, he has good moves. I wish I were up there—they'd never stop me." For the Dolphins it was still the AFL, Coach George Wilson's lame-duck year, and the collapse from injuries into a 3–10–1 season. By 1972, in the short span of three years, the leagues had merged, a great coach had come south to turn the team around, and twelve men, in six Apollo missions, had walked on the moon. "In some ways," said Larry Csonka, "we became associated with the space program. We got to know some of the astronauts on a first-name basis because of their interest in sports and our interest in NASA. I got to go to some of the moon shots." Six manned moon missions in thirty-three months somewhat dulled the fervor of the public and the media, which have a hunger for novelty. Still, in the first week of December 1972, as astronauts Gene Cernan, Jack Schmitt, and Ron Evans—along with five mice conscripted for a science experiment—made their final preparations for the voyage of *Apollo 17*, "America's last lunar explorers of the 20th Century" were big news, especially in South Florida, where the first night launch ever was expected to create "a new moon over Miami." A quarter million people flocked to the viewing areas closest to Cape Kennedy on Wednesday night, as my family had eighteen months earlier for *Apollo 15*, and were rewarded with a phantasmagoric explosion of a blastoff just after midnight. "Go . . . go . . . go!"

shrieked the crowd, as if they were urging Mercury across the Poly-Turf rather than *Apollo* up into orbit and beyond, to the moon one last time.

Back in the stratosphere, yet another earthbound aircraft was hijacked, and Edna Buchanan took a break from the murderers and rapists to check out the new security setups at Miami International. Eastern had set up a metal detector for passengers to walk through, although "airline employees ignored the magnetometer's spectacular display indicating the presence of metal on many of the boarding passengers." Turns out they were only paying attention to the detectors' results on a certain one percent of passengers designated "selectees," whose behavioral profile matched that of hijackers. Pan Am had its X-ray machine going, but at other gates, such as Delta and National, no security system was apparent at all. For the moment, it was up to individual airlines to prevent hijackers from boarding their planes.

Nixon was back in Washington, hell-bent on continuing to bomb the North Vietnamese into submission—or, to be honest, into signing an agreement that was already sure to result in their ultimate victory. The problem for Nixon was not Hanoi but rather Saigon, and the U.S. this week threatened President Thieu that he was risking the loss of future military and economic aid if South Vietnam continued to jeopardize the peace process. Nixon needed some good news to staunch this burgeoning Watergate fiasco. After a post-election lull, the vultures were gathering. John Sirica, the judge presiding over the trial of the seven Watergate burglars, had just announced that the trial should cast a broader net, to investigate whether they were acting on orders from higher up, and just how high. "The jury is going to want to know . . . ," he said, "who hired them? Who started this?" Nixon scowled. No one cared about that. The people wanted peace. The bombs, it seemed, were merely a front; Nixon was ready to sell out South Vietnam, sign a treaty that had at least a semblance of "peace with honor," and get the hell out of there. Kissinger flew back to Paris for more of the endless secret talks with Le Duc Tho, and another six hundred tons of explosives belched from the bellies of the Stratofortresses in one day alone, Thursday.

. . .

The Dolphins were twelve and oh and soaring far above every other team in the league—except the Washington Redskins. George Allen and his team might have been perfect at this point, too, if it weren't for a nightmare finish against the Patriots in the third week. On the same day Griese threw his game-winning toss to Mandich to sneak by the Vikings, Washington's Curt Knight kicked a short field goal to tie the Patriots with a couple minutes left. But the Pats were called for roughing the kicker, and Allen decided to give up the three points and go for the win. Three plays later, Knight tried an even shorter field goal, from twenty-seven yards out—and missed. Such were the vagaries of straight-on kicking; in his five-year career with Washington, Knight made only fifty-eight percent of his field goals, including only two-thirds of the short ones in the twenty-to-twenty-nine-yard range. This game wasn't over, though, as Washington's Bill Malinchak blocked a punt in the final seconds and was certain he recovered it for a touchdown. But the refs ruled that the ball had touched the back border of the end zone, resulting in a safety. The Patriots won, 24–23.

So Shula and the Dolphins knew that the Redskins were right behind them, watching, knowing that but for a quirk of fate there would be two perfect teams this year—so far, at least. There wasn't any rivalry between the two clubs, as they had never played each other outside the exhibition season, this being only Miami's third season in the NFL. But there was certainly a rivalry between the coaches. In 1967, when Shula's Colts went undefeated for thirteen games, it was Allen's Rams who had kept them from the playoffs. The next year Shula returned the favor, beating out a good Rams team for the division title during Earl Morrall's annus mirabilis. And in Shula's final, bitter season in Baltimore, there was Allen on top of the division again, looking down on him. By now both coaches had elite status, but they also shared that hated aspersion: Can't win the big one. In Allen's two best years in Los Angeles, he won the division only to lose in the conference championship game. Shula had done better than that, getting to two Super Bowls, but his seasons too had always ended in defeat. They also shared an uncompromising, obsessive drive to win—and an innate ability to inspire their players to the same passion. Their wives could tell you about it: the unending hours of study, practice, preparation, from breakfast to bedtime. The preoccupation with the one task that mattered: winning the next football game. "Losing," Allen often said, "is like death." And: "The worst moments of my life are when I wake up in the middle of the night and can't remember whether we won or lost. . . . If I remember that we lost, I am destroyed by the thought of it and regret I ever woke up at all." "And if we win," his wife, Etty, said, "he will be up early planning for the next game."

Now Allen had taken Washington, a perennially losing team, and led it to its first division championship since 1945, when the entire league had ten teams. And Shula had responded to the crushing loss to Dallas with twelve straight victories. This week his face was on the cover of *Time*: BUILDING FOR THE SUPER BOWL. Howard Cosell had just told the nation, as if setting up a January show-down, that they were the two greatest coaches alive. But the two best coaches had never won the big one. And now their teams were 12–0 and 11–1, division champs driving toward the same January end zone.

· · ·

On Friday, Bob Griese was put back on the active roster and took his first prac-tice snap, fifty-four days after his ankle gave way on the Orange Bowl floor. He called a run but audibled at the line of scrimmage and shot a crisp completion to Otto Stowe. Since his cast had come off almost three weeks before, he'd been following the rehab regimen prescribed by Dr. Virgin and the team trainer, Bob Lundy: stretching, icing, whirlpools, light weights, gradually more walking. Shula was thrilled to see him jogging with no limp. There was no way he would be playing against the Giants this week, but there was a seven-week limit by which the team had to activate him if he was to play this season at all. That meant someone else had to be taken off the active roster, and it couldn't be Del Gaizo, because he was still the backup that week if Morrall got hurt. (Which was great news for Del Gaizo, because being active for this, his seventh game, meant he was eligible for a full share of playoff money.) So Billy Lothridge, who'd reluctantly answered the call to come out of retirement and lofted four punts in two games, was moved to the taxi squad, and Shula would make do with Dick Anderson's punts for another game or two, despite the wisecracks. ("Dick is inclined to foul one off now and then," wrote Braucher. "In general, as a punter he makes an excellent strong safety.") Larry Seiple's cast was off and he would be ready for the playoffs.

Injury management was a weekly puzzle, and it could present dilemmas, particularly for a team that had clinched the division so early but still wanted to win. As much as Shula insisted that a Super Bowl victory—not a perfect season—was the only goal, it was impossible to call these final games "meaning-less." That loss to New England had given George Allen the luxury of resting players for the playoffs; no one would care much whether the team finished 13–1 or 12–2. But if Shula rested his starters and lost a game, people would forever say he had blown the chance for immortality. And he was starting to get testy when people suggested, as a New York reporter would this week, that the Dolphins might be better off losing one of these final games, to take the pressure off in the playoffs. "I just can't buy that attitude," he shot back. "I don't think there's anything you ever gain by losing. I go along with Jack Nicklaus: he said once, 'You know what breeds winning? *Winning* breeds winning.'"

Larry Little's knee, it seemed, wasn't going to look normal until the off-season. It had been swollen for weeks; he bruised it again in Foxborough and was questionable for the next week, but on Friday he was listed as probable. Doug Crusan, who had replaced his replacement, Wayne Moore, since the Minnesota game, suffered a bad sprain against New England. Luckily, Moore was ready to go again. Paul Warfield might have been a good candidate to rest, as he was still recovering from the sprained ankle and the receiver corps was so deep, but Shula had him scheduled to return to the starting lineup. Some, like Jim Kiick, whose knee and wrist were hampering him, wanted to keep playing for other reasons: with Morris playing so well, he might be in danger of being forgotten. Morris was still shooting for a thousand yards, and Shula admitted: "I'd like to see Merc get it. But as we wind down and prepare for the playoffs, the important thing is keeping everybody in good shape. Whatever I do will be dictated by this thought—a team thought, not an individual thought."

On Saturday morning, as the *Apollo 17* spacecraft sped soundlessly toward the moon, the Dolphins flew up to New York, with an afternoon practice scheduled in Yankee Stadium. "The House That Ruth Built" had been primarily the home of baseball's Yankees since it was erected in 1923, the Babe's fourth year in New York, but it had also been home to various football teams, including five different New York Yankees (or Yanks) football clubs in five leagues. And the Giants had been playing there since leaving the old Polo Grounds in 1956. (They departed for the Yale Bowl mid-1973, after two final games at Yankee Stadium, while they waited for their new stadium in the Meadowlands to be constructed.) Just a few years before, Frederick Exley had written, "To those who understand . . . the place of sports in [American] life . . . the Yankee Stadium can be a heart-stopping, an awesomely imposing place."

The stadium was indeed a monument of American sport, and it was a thrill for the Dolphins to play there for the only time, in their first-ever meeting with the Giants. "It's been a dream all my life to play in Yankee Stadium," said Kiick. "This place just awes you. I'm from this area, and when we were kids that's all we used to talk about—the Giants in Yankee Stadium." Others, like Manny Fernandez, had never even been there. "It has to psyche you up," he said, "to play in a stadium you've heard about since you were a kid. And it's not just Yankee Stadium. It's any big town like New York. That's where you get the recognition." And the pressure. The Dolphins were about to find out how it might have been starting 12–0 in a media center like New York. Whereas the South Florida press were keeping the "undefeated" coverage understated, it's all the big-city boys wanted to talk about. For Earl Morrall, it was a trip back to one of his itinerant professional homes. Of course, there were more than a few NFL destinations that had once been home to him. He had played three years in Yankee Stadium in the sixties, right before going to Shula's Colts for four more. "The last time I was there was in '68 with Earl," said Shula, "and we kidded him as we always did about getting revenge on his various old teams. We beat them 26–0, so maybe we can get him a little riled up this week too."

Sunday, December 10, while B-52s continued to batter the DMZ in Vietnam even as Kissinger and Le Duc Tho held their longest negotiation yet in Paris, and the *Apollo 17* astronauts, after four days hurtling through space, finally felt the gentle tug of the Moon's gravity, the Dolphins and Giants ran out onto the Yankee Stadium grass, already softening in the cold, light rain. This would be the first—and only—Dolphin game of the season in challenging weather. The players didn't mind: it was still a holiday from the Poly-Turf.

The Giants were a solid team and had been in contention for the playoffs until about dinnertime Saturday, when the Redskins, resting some key players in a game that meant nothing to them, lost to a Cowboys team all fired up to secure the final playoff spot. So it would have been understandable if the Giants' disappointment dulled their edge a bit on Sunday. Instead it seemed to loosen them up to play their best, and they came out firing like this was the Big One. Their coach, Alex Webster, had had the *Time* cover with Don Shula on the locker room bulletin board all week to motivate his troops, and apparently he hadn't taken it off on Sunday morning. They ran Yepremian's opening kickoff back to the fifty, and five plays later scored on a one-yard run. At that point, though, the field conditions began to affect this game. Pete Gogolak, a Hungarian immigrant who was the NFL's soccer-style-kicking pioneer in 1966, leading the way for Yepremian and others, came on to kick the extra point. The placement spot for extra points on that end of the stadium was smack in the middle of the Yankees' infield, and the infield was cold, sloppy mud. No matter, one might have thought: an extra point in those days was a *nine-yard* kick. All you had to do was get it over the linemen and you couldn't miss. Gogolak stepped forward, tried to avoid a banana-peel flop, swiped his foot at the muddy ball, and sent it wobbling right into the scrum of players in front of him. Six-nothing, Giants.

"If we want to stop the Dolphins," Webster had told his defense, "we have to stop Csonka. It's that simple." This was both simplistic and quixotic most any week against Miami, but in this game it really wasn't going to do the trick. For Shula mostly rested Zonk and left it to Morris to pursue his thousand and Kiick to impress his homeboys in the stands. The two rivals responded well, and Morrall's offense answered the Giants' score with a ten-play, eighty-yard drive of its own, capped by a twelve-yard Morris sweep around the left end. On an earlier play, Morris had tried to make a cut and slipped right onto his side. As he got back to the huddle, Csonka chided him: "Merc, only a dumb Hunky would try to cut in that stuff." Marv Fleming, next to Csonka, was perplexed: "What'd you call him?" "A dumb Hunky—a Hungarian." Fleming cracked up, and this time when Morris got the ball he negotiated a powerful but delicate sprint for the corner, concentrating on staying on his feet, content with a rare, understated lefty spike as he crossed just inside the end zone pylon. The kicking was easier on that end of the field, and Garo chipped the ball up for a 7–6 lead. On the very next play, the kickoff, special-teams hero Lloyd Mumphord separated the returner and the wet football, and three plays later Garo kicked a thirty-seven-yarder for 10–6.

The weather was supposed to play into the hands of the tough northern home team, but instead it greased those hands. The Giants just couldn't seem to hang on to that wet football. After a long ensuing drive, they fumbled again in Miami territory, and Doug Swift was there to fall on it. "We were backed up to the ten-yard line," said Kiick, "and I felt I could do something if I got in. I had this definite feeling, and darned if Shula wasn't grabbing me and telling me to go." The Jersey boy put his head down and charged right up the middle twelve and then twenty yards through the slog. By now the middle of the field, formerly grass, was as muddy as the infield. Then, after an exchange of punts, Kiick gave Miami two more big pushes through the bog of nine and eleven yards, to set the stage for this game's enduring highlight. With third down and nine to go from the New York thirty-four, Morrall faded back, looking for Paul Warfield.

Although the Dolphins were deep in receivers, the return of Warfield from injury meant the reemergence of a threat like no other in football. One of the most elegant athletes ever—in any sport—Warfield combined world-class speed with a gymnast's body control and an artist's hands. Thirty years old that year, quiet and studious like Griese, he didn't drink, smoke, or curse, and he practiced his pass routes over and over after practice, counting steps, until he could perform them like a dancer. The host of his own radio talk show in Miami and studying for a master's degree in telecommunications at Kent State, Warfield was also "the ultimate in locker-room news management," according to one frustrated local reporter. "Conversationally conservative . . . he smothers the inquirer with technical details. . . . He doesn't speak in headlines, but in footnotes." Another journalist spoke of his "long-winded, forensic explanations that left his interrogators with padfuls of arcane sketches." He liked to compare a football team to a military unit and refused ever to say a controversial word—unless the topic of zone defense arose. Since no one could cover Warfield alone, teams double-covered him at the very least and more recently employed some sort of zone. And to him the zone was an abomination.

"It has no place in pro football," he said—never mind that his own team played zone more than any. "It takes a man who can run the 100-yard dash in 9.6 seconds and assigns him to cover a spot on the field. That's a waste of talent and keeps the fans from seeing the man-to-man competition they want. It takes all the artistry out of pass receiving. When a receiver is running against a zone, he can make a classic move and produce no reaction—the defensive man will just ignore it. All he cares about is his area and the ball. Now it's not man against man, it's man against thing. The duels are gone, and the long passes are gone." Once he got over his umbrage, however, he did what he always did: he went back to the films. And he found ways to beat the zone. He worked harder on the details of his craft than the next-best All-Pro or the last free agent struggling to make the team. Then he quietly did crosswords by his locker while the others were revving themselves up for the game.

His teammates spoke of him in hushed tones—then and decades later—as though he were a guru, or royalty. "He personifies class," said Doug Swift.

"He doesn't talk much. He's very workmanlike." "He's like satin," said Csonka. "Not only in the way he runs pass patterns but in his whole personality." Vince Lombardi's famous exhortation "When you make it to the end zone, act like you've been there before" might have been inspired by Warfield. His end zone celebration was to calmly flip the ball to the ref and head back to the sideline. Swift: "He just glides into the end zone, then casually walks out. Doesn't even jog. He just pulls up his pants and he walks."

"Even when he blocked," said Eddie Jenkins, "he had a way of keeping his feet and positioning himself so as to knock you off stride—just for a second or two, and that was enough. Everything was measured. He'd execute the most powerful blocks that way." Indeed, as phenomenal a receiver as Warfield was, he was just as good a blocker. Not many fans may have realized it, but his team-mates and opponents did. "I did take pride in my blocking," said Warfield. He'd first learned to appreciate the fine art from his college coach at Ohio State, Woody Hayes. Then he played for years in Cleveland with the all-time-great running backs Jim Brown and Leroy Kelly, a similar situation to Miami with its run-based attack. "There were plays designed for me to block, and even though I couldn't overpower a big defensive end, I learned all I had to do was stymie him so we could run outside. And I learned that my blocking helped me as a receiver, when we gave a run look that allowed me to release and surprise defensive backs." He was famous for his crackback blocks—when a play is designed toward one side, and the receiver on that side comes back toward the middle and takes a defender by surprise, launching him back whence he came. Csonka remembered a crackback block Warfield leveled on All-Pro Bear linebacker Dick Butkus in 1971. Butkus himself called it one of the hardest shots he'd ever taken.

"Warfield was twenty-five percent of that team," said Marv Fleming. "He was such a force for us. When he was on that field, everyone was afraid of him." Not of being laid flat like Butkus, but of being left in Warfield's dust. A natural sprinter who'd set Ohio schoolboy records in the 100-yard dash, the 180-yard hurdles, and the long jump, he was ranked fifth in the world in the long jump in his college years when he competed on the U.S. National team. His jump of twenty-six feet two and a half inches would have just barely missed the bronze medal at the next Olympics. The combination of that speed and agility with preternatural body control and the precision born of countless after-practice

hours spent choreographing every step of every pattern resulted in a dream of
a wide receiver. Every defense keyed on him, and only rarely did he find himself
covered by a single man. Despite that, he is the only receiver in the Hall of Fame
with a career average of more than twenty yards per catch.

Lloyd Mumphord, the fifth defensive back, was the Dolphins' best pass
coverage man. On passing downs, Mumphord was usually assigned the opponent's star receiver. His toughest assignment, though, was in practice, where
he had to cover Warfield. Or try. The very first time, in 1970, Warfield left him
high and dry on a simple down and out. "I said to myself, 'Oh, Lord, pull yourself together,'" Mumphord recalled. Another time, he walked up to Mercury
Morris afterward: "I don't know how he did it. I was on him, and next thing I
knew I was all by myself."

Mumphord could have joined a therapy support group of defensive backs
from around the league. And one of the longest-suffering members would
have been Carl "Spider" Lockhart, the veteran two-time Pro Bowler for the
Giants. Just a year younger than Warfield, he'd been doing his best against
him for eight seasons. Now, with just under three minutes left in the half in a
still-close game, 10–6 Dolphins, Miami had that third down and nine at the
Giant thirty-four-yard line. Good chance they'd go to their All-World receiver,
finally back from injury. No way he was going to get single coverage. Cornerback
Willie Williams took him short, and Lockhart had him deep. Earl Morrall
backpedaled in his old straight-on style and watched what was happening
downfield. What was happening was that Paul Warfield had found a way to
exert his artistry even against double coverage. "I slipped under Williams and
straightened up Lockhart," Warfield calmly explained later. "But Spider stayed
back. He wasn't biting." Warfield then executed a tripartite pattern, cutting
inside, outside, and back inside. The last bit did the trick. "That last one was
such a fantastic move that Paul almost faked *me* out," said Morrall. Lockhart
wasn't so lucky, but then, unlike Morrall, he didn't know what play had been
called. "I had Paul covered the first two moves," he said, "but his third was the
greatest I've ever seen." When the pass arrived, deep and high down the middle
of the field, Warfield was all alone, a boy running patterns with his friend after
a rainstorm. Lockhart, trying to get back from the side, could only watch as
the old long-jumper leaped into the air at the five, received the ball into his
belly at the peak of his flight as gracefully as a ballet dancer, and splashed

down on his side, sliding through the mud into the end zone, recumbent and untouched.

• • •

The remarkable 34-yard catch was of only average length for Warfield's day, as he ended with four receptions for 132 yards. This one gave Miami a 17–6 lead and set the tone for the rest of the day. New York did get another touchdown right before the half, after a pass interference call in the end zone, but that was the end of their offensive day. In the second half, as the stadium lights came on, "the vivid reds and oranges, the plaids and tans of autumn clothing," as Exley had noted, suddenly flashed brightly again, like foliage on the final peak day of autumn color, "reminding one that time is passing, that time indeed is running out." As it indeed was running out for the Giants. The Miami defense began to enjoy the mire like the English at Agincourt. "At first we floundered around," said Doug Swift, "and it was close. Then all of a sudden we just got going in the mud and we started to play ball and it was like old-time football. It was great—all muddy, and cold, and dirty. And Nick [Buoniconti] was carrying on and cussing, and he looked more like a Roman gladiator than ever, because he was all mud and he had this shining armored helmet, and I said, 'This is a riot,' watching Nick in there. He was fun to play with, mostly because he was such a nut." The No-Names in the mud dominated the second half. When the Giants did manage to move the ball across midfield, they were befuddled by the mess in Yankee Stadium. They ended up losing four fumbles and two interceptions, which truncated every attempt to catch up.

Meanwhile, Swift and his Dolphin teammates on both sides of the ball were enjoying their visit. Kiick looked as happy as a toddler in a mud puddle as he repeatedly chewed up the middle of the field. No one had to ask Csonka if he preferred this to the Poly-Turf. And Garo Yepremian, although no kicker could pretend to like the conditions, was proving more resourceful than Gogolak. In the fourth quarter, as the astronauts, 250,000 miles from home, finally swung around the far side of the Moon and eased their craft into lower orbit, darkness was falling over the stadium and Yepremian was asked twice to deliver short field goals from the muddy end to seal the game. Unlike Gogolak, he thought to bring out a towel to clean off the kicking surface.

Dick Anderson also had a fine game punting, despite the jokes. All three of his kicks were downed inside the twenty, including a forty-five-yarder and a final short one intended to pin the Giants down near their own goal line in the final minutes. As it happened, it came down shorter than expected and bounced off an unsuspecting blocker's helmet at the twenty and was recovered by the Dolphins. "That's the worst punt I ever saw in my life," Shula said afterward. "It looked like you were trying a field goal." Anderson, who had played on his high school's state championship golf team, looked at it another way: "That was a sand wedge shot that hit the pin."

It set up a Yepremian putt from only sixteen yards out, smack-dab in the middle of the soggy infield. No problem for Garo, who used his towel to "scoop gobs of mud" away from the kicking spot, not unlike how the Patriots would one day commandeer that snowplow for a similar purpose at Foxborough. With the ground relatively clear, Yepremian pushed the short field goal through for the final 23–13 margin of victory.

All in all, a satisfying jaunt up to the big city. Csonka got some rest, Kiick got some work—sixty-nine yards in ten carries, plus four catches—and Morris led with ninety-eight yards, keeping him on pace for a thousand-yard season. Another ninety-five the next week and he was there. The offense, too, with another two-hundred-yard rushing day, seemed to all but guarantee its goal of the all-time team rushing record, only a hundred and four yards away. Warfield had come back gloriously from his ankle injury and did so without aggravating it. The only sore spot was Larry Little, who played despite his hurting knee and had to be removed early on when he bashed it up again. Al Jenkins filled in admirably, but everyone knew how indispensable Little would be in a championship run.

Bob Griese had done no more than warm up a little in the pregame, and had not been expected to; he was still unable to put his full weight on his ankle. Maybe the next week, maybe the one after. But no one was too worried about that, as Earl Morrall continued to play like a championship quarterback. In fact, with this game he had accumulated enough pass attempts to be listed in the official league statistics, and he popped up right at the top: the number one passer in the conference, by a wide margin. Griese should be ready by the playoffs, but, wrote Braucher, "if you can find a sport foolish enough to bet that Earl Morrall won't take the Dolphins the rest of the way, no matter how far it is, lay the mortgage on it. . . . Remember when the people who count exhibition games were retiring Morrall in September?"

Fourteen and Oh

Each year there are a handful of mornings when Miamians wake and, upon stepping outside to get the newspaper or head off to school or work, feel a thrilling coolness in the air. To us kids who had never, or only rarely on winter trips, seen snow, running outside and inhaling air whose temperature was in the fifties—or maybe even forties—was akin to the northern child waking to a fresh blanket of snow out his bedroom window. In a strange way it felt like nostalgia for a past we'd never known.

The morning of December 16, 1972, glittered with multiple exhilarators. Although morning temperatures were in the upper sixties, a winter cold front was hitting, and the air, clean and crisp, shot through with pristine sunshine, would be cooling through the day to fifties that evening. The thrill of a cold front seemed to punctuate the beginning of the holiday season—just one more week of school before the two-week vacation. And above all, the Dolphins had a special Saturday home game in the afternoon, when they would, surely, complete a perfect regular season.

A nine-year-old has his responsibilities, though, and for me this Saturday's excitements were tantalizingly impeded by the necessity of Hebrew school in the morning and a piano recital in the afternoon. While our geochemist father had raised us in an atmosphere of scientific atheism, he had agreed at the last moment that we should be bar mitzvahed after all, and although the semiweekly after-school torment wouldn't begin until the next year, I had begun with Saturday mornings. I remember carpooling with two friends, all in long pants and sweaters, talking about the Dolphins game: we were going to be fourteen and oh!

To us the week had been about anticipation: of the culmination of the Dolphins season and the coming holiday and vacation. We were hardly aware that, a quarter million miles away, three Americans were carrying out the last great human space adventure of our lifetimes. On Monday, Cernan and Schmitt had climbed into the lunar module *Challenger*, separated from the command module *America*, and flown down to the surface of the Moon. For three days they walked, bounded, and drove their moon buggy for a total of twenty-two hours, disturbing dust and rocks untouched through their 4.5-billion-year existence. They collected 250 pounds of samples to bring home, set up a nuclear-powered science station to leave behind, and erected the sixth American flag on the Moon. And Thursday evening (Miami time) they blasted off again to join their colleague on the orbiting spacecraft via a one-chance-only rendezvous that still boggles the imagination. The last humans on the Moon "for a decade, or perhaps a quarter century," or so they thought, left behind a plaque similar to the one left by the first moonwalkers of *Apollo 11* (a replica of which I had mounted above the desk where I did my schoolwork). This new one read, "Here man completed his first exploration of the moon, December 1972, A.D. May the spirit of peace in which we came be reflected in the lives of all mankind." It was signed by the three astronauts and "Richard M. Nixon, President of the United States of America." They also left the final installment of an almost billion-dollar stash of space litter, including three abandoned rover vehicles, five science stations, tools, cameras, and the golf balls Alan Shepard had sliced into the rough the year before.

Back on Earth, Nixon may have wished he could spend more time enjoying watching the Redskins and Dolphins hurtle toward their own rendezvous. But those unrelenting *W*'s, Watergate and the War, continued to besiege him as the year wound down. On Wednesday, December 13, the peace talks in Paris broke down again, and Kissinger flew to Washington with two options for Nixon. One was to wait until January and try more negotiation. The other: step up the bombing campaign to even higher levels to compel Hanoi to come to an agreement.

Nixon was in no mood for option one. The next day he sent a private ultimatum to Hanoi: Either get back to the negotiating table and "begin talking seriously," or face military consequences. And then, before the enemy even had a chance to respond, he gave them an inkling of what was to come. On Friday, American B-52s set another record, carrying out the heaviest bombing of the war; sixteen missions of fifty Stratofortresses pounded enemy troops and supplies over a twenty-four-hour period.

. . .

Before dawn on December 12, sixty-five Haitian refugees in a leaking sailboat hit ground at Pompano Beach, forty miles north of Miami. (A bit farther south and they might have been discovered by Doug Crusan and the Greenbriar gang.) They were five political prisoners who had bribed their way out of jail and sailed, along with their families and some friends, first to Cuba, then to Bimini, and finally toward Florida, getting lost and bailing water for nineteen days. It was hardly a rare occasion for an unsound vessel of desperate souls to wash ashore in South Florida; since Castro came to power in 1959, more than fourteen thousand Cubans had made their way across the Florida Strait, riding everything from yachts to dinghies to inner tubes and logs. The landings would accelerate through the 1970s and culminate in the Mariel boatlift of 1980.

An influx of population, both domestic and foreign, would transmogrify the area in the 1980s. South Beach, in particular, would turn from a haven for elderly Jews to the hottest nightspot in the country. Even in 1972, Miami Beach was looking toward some such rejuvenation. The city council was not pleased at how television coverage of the conventions had exposed "the poor and the old wandering around decaying South Beach." In his dispatch for *Esquire*, Arthur Miller wrote of "old, half-crippled Jews sliding the shuffleboard disks along the baking concrete slabs." Yiddish was heard on the streets and in the parks; on the forearms of some residents you could still see the tattooed numbers from Dachau and Auschwitz. The spirited new arrivals of the 1950s and 1960s were now elderly and dependent on city services. The "Tropical Deco" hotels they lived in—the Carlyle, the Breakwater, the Governor, the Clevelander—were falling into disrepair, and there was little incentive for the owners to renovate for the benefit of fixed-pension retirees. That fall the council had begun deliberating actions that would eventually upgrade their image and rid them of the frail and elderly. They voted 5–1 against saving the failing Shalom nursing home and instead rezoned it to allow conversion to a hospital. Councilman (later Mayor) Harold Rosen spoke for the majority: "We need fewer nursing homes and city-paid doctors, and more beautification of the city. . . . One or two luxury hotels would upgrade the whole area, and the South Beach blight would be removed." Even as local retirees argued in City Hall against "beautification," they could see their fate. Like the Seminoles a century earlier, they were about to be systematically eradicated by real estate visionaries.

. . .

The Dolphins-Colts game, the last of the regular season, had been scheduled long before the season began as a special Saturday national broadcast. It had been expected that this rematch of the previous year's AFC championship game would decide the division title or at least be a playoff preview. However, the early collapse of the Colts—a fired coach, the demotion of Johnny U, and a disastrous 1–6 beginning—had put them out of contention and rendered the final matchup irrelevant. Except that one team had a chance to register the first undefeated regular season in the NFL since 1942, and that was enough for NBC to be glad of the Saturday slot. Furthermore, the Colts had had a bit of a rejuvenation midway through the season. Joe Thomas's insistence that Marty Domres replace the aging Unitas seemed actually to make sense by December, as the Colts had won four out of five games and Domres was the third-rated AFC passer (behind only Daryle Lamonica and . . . Johnny Unitas). Until this week, that is, when Earl Morrall finally had thrown enough passes to qualify for the official stats. Now the old journeyman brought in as an emergency backup had topped them all.

Meanwhile, last year's All-Pro quarterback was getting just about ready to go. Bob Griese was working hard at practice and, though still not at a hundred percent, hoped to get in some plays against Baltimore. He'd probably be fully healthy by the playoffs, but even he didn't seem to expect to take over for the league's new number one. Braucher's challenge to anyone betting on a Griese comeback had not been pure intuition. "I think Earl will start in the playoffs no matter what," Griese had told him at practice. "All three games [including the Super Bowl], even if I'm healthy." By Saturday the official word was that Griese would not be playing against Baltimore; Jim Del Gaizo was still the backup.

Even now, on the cusp of a perfect season, the Dolphins were having trouble garnering respect. Outspoken Baltimore linebacker Mike Curtis said he thought Miami was better back in Shula's first year, although he grudgingly admitted the defense was improved. "If we perform like we can, we've got a damn good chance," he said. Pittsburgh's brash young quarterback Terry Bradshaw was already talking about breaking Miami's streak in the AFC championship game, provided the Steelers could get past the Raiders in the first playoff game. "I'm more worried about Oakland than Miami. [The Dolphins] are not as good as everyone says. They're improved, but so are we." And on his Sunday night radio show, Howard Cosell seemed to have forgotten his attempts to make peace with the Miami fans. His guest, *Sports Illustrated*'s Dan Jenkins, author of the recent bestselling football novel *Semi-Tough*, asked Howard, "Don't you agree there are no great teams anymore? I don't think Miami is a great team. Do you?" "No, I don't," said Cosell. "Though I think it's a risk to say it in Miami, where they think they've become the international capital of the world in a tiny little corner of the peninsular state with eight hundred thousand television sets in use, vis-à-vis New York's eleven million. . . ." His puzzling correlation of team quality with the size of the local television market only underscored the feelings of some Dolphins, especially after their trip to New York, that a 13–0 team in a major city would be experiencing sporting canonization by now.

So Shula had some material for his weekly motivational speech. His team still had something to prove. And the possibility of an undefeated regular season, mindfully ignored for most of the season, could give them a lift today. There was also a rejuvenated Baltimore team to think about, a squad that still had a lot of pride and would be thrilled to give Miami its first *L* and gain a little revenge for last December's championship game and the 23–0 drubbing up in Baltimore earlier in the year. A team that was the Super Bowl champion less than two years earlier didn't take two shutouts lightly. And lastly, it was to be the final game, at least in Colt blue, for the great Johnny Unitas. Surely they'd give Johnny U one sendoff series at quarterback before he was put out to pasture.

None of the action, of course, would be seen in Miami. Perhaps the only silver lining of the blackout cloud was that if you had another commitment that afternoon, you weren't missing as much. It might have been difficult to drag my brother and me along with our sister to our piano recital at Mrs. Prado's house if the Dolphins game had been on TV. Apparently not a football fan, Mrs. Prado had scheduled the holiday recital right at game time. At one o'clock we kids waited as usual in the kitchen/den "backstage" area as each of us ventured out to the living room to perform our "Für Elise" or "Minuet in G" for the assembled parents. At some point, someone had quietly tuned the hi-fi in the den to WIOD.

One by one, presumably after each saw his own little Rubinstein stagger across the finish line, the dads slipped into the den to follow the game.

In the Orange Bowl, the arrival of winter—the sharp sunshine angling obliquely into the stadium, temperatures dropping through the sixties all through the game, with a brisk wind making it even colder—seemed to subdue the crowd somewhat. They were pleased, of course, to see their team systematically dismantle their final opponent, but there was none of the usual craziness, no bare-chested screaming for violence. No gangs of youths storming the turnstiles, and not even the usual misguided young man or two dashing onto the Poly-Turf mid-game. Just a calmly cheering, hanky-waving eighty thousand and ten—in anomalous jackets and sweaters. Until they were unduly provoked, that is, by a traveling Colts fan who strode up and down the aisles in his blue coat proclaiming "Baltimore Colts: Super Bowl Champions." He was hollered at, threatened, spat upon by teenagers, and pelted with paper cups and hot dog wrappers. "Today I got more harassment than anyplace this year," he said. "The only town where they ever treated me worse was Detroit." Still, it was a relatively composed crowd, as one of the ninety police officers on hand pointed out: "Usually a couple of dozen fans get put out of here every game, and a few get arrested for being drunk and disorderly. But not today."

The game unfolded so deliberately, marching toward its inevitable conclusion, there was little occasion for boisterousness. A long kickoff return to open the game, followed by a short drive capped by a forty-yard Yepremian field goal, and it felt already that that would be sufficient. Domres moved the ball well enough, but the No-Names were determined to allow no points. Along with the records the team and offense were chasing, the defense intended to hang on to their league lead in points allowed. They were only two points ahead of Pittsburgh coming in, and they figured if they shut out the Colts, there was nothing the Steelers could do about it. Three interceptions (along with three fumble recoveries) ensured their plan. When Paul Warfield cut across the middle early in the second quarter and leaped up to grab a high Morrall pass, took a shot to his abdomen and thigh, and fell across the goal line, no one doubted the ten-point lead would hold.

Much of the day's drama revolved around two numbers: 95 (the yards needed by Mercury Morris for a thousand-yard season) and 105 (the team rushing yards needed to set the all-time team record). The former, though certainly within Morris's grasp, would require a good day, plenty of carries, and some luck. The team record, though, was a virtual certainty: they normally got close to two hundred. The line was crossed in the third quarter, and not by any of the big three runners. On third down and eight near midfield, Morrall faded back to pass but bobbled the ball and was forced to try to run for the first down. He didn't make it, but his five-yard scramble took the team past the Detroit Lions' old record of 2,885 yards and, more importantly, into field goal range. An official from the Hall of Fame rushed onto the field to confiscate the ball for preservation in Canton, and Garo Yepremian was right behind him to unload a fifty-yard field goal with ease.

If the Hall of Fame could have known that Buffalo, behind O. J. Simpson, would break Miami's record twice in the next three seasons, they might have let Morrall keep the ball. At the moment, however, everyone was excited by the eclipsing of a thirty-six-year-old record that had seemed impregnable. And no one was happier than the infantry who made it possible. "Offensive linemen don't have statistics," said Bob Kuechenberg. "The defense has its tackles. . . . Everybody is measured in some way, but not us. We look at that team-rushing total as a gauge of our efficiency." They needn't have worried about being appreciated by the runners. "Monte Clark did magic with that offensive line," said Csonka. "He did the single best job I've ever seen any offensive line coach do." Clark had done it through teaching, motivation, and hard work, turning a group of largely unwanted players into the best offensive line in the league—perhaps ever. Kuechenberg, Evans, Langer, Crusan, and Moore, and above all—talk about the "best in the business"—Larry Little.

The only hometown boy on the team, Little grew up in the fifties and early sixties in Overtown, the predominantly Black neighborhood just north of downtown. From his home on Nineteenth Street and Fourth Avenue, he could walk to Booker T. Washington High School unimpeded by the monstrous 836/I-95 interchange, which wouldn't arrive until 1969. The surroundings were poor, but Little's mother worked as a maid, his dad worked as a custodian or did odd jobs, and "we never went a day being hungry," he said. "We lived better than others." His parents were tough—they took turns beating on him one night after he was suspended from school "for sassing a teacher"—but they instilled in him and his siblings a sense of confidence and self-worth. (His older brother George became an actor and singer; his much younger brother David would follow Larry's path

to the NFL in the 1980s.) His neighborhood and schools were all Black, part
of a segregated Miami; Larry was unable to sit in the front of the city bus or
drink from the same water fountains as white people. He remembered sneaking over to the "white" water fountain at the W. T. Grant department store to
see if it tasted any different. "It was colder," he said. He'd walk the two miles
to the Orange Bowl to watch the University of Miami football games and have
to sit in the "colored" section of the bleachers to watch the all-white teams.
In high school and then at Bethune-Cookman College in Daytona Beach, he
never played football with or against white players. There was no professional
football in Florida, or anywhere in the Southeast, so the TV showed the two
nearest pro teams, Washington and Baltimore. There were few Black NFL
players in the 1950s, and the Redskins' owner was the very last to integrate
his team, but the Colts had two excellent Black players, Gene "Big Daddy"
Lipscomb and Jim Parker. So Larry Little was a Colts fan, with NFL dreams
of his own.

Although Little was a standout defensive tackle in college,
Bethune-Cookman was no Grambling—the Notre Dame of Black football—and
he was overlooked in the AFL and NFL drafts in 1967. Joe Thomas of the new
Miami team approached him with a $500 free-agent signing bonus, but Little
had already been offered $750 by the San Diego Chargers, another AFL team,
and maybe he liked the idea of getting out of town. He enjoyed his two years
in California, where the Chargers tried him on both sides of the line and even
at fullback (he was so fast for a big man) before becoming frustrated with his
weight problems and inconsistent performance. But Joe Thomas had seen
something in Larry Little. When he was traded back home to Miami, Thomas
told him, "I finally got you." But Little was not happy about it. "I was getting
ready to make my home in San Diego," he remembered. "I loved it out there. It
was a different culture," a relief from the Southern segregation he'd grown up
in, and there were many more Blacks on the Chargers team. "And though we
weren't winning any championships, we were a lot better than Miami." In the
spring of 1969, in an Overtown bar called the Satellite where Black Dolphins
liked to hang out, he ran into his old high school teammate Mack Lamb, who'd
been hanging on with the Dolphins as a reserve cornerback. "That's great!" said
Lamb when he heard the news. "We'll be teammates again." "No, Mack," said
Larry. "I was traded for you." Cut by the Chargers, Lamb was back in Miami in

the fall, coaching high school; within a couple years, Little was the best offensive lineman in football. Another Joe Thomas masterstroke.

What turned Larry Little from a fringe player in San Diego to All-Pro in Miami? The first thing was weight. Only six-foot-one, he had fried-chickened himself up to three hundred pounds by the time he left the Chargers. George Wilson got him back down to 285 his first year. That wasn't good enough for Shula, who mandated 265. "And when I lost that weight," Little said, "it made me a better football player." Then there was the mentorship of Monte Clark, who recognized the talent and newly reacquired speed. As Csonka would note, "People didn't realize how fast he was because of his size. I'm actually pretty fast for *my* size, and I couldn't even keep up with him." Clark taught Little to stop looking all around as he pulled on a sweep, worried about linemen or blitzing linebackers. You focus on one thing, he told him: the cornerback you're going to blast out of the play. Little took that instruction, among myriad others, to heart and became the outstanding pulling guard in the league. His favorite play: Ride 38, in which he'd pull around Norm Evans on his right and lead Morris or another runner on the sweep. Morris would often have his free hand on Little's back, just waiting for the big man to spring him open. Little would isolate his target, usually the cornerback, and then came what Don Shula called the "moment of truth" for the defensive back; the coach knew it from experience. "If you try to finesse it, the guy will just walk into the end zone. You have to try to get down as low and as tough as you can and try to stay on your feet." Against Miami, the cornerback rarely stayed on his feet. Over and over, Larry Little ran into and over those poor guys, plowing them into the ground and then, more often than not, falling right on top of them. "Like a tractor hitting a tree," said Clark admiringly. "I enjoyed knocking a man off the ball and putting him on his behind," said Little later. "That's how we got our thrill." Often it was Csonka riding the Little train, and he appreciated it as much as Morris: "Anytime Larry is out in front of me, the cornerback looks like he wishes he were watching on TV."

A lot had happened very quickly for Larry Little, both good and bad. In just two years he had transformed from an also-ran in San Diego to the consensus number one offensive lineman in football. As a result, he had signed a new contract before the season for $170,000 over two years. His weight was now even lower than Shula's target, usually around 258 or 260, but he was still a large, powerful man, belying the sensitive soul within. "He's a soft-spoken, easy-going guy," said Csonka. "You can hurt his feelings easily." He was back in his hometown as a superstar but always cognizant of how close his luxury apartment near Doral was to his Overtown childhood. "I was exposed to everything [in those years]," he said, "and I'd be lying if I said I didn't do anything wrong." It was his big brother George who had steered him into sports to keep him out of trouble. Larry decided to do the same for other kids in rough circumstances, and in 1970 he and a few friends from the Dolphins started the Gold Coast Summer Camp for kids from Overtown and Liberty City and other distressed areas. There was no charge. The kids slept in tents at the Miami Beach Dog Track, at the southern tip of the island, and Little and his partners chipped in to bring in food for lunch. When Joe Robbie heard about it, he decided the Dolphins should support the camp, and beginning the next year the team staged the first training camp intrasquad scrimmage at the Orange Bowl to raise funds for the camp.

In July 1971, three days before that event, Little's big brother George, who had fallen on hard times and was living in the Imperial Hotel in Overtown, was shot dead in Liberty City the night of his thirtieth birthday. Larry was excused from the scrimmage but showed up and played anyway; more than ten thousand fans came, raising over $20,000 for the camp. "I was broken up," he said, "but I played anyway because I owed it to him, and also the game was to raise money for our boys' camp."

At twenty-seven, Little was entering his prime together with Shula's Dolphins; 1972 would be the second of his five straight All-Pro years. The offensive line called themselves the Expendables, since all but Doug Crusan had been rejects from other teams, but none were expendable now—least of all Larry Little, and also not Crusan and Wayne Moore, who at this point were coholders of the left tackle position. Crusan, a top draft choice in 1968, had been the relaxed, jolly-humored starter on the left side for the last three years. He was nicknamed "Bluto" for his enormous six-foot-four frame sporting a normal-sized head, and Yepremian called him "the comedian of the team. He put on the rookie show every year during training camp, and he gave himself the honor of choosing the ugliest guy on the team. I won't name the people that he picked, but it wasn't me. I didn't make the grade. I must have been below ugly." Crusan had been around long enough to remember the rough years when the offensive line was often the scapegoat for the epidemic of quarterback sacks and ungainful runs. In particular, with Little and Evans already solid on the right, it was the left side of the line that bore the brunt of criticism. Even when the team contributed to a benefit Christmas album, singing "Frosty the Snowman," Crusan said the word around the locker room was that the recording was all right—"except for a suspicious tremolo on the left side." So he was as proud as anyone that by 1971 the left side—he and Kooch—were an equal wing of a supreme line.

But in 1972, when Crusan popped a calf muscle in the preseason opener, some worried about a potential new weakness on the left. Crusan's backup was Wayne Moore, a.k.a. Solomon Moore, the man San Francisco had tried to sneak through waivers two years before. Moore had hardly played in his first couple years—and in college he hadn't played at all. He grew up in Beaumont, in the southeast corner of Texas, and starred in both basketball and football at his all-Black high school. But at Lamar Tech, also in Beaumont, he'd played only basketball, dominating the boards and defense with his six-foot-six, 265-pound body. A Texan on the 49ers, though, remembered what a force he'd been as a high school lineman and recommended the team try him out. San Francisco signed him for a year on their taxi squad, and it was when they were trying to do the same in 1970 that Monte Clark plucked him off their waiver list. Moore was not happy about it. His image of Miami said a lot about that city's reputation among African Americans, even those from Texas: "I hated [the trade], I hated it with a passion. I'd developed a lot of good friendships and I loved the [San Francisco] area, and I loved the team. I didn't want to come down here in the South and just suffer in this heat. It was the heat factor and going to a Southern city, something I didn't know anything about."

Moore came to enjoy South Florida, eventually retiring there after football, and he quickly became one of the best-liked members of his new team. He was close friends and roommates with Larry Little. As physically imposing as he was on the field, Marlin Briscoe called him "a gentle giant and quiet family man who could warm a room with his smile." And Kuechenberg remembered him as "a prince. He was a wonderful human being." He was also another indispensable piece of the perfect puzzle. Monte Clark's 1970 basketball espionage paid off two years later when Crusan went down in preseason. Moore hadn't played much, but he was an imposing physical specimen who had been learning his position steadily over three-plus pro seasons—including three training camps under Clark's wizardly mentorship—and he was ready. By the end of the preseason, Clark and Shula were feeling just as good about the line's left side as they had been before Crusan's injury. Crusan's calf had actually healed up nicely; he was activated for the season opener in Kansas City, but Moore was playing so well, Shula kept him in.

Then, in the third game, up in Minnesota, Moore suffered a dislocated shoulder in the second quarter. So Crusan, the old number one draft choice, stepped in for the free agent and resumed what he must have considered his rightful starting position. "How about Doug Crusan coming in after Wayne Moore was hurt and Crusan had been out with an injury himself?" Larry Csonka was beaming after the big comeback victory. "Crusan and Manny Fernandez, they don't say much, but they're unbelievable team men. That's why it's so beautiful to be on a club like this." For nine games since then, Crusan played the best of his career as the offense rolled up unprecedented rushing numbers and the team cruised through the season without a loss. Up in Foxborough, though, against the Patriots, he had twisted an ankle in that morass of battle between the two lines that many called "the Pit." Most linemen described their work with a war vocabulary: the violence, the intensity of man-to-man combat. But Bluto made it sound like a ten-year-old's birthday party. "In the offensive and defensive line it's like a bunch of bear cubs rolling around—you got some pretty big bodies bouncing around, with all the movement you make—and somebody just rolled me up from the side." So Moore replaced him again for the rest of the season, and for good. After starting for four seasons, Crusan would play only sporadically the next two years before retiring in 1975. But in 1972 that left tackle position was like a championship tag-team wrestling duo; no matter which of them was in, the left side was a rock.

Now that the offensive line had their rushing record, they had another prize in sight. They wanted to be the first line to lead two runners to a thousand yards. Mercury Morris wanted it too. His ankle had been hurting all year, and these last two games offered an occasion for rest. But he'd slashed through the mud for ninety-eight yards in New York, leaving him only ninety-five yards short of the big mark. He let Dr. Virgin inject the Xylocaine cocktail into his ankle again, he popped his Dexamyl—can't mess with the winning formula now—and he started the game. He had asked the local sportswriters, even before the last game, not to play up this individual angle. "I want to sneak in there," he told them. "All of a sudden people will say, 'Hey, he gained a thousand yards, too.' I don't want any hoo-rah about it until after I've done it." But if he really thought he'd be able to sneak his way to a thousand, his illusions were popped during the pregame warm-ups.

He was sitting on the turf near the corner of the Orange Bowl, slowly leaning forward to stretch out his hamstrings, when the Colts came out of their tunnel on the other side. As he stretched, he became aware of one Baltimore player heading in his direction; it was Mike Curtis, walking slowly across the field. Everyone knew Curtis. They called him Animal, or Mad Dog, or Pancake, for the topology he imposed on ball carriers. And poseurs: Morris was in the Dolphins' huddle up in Baltimore the year before when a fan leaped onto the field, grabbed the ball from the line of scrimmage, and began to run off with it tucked under his arm Jim Brown–style. He didn't get far, as Morris recalled: "All of a sudden I see this guy and I hear this POOM and all I see is the guy's feet in the air as he's dropping to the ground, half convulsed. And Curtis is going, 'What the fuck you think this is, the playground?'" Now Morris, refusing to look up, saw a man's shadow and felt a tap on his shoulder pads. "Hey," barked Curtis. "You ain't making no fucking record off me today." And he walked back to his side of the field.

Morris said it was Shula's decision to play him that day and try to get him a thousand, despite the coach's consistent declarations that all he cared about were team accomplishments. Maybe it was the prospect of the offense earning the distinction of the first thousand-yard *duo* that made the difference. In any case, even when the victory was assured in the second half, Morris was still out there, taking carry after carry. In the huddle, his teammates were counting down: "Merc needs twenty-nine more . . . he needs fifteen more. . . ." By this point his secret was out. Everyone in the stadium knew why they kept handing off to Morris, and they listened on their transistor radios for Rick Weaver to give them the updated yardage. At my piano recital, the den was now filled with dads crouched by the hi-fi, and every ten minutes another would peek in and ask how many yards Morris had.

And every time he got the ball, there was Mike Curtis. "Every time I lined up in the I [formation] and scanned the defense," he said, "I could see Curtis looking back at me just waiting for that pitch. You could see it in his eyes. The relentlessness, trying to get to me every time." Maybe it was the ankle, or the Dexamyl, or the anxiousness from trying to get the record, but Morris also kept slipping just as he was about to turn the corner. (Csonka got in one last shot at the Poly-Turf: "As far as I'm concerned, Merc was denied his thousand by the surface he had to play on. Eight or nine times he slipped and fell.") As sympathetic an observer as Bill Braucher called it a "carnival" and a "travesty" as, with the game winding down, the ball kept going to number twenty-two, and it seemed the law of diminishing returns kept shrinking the gains. In the fourth quarter, ankle pain was poking through the Xylocaine cushion. After a three-yard gain with six minutes left in the game, he came limping off the field in obvious distress. But the next time they got the ball he was back in there. After the two-minute warning, he took one more handoff and was slammed to the ground after only one yard. This time he lay writhing on the turf before two trainers helped him off the field for the last time. He had carried the ball more than ever before, twenty-six times, but for one of his lowest averages ever and a total of only eighty-six yards. I remember one of the dads at the hi-fi relaying the disappointing news: "He didn't make it. Nine ninety-one."

Back in game seven, another runaway win up in Baltimore, Shula had refused to leave Csonka in to get seven more yards for a hundred. But then, four games later, way ahead of St. Louis late in the game, he'd relented in the exact same situation and left Csonka in to get his hundred. Now he would take a lot of criticism for letting Morris ruin his ankle in pursuit of a thousand yards. Even the normally reverent NFL Films, in its weekly production *This Week in Pro Football*, bemoaned "an injury perhaps needlessly sustained for individual achievement at the greater expense of the team." After the game, Morris couldn't hide his disappointment: "Hell, everybody was trying to get it for me. They tried so hard. I feel let down, too, because my teammates are disappointed for me. If only we'd been on grass . . ." His voice trailed off. "He never finished the thought," wrote a reporter, "perhaps still wondering where he could pick up another nine yards now that the season had ended."

The game featured two quarterbacking landmarks. One was the final appearance of Johnny Unitas in a Colts uniform. He briefly replaced a shaken-up Marty Domres in the second quarter and completed one short pass, but then on his final pass as a Colt he was intercepted by Doug Swift. The Orange Bowl crowd gave him a standing ovation when he came in and of course cheered the interception, and that was it for Johnny U. Fans up in Baltimore were surely more sorrowful than Unitas, who simply said, "What's to be emotional about? Do you cry when you leave your job? They just don't want me to play football for them." Even Don Shula seemed more moved than Unitas: "I had a lump in my throat," he said. "Do you know I was a cornerback with the Colts when John threw his first NFL pass? That one was intercepted, too."

The other notable appearance was that of Bob Griese, trotting matter-of-factly back onto the Poly-Turf two months and a day after shattering his ankle on it. With a 16–0 lead late in the game, Shula figured it was a good opportunity to get Griese reacclimatized to live action. At the beginning of a series he called him over and was about to send him in, then held on to his arm. "No," he said, "wait one play." The fans had already seen Griese getting ready and were beginning to cheer but now had to suppress it for a play. "You should be writing for the movies," said Griese before finally running to the huddle amid the roar of the crowd. He commandeered the last two short drives, gave Morris his last five shots at a thousand, and even completed a couple of short passes to Otto Stowe. When linebacker Ted Hendricks broke through the line and sacked him, throwing him somewhat violently to the ground, everyone from the upper deck down to Shula must have held their breath. But Griese popped right back up. He was fine. Everyone knew how long he'd been sitting, though, and Earl Morrall was still considered the man to lead the Dolphins through the playoffs.

Above all, of course, the big story of the day was the completion of a perfect regular season. "Fourteen and oh" were words spoken for the first time in football history. (Before 1961, teams didn't play that many—the '42 Bears had gone 11–0 before losing the championship.) When the final seconds of the season ticked off, the players jogged back to the locker room showing little emotion, typical of this team. (The crowd was somewhat muted too. The only fan to storm the field was one dressed as Santa Claus, who tried to congratulate Shula but was respectfully escorted off the field by a policeman.) Shula himself celebrated about as much as he ever did, clapping both hands on Howard Twilley's back as he followed him into the tunnel, and a few players whooped it up a bit in the showers, but most were already thinking about the next week's playoff game with Cleveland. Before the players could even think about giving the game ball to Shula in recognition of the enormous season achievement, he let it be known once again that there was only one game ball he was interested in, and that would be awarded on January 14. So today it went to the offensive line, who insisted their guru, Monte Clark, keep it for them.

The players seemed uncomfortable discussing the 14–0 record. It was a tremendous achievement, but they knew to a man—Shula had been beating it into their heads since summer—that it would mean nothing if they didn't win three more in a row. To be undefeated might make a playoff loss even more desolating. As a team, they seemed even now like a man laboring under the weight of his past failures. "I really can't get too excited over it," said Nick Buoniconti. "We still have an awful lot to atone for." Only Jake Scott was willing to admit the uniqueness of what they had done. "Maybe we don't realize the importance of it now," he said. "We're thinking about the playoffs. But I reckon in ten, fifteen years, when the money's spent, we'll look back on this day with warmth."

Fifteen and Oh

Christmas came a few days early for Mercury Morris. After practice on Thursday, December 21, at the full team meeting, Shula made an announcement. The NFL, after reviewing disputed plays from the regular season, had corrected a call from the October 22 game against Buffalo. Most fans remembered the play, which stood out amid a succession of blunders in the Orange Bowl. Morrall had tossed a lateral pass to Morris that never got there. A defender tipped it and then fell on it, and the refs gave Buffalo possession. The Dolphins were sure it was an incomplete forward pass: Shula screamed and grabbed a line judge and was penalized fifteen yards. What no one outside the officials' box realized was that Morris, who had never touched the ball, had been given a nine-yard loss on the play. Now, in their postseason review, the league officiating committee had changed the status of the play to a "fumble" by Morrall. "So," Shula told the team, "Merc's season total is actually nine yards more than we thought."

Everyone in the room was aware of exactly how close Morris had come on Saturday in his painful mission for a thousand yards. He had come up nine yards short. This seemed too perfect to be true. "At first I didn't believe him," said Morris afterward. "I thought he was goofing on me." Then the room erupted in cheers. Merc had his thousand, and the team was not only the first ever with a 14–0 record and the all-time rushing leader but also the first with two thousand-yard runners.

• • •

The cold wave had passed, and when the Nixon family emerged from Air Force One at Homestead Air Force Base for a Florida Christmas, they felt that blast of warm air on their faces that really was what made Miami magic: you climbed into a metal cylinder in the bitter cold and stepped out of Miami International into a dream of summer. Even the drivers at the taxi stand, waiting in their flapping short sleeves, looked as if they were on vacation. The president was glad to be back, but as he and his family helicoptered from Homestead up to Key Biscayne, he knew he would not be completely on holiday from the pressures of his office. Several groups had already announced that they would be holding protests outside his compound. A few days earlier Nixon had ordered the commencement of the heaviest bombing campaign since the Second World War. As a true football fan, and perhaps inspired by the Super Bowl numbering system, he called it Operation Linebacker II.

The first Operation Linebacker was the bombardment that had raged from April to October, until the Paris peace talks had forged an illusory truce. But the two months since then had seen repeated breakdowns of successive breakthroughs. The demands of the North and of the South, it seemed, were unalterable and incompatible. On December 17, almost two months after Kissinger's "Peace is at hand" announcement, the *Herald* front page was split between the Dolphins' 14 AND 0 and Kissinger's new declaration: NOT YET, BUT WE'RE 99% THERE. But in the same article both Kissinger and his North Vietnamese counterpart accused each other of duplicity and fickleness. Nixon's ultimatum of December 14—get back to negotiations within seventy-two hours, or else—had been disregarded, and on the eighteenth he unleashed Linebacker II.

For eleven days, the U.S. launched over three thousand sorties, mostly by B-52s, dropping forty thousand tons of bombs, mainly on Hanoi and surrounding areas. In Washington, United States senators were opposed to the missions by a two-to-one margin (though mostly on party lines). The *New York Times* called it "Stone Age barbarism," the *Washington Post* "savage and senseless." In general, though, these latest hostilities met with much less public protest at home than earlier ones. "The public response," wrote Stanley Karnow, "was relatively muted; with almost all the American troops home, the war had ceased to be a national torment." Forty-three American airmen were killed and forty-nine more were taken prisoner, but the American people, it seemed, were ready to move on.

Muted, too, was the response to the end of the great endeavor known as Apollo. Since John F. Kennedy had announced the historic mission of "landing a man on the Moon and returning him safely to the Earth," the government had spent about $25 billion achieving it, and now the last section of the last Apollo spaceship parachuted down into the Pacific Ocean after a journey of a million and a half miles. While many still considered the moon landings the greatest achievement of the human race, there was also a growing bitterness regarding where that money might have gone. William Hines, considered "the godfather of NASA space reporting," called it an eleven-year "binge": "And now, thank God, the whole crazy business is over."

· · ·

Christmas week in Miami: warm, sunny days, cool nights with the windows open. Friday the twenty-second, school let out for two weeks of late mornings in bed, days at the tennis courts or throwing the football around the yard in anticipation of the playoffs. Closer to the sea, the sidewalks of Miami Beach and Coconut Grove were swarming with snowbirds. On Crandon Park beach, you might see a flock of pale, beefy young men tramping the sand, a carefree confident look on their faces: the Nebraska Cornhuskers football team, in town to face Notre Dame in the Orange Bowl game on New Year's Day. The hotels and restaurants were full; the paper was calling it one of the biggest entertainment weeks ever in South Florida. All week there was Wilson Pickett at the Marco Polo, Lorna Luft at the Eden Roc, and Lou Rawls at the Newport. Ann-Margret was doing two shows a night at the Fontainebleau. Woody Allen was making a rare return to stand-up after the recent release of his seventh film, *Everything You Always Wanted to Know About Sex* (*But Were Afraid to Ask)*, and was paired at the Deauville with singer Edie Adams. For those who preferred comedy the way it used to be, Milton Berle was headlining at the Diplomat. And of course there were enough nude revues around town, from *The Love Machines* to *Vie Parisienne*, to start a nudist colony. In fact, there was an actual nude play, *Nude Awakening*, at an actual nudist colony, in the wilderness west of Fort Lauderdale, out past Cooper City.

The hottest ticket that week, however, was to get into the Orange Bowl to see the NFL's only undefeated team try to stay that way. Because until 1975 the league didn't award home field in the playoffs to the team with the better record—the divisions took turns getting the home field—the Dolphins might have only one home game: the first one, Christmas Eve against the Cleveland

Browns. If they won, they'd be home again for the AFC championship game if Oakland beat the Steelers but otherwise would have to travel to Pittsburgh. And even in the playoffs, home games would not be on television locally. The First Football Fan had done his best; Nixon had personally asked Pete Rozelle, the NFL commissioner, to lift the blackouts on playoff games that year, provided the games were sold out forty-eight hours before game time. But Rozelle refused: recent playoff games had failed to sell out, he said, due to misguided anticipation of the blackout being lifted. Above all, he wanted pro football to remain primarily a live event and not become "a studio show." He even went on television (of all places) to make his case to the public at halftime of a nationally televised game: football, he said, must remain a stadium spectator sport. Nixon did not take the rebuff lightly; in retaliation, he had Attorney General Richard Kleindienst announce that the administration "would strongly urge the new Congress to examine the anti-trust exemption [enjoyed by the NFL] and seek legislation that is more in keeping with the public interest." Although Nixon surely felt he was fighting for the workingman, a public opinion poll the next week showed there weren't enough football fans out there appreciating his efforts. The public, apparently, felt the president should be spending more time trying to end the war than worrying about watching home Redskins games. And in any case, coincidentally or not, Nixon was on Key Biscayne and at Camp David for Washington's two home playoff games, out of blackout range and parked in front of the tube.

With no television broadcast in Miami, playoff tickets were even more precious. Just as the crowd began exiting the Orange Bowl on Saturday after the Colts game, a line began forming at gate fourteen. Despite previous expectations that no tickets for the first playoff game would be left for the general public, about four thousand were remaining after season tickets and those allotted to the other team and officials, and they would go on sale Sunday morning. Even at the inflated prices of $7 for the end zone, $10 for most of the other seats, and $12 for the "luxury" seats with backs (regular-season prices were $4 to $10), demand was high. About a hundred fans camped out all night, on the coldest night of the year, to be first in line. They piled blankets into their tents or sleeping bags, played chess, strummed on guitars, passed around flasks, and occasionally broke into the chant, "We're number one!" By daybreak there were more than a thousand people in line, and the Dolphins management paid a local café to bring in coffee and pastries for everyone. At nine-thirty, after seventeen hours in line, John Huard of Fort Lauderdale scored the first four tickets, emblazoned with grainy photos of Don Shula and Joe Robbie under the header *A WINNING TEAM*. By eleven, everyone had been served—and still two hundred tickets remained. There'd really been no need to spend the night freezing and sleepless. Another couple of hours and it was an official sellout, a week ahead of time. But still there would be no local television.

TV or not, the Dolphins were still the biggest show in town. The players had made the most of local advertising deals, and Cruise Casuals, the men's clothing store that had been featuring players like Morris, Csonka, Kiick, and Morrall in their newspaper ads, now even ran a big one featuring the *assistant coaches*: Arnsparger, Keane, Schnellenberger, Scarry, and Taseff, with six-foot-six, crew-cut Monte Clark towering awkwardly in the middle, all lined up in their sport jackets and looking about as comfortable . . . well, as Earl Morrall did in his seersucker blazer.

Assistant coaches belonged in dark film rooms when not sweating on the practice field, and those were the only places you could find these guys this week as they prepared for a new season in which a single loss meant—if the set of Shula's jaw was any indication—another year under the weight of his albatross. Although no one on the team would admit it, a perfect regular season only raised the stakes: they were reaching for a higher prize than ever, but a loss now would make the last Super Bowl seem like a minor miscue.

In the first round they were hosting Cleveland, a solid team but hardly the storied dynasty of old. The great championship years of the 1950s and 1960s were long gone. After a rough year in 1970 they had come back with a division title the next year and a wild card this year—10–4 behind Pittsburgh's 11–3—but they certainly were not considered a contender to go all the way. This had been expected to be a rebuilding year, as young quarterback Mike Phipps, in his third year, became a starter for the first time. But a light schedule allowed them to win eight of nine games after a 2–3 start and sneak into the playoffs. The only impressive win, really, had been a tight one over the Steelers, and the Browns came down to Miami as eleven-point underdogs. Even more galling for them and their fans was the announcement of the Pro Bowl team on Wednesday: they were one of only two teams—along with 3–11 New England—who had no players chosen. "You win ten games and don't have a guy on the team make the Pro Bowl?" asked Coach Nick Skorich. This was the kind of thing that gets posted on locker room walls, the sort of incentive that could justify shaving several points off the spread. Owner Art Modell arrived in Miami in a cloud of sarcasm, claiming his team was simply happy "to have a ticket to the dance. . . . I just hope we can make it through the National Anthem."

The Dolphins, not surprisingly, had the most players chosen for the Pro Bowl, tied with Oakland. Stanfill, Buoniconti, Anderson, and Scott were chosen for the defense, and the offense had Little, Evans, Csonka, Morris, and Warfield. Morris was selected as a kick returner, which must have been a nod to his thousand yards rushing, because his fourteen kick returns for a twenty-four-yard average didn't put him even in the top twenty-five. And Warfield's selection, despite being sixtieth in receptions with twenty-nine, was recognition that even though his team threw the ball less than almost anyone, he was still probably the most respected receiver in the league.

Now he had a chance to go against his former team, and although he would downplay any such angle, there has never been a player, traded against his wishes, who didn't want to show that a mistake had been made. Modell was not yet ready to regret his trade of Warfield for the draft choice that gave them Phipps. After all, Warfield was thirty years old, and Phipps, while it had taken him the expected couple of years to get used to the pro game, had had a decent season for a third-year man. The Browns still had every expectation that he would develop into a star quarterback. Coach Skorich's declaration, "I think it was one of the greatest trades the Browns have ever made," may have been more hopeful than definitive, but it could not have sat well with Warfield.

Warfield knew Modell, though, and he wasn't buying the fake playing dead for this game. He told his teammates how back in '64, his rookie year in Cleveland, they were big underdogs against Don Shula's 12–2 Baltimore team in the NFL championship game. "All we heard all week was how great the Colts were," he said, "and we laid it on them, 27–0. You've got to be leery of teams that short-sell themselves." This game was personal for Warfield, who grew up just a few miles from the Browns' training camp, was ecstatic to be drafted by his favorite team, and had taken the trade to Miami hard at first. "If I had to pick five teams in football I didn't want to be traded to," he said, "Miami would have been one of them. I was hurt. I had expected a different kind of treatment from the Browns." But Warfield had learned a lot in Cleveland from Jim Brown, including—in the context of handling physical and verbal abuse from opposing players—"if you think about revenge, you're not concentrating on the objective: to win. Jim Brown knew what he was about. Don't get mad. Get even."

Warfield was not the only Dolphin to whom a Cleveland matchup was notable. Shula, of course, had also grown up a Browns fan and had the thrill of playing for them (before leaving in a similarly heartbreaking trade), as did his college roommate Carl Taseff, the Dolphins' defensive backs coach. Mike Scarry, the defensive line coach, had played for the Browns early in his career as well, and Monte Clark played his seven best years on the Cleveland offensive line. Tight end Jim Mandich idolized the Browns as a boy, watching every Cleveland game on the TV in his father's bar, a forty-minute drive from Municipal Stadium. Bob Matheson had played his first four seasons in Cleveland before Miami traded for him and designed a new defense around him. And Jim Langer had envisioned a long career in Cleveland before the Browns hung him out to dry on the waiver list. Another link was the return to Miami of Bob DeMarco, the veteran center whom Langer had beaten out of a position in training camp. DeMarco left town angry, but several games into the season he was signed by Cleveland, and now he was feeling more magnanimous toward his old team—and looking forward to getting a little friendly revenge of his own. "Everybody's saying we don't have much of a chance. But when I joined the Dolphins, everybody was saying the same thing about us. They were amazed when we got into the Super Bowl."

. . .

All teams were suffering casualties by the end of the long season, and as the first playoff game approached, the Dolphins were no exception. Shula might have been thinking twice about having run Morris into the ground in pursuit of a thousand yards, even after that venture's belated success. The speedster was practicing gingerly, and he even admitted to a reporter, "The situation is not real good." On Wednesday he was listed as "probable" for the playoff game. Friday the team announced that Kiick would start; Morris would play but wouldn't return kickoffs. They might need him, as Kiick's knee had been hurting for weeks, and now Csonka was in bed most of the week with a stomach virus. He returned to practice Thursday but looked a bit weak. The offensive line wasn't a hundred percent either. Doug Crusan was activated for the game but still had a shaky ankle; luckily Wayne Moore was back and playing great. But Bob Kuechenberg was now "doubtful" with an aching back. Al Jenkins, who had spelled Larry Little in New York, would replace Kuechenberg if needed, but that would be a downgrade you didn't want in the playoffs.

In addition to these health anxieties, Shula was facing a quarterback dilemma that felt all too familiar. Bob Griese was back at just about full strength, ready to go if needed. It would have been an obvious decision to reinstall the All-Pro, except that his backup was a former MVP who was the league's leading passer this season. Two of Shula's credos were in conflict: no one should lose their starting status due to injury, and you never change a winning lineup. The situation was eerily similar to his 1968 season in Baltimore, when Shula had stuck with Morrall in Super Bowl III even though Unitas was recovered from injury. After the historic loss to the Jets, many argued he should have put Unitas in much earlier than he did. Shula would start with Morrall in these playoffs as well, no question. The question was how many sluggish drives or errant passes it would take before Shula wouldn't be able to resist putting Griese back in.

· · ·

Playoff weekend finally arrived. The Greenbriar group, including the Morrall, Crusan, and Matheson families, had reached the end of their off-season lease. They left their apartments to the high-paying holiday crowd and moved down from Hallandale to the Kings Inn, right across Northwest Thirty-Sixth Street from the airport, until whenever the playoffs ended. It was a convenient choice, as that was the hotel where the team stayed every Saturday night before home games. The players got to know Art Brun, a popular Miami entrepreneur who ran the hotel along with the adjoining cottages known as the Villas. It was a surprising choice for Shula, as the Kings Inn hosted a boisterous nightlife and was also home for the pupils of Eastern Airlines' stewardess school. The trainees hung out by the pool in the afternoons and the bar at night; the "ongoing music and frivolity" were remembered fondly by Brun's employees and clientele alike. The waitstaff also remembered feeding the Dolphins supper the night before games and breakfast in the morning before waving them good luck as they headed out for the Orange Bowl.

It's doubtful Shula was able to keep Kiick, Csonka, Mandich, Fernandez, and Scott in their rooms at the Kings Inn, but surely he tried. In any case, by six p.m. Saturday, December 23, they were all checked in and ready for the coach's Saturday night ritual of burgers and beer. They may have laughed a bit at the full-page ad in the *Miami Herald* that day, placed by the *Cleveland Plain Dealer*. It featured a large drawing of a football with a fuse attached, all wrapped up for Christmas. "Merry Christmas to the Dolphins," it read. "We hate to see you [fans] plagued by anxiety [about completing a perfect season]. . . . So we're sending you a can't miss antidote . . . the Cleveland Browns. . . . [By] about 6 p.m. Sunday, you can stop getting all worked up over the fortunes of the Dolphins in the Super Bowl. Instead, all you'll have to think about is a 14 and 1 record." The same day, the *Herald* had placed a similar ad in the *Plain Dealer* pointing out how many players slipped through the Browns' hands and ended up on the great Dolphins team. "When the Dolphins play the Browns, we're betting on *your* hometown boys." They particularly dug it in about Warfield, the sight of whom in aqua and orange still was painful for Browns fans: "You remember Warfield. It's worth the price of a ticket just to watch him run one pattern."

Warfield, though, had been having trouble sleeping all week. After the last game, his wife and kids had gone back to their permanent home outside Cleveland for the holidays, leaving Paul in his Miami residence, a luxury high-rise condo on Hallandale Beach just a few blocks from the more homely Greenbriar. "We were not committed to living in Miami," he recalled, "for a lot of reasons." Ohio was home, where extended family was. But also he had never welcomed a move to the South: "I grew up in the North during segregation, and you never wanted to go across the Mason-Dixon Line. Once you went across the Ohio River into Kentucky it was like going into another country. We had no real problems in Miami, aside from one disappointing incident my wife experienced." But still, Cleveland was home.

If the idea had been to let him prepare for the playoffs without distraction, it had backfired. Every night he lay awake for hours, worried about his old team sneaking in to ruin the perfect season. On the morning of the game, Christmas Eve, he woke up even more disoriented. For a moment he was sure he had overslept and would be late to the Orange Bowl to begin his stretching and warm-up routine. Sitting up in bed, he was puzzled by the lack of sunshine behind the blinds; it was 5:23 a.m. "Not since junior high school have I had trouble sleeping before a game," he said later that day. "I must have been thinking about the Browns even in my sleep."

It wasn't just the Cleveland team—solid, but hardly a daunting prospect to the defending AFC champs—that had the entire Dolphins team feeling a bit uneasy. It was the realization that no matter how perfect your regular season was, one misstep now meant total failure. The point had been driven home the day before as they watched the first playoff game, between Pittsburgh and Oakland. Trailing 6–0 with just over a minute left, backup Raiders quarterback Ken Stabler had faded back to pass, scrambled away from pressure, and run thirty yards for the apparent game-winning touchdown. (Earl Morrall's teammates would tell him that night that Stabler's run reminded them of Earl's mad thirty-one-yard dash against the Jets—not Stabler's run as it happened, but rather when they showed it on slow-motion replay.) The game appeared to end 7–6 for the Raiders when Terry Bradshaw, after barely eluding a sack, launched a desperation fourth-down pass with fifteen seconds left. Safety Jack Tatum torpedoed the receiver, Frenchy Fuqua, just as the ball arrived, and the ball went flying out of the TV picture. But Franco Harris appeared suddenly from off-screen. He had somehow grabbed the errant ball a few inches above the ground, and he ran it forty-two yards for a touchdown to win the game. Harris's "Immaculate Reception," considered by many the greatest play in NFL history, instantly erased the possibility of another Orange Bowl game this year—if the Dolphins won they would now have to go to Pittsburgh—and also impressed upon the Dolphins the danger of thinking any game was "in the bag."

The other playoff game Saturday was another stunner and must have had Shula pondering too. The Cowboys found themselves down by fifteen to San Francisco in the fourth quarter when Tom Landry finally brought in Roger Staubach, the previous year's Super Bowl hero, who had been injured and replaced by Craig Morton for most of the '72 season. Staubach threw two touchdown passes in the final two minutes to lead Dallas to victory in a 30–28 thriller. Just like Shula in '68, Landry had been slow to reinstate his injured star quarterback. Fans and the media would be watching Shula every time the Dolphin offense had to punt. What would it take for him to bench Morrall?

• • •

The windchill of last week was gone. As the Orange Bowl filled up on the afternoon of Christmas Eve, a hot sun baked the Poly-Turf well above the air temperature of near eighty degrees. The sellout crowd began filling the stadium two hours before the three p.m. kickoff, but one famous fan would not be there. Rumor had had it that President Nixon would make the ten-mile drive in from Key Biscayne to watch the team he had become somewhat fascinated by, but in the end he stayed home and worked, conferring with White House aides and with Kissinger by telephone. Possibly Nixon felt it would look bad to be out at a ball game while by his order four thousand tons of bombs were being dropped on North Vietnam, although it didn't prevent Kissinger from attending the Redskins-Packers game up in Washington. Nixon even turned down offers from several local supporters to install a long-range antenna to pick up the television signal from Fort Myers, doubling down on his solidarity with the American football fan's struggle against the NFL blackout. "The president feels very strongly that he shouldn't be able to receive anything the normal viewer could not get," said his spokesman.

In the Dolphin locker room, the strain of bringing a perfect record to the trial of a playoff game was palpable. The whole campaign of reclamation could disappear in a quick afternoon. Shula bemused veteran sports announcer Curt Gowdy, who was chatting with Larry Csonka, by asking him to put out his cigar. Who would object to smoking in a locker room? There were even ten Dolphins or so, including Larry Little and Larry Seiple, who still smoked cigarettes. "I don't want the smoke bothering anyone," quipped Shula, and Gowdy complied. "He's got his game face on," said Csonka.

The whole team had their game faces on—a bit too tightly. The Dolphins came out intent on showing the nation why they were 14–0 and instead looked mediocre. Just like the Giants, the Cleveland defensive line had sworn they'd stop Csonka ("The big bastard isn't going to beat us" was their pact), and sure enough they held him to nineteen yards on eight carries in the first half. But unlike up in Yankee Stadium, no one else was picking up the slack. The leading rusher was Warfield, on two end arounds, and Morrall had completed only four passes for thirty-eight yards.

Luckily, there were always the special teams. On Cleveland's second possession they had to punt, and Miami put everybody except returner Jake Scott up on the line. Two or three of them came breaking through to the punter, and Charlie Babb blocked the kick and fell on it at the six-yard line. He looked as if he might just stay there, but Curtis Johnson lifted him right off the ground and gave him a push toward the end zone, where he arrived a few seconds later for the touchdown. "I can't really say whether I would have thought to get up and run or not [if Johnson hadn't been there]," said Babb. Asked whether the famously taciturn Johnson had exhorted him to run, he said, "Hell no. Curtis hasn't said anything to me all year."

Miami also got a forty-yard field goal after a short drive featuring a twenty-one-yard run by Warfield and an eleven-yard pass to Twilley. But Yepremian also missed two long kicks, from fifty-three and forty-six yards, and another didn't count. With the clock running and no time-outs, the field goal team came running on just before halftime, and Garo poked a "gimme" seventeen-yarder through as time expired. But a couple linemen had not gotten set in time, and because an offensive penalty as time runs out does not get a replay, the half was over. But despite the errors and listless play, Miami still led 10–0.

The Browns saw that ten-point deficit very differently. Phipps had been intercepted three times, he'd had one perfect pass dropped in the end zone, they'd had one punt blocked for a touchdown and another ruined by a fumbled snap, and still they were only down by ten? "At the half, we knew Miami was ready to be taken," said Skorich. "After all that had happened, to be only ten points behind . . ."

Of course, the other side of that was Miami's perspective: they'd played an awful half and still had a ten-point lead. They made some adjustments to open up the running game and were confident they'd just widen the gap. However, they had to punt on their first possession, and Cleveland's top draft choice Thom Darden ran it back thirty-eight yards. Five plays later Phipps took the snap, faked a handoff and rolled out right, then ran it in for the touchdown. All of a sudden it was a tight 10–7 game.

With Csonka ineffective, perhaps still weakened from his stomach bug, Kiick and Morris began to step up their game. They provided the bulk of the yardage on the ensuing drive as the game moved into the fourth quarter, and Yepremian lined up for another forty-six-yard attempt. Browns on the field and on the sideline were screaming at him, reminding him of his two first-half misses: "The wind's against you! It's too far! You can't do it!" (In the telling, Garo may have redacted some stronger language.) Well, he said later, "that's one of those things that psyches you up and makes you play better." He knocked this one through for a 13–7 lead. Then, on their next possession, the

Dolphins finally seemed to be taking the game in hand, driving down to the Cleveland thirty-three. Jim Kiick slashed for twenty-five of those yards on four tough carries, and Morrall gave it to him again on one of their core plays, the 36 Trap Left, with Larry Little pulling from the right side to lead the way. But Kiick made a rare error, getting too close to Little, bumping into him and fumbling the ball. This led to a bizarre chain of events. Cleveland drove back into Miami territory, only to see Dick Anderson intercept a long pass at the eighteen-yard line. That might have almost sealed the game, but after eluding one tackle and trying to stretch his return, Anderson fumbled the ball himself and it was recovered by the original intended receiver, Fair Hooker. Two plays later, Anderson and Johnson got mixed up on coverage, and Phipps, just before getting flattened by a charging Bill Stanfill, found Hooker all alone at the goal line. With only eight minutes and eleven seconds left in the game, Cleveland was winning, 14–13. The Dolphins hadn't been behind this late in a game since the third week, up in Minnesota.

"We thought they'd choke at that point," said one Cleveland player. "Sometimes teams will tighten up when they're not used to being behind." But the Dolphins were far from panicking. They'd driven right down the field the previous possession, before the unfortunate fumble. Shula had considered bringing Griese in for the second half, and it occurred to him again at this point, as Morrall had completed only four of eleven passes for thirty-eight yards. "I'd have done it if I felt it would shake us up," Shula said later. "But a lot of things that happened weren't Earl's fault, like Kiick's fumble." And Griese still wasn't quite a hundred percent. Instead, Shula grabbed Morrall by the arm. "We've got plenty of time," he said. "No need to rush."

There was generally little need to remind Earl Morrall to take things slow. The way the Dolphins liked mostly to run the ball, however, which kept the clock running, it was very possible this would be their last possession. If they had any kind of extended drive, they would need it to end with a score. After the kickoff, the ball was at their own twenty. The hot sun was out of view and setting in the Everglades. The Orange Bowl lights were on; it was Christmas Eve and no one was thinking about Christmas. Morrall jogged out to the huddle, which was unusually quiet. But before he could call the play, another voice sounded. "All right, this is it. If we're gonna get anything done, now's the time to do it." Paul Warfield did not speak in huddles. Now it was as though the late

Vince Lombardi had appeared up above in the darkening sky. Morrall just nodded at him and called the play—one of their bread-and-butter passes that he
had neglected all game. It was Dick Nixon's brainstorm from the Super Bowl:
the slant-in to Warfield. He had had two successful runs on end arounds, but
the great receiver hadn't caught a ball all day. Now he ran the simple pattern
into the middle of the field, Morrall never looked anywhere else, fired it in,
and Warfield took it in stride just before taking two hits, low and high, which
flipped him right over onto his back on the thirty-five. He casually tossed the
ball to the ref while lying flat on his back and slowly got up. "Never let them
know you're hurt" was his advice to the younger wide receivers.

With Csonka not at full strength and also being keyed on by the Cleveland
line, the rushing burden had passed to Morris and Kiick, who were up to the
task. Now Morris got the call twice in a row, plowing straight up behind Larry
Little for five yards and then again behind Little on a sweep right for another
five. First down at the forty-five. And then Morrall called Warfield's number
again. As the quarterback executed his awkward backpedal and then stumbled
a bit, double clutching while eluding a blitz, Warfield was fighting cornerback
Ben Davis, who played him bump-and-run for ten yards before Warfield finally
put a fake on him and broke free long up the middle. Morrall's deep lob was
slightly overthrown, and Warfield had to leap for it. His catch was another bit
of performance art—almost identical to his touchdown slide through the mud
in Yankee Stadium, except this time he bobbled the ball for a moment before
cradling it and falling to the hard, dry Poly-Turf. He lay there for a minute on
his back, ignoring his own advice. He had knocked the wind out of himself,
but it was a thirty-five-yard gain, down to the Cleveland twenty. After a short
Morris run, Morrall called for number forty-two again, as if he knew how
badly Warfield wanted this game. He was free for a moment in the end zone,
but linebacker Billy Andrews hung on to him and was called for holding. The
ten-yard penalty made it first and goal at the eight-yard line.

Conservative old Earl Morrall seemed to be making statements with
his calls. He was letting Warfield drive a stake through the heart of the team
that had traded him, and now he decided to bestow on Jim Kiick a chance for
atonement. Kiick had killed the best previous drive of the day with a fumble
deep in Cleveland territory. Now, with the game on the line, Morrall called the
same play, 36 Trap, this time to the right, with Kuechenberg pulling over from

the left. "That really had me thinking," said Kiick afterward. "That fumble earlier really upset me. It could have cost us the game. Now I saw the opening and covered up the ball with two hands. I wanted the touchdown in the worst way." As he took the handoff to the right and cut toward the goal line, he saw Csonka ahead of him cutting down a lineman and plowing him into the ground Larry Little–style. With Evans and Kuechenberg leading the way, he surged forward. Kuechenberg had been considered doubtful for the game most of the week with a badly aching back, but he had taken his painkillers and insisted on starting. Nothing was going to keep him out of this game. Now, at the finish line, he delivered one last sledgehammer of a block, smacking linebacker Charlie Hall three yards backward in the air. By the time three defenders managed to touch Kiick, he was too close, with too much momentum, for it to do any good. He launched himself into the air as he had done so many times before, Mr. Clutch near the goal line, and landed in the end zone, sliding to a halt with his shoulder by the padded base of the goalpost.

As they ran off the field, Kiick slapped Kooch on the back: "What a block!" The first to greet him as he approached the sideline was Mercury Morris, the interloper who had come between Butch and Sundance. Morris, arms stretched out wide, grabbed Kiick and lifted him into the air. "One of the greatest moments of joy I ever had," said Morris, "was when Jim scored that winning touchdown. . . . I was so freaking happy he did that, I ran out on the field. . . . I'm going, 'Jim! Yes!'"

The offense had finally come through with an eighty-yard drive to take the lead. Paul Warfield had assuaged his worries by accounting for sixty of the eighty yards himself. However, they had done it so uncharacteristically fast—seven quick plays using up only a touch over three minutes—that there were still almost five minutes left. Miami's defense forced Cleveland to punt after three plays, but then the offense, bent on running out the clock with running plays, failed to get a first down themselves. The Browns took over near midfield, with almost two minutes left, for one more chance. They needed a touchdown, though, not a field goal, and that's the difference between a good chance and not much of one. They got down to the Miami thirty-four, but on second down Phipps tried to hit Hooker over the middle and didn't see Doug Swift crossing over from the right. Swift, a smart, solid all-around player, wasn't known for having particularly good hands. But when Dick Anderson had batted up Phipps's first pass of the day, Swift had made a great diving catch for the interception. And now, as he put it, "[Phipps] laid it right on my head. I wasn't about to drop it." With less than a minute left, he should have just fallen down, and that would have been that. He admitted as much later: "Anderson's fumble on his interception was still fresh in my mind." But the iconoclastic "Swiftie," as his teammates and even his wife called him, instead took off on a fifteen-second victory scramble. When he got near the sideline he forswore that conservative cop-out as well, cutting back into the field, dangerously switching the ball to his other hand. Finally, with Tim Foley motioning and screaming at him to get on the ground, Swift complied. Or, as he put it, "I got exhausted and fell down."

Finally this first test, which was supposed to be much easier than that, was over. Young fans leaped down from the stands and sprinted around the field, slapping players on the back and celebrating. And the 15–0 Dolphins ran off the Poly-Turf for the last time that season, happy to be alive. The Browns had sworn to stop the "big bastard," but they discovered, as others had, that there was a lot more to the Miami offense than Zonk. They had been stung by their old superstar, Warfield, and those other two runners, Kiick and Morris. Merc had taken the load fifteen times on his throbbing ankle and run for seventy-two yards, and Kiick had had a big day, too, with fourteen runs for fifty yards and the game-winning touchdown. Even with Csonka marginalized, the offense had run the ball forty-seven times for 198 yards. Morrall had only completed six passes, two of which were the Warfield knockout punches in the winning drive. "That last drive," said Morris in the locker room, "was for all the believers."

"We played only as good as we had to play," said Csonka. "We've got to overcome that next week at Pittsburgh." "I was nervous and emotional," Warfield admitted as he got dressed at his locker. "This is normally a relaxed team, but we were all so anxious to get past this first obstacle. I think we were too cautious. Our offense will be better next week." Even after his heroics on the winning drive, he'd had to agonize for the final five minutes of game time, which seemed like an hour. Now he was finally relaxed, showered, and packed, and he excused himself and rushed over to the airport. He would be in Cleveland even before the Browns, to join his family for Christmas.

Doug Swift was in no such rush, savoring the rare attention and the game ball he'd been awarded for his two interceptions. There had been times when he'd brooded over the value of a life in football: "Sometimes you wonder what the hell you're doing out there. You're at the bottom of the pile, with all that armor on, the pads and helmet, and you're sweating your ass off, and you look down at the artificial grass, man, and you really wonder what it's all about." Other times, though, he spoke of his love for the game and his compulsion to play it as perfectly as was humanly possible. The freethinking "new movement type," son of two physicians, liked to joke about how he was only in football because "I like all the money. I can't make money like this anywhere else." Now, referring to the $25,000 or so a run to the Super Bowl might earn, he called his game-saving interception "a big thrill, a big financial thrill." As for his mad zigzagging after the steal when he should have done the safe thing and hit the turf? Maybe it wasn't all about the money after all. There was a boyish jubilation in that runback that belied his wisecracks. He smiled and held up the ball. "Intercepting," he said, "is the only joy a linebacker gets."

Sixteen and Oh

Christmas Week in Miami. The same heightened atmosphere as everywhere, with schools out and the anticipation of the holidays. Hanukkah came early this year, the first week of December, and we lit our candles and received our gifts. Christmas to us is just a big dinner with family friends, a second Thanksgiving. But it's still a special day, with everything closed. Luckily they leave the gate open at the tennis club and we see the Bennetts, the Siegals, Dr. Jay—actually about half the club at Kendalltown. And as the week progresses toward New Year's, there are college bowl games every night, the Junior Orange Bowl parade, the King Orange parade, the Orange Bowl game on New Year's. And the South Florida warmth—mid-seventies most days, only an occasional chill in the night air—lends its own sort of magic. Even we, who have known only these sunny short-sleeved Christmases, know it's not normal. We see the ice storms and snow on the evening news and feel a sense of shelter, a charmed existence, in living down here. For decades, well into a new century, until my parents finally retire, sell the house we've known for forty-six years, and execute a reverse migration back to the Northeast, I will treasure the chance to come back for holidays, to experience each year, once again, that blast of warm air by the taxi stand.

On Thursday, a hundred thousand wholesome folk line the streets of Coral Gables to see the brightly costumed dance troupes, thirty floats, and seventeen high school bands of the twenty-fourth Junior Orange Bowl Parade. Queen Barbara Ann Bowser, age twelve, crowned and bejeweled, rides high on a giant music box float with her two princesses. Anita Bryant is even there, smiling and waving amid what looks like a forest of orange ice-cream cones. Anita Bryant, the former Miss Oklahoma and singing sensation—she sang the national anthem at last year's AFC championship game—now at thirty-two a born-again media personality and national spokeswoman for the Florida orange juice industry. She lives with her husband and four children in a twenty-nine-room mansion on Miami Beach. They're friends with several Dolphins, and she makes more money than any of them: eighty thousand from her OJ work alone. Like Jane Chastain, she's a Miami workingwoman who's made it big and remained as Christian and conservative as you can get. Her agent puts it mildly: "She doesn't go for Women's Lib."

Each day this week, around the clock, six hundred American aircraft make runways tremble in Guam and head for North Vietnam bulging with four thousand tons of high explosives. "Linebacker II" is raging in its final blitz. The bombing campaign over the Hanoi-Haiphong area is more destructive than any in the history of warfare, with the exception of the dropping of the two atomic bombs on Japan. The jets are unheard at thirty-five thousand feet; ruination falls from the sky like summer hail. The last remaining civilians in Hanoi, tens of thousands of them, flee the city "by every conveyance imaginable."

Saturday, Nixon finally calls a halt to the carnage and announces that peace talks will resume in Paris on January 8. (Bombing continues the next day, but only south of the twentieth parallel.) In Egypt, Anwar Sadat announces his country's preparation for renewed war against Israel in 1973 "until God gives us victory." In Miami, Saturday brings the main course after the junior parade: the thirty-ninth King Orange Jubilee. Six hundred thousand line Biscayne Boulevard to see it all. Anita Bryant is back, emerging from a house made of giant oranges on the Florida Citrus Commission float before hopping off to join the telecast crew. Mickey Mouse and Snoopy, ten feet tall, glide by; forty floats in all, thirty-one bands, and the high school beauties. Orange Bowl queen Maria O'Byrne, in a long white gown, and her Court ride high atop the King Orange float, which proclaims in huge white letters: A WORLD AT PEACE. Anwar Sadat: "I declare that the door to battle is the door of the future, and that there is no other path." Twenty-seven years after Hiroshima and Nagasaki, Harry Truman is dead at eighty-eight, in Independence, Missouri.

. . .

Rocky Bleier of the Pittsburgh Steelers was the only NFL player who'd been in Vietnam for more than a USO visit. A year after being drafted by the Steelers in 1968, he was drafted a second time, by the Army, and assigned to a year of duty in Vietnam. Three months in, on patrol in the Hiep Duc Valley, he was shot in the left leg just before a grenade blew through his right foot, knee, and thigh. Following multiple surgeries over the following year, Bleier played the last game in Pittsburgh's 1970 season and was active on special teams in '71 and '72. He would become the starting running back (alongside fullback Franco Harris) in 1974 and even gain a thousand yards in 1976 (he and Harris becoming the second duo to do that, after Csonka and Morris). In 1972 he was still just a special-teams player but already one of the Steeler heroes: the only NFL player with a Purple Heart.

Franco Harris, of course, was the idol of the moment. His miraculous catch off the deflection the week before was the reason Pittsburgh was hosting the Dolphins in the AFC championship game. After "a record of futility unmatched in professional sport," Steelers fans were going nuts this week. One of the oldest NFL teams, they'd joined the league in 1933 when it expanded to two divisions. (They were the Pirates until 1941.) This year, the team's fortieth, it finally won its first division title. And the miraculous defeat of Oakland had set off a weeklong bacchanal that Steelers radio commentator Myron Cope was calling the "Feast of the Immaculate Reception."

Art Rooney, who had founded the Pittsburgh franchise at the age of thirty-two and ran the team for fifty-five years, was a beloved figure in Pittsburgh and around the sports world for his integrity and philanthropy. U.S. Supreme Court justice Byron White, who led the NFL in rushing for Pittsburgh in 1938 (and again in 1940 for Detroit), said simply, "Art Rooney is the finest person I've ever known." Chuck Noll, whom Rooney had hired on Don Shula's recommendation in 1969—Noll was Shula's defensive backs coach in Baltimore—was another universally popular figure. The team's fans were another matter. Their enthusiasm was growing to levels that were frightening to visiting players—and referees. After Franco's sensational touchdown, as hundreds of rabid fans jumped onto the field, referee Fred Swearingen wasn't sure. If the ball had bounced off the offensive receiver, not the defensive back, then the play was illegal. But as Oakland coach John Madden put it, "There was no way he was going to call it the other way, with all those wild people on the field. They'd have killed him on the spot." Three Rivers Stadium was home to an alliance of screaming, banner-waving militias: Franco's Italian Army (Harris's Black

father and Italian mother had met during the Second World War), Frenchy's
Foreign Legion (after the other running back, John "Frenchy" Fuqua), and
Gerela's Gorillas (named for kicker Roy Gerela: they gathered in the end zone
and caused mayhem for visiting kickers attempting field goals). This year the
fans' rabid support had finally been rewarded as the Steelers built their own
unbeaten streak: all eight home games, including the first playoff.

They had sour memories, though, of their last game against the Dolphins,
in Miami the previous year. Griese started on the bench after spending the night
in the hospital with a stomach virus. But he came in after the Dolphins fell
far behind and threw three touchdown passes to Warfield for a 24–21 victory.
Bradshaw had gotten knocked out of the game early with a concussion, though
he came back in later and threw for a touchdown. This week, however, it was
Bradshaw who'd been in the hospital for several days with the flu. On Friday he
met the press with a glucose tube attached to his arm. "We'll beat the Dolphins,"
he said. "I'll be ready by game time, you can bet on that."

Due to league rules for playoff games, the Dolphins flew north on Friday, a
day earlier than usual. They got their first taste of local attitude as they climbed
off their charter flight in Pittsburgh, many wearing hand-painted Yepremian
neckties that featured a dolphin leaping over goalposts: one of the cargo handlers greeted them with, "Fifteen and one!" As they drove downtown to the
William Penn hotel, a plethora of placards and banners in windows showed off
the populace's talent for wordplay: "Zonk Csonka," "Knock Twilley Silly," "Drop
the Mercury," and "Tie Up Garo." Saturday afternoon, a single-engine plane
dropped two thousand leaflets in the area of the hotel. "Surrender!" the papers
ordered. "This leaflet will guarantee safe passage out of town to any member
of the Miami Dolphins football team, if presented to a member of Franco's
Italian Army. Surrender now and enjoy life with your loved ones rather than
face destruction on the field of battle at Three Rivers Stadium."

Manny Fernandez wasn't concerned with armies, foreign legions, or gorillas on Saturday afternoon. He was consumed with relief. That morning, after
riding down the elevator with Kuechenberg, Langer, and Stanfill on the way
to breakfast, he'd picked up a newspaper in the lobby, and the first thing he
saw was the headline: JET WITH 170 DOWN IN EVERGLADES. Just after midnight, an
Eastern Airlines flight crew, approaching Miami International on a flight from
JFK, had gotten distracted by a malfunctioning landing-gear light and didn't

hear a chime warning that they were losing altitude. They thought they were still at two thousand feet as the Lockheed L-1011 crashed into the pitch-dark Everglades, sliding and breaking apart across a thousand-foot swath of grass, water, and mud.

Fernandez didn't say a word to his teammates; he just turned around, took the elevator back up to his room, and got on the phone. He had gotten married a week earlier, the Friday before the Cleveland game, in a small private ceremony for Miami friends before the big wedding planned in California after the Super Bowl. His wife, Marcia, was an Eastern stewardess, and that JFK-to-Miami run was her regular Friday night flight. "I got to my room and called home. I don't even know why, because I knew she was on that airplane. But I did. And she answered." Marcia had traded flights with her friend Adrian the week before because of the Friday wedding ceremony. Manny didn't realize it, but for some reason Adrian had kept the JFK route this week too. Marcia was on a different flight and had landed a half hour before the crash. She'd stayed in the employee lounge with her colleagues all night long, waiting for news. When she finally heard that Adrian was among the eighty or so survivors, she drove home just a little before Manny called. It was her final night as a stewardess.

Three aching ankles, belonging to Morris, Crusan, and Kolen, were pronounced fit to play on Sunday. That was assuming the game-day benefits of Xylocaine, of course. No one was turning down a shot at this point if it would get them onto the field. Even the punter, Larry Seiple, still not fully recovered from his injury, had his knee drained, shot up with painkiller, and wrapped for the game. Two of the injured, Morris and Crusan, were particularly eager to play, as Pittsburgh was their hometown. Morris took the opportunity to visit two of the homes his family had lived in. He was able to get one of those visits in during practice, as one of his old neighborhoods had been razed to build Three Rivers. "I used to live on the twenty-five-yard line," he said. "Shore Avenue." He had bought twenty tickets for family and friends. Crusan had grown up in Monessen, a town just outside the city. He was eager to play in front of family and friends, too, but although he was recovered, Wayne Moore had been playing so well that he would continue to start.

One player had an extra incentive—as if any was needed for the AFC championship game. On Friday, Mean Joe Greene, the awe-inspiring defensive

tackle of the Steelers, was named the AFC's lineman of the year, the most prestigious recognition for those who toil in the Pit. Chosen by a panel of thirty-nine
pro football writers, Greene received nineteen votes. Coming in second with
thirteen votes was the Dolphins' Larry Little. Next best were a couple guys with
two votes. Greene was the cornerstone of the Steeler defense that had led the
league in quarterback sacks, turnovers, and general evocation of terror. "He's
a superstar," admitted Shula. "In a class by himself. You have to talk of him in
the same breath with the greatest linemen in pro football history."

Of course, the same could be said of Little, and he wasn't pleased with the
result of the vote. On Sunday he would have the chance to go directly against
his rival: right guard versus left defensive tackle. "I had a little chip on my
shoulder going into that game," he recalled. "I knew Joe was an outstanding,
tough football player, the best I had played against. But I wasn't gonna let him
dog me out. I considered myself pretty damn good too."

The rest of the offense had something to prove as well, after sputtering
through most of the first playoff game. "We've got nothing to be proud of offen-
sively," said Jim Langer. "The defense won that one," Kuechenberg agreed. "That
game was one of my worst." "We relaxed or something," said Csonka. "We got
up by ten and then got in a rut." And as if they needed reminding, a voice from
the losers' locker room last week had been preserved in the *Herald*: "If they
play like that," said one Cleveland lineman, "the Steelers will murder them."

• • •

Sunday, New Year's Eve. The 15–0 Dolphins had been made to leave their
eighty-degree home and fly north as visitors. But they were at least spared the
raw freeze of a normal Pittsburgh winter's day, as temperatures were rising into
the fifties. If it stayed dry, conditions would be good; if not, the Tartan Turf
was as much of an ice rink in the rain as the Poly-Turf. In an era of the most
miserable playing surfaces ever concocted, the Orange Bowl and Three Rivers
had two of the worst. At least the bruises and rug burns would feel like home.

By the time the teams came out for introductions, Three Rivers Stadium
was quaking dangerously. Still almost new, in its third season, it held just over
fifty thousand—almost all season-ticket holders—plus standing room, and
standing room, as they said, was sold "until the fire marshal arrives." For all the
good he'd done today, the fire marshal might be that guy in the Gerela Gorilla

suit in the front row. "Three Rivers Stadium was loud," said Larry Seiple. "It was kind of scary as you walked on the field."

The day before, Jim Langer had been confident at breakfast. "You know what I would like?" he asked. "I'd like to see them win the toss and receive. Our defense holds them to three and out. They punt. We take it on our thirty-five or forty and ram it right home for a touchdown. That would shock them. They haven't had many power touchdowns scored on them. They'd never catch up." But everything went backward. Miami received the opening kickoff, and after a couple of first downs Earl Morrall overthrew Twilley across the middle and safety Glen Edwards intercepted, giving Pittsburgh the ball at midfield. The Steelers had a tremendous running game but didn't employ it as exclusively as the Dolphins. (Sixty percent of their plays that year were runs, compared to seventy percent for Miami.) But Terry Bradshaw came out, his waistband a little loose from several days in the hospital, and called ten straight rushing plays. Finally, from the three-yard line, Bradshaw faked a handoff and rolled out left, tucking the ball under his arm to try to run it in himself. Jake Scott charged up and hit him low at the two-yard line. Bradshaw flipped over, hit his head and shoulder hard on the turf, and fumbled forward into the end zone, where offensive tackle Gerry Mullins fell on it for a touchdown.

It had seemed like a fortunate drive for the Steelers. They had fumbled twice, needed an offsides call on a third-and-five for a first down, and they were beating the Dolphins 7–0. What the screaming hordes in the stands didn't realize, though, was that Terry Bradshaw didn't know where he was. "Scott really knocked me silly," he said afterward (without reference to the Twilley sign). When he came on for his next series, he barely knew whom to hand off to and had to be replaced with another Terry: Hanratty. "I was pretty loony. I was on the sideline trying to look at the playbook, but it was all Greek to me. I guess I really didn't know what was going on the rest of the half."

The Dolphins weren't about to panic. After all, the Jets had scored the same way back in October, with a lineman recovering a fumble in the end zone on the opening drive. The difference was that this time they had to come back against the defense that had allowed fewer points than any in the league—aside from Miami's. Both defenses held for the next few series, and Seiple came in to punt for the second time, early in the second quarter. It would be the play he would be asked to recall, describe, and expound on for the next fifty years and more.

Larry Seiple had been the Miami punter since the team's second season, his rookie year of 1967. (The inaugural season the punting had been shared by the starting quarterback and coach's son, George Wilson Jr., and middle linebacker Wahoo McDaniel.) Seiple wasn't the most powerful punter in the league, but he might have been the most valuable; Shula had said Seiple could've gotten the game ball in the big win against Minnesota, with two punts downed inside the Viking five-yard line and nothing returnable all day. Seiple had also been an excellent running back and receiver at the University of Kentucky and once, punting in a fourth-and-forty-one situation, ran the ball for a seventy-yard touchdown. Don Shula was less amenable to Seiple taking off on fake punts than the fun-loving George Wilson had been, but it was certainly something they had discussed. They had particularly discussed it that week, as Shula and Carl Taseff had noticed something tantalizing in the films of the Pittsburgh punt-return team. In order to set up the return, their linemen tended to turn around after the snap and sprint downfield to set up their blocking—sometimes even before the ball was punted. "Shula and Taseff both took me aside during that week and showed me what Pittsburgh did on punt returns," said Seiple. "'If we need it,' Shula said, 'we can run on them. I will call it when I want to do it.'" Seiple was enthusiastic, to say the least. On Friday, WIOD's Rick Weaver told him he'd had a dream in which Seiple ran a fake punt for a big play; it was all the punter could do to laugh it off: "Well, we'll see." In the first quarter, on his first punt, he saw the Steelers line turning around just like on the films. He came to the sideline and said, "They're doing it!" Shula just nodded.

Now it was fourth and five from midfield, halftime approaching in a game they were losing 7–0 with the offense unable to throw off its playoff sluggishness. They needed a spark—and yet Shula still had not called the fake. Seiple stood waiting for the snap, the home crowd's roars for their defense still rumbling like a boiling kettle just taken off the fire. And there it was again, as if in slow motion, as the ball came spiraling back to him from between the center's legs. It was even better this time, as there was only one guy rushing; everyone else was spinning and taking off down the field like they missed their bus.

"Well," Seiple said years later. "It was supposed to be called by Coach Shula, but I didn't wait for him to call it. Maybe I had too much to drink the night before, who knows, but I couldn't wait. I think he had told me at some point,

'You can do it—as long as you make it.' And then I saw them all start to roll to my left, and just one guy coming on the right side. Bob blocked him, and as I looked downfield, there was nobody there, so I just took off."

He took his normal left step, right step, and then instead of the third step and kick he ran forward, barely eluding Barry Pearson on the right, whom Bob Matheson had just nudged out of his flight path, obviously unaware himself that Seiple was going to go. The Steelers were busy setting up a return on their right, and Larry Seiple ran down the other side of the field as free as a jogger on the beach. Adrenaline must have been propelling him as fast as he'd ever run, even on the drug-numbed knee, because Pearson, a rookie wide receiver, wasn't even gaining on him. The race began at his own thirty-seven. At the Pittsburgh thirty-five Seiple caught up with one of those linemen, Steve Furness, who was running downfield in the same direction completely unaware of what was happening. Seiple passed him and continued on. Larry Csonka was watching on the sideline: "I could hear the Steelers fans in the stands behind me yelling, 'Turn around!!'" Finally, after about fifty yards of sprinting, Seiple slowed to confront his first would-be tackler—the return man, Glen Edwards—and Pearson finally caught up with him as Edwards forced him out of bounds at the twelve-yard line. He had officially gained thirty-seven yards, and the game had been turned on its end. Two plays later, Csonka, who had caught five passes all year, took a swing pass from Morrall on the left side and ran it in untouched. Both defenses dominated the rest of the quarter, and at halftime the game was tied 7–7.

The mood in the Dolphin locker room was somber. The defense had given up only that first short drive, capped by a fumble touchdown, but for the second straight week the offense seemed lethargic, without its usual confident pop. "The offense was floundering," said Doug Swift, "and Nick [Buoniconti] was beside himself on the sideline, cussing up a storm." Morrall hadn't been too bad: there was that interception, but overall he was seven for eleven with a touchdown. Yet Shula's memory of Super Bowl III, when he'd left Earl in too long, was tearing at him. Down 7–0 at the half, he could've gone with Unitas in the second half but didn't, and when he finally did, it was too late. Now here he was again. Griese wasn't completely recovered yet, but he was close. He wasn't favoring the left foot anymore. He'd told reporters he'd probably be a hundred percent by the Super Bowl. If they got there. Aside from Seiple's mad dash, the Dolphins hadn't got past midfield all day.

Shula walked up to Griese at his locker. "Are you ready?" he asked. Griese looked neither surprised nor unsurprised. "Yes, I'm ready."

Morrall had done so much for Shula over the years, taking him to an NFL championship in Baltimore after Unitas went down, and then filling in for Griese this year without a loss. "Replacing Earl was one of the toughest things I ever had to do," he said later. But he'd made the decision. He continued on to Morrall's locker. "I'm going with Bob the second half," he said. "But stay ready." He was one of the most successful quarterbacks of his generation, a former league MVP, and he'd just led his team to eleven straight victories. Today he'd really only made one bad play, and he was out. But Earl Morrall was the consummate team player, and he was thirty-eight years old, and he knew Griese was prepared. Morrall just nodded. He'd stay ready.

Before Griese could come in, however, Pittsburgh got the opening kickoff of the second half. After two plays they faced third-and-thirteen on their own seventeen-yard line. But then Hanratty, a former Notre Dame star, who hadn't been able to do anything in relief of Bradshaw in the first half, suddenly looked All-Pro, firing two long passes into tight coverage for big gains. Then he gave the ball to Frenchy Fuqua on a draw play for twenty-four yards, down to the Miami thirteen. The Dolphins held, but Gerela's short field goal gave Pittsburgh a 10–7 lead in a tough defensive game.

Asked before the game which quarterback he'd rather go against, Chuck Noll had said, "Griese, because that would mean they'd be behind." With ten minutes and fifty seconds left in the third quarter, he got his wish, as the unprepossessing figure of number twelve came trotting on the field for his first meaningful action in two and a half months. Two plays later, on third and six, Griese called his first pass. It was Nixon's old favorite, yet again. Warfield called it "our money pattern: I take four steps, cut in, and catch the ball on the break." The linemen worked hard on their counterparts so they couldn't get their hands up, Warfield got two full steps inside of linebacker Andy Russell, and Griese threw it quickly and accurately over the middle, getting the ball just barely past the linebacker coming from the other side and hitting Warfield in stride. Warfield saw a defensive back coming from either side, so he took off in a sprint right up the middle of the field. He thought he was going all the way, but the nagging ankle sprain and a slight groin pull slowed him down enough that a cornerback ran him down after a fifty-two-yard gain.

If Seiple's fake punt had changed the tenor of the first half, this long Griese-Warfield hookup from one twenty-four-yard line to the other transformed the second. Griese now took eight more plays for the end of the drive. It had everything you could pack into twenty-four yards, including Dolphin specials like a fourth-down conversion and Griese drawing the defense offsides with his patented cadence call. (Knowing he had a free play, Griese threw for Kiick near the goal line, but Jack Ham stepped in front of it and intercepted. The penalty gave Miami a first down anyway.) Griese then went to the air again, scrambling around for several seconds before finding the oft-overlooked Marv Fleming at the five. With fourth-and-one on the Pittsburgh four, Shula's attitude was the same as when he went for it on fourth down in his own territory against Minnesota: "If you expect to be a world championship team, you've got to make it." Jim Kiick plowed between Little and Evans for two yards, and then a couple plays later took it again on a pitchout right and performed the Kiick special, diving just over the goal line. Bob Griese had made his comeback with a Homeric seven-and-a-half-minute drive that put Miami back on top, 14–10.

Terry Hanratty was able to get his team just past midfield, but as the third quarter ended the Dolphin defense held, and then Maulty Moore, the reserve defensive lineman and special-teams stalwart, "knocked the center back like a bowling ball," got a hand up high above his six-five frame, and blocked Roy Gerela's forty-eight-yard field goal attempt. The Dolphins took over at midfield and proceeded to chew up the fourth quarter.

Griese found Fleming again, this time on the right sideline for a first down. Fleming had not been happy about disparaging remarks in the press concerning his "stone hands" and was pleased to haul in five catches—half the team total—today. "When we play for the big money," said the bejeweled entrepreneur, "the passes come right into my hands." After that throw, though, the drive was all ground control. Morris and Csonka took turns crashing through the middle for big gains. Three effective trap plays, in which the offensive line let Joe Greene, L. C. Greenwood, and Dwight White come through on the outside only to watch the runner disappearing up the middle. Ten yards, twelve yards, eight yards. But the Steelers stiffened up near the goal line, and Miami faced another fourth down, with inches to go for a first down, at the four-yard line. Csonka got the necessary yard there, and then Griese gave it to Kiick again for his specialty, twice in a row. On the second try he followed Csonka and Little, who was pulling to the left, cut inside, bent low, and charged forward, once again lunging just across the goal line.

Monte Clark's offensive line had dominated the infamous Steelers front four, taking eleven slow plays and seven and a half minutes for the second straight drive. Time and again, and particularly on both fourth-down conversions near the goal line, Griese had chosen to run right behind Larry Little—and right over the prizewinning lineman of the year, Joe Greene. Little had said earlier he'd been "in a deep concentration bag" all week. "I know if I don't do the job on him," he said, "we won't win the game. If I do, we'll win. I have a lot of pride, and I can't see myself getting beat." He'd done the job, all right, a task almost no one had even attempted all year: handling Joe Greene unassisted. And when Greene had slid over and lined up over center Jim Langer, Little's future co–Hall of Famer had done just as well. The Dolphins were ahead 21–10. Their two second-half drives had obliterated a full quarter of the game, and Pittsburgh now had only seven minutes left to try a comeback.

The disheartened crowd at Three Rivers stood and cheered at the sight of Terry Bradshaw, who'd been out since bouncing his head in the first quarter, running back on the field. Chuck Noll said after the game that Bradshaw "just wasn't functioning mentally at all [after the injury]. We thought he was all right at halftime, but we wanted to be sure and that's why we waited until the fourth quarter." Hanratty remembered it slightly differently, according to writer Kevin Cook. He recalled a trainer grilling Bradshaw on the bench in the fourth quarter: "Brad, what's the score? Who are we playing?" No response. "What day is it?" Bradshaw looked up and saw his team playing a football game. "Sunday?" "Well, Brad, you got one right." The signal went out to Noll: Bradshaw was good to go.

Though still "wobbling a little," Bradshaw managed to complete four passes in a row—of only five he completed all day—throwing bullets into tight coverage. The last of these was a high, off-target pass that rookie receiver Al Young, who'd caught six passes all year in what would be his only full season in the NFL, managed to snag behind him with one hand as he slid between Jake Scott, Curtis Johnson, and Mike Kolen into the end zone—right under a banner that read FRANCO THE MIRACLE WORKER. Just when it seemed the game was over, Bradshaw had pushed them down the field in two minutes to bring Pittsburgh within four points. The stadium was rocking again, thrumming to the chanting of the faithful.

Fired up by the crowd and Bradshaw's heroic return, the Steel Curtain stuffed two Miami runs, and Griese faced a third and eight from the twenty-two. Instead of playing it safe with another run and punting, relying on the defense, Griese faded back to pass. But no one was open, and defensive tackle Ernie Holmes had gotten by Kuechenberg and was charging the quarterback. With one fake step Griese let Holmes go flying by like a frustrated bull, Kuechenberg in close pursuit. Griese now rolled to his right, but there was Dwight White breaking free of his blockers, so Griese rolled back and around, near the goal line now, as Langer and Moore knocked White to the ground. In Miami, millions of us watching on TV were having flashbacks to Griese's mad scramble in the Super Bowl that had ended in a thirty-yard loss. Now Griese had got himself facing forward again, just in front of the goal line. Holmes had been leveled by Kuechenberg but was up again and closing in; White was back on his feet and coming at him; and Joe Greene, whom Norm Evans had neutralized for as long as could humanly be expected, had finally made his way near his elusive prey. If Griese was sacked on the one-yard line, or even if he was unable to find a receiver to get the ball close to, Seiple would be punting from the back edge of the end zone and the odds of a Steelers comeback would rally considerably. (Quarterbacks were not ever allowed to throw the ball away back then; if no eligible receiver was close to the ball, it was "intentional grounding" and loss of the down.) But a Griese feint sent Holmes sliding to the turf for the third time in one play, and just as Greene and White were about to smother him he finally saw Jim Mandich covered tightly on the right side and threw just close enough to him to avoid a penalty; the ball bounced harmlessly away. Ten million lungs began breathing again in Miami. The crowd groaned—they'd wanted a sack in the end zone—then cheered the defense. Griese was typically unfazed. "That's what the people pay their money for," he said later. "I knew where the end zone was. I wasn't about to get caught in there."

Miami wasn't able to run out the clock, but punting from the twenty-two was better than from the two, and the sack that wasn't was the Steelers' last chance. Bradshaw may have had visions of another quick series of passes down the field, but the No-Names had seen enough of that. On the first play, from the Pittsburgh forty-five, first Stanfill, then Den Herder, and finally Manny Fernandez swarmed over Bradshaw and sacked him for a ten-yard loss. Then, on third down and long, Bradshaw scrambled way to his right and forced a throw into a pod of five Dolphins. Buoniconti made the easy interception at midfield. The Dolphin offense came trotting back on with just over two minutes left, but they were still a little jumpy, a chorus of voices babbling nervously in the huddle: "Watch the offsides!" "Let's punch it down their throats." "Come on, now's the time!"

Suddenly one voice cut off all the others. "Shut up, damn it!" Silence. Bob Griese hadn't sworn since they lost the Super Bowl a year ago. Ol' Earl had been terrific for eleven games, but now they were headed back to the big one, and taking them there was their no-nonsense All-Pro QB. You didn't chatter in a Griese huddle. He proceeded to call Csonka's number four times in a row, in addition to pulling the defense offsides with another cadence call, and when they finally turned the ball over on downs, it was at the Pittsburgh nine-yard line, and only forty-two seconds remained in the game. Mike Kolen intercepted the final Bradshaw pass, and the Miami Dolphins were AFC champs again.

When the gun sounded, the Dolphins calmly jogged, or walked, off the field. In a few hours, in Washington, George Allen would ride his players' shoulders, waving to the crowd in triumph; in the locker room he'd lead his team in a jumping, screaming celebration of their utter dismantling of the Cowboys. After their victory, the 16–0 Dolphins were engaging in their own version of joyous mayhem: pats on the back, smiles, an occasional shout from the shower room. Others were more sober, knowing there was one more victory needed before they could celebrate. It had been a physically punishing contest. Cornerback Tim Foley had separated his left shoulder in the first quarter and watched the rest of the game with his arm wrapped and in a sling. He was already ruled out of the Super Bowl. Jake Scott separated his right shoulder later in the game but said he'd be playing for sure. "Maybe it'll balance out the left one," he said, referring to his other shoulder, separated two years before. Nick Buoniconti sat half undressed, revealing the cast on his right wrist and a wrapped left shoulder he could barely move. "It's just a bruise," he said. "It'll be all right. The wrist is the one I broke last year and again in preseason. It won't stop me." Csonka held out his right elbow, which appeared to have a golf ball implanted in it. "It doesn't do any good," he sighed. "I keep making these speeches and keep running into more damned carpets. This stuff was harder than our own junk." In the other locker room, Mean Joe Greene, who would win four Super Bowls and make ten Pro Bowls on his way to the Hall of Fame, was gracious in defeat. "I said before today's game that this one would be won up front," he said, "and I think it was. At least, I know they won on my side . . . [with] Little and Langer."

On the flight home, complimentary wine, beer, and champagne soothed the bruises, as did satisfaction. Players were walking up and down the aisle, congratulating each other. Even Joe Robbie, perhaps having more than champagne in his seat up front, was staggering around, announcing his team's latest feat: winning two AFC championships in one year, January 2 and December 31. Howard Twilley was holding up a miniature bottle of Mateus rosé and toasting his friend Bob Griese, fourteen months his junior. "The kid won it for us," he announced. "I don't know what magic he's got. But the kid did it."

The kid was his usual placid self. "My most satisfying victory? Well, it was satisfying, but I don't talk in extremes. I don't feel any of the jubilation we felt after we beat Kansas City and then Baltimore last year. We were just so glad to get into the Super Bowl. Now we want to win." This was the Code, the team mantra for the past eleven and a half months. Out of Shula's set mouth, it had a dramatic intensity. Griese recited it with all the gusto of a Sunday school catechism. He got a pillow down from the overhead rack and went to sleep.

The noon game, with less passing and fewer commercials than the league's future would bring, had finished at two thirty-five; when the plane landed in Miami it was still early evening. The crowds waiting for them after each away game had been growing, and the airport authorities had at some point set up the Eastern Airlines parking lot just off Thirty-Sixth Street to accommodate the throngs. They'd begun arriving an hour after Kolen's interception, with their Dolphins shirts and home-painted banners, chanting "We're Number One!" Thousands now were packed behind a chain-link fence. The Dolphin Dolls led them in singing "We Love You Dolphins." The Eastern Airlines jet taxied right up to the fence and parked next to a red-white-and-blue–draped trailer. Shula, in jacket and tie, approached the microphone and shouted, "Happy New Year, everybody! I'm just so proud of the team . . . and now we've got the AFC championship and the right to go back to get even for what happened in last year's Super Bowl. All we want now is to be seventeen and oh!" A few players—Griese, Morrall, Stanfill, Evans—addressed the crowd while the others slipped into a waiting bus to get them across the street to their cars at the Kings Inn.

On the plane ride home, Norm Evans had come over and sat down next to Eddie Jenkins. The rookie had been back on the taxi squad since the end of October. It was a bittersweet feeling to practice with the team all week and travel with them but have to watch the games in street clothes. And Norm knew he had no family in Miami. "Hey, Eddie," said Evans, "would you like to come over and have New Year's dinner with my wife and me?" Jenkins was shocked. "It was so gracious of him to invite me over. And it was the greatest New Year's of all time." Sure, he was just on the cab squad, but he'd made the team, and had been on the active roster enough of the season to get half the playoff spoils: an extra game's salary for the first playoff, $8,500 for winning the AFC, and at least another $7,500 for the Super Bowl ($15,000 if they won). His payout of half that nearly doubled his salary for the year. He had a fine meal with the staid Evanses, then later found a New Year's party to go to. When he woke late the next morning, it was already eighty degrees. "I had no girlfriend at the time, nobody to talk to. I'd sometimes just go drive over the bridge to Key Biscayne, take a beer, just walk around the beach, watch the little houseboats there." At Crandon he walked past the palm trees in the picnic areas and across the wide swath of sand and, stutter-stepping to avoid the little blue bags of poison—Portuguese men-of-war—scattered near the shoreline, ran out into the warm, shallow ocean until it was deep enough for him to submerge himself. A good number of others were spread out on the beach, many of them certainly fans who didn't suspect a Dolphin was in their midst. Sunshine was pouring down between staggered cumuli into the aquamarine. Every ten minutes or so a fat jetliner appeared from the horizon, engines humming at low power, making a gliding descent over the water into Miami. They came in low and slow, and you could see the logos: the big blue Pan Am globe, Varig's blue-and-white compass star, the orange-and-gold National man-in-the-sun. The war was as good as over, the beach was heaven, and the Dolphins were back in the Super Bowl. It was nineteen seventy-three.

Super Bowl Pregame

After a couple of days off, the Dolphins were back at Biscayne College for practice on Wednesday, January 3. Don Shula's first order of business was a delicate matter. No one on the team, in the press corps, or among the fandom now thought there was any chance Bob Griese wasn't starting the Super Bowl. He was the team's All-Pro quarterback, and he'd showed with his game-winning performance against Pittsburgh—in particular that mad serpentine scramble—that he was over his leg injury. But Shula had enormous respect for Earl Morrall, for what he'd done in the past and for how he'd come off the bench to save the season, and he wanted to do this the right way. "You don't fool around with men the stature of Griese and Morrall," he said later.

First he called Griese into his office to make sure he was feeling good and ready to play. Although the quarterback maintained his deadpan demeanor ("I feel fine, Coach"; "I'm ready to play if that's your decision"), Shula liked what he saw when he told Griese he was going to start the big game: "His eyes lit up. It was easy to see how keyed up Bob was." Then he went to find Morrall. This conversation wasn't as easy. Morrall didn't have a Unitas-sized ego, but he must have bristled when he read the *New York Times*'s Dave Anderson calling him "a backup by nature." He was a proud veteran of seventeen seasons who had won an NFL championship and a Super Bowl and had started more than half the two hundred games he'd played in. And when he sat down in Shula's office he was going to take it like a man, but he wasn't going to take it like a natural backup. "I want to play just as much as he does," he told his coach. "I know," said Shula. "I feel I've contributed"—the understatement of the year, even from

Earl—"and I still want to contribute." Shula understood, but he had made his decision. All right, Morrall assured him he would stay prepared and wouldn't make any waves. As for the rest of the team, Griese was surely correct when he told a reporter after practice, "Nobody on the team is going to question it. Some guys might question Shula's views on social activities, but not on football." The very next day, Morrall was chosen as the NFL's All-Pro quarterback for 1972, beating out Joe Namath and Washington's Billy Kilmer.

Practices were light the rest of the week. In accordance with league guidelines, they would fly out to Los Angeles on Sunday to be available all Super Bowl week for media events and other hoopla. Shula didn't like it, but he understood. These last few days in Miami, he kept practices short, hoping to build momentum slowly over the next ten days.

Friday there was nothing before the eleven a.m. meeting, so Manny Fernandez and Bill Stanfill were out in the 'Glades by first light. Riding Manny's swamp buggy through what they called the "pond," a large area with no sawgrass, "there must've been three or four hundred alligators around us," said Fernandez. "Bill lay flat on his belly on the deck of the buggy, reached down and snatched one, stuck it in the toolbox." One of them thought it would be a fine idea to bring it back as a surprise for Coach Shula. The other agreed, so when they got back to the road and got the buggy onto the trailer, they taped the gator's mouth shut and put it in the trunk of Manny's car. Back at Biscayne College, before practice started, they enlisted Csonka's help. Doing his best version of Hogan sweet-talking Colonel Klink's pretty, blond secretary in *Hogan's Heroes*, which had just finished its successful six-year run on CBS, Csonka kept Shula's secretary busy in conversation while Fernandez lugged the gator into the coach's private shower stall in his office. And there it stayed until practice ended, when they knew Shula would clean up before being picked up by Dorothy to go out for Friday night dinner.

Csonka remembers that he and Manny were out fishing that morning, and Manny was the one who went "thrashing around in the reeds like King Kong, and he comes out with this thing wriggling, and he walks up and drops it in the boat." He says Fernandez and Kuechenberg staged a fight in Shula's outer office to distract the secretary while Csonka carried the gator into the shower. What everyone agrees on is that when a bunch of players hung around after practice later than usual for the entertainment, they heard a howl like from the new box-office smash *Deliverance*, followed by Shula running out of his office in a towel, rage in his eyes. He went straight to Jim Kiick. "I always got blamed for everything," said Kiick. "I was from Jersey, and Zonk and Shula were both Hungarians from Ohio. Zonk never got in trouble." "Jim was just the easiest one to catch," said Csonka. "Also, he didn't care about getting away." When Shula confronted Kiick, the city boy who wouldn't have been caught dead in the Everglades just looked up and said, "Coach, the only way I was involved is we had a vote whether to tape the mouth shut. Fortunately for you, I lost by one vote."

Shula, despite his initial reaction, was soon able to laugh about it, just as he was after numerous other shenanigans. Despite his work ethic and stentorian dictatorship on the football side, he liked a good joke. And Kiick was right: Zonk never got in trouble. Not when he told Shula the long strip of rubber he was holding on the practice field was a snake and then threw it at him; not when he hid a bullfrog under a towel on the meeting room podium. Shula came in to address the team, moved the towel, and jumped higher than the bullfrog. Another time Shula strode in and flipped on the projector to a bunch of muffled snickers: the footage didn't look quite like last week's game. Csonka had substituted a pornographic movie for the game film. Shula screamed for lights on, snapped off the projector, and looked as though he'd been in the sun too long. But he couldn't have punished the perpetrator if he'd wanted to; no one was willing to give that one away for fifty years. An alligator, though: after the anger subsided, all he could do was stand there in his towel and shake his head. Only in Miami did a coach get a gator in the shower. Funny place for a football team.

Shula almost welcomed the prank; he was determined to keep things light this time around. Unflagging bloodless preparation hadn't worked out for him in Super Bowls III and VI. They had a final, short practice at Biscayne on Sunday, January 7, before catching their flight. It was hot, up in the eighties, and they were just running half-speed drills to groove the plays they planned to use against Washington. Mercury Morris got a bit overenthusiastic on a sweep, and when Larry Little fell down in front of him, Merc used the guard's back as a springboard to leap into the secondary. That was okay to get a vital first down in a big game, but in a light drill? As Morris walked back to the huddle, Little gave him a look you don't want to get from a man of that size. "Come on, go to it!" shouted Shula with a grin. He wasn't really one of those coaches who thought intramural fights primed the competitive spirit, but he seemed to find the prospect of this matchup amusing. His Dolphins, however, weren't that kind of a team. "Hey," he complained, "why don't you guys go to it?"

"It wouldn't be much of a fight," said the 265-pound Little.

"Bring your lunch," said Morris. Though only 190 pounds, he was possibly the strongest man on the team. "It might last all day." Everybody laughed and lined back up for a few more plays. The plane was leaving at four.

• • •

As their Eastern charter soared westward, Henry Kissinger was high over the Atlantic, heading back to Paris to resume peace talks with Le Duc Tho after almost a month. Hopes for peace were not bolstered by the state newspaper in Hanoi calling Nixon "more dangerous and cruel than Hitler," and as Kissinger prepared to board his plane, the most bravado he could muster was a mumble in his heavy accent, "I'll do my best." Neither side had stirred from their basic demands over the past year, and fighting remained fierce in the first week of 1973. In Washington a few days earlier, the Senate and House had convened. Despite Nixon's landslide, the new Congress was as decidedly Democratic as the last, and it watched with great interest, as did the nation, the trial of the Watergate burglars, set to begin Monday.

• • •

By the third Super Bowl, when Joe Namath pranced, partied, and worked the press in Miami, Super Bowl week was already becoming a frenzied citywide festival. The two-week break after a steady season-long rhythm of a game every week, the infusion of media from around the nation, the influx of fans, and the setting in a warm vacation area in winter (three of the first five Super Bowls were in Miami) led to a party atmosphere and difficulties for disciplined-minded coaches. When the Dolphins went to New Orleans to play the Cowboys, their hotel was like the set of a Marx Brothers movie. The halls were jammed with traffic all day and most of the night: reporters, fans, hopeful hucksters and prostitutes, old friends and new friends trying to rustle up tickets. Room phones rang like the maître d's at Tony Roma's. Most nights those players who were inclined to socialize did just that, frequenting the Bourbon Street bars to "raise a

little hell and get our minds off football." After reports got back to Shula about a
particular raucous interaction long past midnight the night before, the coach let
loose in a team meeting: ". . . And what in the hell is a female impersonator?!"

The entertainment may have had nothing to do with Miami's anemic
performance in the big game, but Shula was pleased nonetheless with the
contrasting atmosphere this year. Unlike New Orleans's concentrated urban
playground, L.A.'s attractions were spread out over a vast geographic area,
and the NFL was using all of it. The game itself would be in the Los Angeles
Coliseum, next to USC in south-central L.A. But the Dolphins were assigned
to stay at the Edgewater Hyatt House, down on the marina in Long Beach,
twenty-five miles to the south, and they'd practice at Blair Field, a college and
high school stadium also in Long Beach. Shula made sure there was security
at the hotel to keep uninvited visitors away, and after the first two nights there
would be a team curfew.

With that in mind, certain players felt compelled to explore the L.A.
nightlife while they could. Monday had no requirements other than Picture
Day in the afternoon, after which Csonka and Kiick drove up to Beverly Hills
to check out the scene there. On the way back they stopped into a bar and
ran into Jake Scott, Dick Anderson, and Jim Mandich. Scott and Mandich
were drinking, Anderson was playing some pinball: they had their designated
driver. After shooting some pool, they piled into Anderson's rental car and
headed for their new favorite bar, the Basement in Marina del Rey. Then it was
off to more Newport Beach locales. When the bars closed, they visited some
massage parlors—just to observe the scene. These joints were more packed
than the bars.

Don Shula had gone to bed at a reasonable hour, but the time change—not
to mention an unending cascade of numbers, images, and formations related
to the reason they were in California—kept him up much of the night. "It was
four in the morning," he said, "and I couldn't go back to sleep, even though I'd
had a couple of beers and stayed up later than usual. So I just lay there, waiting until six a.m., when breakfast opened." At 6:01 he was sitting alone with
a cup of coffee when Mandich appeared like a bad dream, dressed to kill and
smelling like a saloon. The big tight end shuffled over in his bell-bottoms and
fell into the chair across from Shula. "How you doing, Coach?" For once, Shula
had absolutely nothing to say.

. . .

The Redskins were even farther away, out in Santa Ana, which also pleased Shula. And while the Dolphins had a couple of free nights and then just a loose curfew, George Allen had his team barricaded at the Saddleback Inn as if they were on work release. Missing curfew for them meant a hefty fine. He had an even more visible security service working the halls. "Hookers are unwelcome," said one guard. "One of our tasks is to keep them from trying to crash the players' rooms." Edwin Pope visited the Saddleback and said it was "like walking through a room full of convicts waiting for a last-minute stay of execution. When I saw Allen coming down the stairs my first impulse was to send out for oxygen."

That was just George Allen, a man often described as pale, sunken-chested, eyes blinking as though he were coming out of a dark room—which he most likely was, being as devoted to film study as Shula. But the man he resembled even more was Dick Nixon. Of poor origins, the son of a chauffeur in Michigan, Allen had gone to little Alma College and was part of the Navy's V-12 College Training Program. Unlike Shula, a college star who made the NFL, Allen, like Nixon, had barely even made his college team and got into football coaching on sheer desire and hard work. His longest stint before the NFL was at Nixon's alma mater, Whittier College, where he coached both football and baseball from 1951 to 1957. Whether it was the Whittier connection or the common history of rising from humble beginnings with dogged perseverance, the president took a great liking to the new Redskins coach in '71, visiting training camp, calling him once a week to discuss strategy, and even having Allen and his wife, Etty, to the White House for dinners.

Also like Nixon, Allen was not a particularly affable personality but knew how to win. "Coaching is my life, my business, my hobby," he said. "Other than my family, I have no other interest." His favorite drink was milk, and his favorite dinner ice cream—because it gave him more time to work on preparing for next week's game. One owner quipped, "It was more fun to lose without him than to win with him," but most players and fans just wanted to win. And that was what George Allen did. After years as an assistant, he took over the Los Angeles Rams in 1966 and replaced a seven-year losing streak with five straight winning seasons. Then, in 1971, he arrived in Washington to take over a dismal team that hadn't played a playoff game in twenty-five years. He immediately whipped them up to five straight wins to commence a run to the playoffs. Nixon was with them all the way, sometimes attending practice and being photographed with the team.

But still, like Shula and the pre-presidential Nixon, Allen seemed never able to take the ultimate prize. Coming into the 1972 season, despite his tremendous success, he had never even won a playoff game. But staying right on Shula's heels all year with an almost perfect record—just that crazy loss in New England and a couple of meaningless ones at the end—he had finally come through with two big playoff victories and was in the Super Bowl. Nixon was secluded in the White House amid his unpopular bombing campaign and the growing Watergate investigation; cabinet secretaries and congressional leaders alike couldn't get in to see him. But the day after Washington beat Dallas to win the NFC championship, Nixon invited Allen over for a celebration. And now it was the president's two favorites, Allen and Shula, facing off. Somebody was finally going to win the big one.

• • •

After their first couple of nights out on the town, Csonka, Kiick, Mandich, and the rest settled down to business. This wasn't training camp; no one was sneaking out to look for stewardesses in bars. Not with five days left in their yearlong crusade. They all remembered what the festive atmosphere had done to them last year. "Your first Super Bowl," said Larry Little, "the cameras, the attention, the commotion. . . . It has to bother you." Howard Twilley agreed: "Gearing for pregame distraction is the key. This year I go with the idea that nothing, absolutely nothing, will take my mind off the goal of a world championship." Mercury Morris had a weight set in his hotel room and declared he wasn't going anywhere. This experience of having gone through it before seemed to have them calm and focused. Maybe that was the reason that three of the six Super Bowls so far had been won by teams that had been there before and lost.

Every morning at ten, busloads of reporters and cameramen pulled up to the Hyatt. Shula would give a press conference, after which the players were available for interviews. Griese was his usual phlegmatic self: "The Super Bowl is a game, that's all it is. Except if you win this one, you win the world championship. I get psyched up for all games." Buoniconti worked the room each day like the lawyer and entrepreneur he was, joking and explaining—but bristling whenever he was asked about how the Dallas Cowboys said they had fooled him again and again in Super Bowl VI. He had taken such a hit to the head in that game that he didn't really remember playing in it, but that didn't ameliorate his annoyance. "You've got to be an idiot to talk in terms of one individual," he said. "Great, I'm the non-hero," he said. After a while, anytime he heard the word "Dallas," he just said, "Next question." Mercury Morris didn't mind: "Last year we were glad to get in the game and Dallas came to *win* it. Well, we've already been in the game. This year *we* came to win it." But perhaps Doug Swift got to the heart of the matter best: "We need this one. We've got to have it. We've gone sixteen and oh, and if we lose this one people are going to remember us as the biggest bunch of hot air in the world."

The pressure was building, and the relief valve was Don Shula's robust cranium. As if it wasn't enough that he had been to the big show twice before and lost—and, even worse, the Colts finally won it the first year he was gone—his old boss was piling on. Carroll Rosenbloom, the former Colts owner who had swapped franchises with Robert Irsay and taken over the Rams, had never forgiven Shula for jumping to Miami before he could fire him. Now, as the "host owner" of the Super Bowl, he seemed to be taking great pleasure in pillorying him at every opportunity. Shula was a "pig," a "loser of the big ones" who had "walked out on me, hired behind my back by that fellow Robbie. . . . I'm picking Washington. Allen is a winner. The other guy has matured, I guess, but I've seen him freeze up too many times in the big one. I just don't believe he can do it. I'll believe it when I see him do it."

It was like the owner of the *Pequod* taunting Captain Ahab for failing to nab that big white whale. Shula did his best to take a deep breath at the podium: "Anything that man says would not surprise me. He has done nothing for three years but downgrade me not only as a coach but as a human being as well. He has even made remarks involving my family." And if Rosenbloom's calumny wasn't enough, Shula was also distracted by what he was certain was George Allen's attempts to spy on his practices. It wasn't completely paranoia, as Howard Schnellenberger had been an Allen assistant in L.A. and remembered being ordered on such assignments, and Allen had been accused by others in the past of espionage. Two years earlier he'd been caught trading two draft choices that he had already traded away previously. (Somehow the league didn't discover this until draft day, and Allen got off with just a $5,000 fine.) Once, in Baltimore, Shula was convinced that a lady pushing a baby carriage past the Colts practice field was one of Allen's agents, with a camera in the baby clothes. Now, when rain made Blair Field too soggy, Shula grabbed the opportunity to move his team to a community college field, the location of which was "to be announced after we finish practice." He also declared that they were going over the border to practice and that a reporter should "slip the word over to George so he can start looking for our practice field in Tijuana." And when someone else asked if Shula was having his team's practices filmed, he deadpanned, "No, George is handling that."

The Dolphins seemed relaxed this time around, and Shula was doing his best to model a loose confidence. But his nerves were showing through. It didn't help that he had the flu—as did Marv Fleming, who had been hospitalized for five days just before the team left Miami—and was worried it would infect more of his team. (In fact, Wayne Moore would only last a half because of flu, and Buoniconti had symptoms the morning of the game, played sick, and missed the Pro Bowl.) Shula was collapsing into bed at nine each night with a bagful of pills provided by Dr. Virgin. When asked a simple question at one morning press conference, he shot back, "What is the attitude of the coach? The coach is oh-and-two in the Super Bowl and the coach's attitude is damn good." Jim Mandich said, off the record, "I've never seen Shula as uptight as this. My God, can you imagine what life with Shula would be like if he lost another Super Bowl?"

But if he may have been a bit prickly at times, the "good-natured Shula's" "graceful humor" won over the press corps. He certainly won Most Congenial Coach of the Week over the dour, irritable Allen. Members of the Washington press corps weren't surprised, as Allen had been demonizing them for two years now. Back in October, he'd all but blamed them for the New England loss, saying they'd riled up the opponent by calling them the "Patsies." Then, declaring that the papers were giving away his secrets, he closed team practice to reporters, claiming, "All you guys want to do is hurt the team. We didn't have this trouble in Los Angeles." And this was during a glorious season with only that one loss so far. Now, Super Bowl pressure was really popping Allen's cork. On Friday he complained, "Yesterday thirty-one of my players were with the press for an hour and a half, and afterward we had our worst practice of the week." After a few more questions and tight-lipped answers, he turned and said softly to an NFL staffer, "Can I go now?"

Allen's players did not seem to share his tenseness and terseness with the press. They were an older bunch who enjoyed their moniker, the "Over-the-Hill Gang." One of Allen's idiosyncrasies was that, rather than build a team over time with strong young players, he preferred to trade away his draft choices for experienced veterans. That was how he had transformed the Redskins in one off-season: he traded away twenty-four draft picks in nineteen deals—and that didn't include the draft choices he traded twice. Eight of the veterans he picked up were his former Rams players, including the standout linebacker Jack Pardee and guard John Wilbur. Allen was loyal to his men, and they repaid that loyalty. "He loves his men," said his wife, Etty. "He goes around muttering about Billy and Sonny and Larry and his 'geezers.'" One of those devoted veterans was Washington's quarterback, Billy Kilmer, whom Allen had gotten from New Orleans the year before.

Kilmer, you could say, was not uptight about the Super Bowl. He was propped up in his bed at the Saddleback with a Coors one evening as he waved in some reporters who had somehow got past security. "Come on in," he shouted. "The beer's in the bathtub." Known for his nightlife exploits and barroom stamina, his teammates called him "Ole Whiskey." "Aw," he said, "the guys call me that because I get so red in the face. And I don't even like the stuff." During one prolonged afternoon interview with Sally Quinn of the *Post*, he endured four Old Fashioneds (with extra cherry juice "to hide the taste of the whiskey") and two Bloody Marys (extra Tabasco and Worcestershire sauce "to hide the taste"). He also gazed out the window and told her, "Fifty degrees and cloudy, that's my idea of perfect football weather. Good lovemakin' weather, too."

Kilmer was a ruggedly handsome six-foot-two, two-hundred-pound relic, one of the last players to sport just a single bar on his face mask. To us young Dolphin fans he was an ancient figure from another era, still hanging on in Washington, barely able to hobble back to the pocket, from where he would lob a wounded duck in the general vicinity of a receiver. In fact he was thirty-three years old, with five more good seasons ahead of him. He just looked gimpy on the field, the result of a grisly car accident ten years earlier, when he fell asleep and drove his convertible into the San Francisco Bay. Prior to that he'd been a virtuoso running quarterback for UCLA and primarily a runner for the 49ers. He was traded to New Orleans, where he finally got to play quarterback, but he never played for a winner before he came to Washington. When their star quarterback Sonny Jurgenson was injured, Kilmer stepped in and led the Redskins to their first playoff season in a quarter century. "I can't run anymore, though," he said. "I'm strictly a dropback man, a pocket passer. They went from Sonny, the greatest passer in the history of football, to Billy Kilmer who throws floaters." It was true his passes lacked the spin and zip you'd expect from a pro quarterback, but they were accurate and often deadly. In the recent NFC championship game he'd launched two perfect touchdown passes, one a forty-five-yard bomb, that killed the Cowboys.

"I wake up at five-thirty in the morning," he said, sitting up a bit in his hotel bed. "And the first thing that pops in my head is, 'What's Miami going to do on first and ten? On third and ten?'" He was thinking of the No-Name Defense and its propensity to fake coverages and throw unexpected formations at a quarterback. "This is the biggest game of my life. But it won't mean a thing if I lose. It'll turn right around on you, like pissing in the wind. . . ."

Bob Griese was sleeping much better. On Wednesday, in a diary he was keeping for Bill Bondurant of the *Fort Lauderdale News* (to be revealed only after the game), he wrote, "Today I'm convinced that we can beat them. After watching their defense on films, I don't see how we can lose unless we do something to throw it away." Among other things, in practice he was working on two particular pass plays. With Warfield he was grooving a play-action with a two-stage pass pattern designed for double coverage at around midfield. Griese was also drilling a play with Howard Twilley: a slight variant on Twilley's favorite post-corner pattern. Griese felt confident that in certain situations these two plays would work as in a quarterback's fantasy. But he was feeling that way about the whole game plan: "It looks to me like anything we run can be successful against them. Our strength against their strength should work . . ."

. . .

Even before the first "World Championship Game," in 1966, Lamar Hunt, founder of the AFL and owner of the Kansas City Chiefs, had written to Commissioner Pete Rozelle, "I have kiddingly called it the 'Super Bowl,' which obviously can be improved upon." The media, first in Kansas City and then

elsewhere, liked the moniker and used it, and by the third contest, the Jets'
surprise victory in the Orange Bowl in 1969, it was officially the Super Bowl.
Roman numbering began with V, and by VII the event had come into its own.
Tickets were up to $15, and all 93,607 of them had been sold, which was not
always the case in the early years. The day before the game, scalpers were getting up to ten times face value.

For the players, the winner's share was a much bigger incentive than it
would be decades later, when it would be about a third of the minimum NFL
salary and a mere pittance for the wealthy stars. A win in Super Bowl VII would
more than double most participants' annual income; many players, when discussing Super Bowl prospects, talked about the money as much as the glory.
"We had black [players], we had white," said Wayne Moore, "but the color on
our mind was the same. It was green: to get that money and that trophy." Lying
in bed in their room at the Hyatt, Maulty Moore and Vern Den Herder killed
time musing about what they would do with their Super Bowl money. Moore,
from the Black part of Brooksville, Florida, and Den Herder, who'd grown up
working farms in Sioux Center, were one of the odd couples formed by Shula's
enforced-integration rooming policy. They got along well but were from different worlds. "I'm going to take that Super Bowl check and buy a ranch and a
bull," said Vern. Maulty just smiled. He had a different sort of ranch in mind: a
four-bedroom, two-bathroom South Florida–style ranch house that he'd already
picked out, just outside Fort Lauderdale, featuring something his family could
only long for back in Brooksville. "I'm going to buy an air-conditioned house"
was all he said.

In similar fashion, Jim and Alice Kiick had an empty lot in Fort Lauderdale
where they hoped to turn their Super Bowl winnings into a new home. The
Twilleys were building a dream home back in Tulsa, where they would spend
off-seasons and eventually retire. (First, though, they'd spend some of their
share on a Marco Island vacation with the Grieses.) Jim and Lynda Langer were
earmarking their winnings for a cabin up in Minnesota. The Csonkas had moved
into a new house in Plantation (a less developed area west of Fort Lauderdale)
the previous spring, and according to Pam Csonka, Larry was talking about
converting the garage into a game room for his pool table and building a dock
for a boat "that he is not getting." Mercury Morris was thinking of a new Cadillac
Eldorado for his girlfriend Dorothy, black with a black vinyl top. (He preferred

his newest Corvette Stingray, bright yellow.) And Eddie Jenkins, who wouldn't suit up for the big game but was in L.A. to practice with the team, had been thinking of his half playoff share as he browsed the Datsun dealership near his Miami apartment. He couldn't take his eyes off a jet-black 240Z glistening in the showroom. He told the dealer that if they won the Super Bowl, he was going to come back and drive that baby away.

Despite all they had accomplished, though, not everyone thought the undefeated 16–0 two-time AFC champs were going to get that winner's money. The official Las Vegas line did have the Dolphins as slight favorites, by a single point. It was the first time a former AFL team had been favored; after embarrassing losses by the NFL's Baltimore (favored by eighteen points) and Minnesota (favored by twelve) to the Jets and Chiefs, the oddsmakers were finally getting wise to the equality of the two old leagues. But not Jimmy the Greek, kibitzing with Larry King as they sped down I-15 from Vegas to L.A.

King, in addition to his radio, television, and newspaper presence in Miami, had been the color commentator for Dolphin games beginning in 1970. But he had been relieved of that job in December 1971, just before the historic Longest Game with Kansas City, under ignominious circumstances. A devotee of nuptials and the horse track with equal enthusiasm, King had run up big debts, multiple alimonies, and trouble with the IRS by the time he became friends in 1966 with millionaire financier Lou Wolfson. Wolfson got him involved in a scheme to funnel money to JFK conspiracist Jim Garrison, and King used some of it to pay off his own debts. He knew he'd have to tell the truth eventually and pay it back, but he figured by then he'd have finally picked a winner at Calder Race Course.

When Wolfson got out of prison in 1971—he'd been convicted of selling unregistered stock—he filed a criminal complaint against King for grand larceny. A couple of days before King would have flown to Kansas City to work the Dolphins' Christmas Eve playoff game, his picture was in all the local papers with a story about his arrest. When he arrived at WIOD that night to do his show, out on bail, he was told he was suspended until the case was resolved. Ditto, he would learn, for his TV show and his newspaper column.

Three months later the case was dismissed, as the statute of limitations had run out. But King's media employers were unwilling to reinstate him. It was the spring of 1972; Larry King was thirty-seven years old, with no job, no money, and a couple hundred thousand dollars of debt, not to mention rent, alimony, and child support payments due. By August, though, he was back where he thrived: the radio, courtesy of a new show, *Larry's Locker Room*, on "Ocean Radio," WOCN, 1450AM. After games he'd be in the locker rooms interviewing the Dolphins and their opponents. He'd also have his interview show again, nine to midnight six nights a week, live from the Dupont Plaza Hotel. So Larry King was back and able to be a part of the greatest season of the team he had grown to love.

He also still had his gambling debts, but those could be finessed, as he'd always done. And in January 1973, two days before the Super Bowl, he found himself in Las Vegas. "I don't know why I went to Vegas," he said, "but I did." Apparently, Jimmy the Greek preferred the casinos to the Super Bowl hoopla also, and the day before the game the two of them drove to L.A. together, along with Pete Axthelm, a young sportswriter for *Newsweek*. As the creosote flew by, King was giving the Greek the business about the three-and-a-half-point spread he was calling in favor of Washington. (It was two points until he saw how badly Jake Scott was favoring his shoulder. Kilmer was going to pick on that sore spot for sure.) "How can we be underdogs? We're undefeated!" King insisted. "Ahh," the Greek waved his hand, "you're still the AFL. The Redskins played tougher competition." Two years after the merger, with Miami embarrassing the NFL's old powerhouse, the Colts, in last year's playoffs and twice this year, he was still thinking of the AFC as if it were a separate, weaker league. "I said, 'You're making a big mistake,'" King remembered. "Of course I had no money to bet at the time, otherwise I would have made a killing."

The kid in the backseat apparently took the Greek over King plus three, for Axthelm wrote in his next column, "The prediction here is that the fearsome Redskins defense will force Shula to wait for his reward." He was not an outlier by any means. Axthelm was a young gun, and the old boys in the press box were even more enamored of Allen's Over-the-Hill Gang. *Sports Illustrated*'s Tex Maule, pointing out Washington's tougher schedule and far more dominating playoff wins, had Washington by "at least ten points and perhaps by as many as twenty-one." The strangest and most derisive analysis of the Super Bowl matchup came on game day from Jim Murray of the *L.A. Times* in a nationally syndicated column that also appeared in the *Miami Herald*. Murray took the familiar reckoning of the relative anonymity of Shula's squad—which the "No-Name Defense" wore as a badge of pride—and pumped it with yellow-journalistic steroids into a scathing disparagement of the undefeated team playing its second straight Super Bowl. Murray, a revered sportswriter who would later win the Pulitzer Prize for Commentary and join the National Sportscasters and Sportswriters Association Hall of Fame, was known for his biting humor and was clearly having fun. He called the Dolphins "kids . . . in kooky tangerine-and-turquoise uniforms doing impersonations of football players. . . . They're like the drunk that climbs to the top of the ladder at the carnival to do a high dive into a pail of water, the rube who comes out of the audience to wrestle the bear or buck the shell game." He made fun of their names: "What's a Csonka?" He asked, "Will they just stand there like they did in last year's Super Bowl?" and "What is this, the Super Bowl or Amateur Night?" It was all clearly meant to be funny, but if Murray had put money on Washington, it might have been a mistake to write, "Who's that bald-headed guy playing safety?" That one could have riled up *both* Jake Scott and Dick Anderson.

Murray's humor fell flat, as there was obviously no more qualified team than Miami. They hadn't squeaked in as a wild-card team and gotten lucky in two playoff games. They were 16–0. As one might imagine, the Dolphins were not amused. On game day Norm Evans said, "That was the first thing I saw this morning when I got up. I'd like to fold that thing up in a triangle and stick it in Murray's ear." If that's what Pope Norm said, you can imagine what Manny Fernandez and Jake Scott were thinking.

The Dolphins' wives finally arrived Friday night, courtesy of Joe Robbie. By design, probably that of Shula, they were put up at the luxurious Beverly Hilton, a prime spot for shopping and sightseeing—and a $45 cab ride away from Dolphins headquarters in Long Beach. They were not invited for burgers and beer Saturday night at the players' hotel; Shula had learned a lesson from the year before, when there was a big team dinner with spouses at a New Orleans restaurant. "It was a nice affair," said Shula, "but it was too different from our usual pre-game routine. This time we'll have the regular nine-thirty snack." The women didn't seem to mind. Robbie, seemingly determined to shed his cheapskate rep, was picking up their dinner tab, plus a show on Saturday night. Aside from that, the players' partners seemed as hell-bent on success this year as they were. "I wouldn't plan to see Howard anyway," said Julie Twilley. "They know we're here and how we feel . . . and they have to concentrate."

Dick Anderson's wife, Lois, sounded like the veteran she was: "We've gone through some hard times as a team, and it's given us a kind of maturity. Last year we went to the Super Bowl but lost. This time, though, it's like a job. We have to win."

Practice down in Long Beach had gone superbly. Everyone, from the six-foot-six roommates Den Herder and Moore down to five-eight Garo Yepremian, was primed and ready. Yepremian had been kicking smoothly off the natural grass, and since you can't kick footballs all day long, he had been killing time as usual by having catches with thirteen-year-old David Shula. His right arm felt as invigorated as his left leg: "I was throwing the ball thirty-five yards," he remembered later, "and I felt like I was a great quarterback."

The only player unable to play would be cornerback Tim Foley, who needed an operation after severely separating his shoulder against Pittsburgh. He was in L.A. with his arm in a sling, his face lined with frustration. He'd taken the Shula mantra more seriously than anyone, had kept that photo of the losing score on the wall of his home ever since the Super Bowl. To pass the time, Foley was filming some color pieces for one of the Miami TV stations. After he visited a Redskins practice and interviewed some players, George Allen was able to turn the tables and complain that Foley was spying for Shula.

One man's misfortune, though, is another man's opportunity. Lloyd Mumphord, the diminutive but multitalented player, barely larger than Yepremian, who had lost his starting position to Foley the year before, would replace him in the Super Bowl. Mumphord was making the most of it. He was the Dolphins' best pass defender anyway, and wasn't being shy about it. "Taylor never made any big plays off me," he said, referring to Washington's star receiver. As for their gimpy quarterback? "I like the way Kilmer throws the ball. He doesn't throw with much zip, just lays it up there. Maybe one of them will come down in my hands." ("What do you expect him to say?" said Shula. "I'm going out to get my tail beat?") Rookie Charlie Babb, in turn, would be the fifth defensive back to come in on passing downs, and another rookie DB, Henry Stuckey, was activated. For Stuckey, who had been making $300 a week on the taxi squad and had not been eligible for any playoff bonus money, the move would net him $4,000 if Miami won. In a rarity, his first game as a professional football player would be the Super Bowl. "This is going to be one of my biggest games," he deadpanned for the press.

Saturday night, in their hotel rooms, players clicking through the channels on their TVs might have watched some of Marlene Dietrich's first television appearance ever: a tape of the seventy-one-year-old legend's London concert from November. Or they might have come upon President Nixon being interviewed in Key Biscayne about Sunday's game. He reiterated his support for George Allen and his "home team." George would have his defense ready for the return of Miami's great scrambling quarterback, he said: "I wouldn't want to be Griese on Sunday." Hunter S. Thompson, going over his notes while scrambling his brain with coffee, Wild Turkey, and Jamaican cigars, saw this in his hotel room and immediately "began betting heavily on Miami."

Nixon flew to South Florida on Friday, poring over the Dolphins-Redskins matchup, perhaps wondering which coach he should favor with a play call. (Despite his Redskins bravado on television, he admitted to reporters that in his opinion the game was a toss-up.) But he had a lot more on his mind than football. On his orders, B-52s continued to unleash many tons of bombs on Vietnam every day; just the previous day they had destroyed a wide area only forty miles northwest of Saigon, trying desperately to prevent the North Vietnamese from moving heavy artillery and tanks into the South from the Cambodian border. Three months after the supposed peace deal, Hanoi was still refusing to accept any possibility of a divided Vietnam. How much bombing could they take?

Then there was this damn Watergate trial. Howard Hunt had just pleaded guilty to all six charges against him in connection with the bugging and burglary in June, and—good man—sworn that to his knowledge no one high up in the Nixon administration was involved. It looked as though the four Miamians—Barker and company—would do the same. But that still left Gordon Liddy and Jim McCord, and their trial would begin the day after the Super Bowl.

Nixon had left his family behind in Washington and was looking forward to a relaxing weekend with Bebe Rebozo. He would enjoy watching the Super Bowl without distraction. Friday night, Nixon and Rebozo had dinner together and watched a movie. On Saturday they went for a long drive down the Tamiami Trail into the Everglades. After midnight, Henry Kissinger's *Spirit of '76* Air Force jetliner arrived from Paris at Homestead Air Force Base. He helicoptered up to the compound at Key Biscayne and had a brief consultation with the president before retiring. In the morning, Nixon met with Henry again, but then he and Rebozo had lunch and took a chauffeured limousine the sixty miles down to the Ocean Reef Club, Bebe's place in Key Largo. They arrived twenty minutes before kickoff.

• • •

Bob Griese woke up early Sunday and went to Mass as usual. Feeling relaxed and confident after two weeks of preparing for the Redskins, he went to breakfast in the hotel and feasted on steak, eggs, toast, and coffee with plenty of honey. While he was eating, all alone in the room, Larry King appeared and joined him with a cup of coffee. "Good morning, Larry," said Griese. "Hey, what do you think: Can the property values in Key Biscayne keep going up?" King smiled at the young quarterback and said to himself, *There is absolutely no way the Dolphins can lose this game.*

Kickoff was scheduled for twelve forty, even earlier than a regular season game. By eight thirty the rest of the Dolphins had arrived, King and any other outsiders were ushered out, and the team had their official breakfast meeting. When everyone was done eating, Shula called for silence. "He'd get us together at breakfast," recalled one player, "and there'd be a little twitch in his eye as he said a few words and then gave us the first two plays we were going to run in the game. Later in my life I realized he was putting you in a game mentality: *It starts right now. From here on in, we're on.* After that, everyone hit their rooms, got their bags, let's go. No playing around, all business."

Anyone who deviated from this mindset risked incurring Shula's wrath. When the team was all loaded onto the bus outside the hotel, one player was missing. "Where's Jake?" Shula was livid. He went outside and there was his free safety, handing game tickets out to some friends. Shula screamed, "Hey! You're going to be late to the biggest game of your career!" Jake Scott looked over at him. Jake liked to party; he definitely marched to his own damn drummer. But he was never, ever late for anything. His shoulder felt as if a steak knife was sticking out of it; in a couple hours he would be shot up with painkillers to allow him to play football. In the last Super Bowl he'd played with two broken hands; he'd played all this year with one still in a cast. He shouted back, loud enough for everyone to hear, "What's the matter? You worried about going down as the losingest coach in Super Bowl history?" Neither said another word. It was, as it turned out, the beginning of a thirty-five-year silent feud. They got on the bus, and the Dolphins headed for the Coliseum.

Seventeen and Oh: Super Bowl VII

The Los Angeles Memorial Coliseum was even then known as the "Grand Old Lady" of American sports stadiums. A monument to those lost in World War I, it was completed in 1923, a concrete classical palace with an imposing peristyle at one end. Its capacity for the 1932 Olympics was 101,574; later renovations lowered that to just over 93,000, but it was still the largest venue for American football. The longtime home of both USC and UCLA as well as the NFL's Rams, it was also the showcase for the Pro Bowl the past twenty years. When the Dolphins and Redskins came out to warm up in the late morning, the vast bowl was still largely empty. The Dolphins stretched in groups, quiet and serious. On the other side of the field, the Redskins were whooping it up, chanting, clapping their hands. Shula had warned his guys about this, how Allen would try to get every psychological advantage, even during the warm-up. But as Norm Evans said, "We had gone sixteen and oh and survived the ear-shattering bedlam of Pittsburgh. Man, forty guys playing patty-cake wasn't gonna scare us."

The weather that morning in Long Beach was comfortable, but as noon approached in central Los Angeles it was much hotter than normal. It would be eighty-six at game time, even hotter on the field. It made every Dolphin smile. "We had them when we walked on the field," said Marv Fleming. "By the middle of the first quarter they were breathing hard. When teams come down to Miami and start breathing hard, we know they're in trouble. Why? Because fatigue makes cowards of us all. That's what Lombardi used to say." Conditions were perfect for the Dolphins, right down to the playing surface, Bermuda roots seeded with rye. The players were thrilled to be on natural grass for the big one. All of them except the kicker, that is. All kickers prefer artificial turf, as the ball sits up high on the plastic and is easier to loft into the air. Garo Yepremian had never minded grass, though. He'd hit his longest field goal (at the time) up in Minnesota that year and had been doing great in practice on the grass down in Long Beach. But in the Coliseum, he said, "I soon realized I was having problems kicking the ball. I couldn't get it up high enough. . . ." He tried three different pairs of cleats, but he was having trouble planting his right, non-kicking foot properly, and all his kicks were low. Oh, well, he thought. On Broadway they say a bad dress rehearsal portends a good performance.

The Dolphins ran through some plays and headed back into the locker room to gather themselves before kickoff. Just another game—except the locker room was packed with TV cameras, lights, and a platform set up for the post-game show. Evans was reminded of twelve months before, when Shula stood on such a stage and congratulated the Cowboys while his players sat stunned. Now the locker room was quiet, the only sound the ripping of tape as the trainers rewrapped some ankles and wrists. "It was pretty quiet," said Csonka. "The extra people were out of the locker room; it was just players, coaches, and trainers—immediate family. Shula said, 'Well, here we are.' He reiterated that this was the moment he'd talked about back in training camp. He didn't say much else. We weren't a rah rah kind of team, and he wasn't a rah rah kind of guy. But his voice was cracking. And it was pretty self-evident that we were sixteen and oh and what this game meant." Then, as he did before every game, he led the team in the Lord's Prayer.

When they ran back out onto the field, it was a different world. A marching band and cheerleaders welcomed the teams out of the tunnels, photographers and film crews were all over the field, and the enormous stadium was packed—almost. Pete Rozelle had agreed, as an experiment, to lift the local television blackout if the game sold out more than ten days in advance, and it had. As a result, Rozelle had the satisfaction of smugly noting that 8,500 ticket holders had stayed home to watch on TV. The televising also hit the scalpers hard: they were getting only the $15 face value for most tickets, and even prime fifty-yard-line seats were down from $300 early in the week to barely a hundred at game time.

Still, the place *felt* full, with more people than fit in the Orange Bowl. And there was no mistaking this for a normal football game. The *Apollo 17* astronauts were there to take part in the pregame ceremonies, which ended with the Michigan Marching Band morphing into an enormous *VII*. It was the third Super Bowl with Roman numerals, and the first with no ties—no neckties, that is. Shula continued his '72 casual look with a white polo shirt; Allen wore the same, the only difference the team logos on their chests.

No matter how much pomp and circumstance they could pump into the event, at some point someone had to kick the ball off a tee and it became a football game. The Dolphins could hardly believe twelve months and sixteen victories had gone by, and they were back with their chance at redemption. The ball came spinning down into Mercury Morris's hands at the eight-yard line, and he somewhat nervously let it slide through his fingers; it bounced straight up, though, like he was dribbling a basketball, and he ran it back to the twenty-four. Miami huddled up, and Griese called the opening play that Shula had announced at breakfast. Their offensive strategy today was to try to surprise Washington by passing in running situations and running in passing situations, but not immediately. The first two plays were runs by Kiick and Csonka, and on third down Griese threw a short swing pass to Csonka, but it wasn't enough. Three and out on their first series was not exactly what they were looking for. Yet they still felt confident. "I know it sounds strange," Shula said, "but I felt like the team was very relaxed despite the slow start." Seiple came in to punt.

Now came the first odd play of the game. It appeared initially that long-snapper Howard Kindig had fumbled the ball before even hiking it. Washington jumped on it for a huge early turnover. A flag was down, however: illegal procedure against Washington. Officials made no verbal explanation in those days, just a silent hand signal to each sideline to indicate the penalty. What had happened, though, was that Harold McLinton, anticipating the snap perfectly, reached over and slapped the ball away just as Kindig lifted it. The slow-motion replay made it obvious, but NBC's Curt Gowdy still didn't realize and announced: "He was so nervous he pulled his hands back but left the ball on the field!" It was a classic bit of George Allen chicanery. Not only had he planned it, he had asked the league officiating office about it before the playoffs and was told it was illegal. But he went for it anyway: maybe the refs wouldn't notice. They did. It was still fourth down, though, and Seiple punted it away.

Both defenses held twice, until things finally started to happen on Miami's third possession. Shula was alternating series between Kiick and Morris, and this one was Kiick's. He ran twice for ten yards, giving Miami a first down near midfield. Then Griese finally went with the unexpected. Just when the running game was getting going, and you'd think the conservative Dolphins would keep hammering it on the ground, Griese sent Paul Warfield semi-deep against the despised zone defense. Mike Bass had him short, and Brig Owens had him deep—but to the inside—and Griese found him with a soft pass down the left sideline for nineteen yards, down to the Washington thirty-four. Warfield calmly jogged back, and Griese walked downfield like he'd just dropped a few letters off at the post office. He was probably already thinking about Howard Twilley.

Csonka for two up the middle; Kiick for four to the twenty-seven. Even through the growing din of eighty-five thousand fans, the players could hear Shula's foghorn: "Take it in, offense!" Just before Kiick's run, color commentator Al DeRogatis said he'd been "watching the two little men on this side, Twilley and Pat Fischer. Pat is playing him bump-and-run. I guess it's nice when you're five-nine to at last be able to play a smaller man bump-and-run. He could get burned, though. Twilley can fool you." Thirty seconds later, Griese stepped into the huddle. "Before Bob uttered a single syllable," said Twilley later, "I knew what play he was going to call." The moment was here: they'd be double-covering Warfield on third down, leaving only Fischer on Twilley. If anything, Fischer would be expecting the Twilley special: a quick slant to the inside. He would also know, as a smart three-time All-Pro cornerback, that they liked to fake that and run a post-corner pattern: three steps slanting inside, then a break to the outside. (Twilley had done it for Morrall's first touchdown of the year, when he came in for Griese against San Diego.) But Griese and Twilley had been drilling a slight variant of that pattern. Instead of three steps, Howard was taking five steps before breaking to the corner. Just two extra steps. "We probably ran that a hundred times in the week before the game," said Twilley.

Griese spoke the words he was waiting for—"Brown right, sixty double-Q, on two"—and theory and practice became reality. Fischer said those extra two steps to the inside "had me convinced he wanted to stay inside." "He turned him inside out!" cried Gowdy. Griese lobbed a perfect pass over a linebacker right into the wide-open Twilley's hands. Fischer caught up and hit him hard at the one, but the receiver's momentum carried him into the corner of the end zone, where he rolled onto the ground just past the flag. "I'm in!" he screamed at the referee, but the ref was already signaling touchdown: "Don't you see my hands in the air?" he yelled back. Howard jumped up, handed him the ball, and patted him on the back: nice job.

After a stalemate for most of the first quarter, Miami finally seemed to have taken charge with a masterful drive. The quarter ended on the ensuing kickoff, and the Dolphin defense quickly pressed the advantage. They had stopped Washington cold their first two drives, and now on third and long Kilmer tried to throw to his perennial Pro Bowl wide receiver, Charley Taylor. "Usually, I know where I want to throw before the snap," he had said during the week. "But with Miami I'll have to wait until the snap of the ball to decide. A quarterback can get mesmerized and lose his train of thought trying to figure out their defenses. They do that to people." It happened now: Miami was in their 53 defense, and if the throw had been accurate Taylor would have been hammered head-on just as he touched it by number 53 himself, Matheson, who had dropped back from the line into coverage. But Kilmer overthrew Taylor, and Jake Scott leaped up, tipped the ball with both hands, fell to the ground, and caught the ball with his right hand before getting back up and running it eight yards to the Washington forty-eight. It was a spectacular interception.

Scott, after his untimely taunting of Shula that morning, had given his coach a few gray hairs already during the game. He had fielded Washington's two punts like a tightrope walker with a death wish. Never mind his separated shoulder and a wrist waiting for postseason surgery. On the first one, instead of allowing a short punt to bounce safely, he came sprinting in and caught it in a crowd like a sliding outfielder. And the next time, with another short, high punt, he should have called for a free catch. But Jake Scott rarely called a free catch. "You talk about reckless abandon—that's Jake Scott," special-teams coach Carl Taseff had said the previous summer. Coaches of punt returners rarely utter the phrase with that tone of admiration. "Jake has soft hands. When the ball hits, it's like falling into a pillow. Even when his hand was in a cast he never dropped a ball." He caught this one just as a Redskin nailed him, however, and he fumbled the ball forward; luckily his buddy Dick Anderson recovered. Either of these plays could have been a calamitous early turnover, but the gambler had survived and now with his artful interception had given his own team the big break. On the sideline all was forgiven: Shula grinned and clapped his hands like a kid at the circus and gave Scott a grateful slap on the back as he came off.

Scott, as he explained it, was taking to heart the defensive strategy Bill Arnsparger had cooked up for this game: "Arnsparger changed the whole defense for the Super Bowl and clogged up the middle of the field. He said, 'We're not going to lose this game like we did last year by sitting back. We're going to go after them.'" That's exactly what Scott had done, and now, with great field position, Griese again called for a pass on first down and found Marv Fleming crossing over to the right sideline. It was a twenty-yard completion down to the twenty-seven-yard line. But in a rare throwback to his scapegoat days, Bob Kuechenberg had drifted downfield where linemen were not allowed to roam. This seemingly minor infraction was at the time still a fifteen-yard drive killer. Instead of a first down at the Washington twenty-seven, Miami had a first-and-twenty-five back at their own thirty-eight. Three plays later, Seiple punted into the end zone.

Kilmer had no better luck this drive, though. Washington got one first down, but then Manny Fernandez single-handedly dropped league MVP Larry Brown twice for a short gain and a loss, and Washington was punting again. In four possessions, they hadn't gotten past their own forty, and it was largely due to Fernandez. Most of the season Miami's opponents had double-teamed him, knowing no one could handle Manny alone. But George Allen had two Pro Bowlers in the middle of his offensive line—center Len Hauss and guard John Wilbur—and he was letting whomever Fernandez lined up against take him on unassisted. It wasn't working. "Manny was too quick for them," said Scott. "He was in their backfield the whole day just doing whatever he wanted to do." Like Larry Little battling Joe Greene, Fernandez turned it into a personal challenge. "I never did make a Pro Bowl, so going up against a couple Pro Bowlers always gave me extra motivation. They were trying not to double-team me in the first half, but they changed that strategy at halftime."

Ever since his stunning touchdown catch, Howard Twilley had been out of the game. His thigh had been cramping and spasming, and he spent most of two series lying on his stomach, getting leg massages and downing salt pills. As good as Twilley was, his loss cost the Miami passing game little, as Marlin Briscoe came in to relieve him. In any case, Griese went back to the run, and a bruising Csonka charge up the middle for thirteen followed by a seven-yard Kiick sweep—after faking to Csonka up the middle—gave him a second down and three from just past midfield. Morris came in for Kiick in an obvious running situation for these Dolphins. All week Griese had been practicing another special pass play, though—this one with Warfield—and again the ideal moment had arrived. The defense was expecting another run, and there was just enough field in front of Warfield to fake out three defensive backs. Griese looked at his linemen in the huddle and said, "I'm going to need a little more time on this one." Then he called it: Sixty-six Dig Split Post.

Warfield just smiled. He had heard from friends on the Redskins that George Allen had told his defense that no matter what else happens, he didn't want Warfield catching a single pass. Well, he'd already taken that sweet one up the left sideline. Now would come the big one. In the coverage they knew Washington would employ in this situation, a cornerback would play him right on the line and try to take him out of the play immediately. Before the late 1970s, defenders were allowed to hit a receiver as many times as they liked, all the way down the field. Warfield knew Allen wanted his cornerback to try to take him right out of the play with what he called the "Axe," taking his legs right out from beneath him. If he got past that "terrorist action," as he termed it, there would still be two safeties to deal with. He would have no problem faking out the one on the left, Rosey Taylor, and cutting to the right post, but there would be another safety, Brig Owens, over there. Knowing what an aggressive player Owens was, Griese would run a double play-action, faking both a handoff and a pitchout, to bring Owens forward just enough for Warfield to break beyond him.

It felt just like in practice, or in a dream. Griese faked the handoff to Csonka up the middle as Warfield maneuvered past his would-be terrorist. Then he feigned a pitchout to Morris just as Warfield made his move to the right post. Owens bit, and Warfield sprinted deep behind him, taking in Griese's perfect pass and running into the end zone with no one close enough to be in the photo. He turned around and headed back, walking casually as always but holding the ball and looking concerned. A yellow flag was on the ground back at midfield. As Griese had called his cadence, Marlin Briscoe had made the slightest of false starts, not even taking a step but shifting his weight forward and then catching himself. The line judge had seen it, and the illegal procedure brought the whole play back. All that preparation and perfect execution was for naught; at least Warfield was able to get a gibe in after the game: "How'd I get so open? I imagine the president must have given George some coverages. . . ."

No one, of course, felt worse than Briscoe. He knew that play wasn't going to him and that if he wasn't sure of the count to just watch the ball for the snap. But he was lined up against Pat Fischer, from his hometown of Omaha, whom he'd idolized as a kid, whose brother Ken was Marlin's college coach and close friend. And now Marlin was supposed to neutralize Fischer to help free up Warfield. His mind tightened up and he just jumped the gun. He couldn't believe it. Shula yanked him out of the game and put Twilley back in, cramp or no cramp. As Briscoe came off, Shula screamed at him: "Just get set! What the hell are you doing?" Briscoe, who had declared himself the happiest Dolphin to be in the Super Bowl after playing for 1–13 Buffalo the year before, was now out of the Super Bowl, benched for the rest of the game. Two plays later, Seiple came in to punt; it was the second time in three possessions that a penalty had nullified a big pass play and killed a drive.

Miami had completely dominated the game so far, but now Washington was moving for the first time, crossing over midfield as the two-minute warning sounded. The score could easily be 17–0 or 21–0, but instead a touchdown now could tie it up. Then, at third and four from the forty-nine, with Miami in its 53 defense, Bill Arnsparger sent his "Swap" signal, as he would four or five times that day. Instead of Matheson rushing from the line, he backpedaled into coverage, and Doug Swift blitzed the quarterback. Guard John Wilbur, expecting to block Matheson on the outside, was unable to pick up Swift coming in the middle, and with Swift bearing down on him Kilmer had to unload his pass early. Kilmer's two receivers breaking up the middle had no idea the ball was on the way, but Nick Buoniconti was right in the middle of the field watching the whole thing. He stepped forward to make the easy interception and run it all the way back to the Washington twenty-eight.

Now, instead of facing a looming tie, Miami was back in scoring position. Kiick for three, Zonk for three, and with third and four Washington was looking for a pass to Warfield or Twilley, both lining up on the left side. But Griese was looking all the way for tight end Jim Mandich, who faked a block, then ran a crisp down-and-out to the right and made a diving catch at the two-yard line. They were in Jim Kiick territory. Although he'd been somewhat upstaged by Morris that season, he had taken it in from short yardage for the winning touchdowns against both Cleveland and Pittsburgh in the playoffs. On his first try now he found himself in a rugby scrum against four Redskins and could only push it down to the one. Then he followed his sidekick Csonka up the middle, between Langer and Little, and was buried under a mound of rocks right near the goal line. Lying on the ground, unable to see the referees, he just looked up at Csonka, who himself was trapped under three or four maroon boulders. But Csonka could see the ref's upstretched arms. To dispel any doubt his friend might have, Sundance pounded joyously on Butch's helmet. With just nineteen seconds left in the half, the extra point made it 14–0 Miami.

· · ·

The halftime "extravaganza," entitled "Happiness Is . . . ," began with the Michigan marching band forming first a happy face, then a saxophone to play along with Woody Herman, then "NFL," as twenty-six golf carts, each covered with one team's helmet and sporting a dancer kicking her bare legs out the back, paraded around the field. Andy Williams and the Citrus College Singers belted out "This Land Is My Land" as the band formed a map of the United States and a model airliner carried by four men "flew" from the New York islands to California via several major cities. (Miami was not indicated on the map.) A couple more songs, then three thousand pigeons and about as many balloons were released and disappeared into the Greater Los Angeles area.

Richard Nixon missed the extravaganza. It had been a rough first half for Redskins fans, and he and Bebe took a swim in the ocean at halftime to shake it off. In our front yard on Kendale Boulevard, it was Warfield versus Kiick, one on one, to stretch the legs and blow off some steam. I don't know if the "quarterback for both teams" was still Morrall or if we made him switch back to Griese. But there was no doubt in our excited imaginations: the Dolphins were going to win the Super Bowl.

The Dolphins themselves were confident but wary. In the locker room, they cooled off with cold cans of soda. They hadn't expected this kind of heat but were glad for it. They'd already seen the Redskins flagging in it. The offense gathered on one side of the room, and Griese delivered a briefing. "Time's on our side," he said. "If we can keep the running game going, we'll go with that. We'll pass only when it's a sure thing." Griese had called for a pass only eight times in the first half. He completed all eight, although two long ones, including the Warfield touchdown, were called back by penalties. The rest was Csonka, Kiick, Morris, and the offensive line. No need to change a winning game.

On the other side of the locker room, Shula was exhorting his defense not to ease up. He knew George Allen's skill as a motivator, and he could imagine the rhetoric bouncing around the other locker room: Two lucky interceptions, otherwise it's at least a tie game, maybe a Washington lead. George wouldn't mention the Miami scoring opportunities called back or the fact that Miami had double their yardage. What coach would?

Sure enough, when the teams came back out, Allen had his old guys swarming around him like college kids, jumping up and down and smacking each other on the back, all pumped up for a comeback. And they took the second-half kickoff and seemed more than refreshed by the break. With Larry Brown unable to break through the stone wall of Fernandez, Stanfill, and Den Herder, Kilmer went to the air and led his team on their best drive of the game. Four passes of intermediate range, finding the seams in the Miami zone, brought them down to the seventeen-yard line with a first down. But then Kilmer slightly overthrew Taylor, who was blanketed by Scott and Mumphord at the goal line; missed a screen pass to the running back Charley Harraway; and was unequivocally sacked by Manny Fernandez, who was giving the Pro Bowl committee a national scolding. In came Curt Knight, the toe kicker with a Mark Spitz mustache and a Billy Kilmer single-bar face mask. Knight had been the Pro Bowl kicker a year before but had made fewer than half his field goals this year, his career seeming to fade along with his straight-on style. (He was twenty-nine but would play only one more year. He was replaced, though, by another toe kicker, Mark Moseley, who would be one of the best kickers of the next decade and the last in the league to kick straight on.) Knight had had a poor year but a good playoffs, making all seven kicks. Still, no one should have been shocked that he shanked this thirty-two-yarder right. He only made about half from that distance his last two years, and special-teams hero Lloyd Mumphord, whom Knight must surely have been watching in the film room, came rushing hard from the left side and probably had something to do with the kick soaring off to the right.

Bob Griese took over for his first possession of the second half, and like a conservative politician who knows his base, he made good on his locker room promise: he ran the ball. Three straight handoffs to Csonka for seven tough yards, then a punt. Kilmer went back to the run himself, much more successfully, and Washington moved right down the field to the Miami forty-four before stalling with a few incomplete passes. They punted, but they had to be feeling a lot better about their chances. At this point they had run eighteen plays in the third quarter, compared to Miami's three. Surely they agreed with Curt Gowdy, who pronounced, "Washington has completely dominated this third quarter."

But they had dominated without scoring any points. And now Griese continued his conservative agenda, this time with results as thrilling to Dolphin fans as any flea flicker reverse. Merc cutting inside for six. Zonk on the delay trap, behind Evans pulling left, for eleven. And then, just as the defense might be expecting something different—say, a pitchout to Morris, or even a pass—back to Csonka right up the middle. Morris did flare left as if for the pitch, and Griese went that way too. But not before making the lightning-quick handoff to the big man on the P10 Express. This time it was Larry Little pulling into the middle to lead the way, but as he broke through the line and looked for someone to block, Csonka lost patience and blew right by him. Both Little and Fleming, intending to block for Csonka, found themselves chasing after him downfield. Csonka must have felt just as he had on his cross-country run in overtime against Kansas City the previous Christmas, bereft of tacklers as he bowled down the field. He finally found one to pick on, though hardly someone his own size. Pat Fischer had an idea to run him out of bounds at the Washington thirty, but Csonka instead cut back, right at him, and sent him ten yards out of the play with a right forearm. ("Now, watch this violent attack here," cried Al DeRogatis when they showed the replay.) Owens and Pardee finally brought him down on the sixteen-yard line. It was a forty-nine-yard gain, his longest run of the year, reminiscent of that game-breaking gallop in Kansas City. Once again, it felt as though Csonka had knocked the wind out of the other team.

The ground assault continued: Morris up the middle for four; Morris sweeping right, cutting back, and fighting hard through tacklers for five more, down to the seven-yard line. On third down, with both tight ends in and the entire line bunched up tight, everyone knew Kiick would get it, and he did, following Csonka for a one-yard plunge for the first down and goal at the four. Csonka was stopped for no gain, but there seemed little chance of stopping Miami's running attack. For ten plays in a row now to start the second half, Griese had called run. And they could not be in a better position. Mandich had hurt his leg on that last play and had to go out, but Griese was so set on his power formation with two tight ends that in came Larry Seiple, who had

had a stellar year at tight end in '69 but hadn't played the position all year. It turned out Griese wanted that formation for the third straight play for purposes of deception. He faked the handoff to Morris and looked for Marv Fleming, breaking to the left side of the end zone. It looked for a moment as though he had him, and the throw was on target, but he hadn't seen Brig Owens sprinting across, and the pass was softer than it might have been. Owens arrived at the last moment, leaped, and corralled the ball with his right hand for a brilliant interception.

Griese walked dejectedly back to the sideline and Shula's tightly held displeasure. The coach might have acerbically pointed out the quarterback's promise to "only throw if it's a sure thing." Instead he blurted out, "We needed at least three [points] out of that!" Griese gave him his best deadpan face. "Nobody knows that better than I do." End of conversation. The long drive had been far from useless, though: they'd chewed up the last third of the third quarter, and Washington was left with one quarter to make up a fourteen-point deficit.

Nixon and Rebozo ordered a dinner of fresh fish at the Ocean Reef Club as the fourth quarter began and watched as the defenses dominated the first two series. Three and out for both teams, but time was running out for Washington as they took over at their own eleven with about twelve minutes remaining. They proceeded upon a prolonged campaign that would absorb most of the final quarter and either bring them a chance at final heroics or leave them gasping short of the prize. Larry Brown finally ran like the league's leading rusher, battling for thirty-one yards on five carries. Harraway got thirteen more on two runs. "But Washington's using a lot of time on this drive," warned Gowdy. They ran a tight-end reverse for six. Twice Kilmer eluded sacks and scrambled for nine and ten yards. "I can't run anymore," he'd told reporters, but with the game on the line the battered old quarterback looked like he was still Cal's single-wing man; on the second scramble he dodged a blitzing Swift and brought out his old open-field moves, fighting down to the nineteen-yard line. Shula watched with both hands on hips as the action moved like a slow tank division down the field, five and ten yards at a time. About half the Dolphins on the sideline had their hands on their hips. Larry Csonka sat on the bench, watching with a face devoid of emotion. Kilmer completed one short pass from his own eleven to start the drive, and another a long time later for a first down at the Miami fourteen-yard line. Brown took it to the ten. "Washington has had the ball about eighty to eighty-five percent of this half," said Gowdy. DeRogatis pointed out that although the Redskins had moved all the way down the field, the Dolphins had forced them to use up seven minutes, allowing no big plays.

After this last Brown run, Manny Fernandez, who had been ravaging the offensive line like an act of God, needed some help from Buoniconti and Scott getting up. He had just made his seventeenth tackle of the afternoon. Earlier, at the beginning of the fourth quarter, he had finally met his match: Nick Buoniconti. Manny had grabbed Brown by his shirtsleeve and was trying to bring him down when everything went blank. "I guess I got a concussion," Fernandez said later. "I swung him around and Nick came in to finish him off and finished me off. I was hit harder than I've ever been hit in my life. I was in another world. I could hear someone yell, 'Manny's hurt—he's down!' Then I heard Shula: 'No, goddamnit, no! He can't be hurt!' So I figured I better get up. I tried to join the Redskins huddle, and Nick had to go get me and drag me back to our huddle." He was still visibly disoriented several drives later, although he continued to make tackles. "Hey, you okay?" Jake Scott looked concerned. Manny just nodded and trudged back to the huddle.

The clock dropped below six minutes and was ticking away. On second down, Kilmer faded back, and just as Stanfill smacked into him he threw for the back of the end zone. Jerry Smith was cutting across the back line; he had Anderson chasing him, Scott coming over from the other side, and Buoniconti playing him short, just outside the end zone. A perfect pass had a chance to catch Smith in between all three of them, and it looked as though Kilmer's throw might just be that perfect. Until it was knocked down—by the crossbar of the goalpost, which still in 1972 hovered right above the goal line. After twelve straight plays this drive gaining four yards or more, the crossbar had finally stalled the march.

Third down from the ten. Two plays left to get at least six yards and a first down, since a field goal was useless at this point. "I can't get greedy or lightning will strike," Kilmer had explained to those reporters in his hotel room. "They make you grind it out, get down to their thirty or so, and then make a mistake. We can't make the mistake. . . ." Instead of going for the first down, though, he called another pass route deep into the end zone. Charley Taylor this time, a post pattern from the right, slanting behind the goalpost again. He had a step on Mumphord, and this time, perhaps wary of that yellow crossbar, Kilmer threw early, to the right of the post and a little behind Taylor. He didn't see Jake Scott waiting there for his ride. Scott jumped straight up, grabbed the interception a few yards deep in the end zone, and took off on a sprint. One nice move between three Redskins and he was off down the left sideline. Only one man was left, running back Charley Harraway. Scott tried to outrun him down the sideline, but Harraway had the angle and trapped him just past midfield. It wasn't the 103-yard touchdown Scott was looking for, but it was a momentous interception and runback that all but sealed the victory for Miami. His teammates mobbed him on the sideline, and as he made his way back to the bench for a drink, Don Shula finally caught up with him, tapped him on the shoulder, and then gave him a little hug and a "Way to go." He wasn't going to be the losingest Super Bowl coach after all.

The Washington drive had been impressive until then, but it had eaten up half of the fourth quarter. Miami now had the ball at midfield with five minutes left and a two-touchdown lead. Csonka for seven, Kiick for three. Kiick for four, Zonk for no gain. The clock was almost down to three minutes. "What a frustrating feeling this must be," said Gowdy, "when you're behind like this, the other club's got the ball, using up thirty seconds each play. . . ." Now, on third and six from the thirty-four, Griese decided to let one fly. After all, they must be expecting nothing but more clock-killing runs. He sent Twilley on my brother's favorite front-yard play: down and out, then break long along the sideline. Twilley fooled Fischer again, getting him to bite and sprinting for the goal line two yards in front of his man. But this time Griese threw a little short, and Fischer was just able to deflect the ball. "Well, Curt," said DeRogatis, "Griese figured if he missed it, he always has his other little guy, Garo." And on came Yepremian to try a forty-two-yard field goal.

Joe Robbie was pacing the sideline, ecstatic at the prospect of his mad gamble of a football team in Miami paying off with a Super Bowl triumph. "Field goal makes it seventeen oh, and seventeen and oh," he kept repeating to anyone who would listen. The word got around. They were about to finish off the perfect season with the perfect score: 17–0.

The kicker was slightly less confident. Normally he would have no doubts about a forty-two-yarder—although to be honest he, like the other top kickers, only made about half their kicks from this distance. But he'd had those problems getting the ball up in the pregame warm-up kicks. Something about this field . . . No matter. Bad dress rehearsal, good performance. He'd lifted both extra points nice and high. The snap came a little low, but Morrall got the ball in place fine. Yepremian swung through it and kicked it differently than in the warm-ups: he kicked it even lower. It hit Bob Heinz's back and bounced back and to the right. Morrall and Yepremian both ran after it. It happened to bounce straight up, and Morrall would have had it right in his hands except that Garo didn't notice the veteran quarterback there and reached in and grabbed it away from him. That was mistake number one (if you don't count the low kick).

It's possible to imagine what sorts of impulses were firing across Yepremian's neural synapses at that moment. Perhaps there was a flicker of the fantasy he had shared with teammates earlier in the year: that he would someday grab a botched snap and punt it. Maybe he had a flashback to the St. Louis Monday night game, just seven weeks before. A blocked kick had bounced back to him on the right side, just like this, and he'd bungled a pass attempt. In a rare failure to iron out every potentially costly defect, Shula neglected to drill Yepremian during the next week's practice in dealing with a blocked kick. Ten, twenty, thirty times a day he could have had him practice falling on the ball. But he did not. So when Garo got this one in his hands, with a couple of minutes left in the Super Bowl, he didn't fall on it. Even this week at practice, instead of disaster prep, he was playing catch, tossing beautiful thirty-five-yard passes, imagining himself a famous quarterback. Now he had a vague glimpse of Csonka looking back at him dumbfounded from fifteen yards downfield, and he decided to throw to him. "As soon as I picked up the ball," he said, "I saw [six-foot-five, 270-pound] Bill Brundige coming towards me with smoke coming out of his ears and mouth. I had no time to adjust the laces or get my legs set . . ." As Morrall gave Brundige a pretty good block, Yepremian tried to pass, and it went even worse than in the Monday night game. The ball slipped out of his hand, but instead of falling to the ground, it hung for a moment right in front of him, and he shoveled it back up into the air with both hands in what can only be seen as a reaction of pure panic. Curt Gowdy and Al DeRogatis broke into laughter. Cornerback Mike Bass came running by, swiped it right out of the air, and headed downfield. Morrall had a bead on him, but Brundige got him back for the previous block, laying the old man flat on the field. The only Dolphin with a chance to stop Bass was Yepremian.

Garo had a reputation for something less than courage in circumstances like this. But in the Longest Game he'd gotten in Ed Podolak's way on a potential game-winning kickoff return, slowing him down enough for Curtis Johnson to catch up and save the day. And he'd done a similar job just two weeks ago in the AFC championship game. Now, with Bass sprinting down the sideline, Yepremian had a chance to force him out of bounds. But Bass made a little fake back to the middle of the field, Garo hesitated, and Bass flew right by him to the end zone.

"Damn!" yelled Al Jenkins on the sideline, in the most family-friendly reaction available to NFL Films. "What a kooky play that was!" cried Curt Gowdy. "Garo Yepremian lost his head and tried to throw a pass!" It would forever be the most remembered play from Super Bowl VII. Not Twilley's touchdown, not Csonka's forty-nine-yard blast, not Jake Scott's game-icing interception and run. And now, instead of beginning their celebration on the sideline, the Dolphins had to squirm through another two minutes of football. "When that happened," said Scott, "it made you sick to think about it. We'd had the game in control. We didn't even have to use the clock." They were still in control, up 14–7, but now they would have to do something. They would have to get a first down if they didn't want to give Washington time for a reasonable chance at a tying touchdown.

Some Dolphins were angry at their little kicker. For decades Bob Kuechenberg would grumble about that "coward" who "wasn't man enough to fall on the ball and take his lumps." A legend endured that Manny Fernandez had gone up to Garo on the sideline and told him, "If we lose this game, I'm going to string you up with one of your ties." Others—or sometimes the same person—would say that it was Buoniconti who made the threat. Either way, it's unlikely. Why would you terrify and undermine the confidence of a teammate you might still need to make a pressure kick in overtime? Shula was probably already thinking of that when he simply told Yepremian, "You should have fallen on it." (To Morrall he barked, "If he ever gets the ball again, don't block for him—tackle him!") Garo himself said right after the game, "Nobody panicked. Nobody yelled at me. Norm came over and said, 'Don't worry, God loves you. And we'll hold them.' In those last two minutes I never did such praying in my life. I felt as if my life was over. If we had lost, it would have haunted me forever. " Morrall stood right by him on the sideline for several minutes, talking him down, telling him to just fall on it next time, but don't worry, we still got this game. . . . Marlin Briscoe came over and joined them, a sympathetic soul. His own blunder had canceled the most beautiful touchdown pass in seven Super Bowls, at a moment when the game was still up for grabs. "Everybody remembers Garo's guffaw," he said almost fifty years later. "But he saved me from being the scapegoat of the day."

What they both needed was for their team to take possession of the ball and churn out a first down. That would use up Washington's time-outs and leave them with virtually no time. If Washington recovered an onside kick, however, they would have two full minutes to score a tying touchdown. Shula put Scott, Twilley, and his other talented ball handlers up on the front line in case George Allen went for it, but instead Curt Knight kicked it high and deep. Morris ran a scary little scatterbug return, the ball held precariously in one hand, to the fifteen. The two-minute warning was issued at one minute fifty-seven seconds. As Griese brought his offense out one more time, they had two things to keep in mind: Don't fumble, and, as Shula barked at Mercury Morris, "Stay in bounds!" Even if they didn't get a first down, if they stayed in bounds they would force Washington to use all its time-outs, and they would punt with about one minute thirty-five seconds remaining.

The infamously predictable Dolphins, however, had a couple of surprises left. Shula sent Morris, who had led the team in fumbles with eight, instead of Kiick to join Csonka in the backfield. And instead of sending Csonka safely up the middle, Griese gave it to Morris on a sweep out right. Morris ran near the sideline and tried to cut back in, but Pat Fischer succeeded in pushing him out of bounds after a three-yard gain. Clock stopped, no time-out necessary. On second down, Griese stunned everyone in the stadium by throwing to Warfield on a dangerous down-and-out pattern. Even in this situation Mike Bass had been giving Warfield a generous cushion, and it was an easy completion for a first down. However, the pattern brought Warfield out near the sideline, and just like Morris he was unable to stay in bounds while eluding Bass. This play was forever hailed as a brilliant call that secured the game. However, because Warfield went out of bounds, it actually achieved very little. Washington still had all three of its time-outs, which it called after each of the next three runs. So Larry Seiple came out to punt with one minute twenty-four seconds left.

Disaster almost struck in any case, because of a rare lapse on the part of the Miami special teams. Mack Alston broke through the middle of the line, leaped in front of Seiple, and came within a hair of blocking the punt. A less experienced punter might have panicked and blown the punt or tried to run with the ball, but Seiple calmly blasted a forty-one-yarder, and Washington took over on its own thirty. They had to hurry, as in those days the clock continued to run after a punt, as soon as the ball was set. In fact, Kilmer overthrew his first pass on purpose just to stop the clock. On second down, he overthrew a well-covered Taylor. With a minute left, he managed to dump a screen pass to Brown as Den Herder knocked his helmet right off his head, but Stanfill dropped Brown for a loss. Fourth down, with the clock running. With Curt Gowdy invoking the Steelers' Immaculate Reception, Kilmer faded back one last time, but Den Herder and Stanfill were both on him before he could even throw a desperation pass. The three of them went down in a bundle. Stanfill began slapping the supine Den Herder and hugging him, paying no attention to poor Kilmer, who was between them and who had once again lost his helmet with the single bar. The referee was telling them to get off Kilmer or there'd be a penalty.

The rest of the defense was running jubilantly off the field while players on the sideline shouted, "That's it! World champs!" Nick Buoniconti ran right into Shula's outstretched arms as someone yelled, "Way to go, Nicky!" DeRogatis intoned, "Garo Yepremian has got to be the happiest man in the stadium," but no one could have been feeling more joy than Don Shula. His extraordinary diligence and motivation had transmuted into monomania a year ago in New Orleans; now he had his white whale. Shula stood grinning, clapping, but also making a show of watching the clock as if it mattered. Griese didn't even need to take a snap and fall on it; as soon as the ball was set, the clock started running. Everyone just watched until it hit zero. Buoniconti and Al Jenkins lifted Shula on their shoulders as hundreds of fans stormed the field.

Shula waved with one hand, hanging on with the other, as they made their way through the crowd. Fans were swarming him, reaching up to shake his hand. One swiped his watch. He dropped to his feet and looked around for the thief, but before he could go after him a young man came running back with the watch and returned it with a big smile. Otherwise the TV cameras might have caught the best tackle of the day.

At six twenty-eight in the evening, in a suburban Miami neighborhood, a car horn sounded. Dark had fallen sometime in the third quarter, and with the game now over, many families, like mine, were setting the table for a late dinner. Another horn went off, and we looked out the open window to see if there'd been an accident. Then another horn, and another down the street. We went out into the evening yard, where the temperature had dipped into the mid-sixties, a little winter thrill. All around us, from up and down the street, cars parked in driveways and on grass swales were bellowing like a gaggle of celebrating geese. Ten miles away, in Little Havana, fifteen-year-old Gloria Estefan, who'd been watching and cheering with her family, heard the same thing. "I remember going outside and lying on the roof of my mother's Monte Carlo and staring up at the stars and hearing the city exploding in horn-honking and celebration."

All around South Florida, impromptu parades were forming. A *Miami Herald* reporter phoned in to the office from a raucous bar on Eighth Street, barely able to be heard, as if he were reporting from Paris on VE Day: "There are hundreds of cars driving up and down the street, blowing their horns and waving white hankies like they're looking for someplace to surrender!" They were sitting up on the window jambs of their Chevys, leaning out and waving those hankies, waving towels and sheets, whatever they had. In the next century, during such disturbances, people would go online to see what was going on; in 1972 they called in to the local newspaper. "Has peace been declared?" one woman asked the *Herald* switchboard operator. "No, ma'am," came the beleaguered reply, "the Dolphins just won the Super Bowl." Other callers wanted to know if there would be school the next day.

On Key Largo, Richard Nixon switched off the television set and sighed. No more football. He and Rebozo went back to Key Biscayne by helicopter. Kissinger was waiting there; the next day would be filled with meetings with Henry and telephone calls with Bob Haldeman back in Washington.

As the Dolphin players came off the field and entered the locker room, their mood seemed somewhat subdued, considering the moment. "I think we were in shock," said Larry Seiple. "There was some celebration, but for the most part it wasn't as jubilant as it probably should've been. I think we had been so focused on getting there that when we finally got there and won it, it just felt like 'Well we're supposed to do that.' It didn't all sink in until a couple days later." As they ran into the tunnel of the Coliseum, Jake Scott turned to Howard Kindig: "No one seems to realize what we just accomplished. Our team doesn't even realize we've made our place in history." A bit later one reporter conducting an interview said, "If I didn't know better, I'd think you lost." Partly it was just the nature of this team. Player after player would repeat that it "wasn't a rah-rah type of team," that they simply went out there and took care of business. "That's the level of maturity that this team had reached," said Warfield. "It was just the mindset of that team," said Doug Crusan. "It was a mature team with players that just took everything in stride. Although to be honest, it was a relief more than anything. We had finally done it." A few years later, the film *Chariots of Fire* would dramatize that feeling. When British sprinter Harold Abrahams finally wins the Olympic gold medal, he shies away from the hugs and backslaps of his teammates. That night he and his coach sit alone in a bar until closing time, subdued and contemplative: their long struggle is over.

Not that the Dolphins were emotionless. When Shula first entered the locker room, he found Bill Arnsparger, and they looked at each other and just hugged, tears in their eyes. When all the players arrived, Shula led them in the usual team prayer and said a few words. "It was the first time ever," said Kiick, "he didn't talk about the next game." Then the reporters flooded in, and Shula jumped up onto a table to hold court: "Let the record speak for itself. It has entered an area no other team has ever gone into. When you're the *first*, it's something special." Across the room, Larry Csonka looked like he'd finally finished that barn for his dad. "I just want to go to sleep," he said. How about Yepremian's field goal fiasco? Everyone wanted to know. "Garo thought he was a quarterback," said Csonka. "He thought he was six-six like Roman Gabriel, with hair down to his shoulders." "I've got to work with Garo in the off-season," Griese joked as the kicker walked by. "Now listen, Garo, you've got to grip the laces, and then you hold the ball back of your ear. . . ." Yepremian characteristically went along with the ribbing: "This is the first time," he announced, "the goat of the game is in the winners' locker room." Inside, though, he was dying. He let his mask of bonhomie drop for a moment and sighed, "That championship ring will hang heavy on my hand." A few hours later he would reluctantly let his brother convince him to attend the team party at the Beverly Hilton, but when he got there he began experiencing anxiety-induced pain all down the left side of his body and had to leave.

The announcement came through of the Super Bowl MVP, and many were surprised by the selection of Jake Scott. Yes, he'd had two interceptions, including the game breaker. But he'd also had a bad fumble on a punt return (luckily covered by Anderson). And then there was Manny Fernandez, with an astonishing seventeen tackles (eleven of them solo), who had dominated the line of scrimmage to an extent not yet seen in a championship game. He stopped the unstoppable Larry Brown cold; he was in the backfield, sacking Kilmer; he was helping out on short passes. Gowdy called his name so often that no one in America could have overlooked his performance.

Except for Dick Schaap. In those days the MVP was chosen by a single man, the editor of *Sport* magazine. And the new occupant of that position in 1972 was Schaap, an accomplished sportswriter and bestselling coauthor of sports memoirs by Joe Namath and others. But Schaap had enjoyed himself a bit too much on Saturday night, and he spent most of the Super Bowl nursing a hangover, even dozing in the press box through much of the game. He said later he was awake for Scott's interceptions; others said he woke up and asked who had played well. He was glad to see Hunter Thompson wasn't there; he could barely recall what bet he'd made with him at two a.m. at Tony's Saloon downtown. (A year later he'd bet against Miami again and lose another $25 to him.) Today Thompson had left the Coliseum at halftime, secure that his wagers would come through. He abandoned the sportswriters, whom he considered "a kind of rude and brainless subculture of fascist drunks whose only real function is to publicize & sell [the product of sports]," and watched the rest of the game at an alcohol-and-drug-soaked party at his friend Bill Cardoso's apartment in West Hollywood. And apparently no one left in the press box mentioned to Schaap that Manny Fernandez had just played the best game they'd ever seen a defensive lineman play.

It didn't bother Manny that day. Nothing did, after the head shot he'd taken from his own teammate, Buoniconti, early in the fourth. "I don't remember the last nine, ten minutes of the game," he said later. "I didn't make another tackle." (Not true.) "I don't recall the party after the game. The first thing I remember is waking up the next morning." A great starting tackle for Miami for over seven years, Fernandez never did get that Pro Bowl selection. But at least his teammates knew who should've been Super Bowl MVP. "The best Super Bowl I ever saw a defensive lineman have," said Csonka. "Maybe I should have shared the

MVP with Manny," said Scott. "But at least I gave him a set of keys to my pickup truck that I got for winning the award."

Speaking of prizes, Don Shula was up on the platform, accepting the Vince Lombardi trophy from Commissioner Pete Rozelle. Normally not one for ceremonies, the coach couldn't get enough of this one. All the flack he'd taken from his old boss, the comments of the "experts" who said he couldn't go all the way, the mission of atonement for the previous year's loss, and the growing burden of perfection since sometime in mid-autumn—all the weight was suddenly lifted from his shoulders. As he took the trophy, he resurrected the many weeks of questioning about his team's perfect record: "We didn't think about fourteen and oh, or fifteen and oh or sixteen and oh. But we're thinking about seventeen and oh right now."

•　•　•

Twenty-four hours later, Shula was up on another makeshift platform, this one at the Eastern parking lot, the Dolphins' now-familiar unloading spot just across Thirty-Sixth Street from the Kings Inn. The crowd had been waiting for hours. It was Monday night, and at seven thirty the Carol City High School marching band had begun playing, followed by the Fred Shannon Smith orchestra. Finally, an hour later, the Eastern DC-8 carrying the perfect team came taxiing in from the runway, and the cheers began to swell. First out of the jet was Shula, relaxed in a navy blue blazer, no tie this time, carrying a black bag. He made his way to the floodlit platform and was the first to speak. He reached into the black Puma shoe bag and pulled out a trophy: a silver football atop an obelisk. "This is the Vince Lombardi trophy for the winner of the Super Bowl," he said into the microphone and held the trophy up high. Then his voice rose with fervor: "Seventeen and oh says it all! The world championship, the best team ever in professional football!"

He handed the trophy to his son David, who put it back in the shoe bag. Several other players spoke, and as the event wound down, someone from Eastern turned to the players and said, "By the way, you're not getting out of here for about three hours." And they brought them inside and served them drinks until the crowd dissipated. It was the beginning of their new existence as the Perfect Team. Whatever they did with the rest of their lives—farming, lawyering, running businesses—it would always be noted that they had played for the 1972 Dolphins. Even for the Hall of Famers Csonka, Griese, Warfield, Little, and Langer, their prodigious individual achievements would take a backseat to this team accomplishment. In the Post Perfect, the dimension they would inhabit from this point on, all anyone would want to hear about was nineteen seventy-two. They couldn't know then that their mark would remain untouched for fifty years and more, and perhaps as Jake Scott had intuited they didn't even realize yet what they had done. As the tumult had began to grow in the locker room after the game, just before the players were engulfed by the phalanx of reporters from around the country, Larry Little was sitting at his locker, forearms on knees, head hanging down, exhausted. "Can you believe it?" asked Norm Evans, coming up to him. "Not yet, man," said Little. "But I think I'm learning."

Past Perfect

How many things by season season'd are
To their right praise and true perfection!
—*The Merchant of Venice*

The day after the Super Bowl, from Key Biscayne, President Nixon ordered a halt to the bombing of North Vietnam. That same day, in Washington, the four Miami defendants in the Watergate trial pleaded guilty, telling an incredulous judge that the break-in was part of their struggle against Fidel Castro and communism and that the Nixon administration had had nothing to do with it. On January 27, the White House announced the suspension of all offensive operations in Vietnam, as the Paris Peace Accords were finally signed. Three days later, G. Gordon Liddy was convicted and sentenced to twenty years in prison.

In the spring and summer of 1973, even as Nixon might have been celebrating his triumph, however specious, in finally getting America out of Vietnam, his administration was collapsing around him. From May to August, the nation was transfixed by the live broadcasts of the Senate Watergate Committee's hearings. Over the next couple of years, as Nixon and Kissinger knew would happen, South Vietnam was unable to survive without U.S. support, and on April 30, 1975, Saigon fell to the North. The press didn't have Dick Nixon around to grill, however. On August 9, 1974, he had resigned the presidency, insisting even then, like a coach already trudging toward the tunnel early in the fourth quarter, "I am not a quitter."

. . .

The Miami Dolphins were still the reigning champions of football. In 1973 they weren't perfect, but they weren't far from it. Another commanding season ended this time with a blowout of the Vikings in the Super Bowl. They were still a young team, and it looked like they might win four or five in a row before they were done.

Before that season, in the early summer of 1973, Don Shula was having his Nixon '68 moment. After an early career that was both exceptional and frustrating, as each year ended with an agonizing loss, he had finally felt the ultimate satisfaction. It was six months now since his team had done the impossible, finishing off the NFL's only perfect season. Now, with a new preseason about to begin, he sat at the bar of his expansive home on the edge of the Miami Lakes Country Club golf course. Dorothy and the kids were out, and he had a rare moment of quietude before his passionate intensity roused itself again with the onset of training camp. He was forty-three years old and would coach the Dolphins for twenty-three more years. Only twice in his thirty-three seasons as a head coach did he have a losing season. (With Shula gone, the Dolphins would begin the twenty-first century with twelve losing seasons out of twenty-one.) He finally retired in 1995 after winning 328 games. In 2020, shortly after his ninetieth birthday, an occasion widely celebrated in the South Florida media, Don Shula died. It was a good life to the end, after a long, satisfying career. But for a man so devoted to winning above all else, the pinnacle had to be those two years of 1972 and 1973. In the midst of it, poised halfway between his two greatest victories, he sipped a Scotch and gazed out from the air-conditioning to the lush lawn sloping down to the sixteenth fairway. "This is everything I ever dreamed of, everything I ever wanted," he said. "I have to shake myself to realize it happened."

. . .

If anyone thought this fulfillment would mean a less relentless training camp, he was quickly disabused of this notion in July. At the very first meeting after the veterans had reported, Shula stood at his podium. The year before, he had gone on and on about the failure in the Super Bowl and how it must be redeemed. Everyone wondered what he was going to come up with after the perfect season. Shula made a few pleasantries and then announced, "Now, our objective this season is to do exactly what we did last season." Players looked around and at each other. Uh-oh. Larry Csonka raised his hand. "Coach, who's going to break Griese's leg in the fifth game?"

The irony of the perfect season is that the 1972 Dolphins can never be called the greatest team ever, because they weren't even the best Dolphin team ever. Most players and observers agree that the 1973 team was even better. They lost a tight one in the second game, 12–7 to Oakland, and another to Baltimore at the end of the season, with the division wrapped up, when they rested Griese and other starters. Other than that, there weren't even any close games. What appears on the record to be tight victories over Dallas and Pittsburgh were actually fourteen- and twenty-point Dolphin fourth-quarter leads that closed up a bit at the end. In the playoffs there was none of the nail-biting of the year before as they crushed Cincinnati 34–16, Oakland 27–10, and Minnesota 24–7 in the Super Bowl. The running game had become even more dominant: against the Raiders in the AFC championship game, Griese felt compelled to throw the ball only six times, completing three for thirty-four yards. (They ran for 266.) In the Super Bowl, the offensive line handled the famed Viking front four with astonishing ease, and Griese probably didn't have to pass at all. He went six for seven, just to show a little versatility. But the dynasty that appeared set to rule for another several years would never be.

CSONKA, KIICK, AND WARFIELD SWITCH TEAMS, blazed the *Herald*. This was still the middle of the 1972 season, and it was just an ad for Surreys, "the snazziest designer clothes south of New York." The unthinkable became reality, however, just eighteen months later, when those same three stars announced on March 31, 1974, that they had signed with the Toronto Northmen of the new World Football League for over $3 million. Their Dolphin contracts were up, and Joe Robbie had made no overtures since the Super Bowl to renew them, so when the trio were drafted by Toronto in March, they flew up there to negotiate, probably just hoping to drive up their market price in Miami. But when their agent phoned Robbie and told him they were about to sign with Toronto and gave him two days to make a counteroffer, Robbie balked. He wouldn't negotiate over the phone, and he wouldn't fly to Toronto, and they wouldn't meet him in New

York. And so came the announcement that shocked the league and appalled Dolphin fans. The three would return to Miami to play out their option year, but in 1975 they would be gone.

The Dolphins played the 1974 season under the cloud of this imminent defection. Shula's two primary assistants were already missing: Arnsparger was head coach of the Giants and Schnellenberger of the Colts. But even with a notably less impregnable defense (only sixth in the league after two years on top) and offense (Morris missed most of the season with an injured knee), the Dolphins still were 11–3 and found themselves leading the Raiders 26–21 in the first playoff game out in Oakland with thirty-five seconds to play. When Vern Den Herder sacked Ken Stabler with no time-outs left, it seemed Miami was headed to another AFC championship game. But as he fell to the ground, Stabler pushed a desperate pass into the end zone, hopelessly aiming at a covered Clarence Davis. Somehow the ball found its way between the hands of Mike Kolen and Charlie Babb and into those of Davis, who held on for an unimaginable victory. Oakland had exorcised the Immaculate Reception, and the Dolphins' glory years ended with the Sea of Hands miracle.

My brother screamed so loud, he got sent to his room. Raiders fans, who had been "throwing beer bottles and other missiles [at the Miami sideline]," according to Buoniconti, poured onto the field. A particularly inebriated one, you'd have to assume, caught Buoniconti with a sucker punch, and Manny Fernandez made like Mike Curtis and laid him on the ground with one hit. "We literally had to swing our way to the locker room," said Jim Mandich. "It was like a feeding frenzy or something. . . ." An ugly end to a golden age. Tensions that the panacea of winning had kept in check began to split the seams. Jake Scott, unhappy with new defensive coordinator Vince Costello, had cursed him out at a practice, and when Shula tried to intervene, Scott lashed out at him too: "I wasn't fucking talking to you!" Mumphord had a shouting match with Shula during the Oakland game about a missed tackle on a punt return, and Shula, in a rare instance of letting emotion cloud a game decision, left his best pass defender on the bench when Curtis Johnson got hurt. Henry Stuckey went in and got burned on a fluke touchdown catch by Cliff Branch, who fell down, wasn't touched, got back up, and ran it in. Costello resigned on the plane ride home.

Mumphord was playing in Baltimore the next season. Buoniconti and Anderson missed the entire 1975 season with injuries and played only sporadically the next year or two. Jake Scott and Doug Swift played one more year and then Scott was traded to Washington and Swift went to medical school. Mike Kolen was much reduced by injuries in 1975, missed all of 1976, and was all but gone. Bill Stanfill's body began to give out, and he only started half the games his next two seasons before retiring. Marlin Briscoe was also gone in 1975, Mercury Morris a year later. Although they still had mostly winning seasons after 1974, the Dolphins missed the playoffs the next three years and didn't win a playoff game until 1982.

By then, Miami had begun its makeover from a sleepy vacation land to an international business hub and mecca for the wild and the beautiful. The Mariel boatlift, combined with a heavy flow of Cuban Americans from around the country down to Miami as well as immigration from a number of other Latin American countries, transformed South Florida's population in the 1980s. International trade boomed, including that of illegal substances, above all cocaine. Guns proliferated, crime skyrocketed, and Miami soon had the highest murder rate in the country. South Beach, meanwhile, fulfilled the aspirations of those city councilors in the early 1970s. The elderly Jews and others of low or limited income were forced out by renovation and rising rents and were eventually replaced by the wealthy and fashionable.

This newest Miami resurrection, however, like those of the 1920s and 1940s, didn't lift everyone. Don Shula may have ameliorated racial tensions on his football team, but South Florida was still "not a good [place] in which to be black." Although there were no more major racial disturbances in the 1970s, resentment among the Black community continued to build, and it exploded in 1980 when four white police officers were acquitted by an all-white jury of the brutal killing of insurance salesman Arthur McDuffie, who had run a red light. Rioters in Liberty City and surrounding areas smashed windows, attacked motorists and burned their cars, burned down buildings. Eighteen people died, hundreds were injured, and a hundred million dollars of damage was done. All over South Florida—even down in Kendall, where I never noticed much tension in my racially mixed high school—schools were closed for three days. The construction of freeways had long ago fractured the Black communities in Liberty City and Overtown, decomposing bustling business communities into vacant lots of rubble. It seemed the McDuffie riots would finish off the job, leaving more burned-out, ransacked buildings in their wake. Where once there was a thriving nightlife with theaters and nightclubs, now were just dark streets, rife with drug dealers. As Mario Alejandro Ariza put it, the land under and around those superhighways became "Miami's skid row, a dangerous, first-circle-of-hell-like demesne for the addicted, the down-on-their-luck, the deranged, and the utterly dispossessed." Not long after the McDuffie riots, the Jet-A-Way, where Larry Little had introduced rookie Eddie Jenkins to the music of Betty Wright, to fried chicken and souse, and to the Black Miami nightlife, collapsed under a wrecking ball.

· · ·

The perfect Dolphins were smart and motivated to succeed, and that didn't end with football. Doug Swift took premed courses at the University of Miami while playing pro football, studied for his MCATs during the 1975 season, started med school at Penn the next year, and had a long career as a cardiac anesthesiologist. Dick Anderson was elected to the Florida Senate as a Democrat in 1978, served one term, and then got back to the successful business career that he'd begun even while playing football. Marv Fleming, too, maintained his business success, flourishing in real estate in California. Nick Buoniconti hit retirement in stride, continuing his lucrative off-field career as an attorney and agent for a number of professional athletes, lobbyist for and eventually president of the U.S. Tobacco Company (manufacturer of smokeless tobacco products like Skoal and Copenhagen), and cohost for two decades of HBO's *Inside the NFL*. Howard Twilley earned his MBA at the University of Miami while he was playing for the Dolphins; when he retired, he moved back to Tulsa, where he'd starred in college, and bought a local Athlete's Foot franchise. He eventually owned thirty-one outlets before selling them all and retiring back to Texas. Tim Foley became an Amway distributor and made millions as he played that pyramid-style business model like a complex Arnsparger defense. Vern Den Herder never got around to veterinary school, but he did buy that land he dreamed of back in Iowa and became a successful farmer well into his seventies.

Of course many are gone now. After retiring from the Dolphins in 1978, Wayne Moore worked as a salesman before becoming the first of the perfect team to die, of a heart attack at forty-four. His right-hand man on the line, Kuechenberg, said, "I have never met a finer person than Solomon. He was far too nice a person to be in football." The next was Bob Matheson, eponym of the

53 defense, of Hodgkin's disease at forty-nine. Cancer also took Jim Mandich and Garo Yepremian. Mandich was a beloved figure among Dolphin fans not just for his eight seasons at tight end but also as a radio talk show host and color commentator for Dolphin games from the 1980s until he became too sick in 2010. Yepremian was traded to New Orleans after the 1978 season despite making the Pro Bowl that year and being in the middle of a league record string of consecutive field goals. He finished off his career in Tampa in 1981 and became a sought-after motivational speaker. To the consternation of some former teammates and the amusement of most, he cashed in on his Super Bowl blooper for the rest of his life. It was a cornerstone of his speeches and the punch line for a slew of TV and radio ads he did. "President Nixon suggested I throw that pass," he liked to say. "Since I didn't have my citizenship papers yet, I thought I'd better throw it." In 2001, when his daughter-in-law was battling brain cancer, he founded the Garo Yepremian Foundation for Brain Tumor Research. In 2014 he was diagnosed with a brain tumor himself and died the next year, at seventy.

Marlin Briscoe and Mercury Morris soon found themselves battling a different disease: addiction. When Briscoe retired in 1977, he had invested his money well and was living a good life in Los Angeles. He got married and was working for a brokerage firm, hanging out with the likes of Jim Brown, O. J. Simpson, and Hollywood VIPs. But the cocaine craze of the 1980s reached him, and before long he was addicted to crack. He lost his job and his marriage, eventually his home too. As he used his NFL background—particularly his association with the perfect team—to scrounge money and drugs, the dealers on the streets would start saying, "Hey, look who's coming. Look at him. It's Seventeen-and-Oh." When he watched Doug Williams become the first Black quarterback to win the Super Bowl, in 1988, it was on a TV set in prison.

After his second short jail term, Briscoe managed to pull himself out of the hole. Among others, Howard Twilley—the very man Briscoe was brought to Miami to replace—gave him financial support so he could afford an apartment and take a high school teaching position. He taught math and coached football, remarried, and later was director of the Boys & Girls Club in Long Beach, where he is now retired.

Mercury Morris, too, marked an important historical moment behind bars. It was November 1982, and the window in cell 5A3 was close enough to the Orange Bowl that he could hear faint sounds of the ceremony celebrating the tenth anniversary of the perfect season. It was his third day in the Dade County Jail, after being arrested for drug trafficking.

His downward spiral can be traced back to the peak of his career, when he injured his neck during the 1973 season. Dr. Virgin diagnosed it as a sprain, and Morris kept playing through the playoffs and Super Bowl. He would have gained a thousand yards again that year, except this time Shula kept him out of the final game of the season. And Morris responded by having his best playoff games ever against Cincinnati and Oakland. The Dolphins won their second Super Bowl, but Morris was in intense pain. At the Pro Bowl, doctors found that his neck was in fact fractured. He played very little in 1974 due to a knee injury, but in 1975, with Csonka and Kiick gone, he was the Dolphins' workhorse, shouldering the payload for the first time with 219 carries. With everyone keying on him, though, his average suffered, dropping from his usual spectacular to just a solid 4.0. In 1976, with hard feelings growing between him and the team regarding his role in the offense and his neck injury, the Dolphins traded him to San Diego. After one year there, the pain in his neck was too much, and he retired in Miami.

By 1980 he was taking all sorts of pain relievers, including emergency midnight Xylocaine injections. Spinal fusion surgery late that year helped, but by then he was facing another problem: cocaine. He had started using it socially, then to alleviate his pain, and now found himself hopelessly addicted. By 1982 he was in dire financial straits, having abandoned his business investments to his addiction, when an acquaintance offered him a chance for some quick money. Just introduce a friend to the guys who were supplying him with his coke. The friend, it turned out, was an undercover cop, and Morris was sentenced to twenty years for cocaine trafficking.

He spent more than three years in prison before the state supreme court overturned his verdict—Morris's lawyer had not been allowed to introduce evidence of entrapment—and granted him a new trial. With plea bargaining, he was sentenced, for a lesser charge, to time served, and was released. Like Marlin Briscoe, Mercury Morris had hit rock bottom and come out determined to rebuild his life. And he did, becoming a successful motivational speaker. Eddie Jenkins remembers inviting Morris up to Boston to speak to prisoners at the Suffolk jail: "He had them so wrapped up, almost crying. 'Your ass is not here because of someone else's failure. . . . You're here because you made a big mistake. So let's stop with the bullshit. Let's start at the beginning.' And they couldn't hear enough of it. I took him to Suffolk Law School, and they thought he was a damn law professor. 'Which law school did you go to? Did you clerk for a federal judge?'" Morris also became, along with Csonka, one of the most willing and articulate spokesmen for the perfect team. Any year a team gets past 10–0, Mercury Morris is answering questions somewhere, with intelligence and humor, sometimes with modesty—"Sure, we were lucky"—sometimes goading a little bit: "Go ask the Patriots how difficult it is to do it and how they feel about some kid in Guatemala wearing those 'Perfect 19–0' tees."

Morris's neck pain will always be there to remind him of the violence of the game he mastered with speed and agility. But he is one of the lucky ones. Manny Fernandez is also one of the lucky ones. True, football took apart his body in a ten-year demolition job. "I've had twelve operations and counting," he said. "It's like taking the car in." And that was when he was in his forties. By his fifties, his shoulders had no rotator cuffs, his knees had no cartilage, and his back had two metal rods with screws in it. He had his ninth back surgery in 2020, pushing the overall total to nineteen. Most recreational activities had gone by the wayside by the time he was forty, but he was still able to hunt and fish on his eighty acres in southwest Georgia, where he moved when he retired from the insurance business in 2010. He lost his wife to cancer in 2015. Yet he was one of the lucky ones; it had been a good life, and as he approached eighty he was still of sound mind if not body.

Jake Scott was one of the lucky ones, too, or at least he seemed to be, after all those years of popping running backs and receivers and then taking his own licks while returning punts. He recalled one game against Buffalo when he had to repeatedly throw himself against massive fullback Jim Braxton. "We finish the game," Scott said years later, "I go off the field, I go to the wrong locker room. O.J. [Simpson] takes me over to our locker room and says, 'I think he belongs to you.'" Yet as he entered his sixties he was still in good shape physically and mentally. In 2006 Dave Hyde made like A. E. Hotchner, who'd famously sought out Hemingway in Cuba, and flew to Hawaii uninvited to find Scott. After his feud with Shula, Scott was traded to Washington in 1976, where he roomed with Billy Kilmer—the victim of his MVP interceptions—and played three strong years. Then he retired to his remote log home in Vail and cut off ties with team PR departments, reporters, even most of his old teammates. He invested his football earnings so well that he never had to work. In 1982 he moved to the tiny town of Hanalei, on the westernmost Hawaiian island of Kauai, where Hyde found him twenty-four years later. "I live the simplest life you can imagine," he said. "I wake up every day and decide whether to golf, fish, or have a drink." He spent half the year on Kauai, the other half visiting friends and family and traveling the world. He finally buried the hatchet with Shula in 2010 and attended some team and league events. He began suffering from dementia in his late sixties, but he retained his reclusive and seemingly idyllic lifestyle until the end. It came for Jake Scott just before Thanksgiving 2020, when he suffered a head injury, had complications after surgery, and died in the hospital some days later. One of the great athletes of his time, with better balance and body control than almost any human, had fallen down some steps while visiting friends in Atlanta.

For his old college buddy Bill Stanfill, the end came much slower. The big Georgian was always so fun-loving, a delightful person to be around. By 2010 he was a broken man. Even back in his fifties he had four fused discs in his back and could barely walk upstairs. His hips were wasting away with avascular necrosis, possibly from the incessant cortisone injections in his playing days. Now, though, came the onset of dementia and Parkinson's disease in his sixties. "Stan," he said to his son, "I can deal with the pain. But this losing your mind, I can't handle that." His legs became too unsteady to hunt or fish, his last pleasures. Manny Fernandez now lived not too far away, and they'd get together regularly. Fernandez retired to southern Georgia partly because of his old friend and comrade in the trenches. They'd been training camp roommates and had shared an apartment near the airport back in '69, two young men running the town, having a blast. There was no running around now. "I'd try to cheer him up," said Manny. "He would pretty much just sit in his man cave in his garage and watch TV and do nothing else." In 2016, when Stanfill was sixty-nine, he became disoriented stepping out of his truck and had a bad fall, just as Scott would. He died from complications after surgery to put a pin in his broken leg.

Yes, Manny Fernandez is one of the lucky ones. Even if he doesn't remember the last ten minutes or so of Super Bowl VII or the party after the game. But his mind is still sound, faring much better than the rest of his body. An autopsy showed Scott's and Stanfill's mental declines to be the result of severe chronic traumatic encephalopathy, CTE, football's fatal calling card. "Bill had a hundred and twenty confirmed concussions," Fernandez says. They played almost exactly the same number of NFL games. "And I made more tackles, was double-teamed much more than he was. How many concussions did I have?"

. . .

A football fan today would have to be willfully oblivious to be unaware of the connection between the sport and brain damage. The articles by Jeanne Marie Laskas (which led to the film and book *Concussion*) and the exhaustive and definitive book *League of Denial* (and subsequent ESPN documentary) by Mark Fainaru-Wada and Steve Fainaru—not to mention the copious news coverage of the subject—have laid bare the tale. The retired players who found their minds deteriorating along with their bodies. Unexplained depression, rage, dementia. How Hall of Fame center Mike Webster went from a happy family man with good retirement prospects to living in parking garages, lost in a catatonic state, Tasering himself just to get a half hour's sleep. How Dr. Bennet Omalu discovered CTE in Webster's brain during autopsy. Just like dementia pugilistica—the famous "punch-drunk" syndrome of old boxers—but in football players? Yes, it turned out that not just the recorded concussions but the constant banging on the helmet throughout a game—an estimated twenty-five thousand mini concussions over a career for a player like Webster—were slowly ruining the brains of football players.

The NFL became a twenty-first-century analog of Big Tobacco, throwing millions into legal battles and funding its own research to show that football isn't causing dementia, even while paying millions to damaged former players in out-of-court settlements. But, like tobacco companies and climate deniers, they were finding the scientific consensus was a tidal wave unable to be rationalized away. One study found NFL players four times more likely than the general population to develop Alzheimer's or Parkinson's diseases. Another, originally commissioned by the NFL itself, found dementia nineteen times more prevalent than normal in former NFL players. A lawsuit by seventy-five former players (or families of deceased players) in 2011 alleged an NFL campaign of "fraud and deceit" regarding what the sport was doing to its players. By 2013, nearly six thousand families had joined the suit. In a 2015 settlement, the league agreed to pay about a billion dollars over sixty-five years. At an average of about $190,000 per player, many found this a paltry sum to make up for ruined lives, especially considering that the NFL was projected to pull in a hundred billion dollars or so during that time period. And since then, players and their families have found it very difficult to collect even that amount. "They say they'll pay for it," said Nick Buoniconti in 2017, "but do you know what that's like, actually getting the money?"

. . .

The 1972 Dolphins set themselves apart from every other NFL team, but of course they were no more impervious to the suffering than other players. Earl Morrall retired in 1976 and after coaching the quarterbacks at the University of Miami for a while got into politics, becoming mayor of Davie, Florida, and just barely losing the 1992 race for the Florida House of Representatives. He lived to age seventy-nine, but his later years were riddled with dementia and Parkinson's disease, and an autopsy showed he had the most severe stage of CTE. Mike Kolen, the youthful bone-crunching linebacker in '72, was diagnosed with Alzheimer's at the age of sixty-nine despite no family history of it. Hubert Ginn and Lloyd Mumphord "have quietly dealt with cognitive impairment" in their seventies. Mumphord came in for Tim Foley that time when Foley "heard chapel bells" after a rough hit. Foley, who made up for inferior size and speed with intelligent play and later became a multimillionaire businessman, suffered a rapid mental decline in his sixties and now has retreated into a cloud of dementia, out of touch with his friends and former teammates.

No player embodied the role of willing warrior in a savage crucible more than Bob Kuechenberg. When he broke his arm late in 1973, he had the bone marrow drilled out and a steel rod inserted to allow him to play through the Super Bowl. In retirement, he would blithely stir his guests' cocktails with that rod. He might have been safer being a human cannonball like his dad, but he never regretted his choice. "Every Sunday was a dream come true," he said. "The truth is if they fed me and paid my rent, I'd have gone out there for nothing. My only regret is that my body won't let me go out there another Sunday and play." He was unaware then what destiny was unfolding in his brain. He died at seventy-one of a heart attack, but only after years of mental decline and depression.

Kuechenberg was able to hide his symptoms and keep up a public façade of good health, even up to a year before his death. But by then the toll taken on the perfect team was well-known, thanks to a 2017 *Miami Herald* article and the two poignant *Sports Illustrated* profiles by S. L. Price that prompted it. Price detailed the woes of two of the heroes of '72, Kiick and Buoniconti.

Butch was actually outplaying the higher paid Sundance for the WFL's Memphis Southmen in 1975 (the Toronto Northmen had had to relocate), with more carries for more yards, and of course more receptions. But when the league folded after eleven games that year—its second—Jim Kiick was all but finished. He'd played with broken toes and fingers, bad ankle sprains, a punctured elbow, and a dislocated hip, missing only one game in seven Dolphin seasons. But as he neared the age of thirty, the toll was showing. He got the ball forty times for Denver in 1976, played even less in 1977, got a tryout with George Allen's Redskins, where Jake Scott was, didn't make it, and retired. He still preferred pickup basketball to job hunting, but he eventually latched on as a private investigator in the Broward County Public Defender's Office. It was when he was in his sixties that his mind began to slip. His son had to move in and help him remember appointments and medications. His second ex-wife had remarried to a neurologist with the notable name of Curtis Johnson, and he arranged for a series of exams and imaging in 2011. The diagnosis: dementia, early-onset Alzheimer's, and suspected CTE. (CTE can only be definitely determined via autopsy.) "I got dizzy, got dinged a few times," Kiick allowed, regarding his playing days. "You'd come to the sidelines and they'd ask, 'How many fingers have I got up?' And you'd say four or three or whatever, and they'd say, 'Close enough.'" "He has holes in his brain," said his neurologist now. "There's no question that he suffered significant brain trauma." By 2016, Kiick was living in an assisted-living facility. Every few weeks Mercury Morris, a friend for far longer than the couple of years they were forced to share one position, drove over an hour up from Homestead to visit his old battery mate. "We made a great running back together—1,597 yards and 18 touchdowns in the undefeated season," he said. "We had a bond then, and we have that same bond today. It was all about the team then. . . . It's still about team." In June 2020, isolated in his room by the Covid-19 pandemic, Jim Kiick died at seventy-three.

When the seconds ticked down on Buoniconti's final game, in 1976, he later said, "I got on my hands and knees and kissed the ground and thanked God that I'd never gotten seriously hurt. A fourteen-year career? I could've been maimed." He wasn't thinking then of the hit in Super Bowl VI that knocked him out—he never remembered playing in that game—or the countless other blows to the head. His career as an attorney, agent, and corporate president barreled confidently along for more than thirty years, marred only by the unthinkable tragedy of October 26, 1985. A parent's worst nightmare came true for Nick and his wife, Terry: a phone call told them their son Marc, a linebacker at the Citadel, had injured his neck making a tackle and would be paralyzed for life. After the initial shock had passed, Buoniconti reacted in typical alpha-personality fashion, founding the Miami Project to Cure Paralysis, which would raise half a billion dollars over thirty-five years. But even as he spearheaded this massive drive to alleviate the ravages of such spinal cord injuries, he wasn't thinking of the more common, less spectacular insults to the brain occurring on football fields all the time.

As Buoniconti reached age seventy, he must have felt as fortunate in his own health as he had when he knelt down on the Orange Bowl field after that final game. He was as vigorous and confident as ever, flying around the country for speaking engagements. But a couple of years later he began losing his balance and falling, forgetting simple things, having difficulty dressing. In 2015, when he was seventy-four, his doctors concluded that his symptoms suggested Alzheimer's disease and/or CTE. Two years later, although he was still able to give speeches and hide his disease from casual observers, he told S. L. Price, "I feel lost. I feel like a child. . . . I didn't have any idea the price would be this debilitating. Had I known, would I have played?" The game had given him so much: a college education, a lucrative career he loved and was great at. "Football kept rewarding me—I can't deny that. But I'm paying the price." He shrugged and grinned. "Everybody pays the piper." Two years later, at seventy-eight, he died under hospice care.

. . .

In the wake of the revelations linking football and brain damage, the sport has often been compared to smoking. A game and a habit, each become a multibillion-dollar business, each found to cause immeasurable misery in a significant percentage of its devotees. In both cases, though, some people never pay the piper. Some can smoke a pack a day and die peacefully at ninety-five. And although few football players can avoid the orthopedic consequences, many can compete through high school, college, and long NFL careers and never lose their mental acuity. Forty-five years after retiring, Manny Fernandez's mind was sharp, even with a quarter of a Super Bowl missing from his memory bank. The same for Larry Little, who absorbed just as many whacks on the head as Mike Webster. He and Jim Langer, who edged out Webster, were chosen for the NFL's All-Decade team of the 1970s; they were the top two among all offensive linemen. In 1993, Little joined Langer, Csonka, Griese, and Warfield in the Hall of Fame. (Buoniconti and Shula would be inducted later.) Little was a college head coach for many years, at his alma mater Bethune-Cookman and then at North Carolina Central, and has been running his Gold Coast Summer Camp for underprivileged kids ever since 1970, when he and a few teammates chipped in to get it started. Retired in Miami, he does crossword puzzles "to keep [his] brain fresh" and gives as cogent and upbeat an interview as anyone. "I would do it all over again," he says when confronted with the specter of his teammates' decline. "I could not have had a better profession at that age than playing in the NFL. I loved playing the game."

Two others who appeared to have escaped the ravages of the sport were Little's fellow Hall of Famers, the brain trust of Griese and Warfield. Griese continued to lead the Dolphins through the 1970s and had two of his best years in 1977 and 1978, although the Dolphins never got past the first round of the playoffs. He remained Miami's quarterback into the 1980 season, when he tore up his shoulder in the fifth game and eventually retired. After a brief stint as the Dolphins' quarterbacks coach, he had a long second career as a television commentator, primarily for college football. He also did radio for Dolphins games for most of the 2010s. The shy Indiana boy who had lost his father early and found something of a father figure in Don Shula became even closer with Shula in retirement. The two played golf together and met regularly for lunch throughout Shula's life. They comforted each other when each lost his wife to breast cancer (Judi Griese in 1988, Dorothy Shula in 1991). When Shula passed, Griese said, "I will remember him first as a savior when he came to the Dolphins, then as a mentor and head coach, then as a friend, and finally as a great friend."

After his partial season in the WFL in 1975, Paul Warfield returned to his old team, the Cleveland Browns. Back on an offense that needed to pass the ball more than a third of the time, he had more catches and yards than he'd had since 1971. But the next year, at thirty-five, he began to slow down, and he retired after the 1977 season. After following up on his telecommunications degree for a few years as a sportscaster for Cleveland's WKYC TV station, he ran a company that manufactured official NFL merchandise. He was also a personnel consultant to the Browns, and director of player relations for a few years, before eventually retiring to Rancho Mirage, California. In a 2020 interview, while sequestered with his family during the pandemic, Warfield was as thoughtful and expansive a speaker as ever. And five decades down the line, he was the only perfect Dolphin who didn't get those daily memos from the knees, back, or neck reminding him of his perilous former occupation. "Just kind of old-folks pains and so forth, nothing major," he said. But then, one would not have expected him to be as susceptible as others to the violence of the game. Playing five years for the Miami Run Machine must have kept his jolt count down. But also, as you review the footage, it's rare to see Warfield absorb the destructive collisions so many receivers suffer. Where another man would be reaching up for the ball and taking a hit in the back, Warfield is flying four feet in the air, cradling it in his midsection, offering the defender only his legs to grasp at. He was so fast, so fluid, so graceful, that, as Tim Foley said, "nobody could get close enough to him to hurt him."

Some smoke like a chimney and live to a hundred. Larry Csonka was as famous early in his career for concussions as for yardage gained. His first two years, doctors speculated whether he'd be able to continue in his chosen profession, so often was he rendered unconscious. "My headaches went away when the blocking got better," he said many years later. But even after the apotheosis of the Monte Clark offensive line gave him some relief, most runs still concluded with a traffic accident. Yet fifty years later, Csonka remained, along with Morris, one of the leading articulators of the perfect season. He certainly carried the physical mementos of his two thousand plunges into the fray, including the Roy Winston backache. But his wit, and his memory, had survived. After the WFL folded, Csonka wanted to return to the Dolphins, but Joe Robbie still had hard feelings about how his three stars had blindsided him. So Csonka signed with the New York Giants and played three years there for a losing team, recording his worst three seasons, statistically. Released by the Giants, he contacted Shula directly this time and received an offer to come to camp and try out for the 1979 season. Asked by a reporter whether Thomas Wolfe was right when he said you can't go home again, Csonka quipped, "Was that the same fellow who said, 'You can't win 'em all'?" Delighted to be playing on natural grass, which had returned to the Orange Bowl in 1976, he had one final year taking the ball from Griese and running behind Little, Kuechenberg, and Langer and almost had another thousand-yard season, running for 837 as the Dolphins went 10–6 and won the division before losing to Pittsburgh in the playoffs.

In retirement, Csonka fell back on his speaking skills. Instead of delivering wisecracks to reporters—"My left leg is turning yellow. My back is turning blue. Sometimes I wish I'd studied harder in college"—he appeared in commercials and on various television programs, kept a busy schedule of speaking engagements, and hosted *American Gladiators* and two hunting-and-fishing shows, *North to Alaska* and *Csonka Outdoors*. For many years now he has lived half the year in Alaska and the other half in Ohio and Florida. Like Griese, he developed a close personal relationship with Shula after both were retired. He still liked to complain about him—"He was so obsessed with winning, frankly, we thought he was on drugs," and "I've spent the last thirty years getting Don Shula's voice out of my ears"—but he also came to call him "an absolute family member." He came down to be part of the coach's surprise ninetieth-birthday party in January 2020. "It was the first time we ever saw him surprised about anything," he said, momentarily forgetting the gator and the bullfrog. "We jumped out of the bushes, and his jaw dropped. It really tickled the fire out of him." Two months later Csonka was trimming his hedges in Ohio when his wife came out with the bad news. "It cut my feet right out from under me," he said. "I had to sit down. . . . I guess I thought he'd live forever. . . . " At the birthday party, Csonka had talked about hoping to be around for Shula's one hundredth. He was sure his coach would be there. "Because can you picture a world without Don Shula in it?"

•   •   •

As a half century arrives to sweep the perfect season ever further into the past, we are forced to imagine a world without even Miami in it. The residue of our unbridled thirst for energy collects into an invisible blanket in the atmosphere; temperatures rise, glaciers melt, the sea rises. Miami developed, Miami Beach flourished, and Csonka and Kiick hurled themselves into the line all about six feet above sea level, on average. Nothing but a bit of dirt and porous limestone underneath. The National Climate Assessment as well as independent climate scientists expect that by 2100 sea levels will have risen by four to six feet, possibly even eight or ten feet. Already "sunny day floods," which inundate Miami streets at high tide, are four times more common than they were in 2000. Many buildings and roadways are already being raised. Yet, just as Americans ignored warnings of the greenhouse effect in the 1990s and kept buying their trucks and SUVs, developers keep pouring money into the South Florida real estate market. Just as I, and millions of other Americans, keep watching football.

Howard Cosell, the voice of boxing as the great bouts between Ali, Frazier, and Foreman were aired in my youth, eventually called for the sport to be banned. Should football be banned? Or should players (and their parents) be given a warning like that on cigarette packs: "The Surgeon General has determined that playing football is dangerous to your health"? The difference between football and smoking, as the Fainarus pointed out, is that "we love football. Americans by the millions are complicit in making the sport what it has become, for better or worse." And "the outcome of the NFL's concussion crisis . . . will be determined not by the 'enemies' or 'opponents' of football but by those in love with the sport." Smokers say that they love smoking, but they may be confusing enthusiasm with chemical addiction. On the other hand, isn't my attraction to football a form of addiction, from having grown up watching Griese and Morris and Warfield? If Joe Robbie had never brought football to Miami—if football didn't even exist—wouldn't I be just as happy to watch baseball or basketball?

Maybe football will find a way to prevent, or at least minimize, brain injuries. Or perhaps the sport will gradually fade away, like boxing, especially if fewer and fewer parents allow their kids to play. Maybe Miami will find a way once again to flourish in the face of natural disaster as this fateful century unwinds and the waters rise. As the city faces the payback of chemistry and the players on its greatest team deal with the consequences of a sport—and, simply, of the passage of time—it is ever more tempting to look back on the high ground of the past. Riding bikes to school all year, drive-in movies out on South Dixie, Bill Haast's show at the Serpentarium with his twenty-six-foot king cobra. Tailgating with Csonka and Kiick and Little in the Orange Bowl parking lot. Watching innocently, without an inkling of the damage being done, a team that seemed without flaw.

Despite Don Shula's insistence during the 1972 season that going unde-feated was not the goal—that in fact it meant nothing next to his team's quest to avenge a loss and win the Super Bowl—it was in fact that secondary feat, completing a perfect season, that would be most important to him and his team. They are not celebrated for having followed a Super Bowl loss with a victory, although only three teams have done it. Their two championships in a row, which seemed likely to stretch to more, were immediately matched by the Steelers, who then eclipsed them by winning four in six years. What has set the 1972 Dolphins apart from all other teams, and what they have relished more than any other accolade, is their perfect record. "Seventeen and oh just happened," said Manny Fernandez, reflecting before the next season. "There was no script, no plan. Whether it ever happens again, we'll just have to wait and see."

We're still waiting. There have been a number of predominant teams since then: the Steelers of 1974–79 (best record 17–2), the late-eighties 49ers (18–1 in '84; they lost their seventh game), the Cowboys of the 1990s (best record 16–3). Seven teams finished the regular season with only one loss, but only three of those won the Super Bowl. One was the 1985 Bears, who made it to 12–0 before Don Shula's own Dolphins gave them their only loss, on a memorable Monday night in Miami with guests Csonka and Kuechenberg watching from the sideline. The year before the Chicago game, the Dolphins themselves, with Dan Marino in his second year, got to 11–0 and were leading San Diego 28–14 in the fourth quarter before they lost in overtime (and lost the Super Bowl to San Francisco).

Then, of course, there were the New England Patriots of 2001–2018. Nine Super Bowl appearances and six championships. Three of those winning years they lost only two games. And in 2007 they became the second team to finish the regular season with a perfect record and were leading in the Super Bowl, 14–10, when the Giants got the ball with two minutes left. A fourth-down conversion, an amazing catch by David Tyree—who trapped the ball against his helmet with one hand—and a touchdown pass from Eli Manning to Plaxico Burress with thirteen seconds left ended New England's hopes of perfection. They had their "Helmet Catch" to rue forever, like Oakland had the "Immaculate Reception" and Miami the "Sea of Hands." Few will recall, however, how lucky New England was to get through the regular season without a loss. They lost one game three times before winning it. In Baltimore on December 3, the Patriots were losing in the final two minutes and were stopped on a fourth-and-one play. However, it turned out the Ravens' defensive coach had furtively called time-out just before the snap. Then the defense stopped them again. But a flag had flown: New England had saved themselves by making a false start. Replay again. This time Tom Brady scrambled for a first down. But he soon faced fourth down again, and his pass over the middle was blocked. Another yellow flag, though, indicated holding on the defense back. Finally, on the ensuing play, Brady threw a miraculous winning touchdown pass in the corner of the end zone. Even that looked on instant replay as if it may have been bobbled, but it was too close a call to overturn.

So the luck evens out. In 1972, the Dolphins got a roughing-the-passer call late against Minnesota to keep the winning drive alive. On the other hand, in the AFC championship game, Pittsburgh scored on a fumble and had another lost fumble ruled out of bounds. And in the Super Bowl, an easy field goal to secure a 17–0 victory was flubbed and bobbled into an interception TD that suddenly threw the outcome into doubt. "We were lucky," Mercury Morris laughs. "But when preparation meets opportunity, you make your own luck." "That's what makes it really fun," says Csonka. "That other people know they can do it, but then they don't. We're still the only one on the mountaintop."

In the early 2000s, word got out that each year when the last undefeated team finally lost, the old Dolphins got together for a champagne toast. In fact, it was just Buoniconti and Anderson. Maybe there were a few phone calls between friends. As the 2020s began, and the fiftieth anniversary of the perfect season approached, fewer and fewer of its heroes were still around to celebrate. A global pandemic prevented those who were from grieving together in person as Don Shula, Jim Kiick, Jake Scott, and Howard Schnellenberger passed away. In Wasilla, Alaska, Larry Csonka filmed himself on Twitter having a celebratory Scotch as the 12–0 Steelers finally lost in November 2020. All in good fun. As he'd put it a few years before, "The fact of the matter is, by going undefeated, we live on. Every year when anyone gets past that five-and-oh mark, the '72 Dolphin ghosts start to appear. And that's a hoot. I like being a ghost."

Quarantined at home in Los Angeles, eight months before succumbing to an infection while hospitalized for Covid, Larry King reminisced about that time in Miami so long ago, when his remarkable life coincided with a remarkable team. "I'm eighty-six now, and I still follow sports closely. But that year is just embedded in me. I don't think we'll ever see a season like that again." "Embedded" is the right word. For those of us who were there—especially, I think, for those who were kids growing up in Miami when the impossible happened—everything about that season imprinted itself in our minds: Griese handing to Csonka on the misdirection; Merc dancing just inside the sideline; Buoniconti resolute in the mud with his feet crossed; the radio voices of Rick Weaver and Henry Barrow. The suburban horns bleating with joy on a January evening.

That magical season is long gone now, along with that quieter Miami, that simpler America. Nostalgia bends the memory into thinking it was a better time, though of course much has improved in society and in people's lives. Larry Csonka's life has been good, and he has few illusions about the backbreaking sport that was his livelihood. But that year, and that team, are embedded in him too. "The only thing I miss about football," he says, "is about five seconds in the huddle right before you break, when you have five of the best offensive linemen ever, who are right in tune with you, and I'm looking across at them, [and] each one of them is mouthing words—they can't talk in the huddle because of Griese—and they're mouthing, 'Run behind me.' If I could go back for anything, I'd like to go back in a time machine just to live those five seconds and look in the eyes of those men, because that was the most confidence I've ever felt in my life about anything."

Seventeen and oh. Those three words encapsulate a time like no other in all fifty previous NFL seasons. And, improbably, like no other in fifty seasons since. But it wasn't just the fact of no games lost or tied. It was the assembling of a disparate bunch of players and coaches into a unit of cohesive excellence that felt as though it *couldn't* lose. It was the sight of Larry Little pulling to the left, leaning into a matchless block. The memory of Paul Warfield coaxing the football from the air and then spinning like a ballet dancer, leaving the defender alone on the turf. Csonka hitting the middle again and again, inexorably moving the chains down the field. Blind to the future, ignorant of the terrifying brain disfunction many of them were setting in motion, dismissive of whatever might be waiting for them after football, these football players were here now, together in their youth, extracting everything from the moment.

Csonka would be standing sometimes shoulder to shoulder with Mandich, waiting for Griese to arrive from the sideline and commandeer the huddle. "Isn't it great, Mad Dog?" he'd say, looking all around the stadium. "Isn't it just great?" Sunday afternoon in Miami, a solid blue sky, sunshine pouring down on the gargantuan horseshoe of the Orange Bowl. The sea of fans roaring in anticipation of the first play, waving white handkerchiefs, waving their shirts. The week's aches and pains dissolved in drugs and adrenaline, eleven teammates in a circle who can't wait to begin. Palm trees swaying behind the squat electric scoreboard in the open end of the stadium. The orange bleachers shaking and the comforting heat and young men in their prime playing a game like no one has ever played it.

Perfect.

ACKNOWLEDGMENTS

I want to thank the following "perfect" Dolphins for being so generous with their time: Marlin Briscoe, Doug Crusan, Vern Den Herder, Manny Fernandez, Eddie Jenkins, Larry Little, Eugene "Mercury" Morris, Larry Seiple, Howard Twilley, and Paul Warfield. Larry King also was as engaging and voluble an interviewee as you might imagine when we spoke, just a few months before his death.

Thanks to Betsy Willeford, Judy Boyett, Micki Gruber, David Moscato, and Jan Prospero for anecdotes, fact-finding, and Dolphin connections. Also, for their donation of photographs, thanks to Edward Christin of the Andy Sweet Photo Legacy and Mike Scanlan at John Carroll University.

I am indebted to the earlier efforts of my fellow perfectologists Bill Braucher, Francis and Raymond Lodato, Mike Freeman, and, above all, Dave Hyde of the *South Florida Sun Sentinel*. Their work is amply credited in the text and endnotes.

My brother, Ron Fisher, checked the manuscript for errors and inconsistencies, clarified some medical information, added memories of his own, and found the best Warfield photo. My wife, Mileta Roe, as always provided advice (editorial and otherwise) and encouragement throughout.

Finally, thanks to my parents for, among so many other things, moving to Miami in August 1966, during the Dolphins' very first preseason.

SEVENTEEN AND OH ROSTER

No.	Name	Pos.
1	Fisher, Marshall	Author
12	Stoltz, Jamison	Editor
22	LaFarge, Albert	Agent
25	Chesanow, David	Copy Editor
66	Brunn, Jennifer	Media
85	VanLangen, Mamie	Digital
88	Mock, Eli	Book Design

NOTES

Introduction

2 "Let's just line up": Dave Hyde, *Still Perfect: The Untold Story of the 1972 Miami Dolphins* (Miami Springs, FL: Dolphin/Curtis Publishing, 2002), p. 88.

3 "They went 17–0, and it won't happen again": Dave Anderson, *New York Times*, Jan. 20, 1973.

Preperfect I: Who Are These Guys?

6 Eddie Jenkins at Democratic National Convention: Eddie Jenkins telephone interview, May 12, 2020.

6 The scene at Flamingo Park: Robert Stulberg, "Flamingo Park Tents Folding Up," *Miami News*, July 14, 1972, 11-A.

7 "We smoke pot, and we like it a lot": Robert Stulberg, "2,000 Protesters Outnumbered," *Miami News*, July 10, 1972, 8-A.

7 PEACE POT PROMISCUITY: Rick Perlstein, *Nixonland: The Rise of a President and the Fracturing of America* (New York: Simon & Schuster, 2008), p. 713.

7–8 "Demonstrators were starting fires" . . . "Shula's looking for you": Jenkins interview.

8 "I couldn't understand" and "Shula was irritating": Steve Perkins and Bill Braucher, *Miami Dolphins: Winning Them All* (New York: Grosset & Dunlap, 1973), pp. 46, 47–48.

9 "Griese was throwing long patterns . . . Shula's foot in your ass.": *Winning Them All*, p. 23, and Bill Braucher, *Promises to Keep* (New York: Dodd, Mead, 1972), p. 185.

9 "ran on Shula time": Manny Fernandez telephone interview, April 6, 2020.

9 "What the hell's wrong with our snap count?": *More Than Perfect*, DVD, directed by Paul Doyle, Jr. (2012, Bombo Sports & Entertainment), 44:30.

9 "I'm twenty-six years old": Larry Csonka and Jim Kiick, *Always on the Run* (New York: Random House, 1973), p. 34.

9 "The day before you went in": Francis J & Raymond M. Lodato, *But We Were 17 and 0* (Lake Worth, FL: IQ Publications, 1986), p. 170.

9 "This was the year": Don Shula, *The Winning Edge* (New York, Dutton, 1973), p. 212.

10 "If I wanted to run cross-country" . . . "It's humiliating": Edwin Pope, "Dolphins' Day: Fun, Frustration for All," *Miami Herald*, July 13, 1972, 1-F.

10 "one of those outdated ideas": Paul Zimmerman, "Sportsman of the Year: Don Shula," *Sports Illustrated*, Dec. 20, 1993.

10 "In six years, not a drop of water": Mercury Morris telephone interview, April 23, 2020.

10–11 "He told us we have two ways," "and we knew we had them," and "I faked it": *The Fish Tank* podcast, "Larry Csonka, Larry Little & Mercury Morris: Perfection," Jan. 14, 2020, www.thefishtank81.com/all-episodes.html#/.

11 "A true Hungarian": Braucher, *Promises*, p. 183.

11 "Shula was amazing": Marlin Briscoe telephone interview, May 11, 2020.

12 "the beneficiary of venal circumstance": *Winning Them All*, p.6.

13 "could squeeze more words into a split second": Tom C. Brody, "Win One for the Flipper," *Sports Illustrated*, Aug. 8, 1966, p. 25.

13 "He's running a two-million-dollar-a-year business like a fruit stand": Mark Kram, "This Man Fired Flipper," *Sports Illustrated*, Dec. 15, 1969.

14 "Because when I sit across from Csonka": Hyde, *Still Perfect*, p. 43.

14 "I liked Joe very much": Larry King telephone interview, May 29, 2020.

14 "He doesn't light up any rooms": Kram, "This Man Fired Flipper."

16 "man to man type of coach": Shula, *Winning Edge*, p. 80.

16 "So, Bobby, what are we going to cook up for Sunday?": *Winning Them All*, p. 52.

16 "If you got something good going": *Always on the Run*, p. 6.

16 "Lord help me": *But We Were 17 and 0*, p. 96.

16 "It was a free atmosphere": Mike Freeman, *Undefeated: Inside the 1972 Miami Dolphins' Perfect Season* (New York: HarperCollins, 2012), p. 140.

16 "We're all getting sick of the rookie bit": Mercury Morris, "Diary of a Rookie," *Miami News*, Aug. 14, 1969, 1-B.

17 "Did I just hear Coach say" . . . "this is pro football?": Morris interview.

17 "increasingly boring, hypocritical": Bill Braucher, "Dolphins Come in on Wing, Prayer," *Miami Herald*, Oct. 16, 1969, 4-E.

17–18 "I don't know what, but something's up" and "The boss is not himself": Braucher, *Promises*, pp. 136 and 147.

18 "determine if his pro football career is at an end": "Csonka's Fate up to Doctors," *Miami News*, Sept. 4, 1969, 2-D.

18 "The Man upstairs" and "This is gonna be a hell of a football team": Braucher, *Promises*, pp. 152 and 155.

19 "Has there ever been a better 1–6–1 team": Larry King, "'Butch' and 'Madwoman' El Smash and El Bombo!," *Miami Herald*, Nov. 6, 1969, 16-D.

19 "Wilson is a great leader" and Csonka swore: Braucher, *Promises*, pp. 158–59.

19 "You boys have a good practice": *The Fish Tank* podcast, "Larry Seiple: Taking Candy from a Baby," Oct. 8, 2019, www.thefishtank81.com/all-episodes.html#/.

20 "Hell, why don't you go right to the top": *Winning Them All*, p. 51.

20 "I remember him just about jumping out of his seat": *More Than Perfect* DVD.

20 "Don, would you be interested in coming down to Miami": Shula, *Winning Edge*, p. 119.

22 "I'm no miracle worker": Braucher, *Promises*, p. 176, and many newspaper accounts.

22 "First I plan to sit down and watch": Bill Bondurant, "Ownership in Dolphins Lures Colts' Coach," *Fort Lauderdale News*, Feb. 19, 1970, 7-D.

22 "Coach, I'm your right guard": Little interview.

22 "I haven't been that light since high school": "Miami's Unmiraculous Miracle Worker," *Time*, Dec. 11, 1972.

22 "But I just ran a four-seven forty": *Always on the Run*, p. 24.

22 "Bubba was a great athlete who was too fat": Morris T. McLemore, *The Miami Dolphins* (New York: Doubleday, 1972), p. 138.

22 "I feel like I've lost a father, I really do" and "Wilson treated you like a man": Braucher, *Promises*, p. 162.

23 "I know you guys are used to having a big party": *More Than Perfect* DVD, and *Zonk! Zonk's NFL,* video previously available at larrycsonka.com, accessed February 2020.

23 "Until dark" was the official quitting time: *Always on the Run*, p. 23.

23 "Okay, everybody!": Braucher, *Promises*, pp. 175–76.

23 "We were all so bushed": Norm Evans and Ray Didinger, *On God's Squad* (Carol Stream, IL: Creation House, 1971), p. 147.

23 "Guys hated to go to bed at night": Morris interview.

23 "You'd say to yourself skip breakfast": *Winning Them All*, p. 53.

24 "We were bitching all the time": *The Fish Tank* podcast, "Larry Seiple: Taking Candy from a Baby."

24 "If it's too tough for you": Evans, *On God's Squad*, p. 146.

24 "You and your goddamn Shula": Braucher, *Promises*, p. 183.

24 "As grueling as practices were . . .": *Zonk! Zonk's NFL* video.

24 "This guy is something else": Braucher, *Promises*, p. 177.

24 Like going from sandlot ball and "We were impressed": Greg Cote, "How Shula Made the Dolphins Perfect and Made Miami Matter, and the Coach Today at 90," *Miami Herald*, Jan. 31, 2020.

24 "Come over here! What kind of a call is that?": Norm Evans and Edwin Pope, *On the Line* (Old Tappan, NJ: Revell, 1976), p. 20.

25 "Miami is not a good city in which to be black": *Economist*, Oct. 16, 1982, p. 22.

25 "if you were Black and didn't have business": Morris interview.

26 "There's a de facto segregation": Morris, "Defacto Segregation at Dolphins' Camp," *Miami News*, July 30, 1969, 2-C.

26 "substantial oil, real estate": "Eligible Bachelors for 1970," *Ebony*, June 1970, p. 112.

26 "All the blacks over here?": Hyde, *Still Perfect*, p. 64.

26 "He even put afro picks": *More Than Perfect* DVD.

26 "fairly liberal": Morris interview.

27 "It was so different from any other team": Freeman, *Undefeated*, p. 91.

28 "If we beat the Colts" and "Much of the second half": Maule, "Miami Gets a Miracle Worker," *Sports Illustrated*, Sept. 7, 1970.

30 "It happened instinctively": Braucher, *Promises*, p. 196.

31 "If wily Butch Cassidy": Bill Braucher, "Butch Kiick and the Sundance Csonka Running Like Pair of Bandits," *Miami Herald*, Dec. 10, 1969, 1-E.

31 "Those guys were in a dangerous profession": *More Than Perfect* DVD.

31 "Who *are* these guys?": *Always on the Run*, p. 8.

32 "I'm no bargainer, and neither is Larry" . . . "we'd have played for nothing": Braucher, *Promises*, pp. 211–12.

32 "Garo came out": *Zonk! Zonk's NFL* video.

32–33 "a ready-made team that any Joe Doakes . . .": Bill Braucher, "Shula Took Ready-Made Team to Super Bowl, Says Wilson," *Miami Herald*, Jan. 12, 1972, 1-E.

33 Griese's Super Bowl VI scramble: Griese liked to tell the story that his gaffe made it third and thirty and that he called time-out, came to the sideline, and told Shula, "Okay, you always want to call the plays, you can call this one." If he ever did that, it couldn't have been after this play, as it was fourth down.

34 "I can't explain it": *Winning Them All*, p. 153.

34 Fernandez stopping to weep: told in Freeman, *Undefeated*, p. 11 and Bob Griese and Dave Hyde, *Perfection* (New York: John Wiley, 2012), p. 9.

34 "I don't think I've ever been more humiliated": *But We Were 17 and 0*, p. 172.

34 "But I don't want you to forget": Shula locker room peroration recounted in many sources; this quote is from Freeman, *Undefeated*, p. 3.

34 "You've got to remember": "Shula Reaction," *Miami Herald*, May 5, 2020.

35 "And he's reaming us out" and "Oh, this is going to be a beauty": *The Fish Tank* podcast, "Larry Csonka, Larry Little & Mercury Morris: Perfection."

35 "Head on elbow pose": *But We Were 17 and 0*, p. 145.

Preperfect II: No Weakness

36–37 "I was afraid they'd pull it back," "A coach on the field," and "You're making a terrible mistake": John Underwood, "Sitting on Top of the World," *Sports Illustrated*, Sept. 17, 1973, pp. 122–42.

37 "What's the matter with you guys?": *Winning Them All*, p. 49.

39 "Every July, I think about the fact": Charlie Nobles, "1972 Dolphins: Undefeated on Field, Undeterred off It," *New York Times*, Feb. 3, 2008.

40 "The clock reads zero seconds": Bill Braucher, "Foley Feels 'Separated' from Team," *Miami Herald*, Jan. 9, 1973, 1-C.

40 John Stofa recruited two local strippers": Fernandez interview.

41 "Far out": Elizabeth Duff, "Conservatives Back, and All Is Serene," *Miami Herald*, July 16, 1972, 34-A.

41 "Fellas": Perlstein, *Nixonland*, p. 686.

43 "It's easily digestible": Al Levine, "Dolphins Blending Together," *Miami News*, July 27, 1972, 1-C.

43 "We liked to joke": Jenkins interview.

44 Briscoe liked to set up the pieces: Al Levine, "Briscoe Calls His Slow Start Typical," *Miami News*, Aug. 22, 1972, 1-B.

44 "In the past" . . . "Mandich's path": Bill Braucher, "Shula's Camp Relaxed as Dolphins Become Pros," *Miami Herald*, Aug. 9, 1972, 1-E.

45 "I think I'm going to be around here" . . . "to get my family down here?": *But We Were 17 and 0*, pp. 23–24.

45–46 Bernstein in Miami, "A $25,000 cashier's check": Carl Bernstein and Bob Woodward, *All the President's Men* (New York: Simon & Schuster, 1974), pp. 37–42; Bernstein and Woodward, "Check Tied to Suspect in Break-In," *Miami Herald*, Aug. 2, 1972, 1-A.

46 "First and foremost is winning": Bill Braucher, "Shula Was Tempted, Now He'll Call Griese," *Miami Herald*, Aug. 7, 1972, 1-D.

47 "Ol' Lem": Al Levine, "The Wrong Quarterback Does Job for Shula," *Miami News*, Aug. 7, 1972, 1-B.

47 "If you noticed": Al Levine, "Even the Lions Were Nice in Garo's Return 'Home,'" *Miami News*, Aug. 7, 1972, 4-B.

47 "It comes to me": Pope, "Csonka 'Hates' Camp, Misses His Home," *Miami Herald*, Aug. 10, 1972, 1-D.

48 "And they'd be there after the game": *Zonk! Zonk's NFL* video.

47 parking lot scene after games: *The Fish Tank* podcast, "Larry Csonka, Larry Little & Mercury Morris: Perfection." Also Briscoe interview, May 11, 2020.

48 "My wife Alice wants me to get a job": *Always on the Run*, p. 86.

48 "We'd show up": David Moscato text message, Oct. 28, 2020.

49 "I hoped it would bounce into my arms": Al Levine, "Error Inexcusable, Says Bob DeMarco," *Miami News*, Aug. 14, 1972, 1-C.

49 "no competition for DeMarco's job": Levine, "Error Inexcusable, Says Bob DeMarco," 6-C.

49 "He's the best darned center in pro football": Gary Long, "'Winning Edge' Means Ring, Job for Langer," *Miami Herald*, Sept. 16, 1972, 3-E.

50 "DeMarco's age and experience": Edwin Pope, "Maturing Line Prepares for King Kong Himself," *Miami Herald*, Aug. 22, 1972, 1-D.

50 "Not this again": *Winning Them All*, p. 33, and Hyde, *Still Perfect*, p. 69.

50 "Luckily, it popped right back": Bill Braucher, "Back Injury Sidelines Heinz," *Miami Herald*, Aug. 16, 1972, 3-D.

50 "All-Ugly" airport scene: Bill Braucher, "Not Even Airline Delay Can Stew Dolphins," *Miami Herald*, Aug. 21, 1972, 1-D.

51 "However, I'm enjoying that problem": Braucher, "Morris Gives Shula Problem He Enjoys," *Miami Herald*, Aug. 20, 1972, 1-F.

51 Scene at Flamingo Park: Robert B. Semple Jr., "Youths for Nixon Contrast with Protesters in Park," *New York Times*, Aug. 22, 1972, p. 1.

52 like decadent ancient Romans: Hunter S. Thompson, *Fear and Loathing: On the Campaign Trail '72* (San Francisco: Straight Arrow, 1973), pp. 381–82.

52 "three hundred close friends": Jean Wardlow, "Reagans, Rain Greet Close Friends," *Miami Herald*, Aug. 24, 1972, 1-B.

53 "If the senator persists": William Montalbano, "GOP Opens Up—on McGovern," *Miami Herald*, Aug. 22, 1972, 1-A.

53 "I'm just not doing the job": Al Levine, "A Disappointing Morrall to the Story," *Miami News*, Aug. 26, 1972, B-1.

54 "thousands of dollars": Shelby Coffee III, "Indians Open War on Redskins," *Washington Post*, March 30, 1972, F1.

54 "This is getting silly": Russ White, "Williams' Answer: What's in a Name?" *Washington Evening Star*, Jan. 27, 1972.

54 "Within the next week": John Crittenden, "Dolphin Strengths Are Now Stronger," *Miami News*, Sept. 1, 1972, 1-D.

55 "They're making a mistake" . . . "Be sure to tell Buoniconti": *Winning Them All*, p. 34.

55 "Langer's too good not to play": Bill Braucher, "Dolphins' Langer Center of Action," *Miami Herald*, Nov. 4, 1972, 1-D, and *Winning Them All*, p. 34.

56 "We felt it was important to win": Bill Braucher, "Dolphins Overtake Vikings, 21–19," *Miami Herald*, Sept. 11, 1972, 5-F.

56 "We needed this win psychologically": Gary Long, "Griese Gambled on Merc's Dive," *Miami Herald*, Sept. 11, 1972, 5-F.

56 "they were trying harder than George McGovern": Al Levine, "Csonka Says Backfield Is Becoming Overcrowded," *Miami News*, Aug. 26, 1972, 5-B.

56 "We're ahead of where we were" and "The other thing that I've found": Al Levine, "The Dolphins: The Thinking's Super," *Miami News*, Aug. 29, 1972, 2-D.

One and Oh

58 "Goddamned old fool": John Farrell, *Richard Nixon: The Life* (New York: Doubleday, 2017), p. 278.

58 A whopping seventy-four percent: Louis Harris, "Majority of Voters Supports Bombing, Mining of N. Vietnam," *Miami Herald*, Sept. 11, 1972, 5-D.

60 "It's all over": *Always on the Run*, p. 194.

60 "I kept hearing the Chiefs yelling": NFL Films, *History of the Miami Dolphins*, 17:30 mark, on YouTube: youtu.be/DffYLUXxL5Y.

60 Griese . . . saw his eyes light up: "The Longest Game Ever: 1971 AFC Divisional Playoff Dolphins vs. Chiefs," NFL Films, 33:00 mark, on YouTube: youtu.be/GeUBqI5Weh4.

60 "I took the ball": *Zonk! Zonk's NFL* video.

60–61 "The ball felt very good off my foot" and When the Yepremians finally got home: Bob Rubin, "Christmas Dinner Delayed in '71, Dolphins-K.C. Played On and On," *Miami Herald*, Dec. 22, 1989.

61 "Do you want to talk about my mother's funeral, too?": Robert Weintraub, "Endless Emotions over N.F.L.'s Longest Game," *New York Times*, Dec. 25, 2012, B8.

61 "People are always going to remember the last game that you've played": Al Levine, "Everyone Has a Memory, Not All Fond," *Miami News*, Sept. 16, 1972, 1-B.

62 "Stealing their money the way we did": Jonathan Rand, "Chiefs Are Poorer Because of Fleming," *Miami News*, Sept. 14, 1972, 2-D.

62 "The guy who designed this stadium," "If it's this hot tomorrow," "As far as I'm concerned," and "That breaks up your evening pretty good": *Winning Them All*, pp. 10–11, 37–38.

63 "Gentlemen": *Winning Them All*, p. 5.

63 "You get that thrill nowhere else": *But We Were 17 and 0*, p. 285.

64 "The thing I remember": Jason Reid, "Marlin Briscoe Carved a Path for Black Quarterbacks to Follow," TheUndefeated.com, Sept. 14, 2017.

65 "By the time I got to Miami": Briscoe interview.

65 "In Buffalo" and "I suffered": John Crittenden, "Exhibitions Count in New Orleans," *Miami News*, Sept. 15, 1972, 1-B.

65 "I've never played in a more miserable": *But We Were 17 and 0*, p. 172.

66 "No need for the fancy stuff": Hyde, *Still Perfect*, p. 88.

66 "I used to hoe beans": Lou Sahadi, *Griese/Csonka: The Miami Dolphins' One-Two Punch* (New York: Scholastic, 1973), p. 103.

66 "If my father liked you, he hit you on the arm": Sahadi, *Griese/Csonka*, p. 104.

67 "Out west it was wide-open back then": *Zonk! Zonk's NFL* video.

68 "That's just the Hunky": Braucher, *Promises*, p. 127.

68 "If this keeps up" and "Most concussions": Braucher, *Promises*, pp. 130–31.

68 "Jake exited with a dreamy smile": Bill Braucher, "Scott Resigned to Another Painful Season," *Miami Herald*, Sept. 24, 1972, 1-E.

68 "Mumphord dashed in": Bill Braucher, "Backup Men Help Preserve Dolphins' Unbeaten Record," *Miami Herald*, Oct. 3, 1972, 1F.

68 "a questionable abnormality": "Csonka's Fate up to Doctors," *Miami News*, Sept. 4, 1969, 2-D.

69   "it was really bleeding bad": *Always on the Run*, p. 65.

69   "Zonk was the blood and guts": Bob Hill, "Rush to Limelight: It'll Be Like Old Times . . . ," *Fort Lauderdale Sun-Sentinel*, Aug. 4, 1987.

69   "If you weren't excited before the game": *But We Were 17 and 0*, p. 287.

69   "I'm afraid if I don't block enough": Evans, *On God's Squad*, p. 179.

69–70   "My collision with Csonka": Peter Golenbock, *Cowboys Have Always Been My Heroes: The Definitive Oral History of America's Team* (New York: Warner Books, 1997), p. 636.

70   "It folded him up" . . . "Look what he did to that defensive back": *America's Game: The 1972 Miami Dolphins*, NFL Network, 12:00 mark, on YouTube: www.youtube.com/watch?v=ld7OV0925Zg&t=2051s.

70   "I'm driven by common sense": *Winning Them All*, p. 23.

70   "one of the most articulate athletes I have ever known": Howard Cosell, *Like It Is* (Chicago: Playboy Press, 1974), p. 75.

70   "I resent being called a bulldozer": Sahadi, *Griese/Csonka*, pp. 90–92.

70   "The meanest looking of the man-mountain people": Mercury Morris, "Diary of a Rookie," *Miami News*, July 25, 1969, 1-B.

70   "I thought I had big thighs": Jim Huber, "No Jealousy: Csonka, Kiick Perfect Roommates," *Miami News*, Aug. 29, 1969, 1-B.

71   "I like to run where there are holes" and "the very image of manhood": John Underwood, "The Blood and Thunder Boys," *Sports Illustrated*, Aug. 7, 1972, pp. 28–29.

71   "On that rug": Al Levine, "Scorching Heat Is No Sweat to the Dolphins," *Miami News*, Sept. 18, 1972, 1-C.

71   "you could hear the feet squishing away": Garo Yepremian and Skip Clayton, *Tales from the Miami Dolphins Sideline* (New York: Sports Publishing, 2012), p. 73.

71   "We almost had to call a timeout after that": *But We Were 17 and 0*, p. 55.

Two and Oh

73   "I'd like to take you out there": *Winning Them All*, p. 12.

73   "maybe watching the second game on TV": Bill Braucher, "'Chicken Little' Guards the Top Perch," *Miami Herald*, Nov. 17, 1972, 5-F.

73   "From July until the end of the draft": "Miami's Unmiraculous Miracle Worker," *Time*, Dec. 11, 1972.

74   "I don't want to take anything away from Merc": Bill Braucher, "Kiick's Pride Stung by Lack of Activity," *Miami Herald*, Sept. 21, 1972, 1-F.

74 "Well, Jane, this is a touchy subject": Csonka interview with Jane Chastain of Channel 4, on *America's Game: 1972 Miami Dolphins* (2007, NFL Productions, Inc.), 12:10 mark, youtu.be/wtBXOm0XXnE.

75 "We have to establish the ground game": *Winning Them All*, p. 14.

75 "The thing this ball club must realize": Bill Braucher, "'72 Dolphin Lines Busy with New Faces," *Miami Herald*, Sept. 19, 1972, 1-C.

75 "In Miami, a few figures": Calvin Trillin, "Covering the Cops: The World of Miami's Top Crime Reporter," *New Yorker*, Feb. 17, 1986, p. 39.

76 "A man wandering": Edna Buchanan, "Wanderer with Knife: 'I Just Killed a Man,'" *Miami Herald*, Sept. 18, 1972, 1-B.

77 "together they transformed a slender" and "a dowdy refuge of retirees": T. D. Allman, *Miami: City of the Future* (New York: Atlantic Monthly Press, 1987), pp. 185, 240.

79 "When Kiick and I got there" and "Most football fans down there": *Zonk! Zonk's NFL* video.

79–80 "Who thinks of apple-cheeked American youth" and "vermilion-trousered gents": "Miami's Unmiraculous Miracle Worker," *Time*, December 11, 1972.

80 "People had no confidence in Miami": Gene Miller and William Montalbano, "Dolphin Fever," *Miami Herald*, Jan. 7, 1973, 20-A.

80 "the Dolphins used to give tickets": *More Than Perfect* DVD.

80–81 "Oh, what that team did for that city" . . . "and the way that city adopted them": King interview.

81 A letter from the Florida Barbers' Association: Morris interview.

83 "If they don't do something about these damn rugs" and "The stuff is falling apart": Braucher, *Promises*, pp. 223–24.

84 "Our greatest opponent was the field" and Little felt "ashamed": Terry Galvin, "Kiick Has Busy Day on Slippery Turf," *Miami Herald*, Jan. 12, 1973, 4-SB.

84 "or maybe the other guys could bring their hairdryers" and "It's the worst": Al Levine, "Dolphins Rage Against Surf in Poly-Turf," *Miami News*, Sept. 25, 1972, 1-C.

84–85 "We are going to drive the ball": Edwin Pope, "Maturing Line Prepares for King Kong Himself," *Miami Herald*, Aug. 22, 1972, 1-D.

85 "It doesn't look like Evans can play": *Winning Them All*, p. 52.

85–86 "That's a hell of a feeling": *But We Were 17 and 0*, p. 101.

86 "I could always run faster than anybody else": Mercury Morris, *Against the Grain* (New York: McGraw Hill, 1988), p. 23.

88   "As long as Csonka and Kiick are around": Edwin Pope, "Shula's 3 Backs: A New Dimension," *Miami Herald*, January 12, 1973, 2-SB.

89   "Shula didn't have enough confidence in me": Morris interview.

89   "The only time I got off the bench": Morris, *Against the Grain*, p. 62.

89–90   "If you have something to say" . . . "So be ready for it" . . . "with anticipation burning in his eyes": Shula, *Winning Edge*, pp. 205–206, 213.

90   "I'm five-ten, one-ninety": Morris interview.

90   "would have been astonishing": Bill Braucher, "What Makes Mercury Run?," *Miami Herald*, Aug. 23, 1972, 1-G.

91   "Morris off his summertime exploits": Bill Braucher, "Dolphins Well-Equipped for Another Super Charge," *Miami Herald*, Sept. 13, 1972, 5-E.

91   "It wasn't a spike": *America's Game,* 16:10 mark.

91   "He's like a time bomb": *Winning Them All*, p. 111.

91   "He's a real character": *But We Were 17 and 0*, p. 161.

92   "This will never do, Danny!": *Winning Them All*, p. 24.

92   "it was a locker-room battle": *America's Game,* 9:45 mark. Morris was probably thinking of WEDR-99 (soul music), which didn't become Power 99 until the 1990s.

92   "Merc was living on his own planet": Jenkins interview.

92   "going to upset that balance of Butch and Sundance" . . . , "this is how we're gonna roll here": NFL Films, *A Football Life: The Perfect Backfield*, 26:00 mark, accessed on YouTube, January 2020, no longer available.

92   "grinning at [Morris]": *Winning Them All*, p. 22.

Three and Oh

93   "Football weather" and "We're going to eat, drink, and celebrate": Edwin Pope, "Viking Fans Enjoy Game—28 Hours Early," *Miami Herald*, Oct. 1, 1972, 2-F.

94–95   "The fiercest game I was ever in" . . . "He hit me in the kidney" . . . "I *am* hurt": *Zonk! Zonk's NFL* video.

94   "It was the hardest hit": Sahadi, *Griese/Csonka*, p. 138.

95   "You can't get hurt, Csonka!" and "I think my goddamn back is broken": *Always on the Run*, p. 60.

95   "That was Shula": Little interview.

95   "I've been in this league eleven years" and "They ought to know you can't kill a Hunky": Bill Braucher, "Winston Tries His Hand at Sawing Csonka in Half," *Miami Herald*, Oct. 4, 1972, 5-D.

97   "I want to thank you very much": Braucher, *Promises*, p. 194.

97   "A beautiful little guy to have around": Evans, *On God's Squad*, p. 187.

97   "He believes he is funny, to a fault" and "A lot of people want me to shave it": Al Levine, "Garo Seriously Thinks He's Funny," *Miami News*, Aug. 1, 1972, 1-B.

98   "If this was Buffalo": Randy Campbell, "Absolute Perfection—the 1972 Miami Dolphins—Game 3," at finsmobunleashed.com/2015/02/18/absolute-perfection-the-1972-miami-dolphins-3/.

99   "The guys looked like they were coming back": *Winning Them All*, p. 32.

99   "We've had this play ready since the season opened": Mike Schwebel, "Grant: It Was a 6-Minute Ball Game," *Fort Lauderdale News*, Oct. 2, 1972, 6-D.

100   "For me that play was more or less routine": Briscoe interview.

100   "I was so shook up": *But We Were 17 and 0*, p. 307.

101   "Six years and this has never happened to me": Mike Schwebel, "Grant: It Was a 6-Minute Game" *Fort Lauderdale News*, Oct. 2, 1972, 6-D.

101   "My momentum carried me into Griese, who had fallen down": William N. Wallace, "Dolphins Defeat Vikings, 16 to 14," *New York Times*, Oct. 2, 1972.

101   "I turned around to watch the ball": Chris Tomasson, "Bob Lurtsema: 1972 Dolphins Would Not Have Gone Undefeated Without Bad Call Against Vikings," *Pioneer Press*, Dec. 13, 2018.

101   "Shula says 'Howard, you're in'": Howard Twilley telephone interview, April 10, 2020.

102   "a student manager pressed into uniform": Tom C. Brody, "Win One for the Flipper," *Sports Illustrated*, Aug. 8, 1966, p. 25.

102   "Twilley's relentless blocking and able hands": Braucher, *Promises*, p. 205.

102   "I wonder who we'll get to replace Twilley this year": *Winning Them All*, p. 26.

102   "We were going to name him Don": Twilley interview and *Miami News*, July 13, 1972, 4-C.

102   "You don't trade a number-one draft pick": Bob Kearney, "Warfield, Twilley, Briscoe and Stowe . . . That's Depth," *Miami Herald*, Jan. 12, 1973, 14-SB.

102   "You'd look at him": Jenkins interview.

102   "They called him Bob's son": Yepremian, *Tales from the Miami Dolphins*, p. 85.

103   "Bob! Bob!": "Twilley Yells, Griese Hears," *Fort Lauderdale News*, Oct. 2, 1972, 6D.

103   "I thought we'd just pound the ball to Csonka": Randy Campbell, "Absolute Perfection—the 1972 Miami Dolphins—Game 3," at finsmobunleashed.com/2015/02/18/absolute-perfection-the-1972-miami-dolphins-3/.

103–4 "You'll see him looking over at the other team": *Always on the Run*, p. 166, and Edwin Pope, "'Difference Was Simple: Griese'—Csonka," *Miami Herald*, Sept. 18, 1972, 4-C.

104 "I-19 split delay on two!": Griese and Hyde, *Perfection*, p. 29.

104 "strangely businesslike atmosphere": Bill Bondurant, *Fort Lauderdale News*, Oct. 2, 1972, 1-D.

104 Forty years afterward: *America's Game*, 8:50 mark.

105 "Nothing serious, just a broken back": "Csonka Bends But Doesn't Break," *Fort Lauderdale News*, Oct. 2, 1972, 5-D.

105 "Zonk should never have dropped that ball": Bill Braucher, "Winston Tries His Hand at Sawing Csonka in Half," *Miami Herald*, Oct. 4, 1972, 5-D.

Four and Oh

106 "Almost every minute of every day": *Winning Them All*, p. 64.

106 "In a game, I think of myself as looking down": "Bullet Bob v. Roger the Dodger," *Time*, Jan. 17, 1972.

106 "I don't think I had any great assets": *But We Were 17 and 0*, p. 112.

107 Cazzie Russell: Bill Gutman, *Staubach Griese Plunkett Gabriel* (New York: Grosset & Dunlap, 1972), p. 57.

107 "The kind you really need": John Underwood, "This Joe Had Better Be Good," *Sports Illustrated*, Dec. 13, 1971, p. 47.

108 "Make me a pocket, and I'll stay in it": Griese and Hyde, *Perfection*, p. 28.

108 "All these are better than the Dolphins' No. 1 quarterback": Jeffrey Denberg, "Charlton Heston Where Are you?," *Miami News*, Nov. 10, 1970, C-1.

109 "I'd rather work it out by myself": Gutman, *Staubach Griese Plunkett Gabriel*, p. 82.

109 "Sure, I'm quiet and introverted": Gutman, *Staubach Griese Plunkett Gabriel*, p. 84.

109 "Helluva pass!" . . . "Thanks, Zonk": *Always on the Run*, p. 167.

109 "I'm not emotionless": *The Don Shula Show*, WPLG Miami, Jan. 15, 1973, 3:00 mark, on YouTube: www.youtube.com/watch?v=Q7NLRpatx9c.

109 "This is a damn disappointing way to end the year": Bill Braucher, "Disappointing Way to End a Successful Season," *Miami Herald*, Jan. 17, 1972, 1-D.

109 "What's the matter with that guy?": Braucher, *Promises*, p. 263.

109 "I had no idea what was going through Bob's mind": *Always on the Run*, p. 165.

109   "kind of a strange person, aloof": *But We Were 17 and 0*, p. 295.

109   "the kind of a guy who wouldn't even talk about himself": Morris interview.

110   "I've never seen any quarterback like him anywhere" and "I might send in five or six plays": Bill Braucher, "Bob Griese the Key for Dolphins Against Redskins," *Miami Herald*, Jan. 14, 1973, 1-D.

110   "laser look": Morris interview.

110   "Bob is so in command at all times": Sahadi, *Griese/Csonka*, p. 17.

110   "Griese's hut-hut trickery": "Griese Is Master of Hut, Hut-Hut No-Play Offense," *Long Beach Independent* (AP), Dec. 24, 1970, C3.

110   "hut" being short for "hike": In football's early days, the quarterback would scratch the center's leg to signal him to pass the ball back (which at that time meant rolling it over the ground). In addition to other drawbacks, such as that the rest of the offense was as clueless as the defense as to when the play would begin, this practice left itself open to subterfuge. John Heisman, future eponym of college football's greatest prize, noticed in 1890 while playing center for Penn that the defensive tackle was trying to trick him into a premature snap by scratching his leg himself. (That's the story, anyway.) So he instructed his quarterback to yell "Hike!" when he wanted the play to start. By the mid-twentieth century, "Hike!" had given way to the military "Hut!" See Ben Zimmer, "Hut! The Story Behind a Football Interjection," Thinkmap Visual Thesaurus, Sept. 14, 2009. www.visualthesaurus.com/cm/wordroutes /hut-the-story-behind-a-football-interjection/.

110   Shula, while with Baltimore: "Griese Calls Signals, Jones Jumps the Gun," *Boston Evening Globe* (AP), Nov. 2, 1971, 28.

111   "wanted to call the best play on every down": Paul Warfield telephone interview, April 18, 2020.

111   "It's a feeling": *Winning Them All*, p. 12.

111   "Well, Jim went to see his buddy Joe Namath": Edwin Pope, "3 Wide-Outs Confused Even Twilley Himself," *Miami Herald*, Oct. 9, 1972, 5-C.

111   "I know people expect a quarterback to be flamboyant": Gutman, *Staubach Griese Plunkett Gabriel*, p. 84.

112   "After I read that" and "I knew the worst they could do was score": *Winning Them All*, p. 38.

112–13   "Shoot": Pope, "3 Wide-Outs Confused Even Twilley Himself," 5-C.

113   "That's my boys, all right": *Winning Them All*, p. 40.

113   "Our defense in 1972 was so good that they spent little time on the field": *Zonk! Zonk's NFL* video.

114 "a pipe and slippers kind of guy": Briscoe interview.

114 "a genius of defensive coaches": Braucher, *Promises*, p. 165, and Robert Hardin, "The Selling of a Pro," *Tropic*, Nov. 26, 1972, p. 53.

114 "I was a technician and awful compulsive": *But We Were 17 and 0*, p. 170.

114 "I know it's only four months after the Super Bowl": William N. Wallace, "Dolphins Dominate Chiefs in 20–10 Victory Before 79,829 at Kansas City," *New York Times*, Sept. 18, 1972, p. 34.

115 "We love that 'No-Name' business, honest": Edwin Pope, "Without a Label, Defense Still Sticks," *Miami Herald*, Oct. 9, 1972, 1-C.

115 "Most defenses show me two basic looks," "The way we kept moving around," and "They used a lot of zone variations": Bill Braucher, "No Names Bend, but Don't Break," *Miami Herald*, Jan. 12, 1973, 5-SB.

115 Namath got so frustrated that he started screaming obscenities: Freeman, *Undefeated*, p. 52.

116 "Who'd he marry, a refrigerator?": *Winning Them All*, p. 33.

116 "What do you think of this?": Dave Hyde, "Bill Arnsparger Was the Perfect Match for Don Shula," *South Florida Sun Sentinel*, July 18, 2015.

116 "in the twilight of a mediocre career": Griese and Hyde, *Perfection*, p. 123.

116 "The easiest thing . . . but we were forced to": Jonathan Rand, "Shula Has Scarcity of Defenders," *Miami News*, Aug. 17, 1972, 2-C, and Al Levine, "Matheson Does Just Fine at End," *Miami News*, Aug. 28, 1972, 2-C.

117 Arnsparger and the "zone blitz": James Dudko, "Bill Arnsparger: Remembering the Godfather of the Zone Blitz and Hybrid Defense," BleacherReport.com, July 19, 2015, and Tim Layden, "Inside the Zone Blitz: LeBeau and Capers Help Modernize NFL Defense," *Sports Illustrated*, Jan. 31, 2011, www.si.com /more-sports/2011/01/31/zone-blitz.

117 "We put people in catch-up situations": *But We Were 17 and 0*, p. 183.

117 "That Dunaway really stopped up the middle": *Winning Them All*, p. 40.

118 "Miami's tough": Bill Braucher, "Namath Salutes Dolphins but Weeb Weeps at Calls," *Miami Herald*, Oct. 9, 1972, 5-C.

118 NO NAMES MEAN NO NAMATH: *Winning Them All*, p. 43.

Five and Oh

120 The Betsy Ross "was a power center" . . . "in faded red paint": Theodore H. White, *The Making of the President 1972* (New York: Atheneum House, 1973), p. 168.

122 "But honey, I'd much rather look at you," "I figured they were impressed

because here was a good-looker," and "delicately flowing shoulder-length hair": Malcolm Balfour, "Jane Chastain: Just One of the Boys," *Tropic*, Jan. 16, 1972, pp. 14–18.

122 "no hard sports, nothing live, no anchoring": Jane Chastain, *I'd Speak Out on the Issues if I Only Knew What to Say* (Ventura, CA: Regal Books, 1987), p. 15.

123 "the lack of normal sex relationships": Ian Ridpath, "Girls . . . a Place in Space," *Province* (Vancouver), Gemini News Service, Oct. 23, 1972.

123 "Nobody has a better chance at a job [here] than a good-looking woman": Frank Greve, "Is Justice Blind?," *Miami Herald*, Jan. 15, 1973, 21-A.

124 "anything you can say about Miami is true": Betsy Willeford, *BookPage*, ca. 1998.

124 "Miami was the perfect place for Charles to live": Betsy Willeford interview, Miami, March 1, 1998.

124 "the world of American bad actors": Thomas McGuane, *Ninety-Two in the Shade* (New York: Farrar, Straus & Giroux, 1973), p. 9.

124 "massive campaign of political spying": Carl Bernstein and Bob Woodward, "FBI Files Link Nixon Aides with Spying," *Miami Herald*, Oct. 10, 1972, 1-A.

124–25 "orderly withdrawal of all American forces": Saul Friedman, "McGovern: Nixon Win Means War Won't End," *Miami Herald*, Oct. 11, 1972, 1-A.

125 "somewhat arrogant campaign apparatus" . . . "can't even charm a garter snake": "For the Next President, the Herald Recommends . . . ," *Miami Herald*, Oct. 8, 1972, 6-A.

126 "When the offense would drive down": *Zonk! Zonk's NFL* video.

127 "became something of a weapon": *The Fish Tank* podcast, "Larry Csonka, Larry Little & Mercury Morris: Perfection."

127 "Kill Them!" . . . Depuy and Quigley: Gene Miller and William Montalbano, "Dolphin Fever," *Miami Herald*, Jan. 7, 1973, 20-A.

127 some fans in the stands were erupting into a precursor: "Shula's 100th, Miami's Pride," *Miami Herald*, Nov. 14, 1972, 6-A.

128 "it's a completely different problem now, almost the reverse": Terry Galvin, "Biltrite Officials Slip into Poly-Turf Picture," *Miami Herald*, Oct. 7, 1972, 5-E.

128 "I'm tired of the buckpassing": Pope, "Despite Win, Shula Sizzles over Turf," *Miami Herald*, Oct. 16, 1972, 5-E.

128 "Okay, go get 'em": Griese and Hyde, *Perfection*, p. 79.

128 "It's no longer a wholesome thing": Dave Brady, "Dolphin Dolls Retire from Sidelines," *Washington Post*, April 2, 1978.

129   "Norm Evans is having a tough time with Deacon": Oct. 15, 1972, television broadcast video with WIOD radio audio: www.youtube.com/watch?v=zT9aRmkoUpU.

129   "felt a riot of pain": Griese and Hyde, *Perfection*, p. 65.

129   "Cuz, we're in deep shit now": *America's Game*, 15:40 mark.

129   "I wanted to throw up": Griese and Hyde, *Perfection*, p. 65.

129   "Better loosen up, Earl" . . . "No, I'm fine": *The Perfect Season*, 8:00 mark, www.youtube.com/watch?v=EBB5RGhRCz8&t=492s.

130   "Our fathers had talked about this guy" and "What do you think?": *Zonk! Zonk's NFL* video.

130   "Okay everybody . . . stay calm": Twilley, Little, Morris interviews and Luther Evans, "Griese Goes Down, but up Pops Morrall," *Miami Herald*, Jan. 12, 1973, 7-SB.

130   "Old man, get those cataracts in motion": Edwin Pope, "Earl Tunes Hearing Aid," *Miami Herald*, Oct. 16, 1972, 1-E.

131   "I knew he could handle the quarterbacking": *America's Game*, 17:05 mark.

131   "We've got to shut the bastards out!": *Winning Them All*, p. 56.

132   "Hey, what are you doing here Julie": Griese and Hyde, *Perfection*, p. 65 (although he incorrectly remembers he was watching television; see *Herald* reports).

133   "A lot worse things could happen": Bill Braucher, "Griese Knew Injury Bad," *Miami Herald*, Oct. 17, 1972, 1-D.

Six and Oh

134   "The reason he's doing it": "Dolphins Land Surfer, Sea to His Needs," *Miami Herald*, Oct. 18, 1972, 1-E.

135   "The Stanfills and their kids lived right above us": Doug Crusan telephone interview, April 28, 2020.

135   "wall to wall beds": Sarah Elder, "Earl Morrall: A Family Man off the Field," *Miami Herald*, Nov. 28, 1972, 1-C.

135–36 "I wear it this way because it's comfortable": *Winning Them All*, p. 98, and "Morrall Takes Passing Lead by keeping Hair out of Eyes," *Miami Herald*, Dec. 11, 1972, 4-C.

136   "Earl was just like Bob": Morris, *Against the Grain*, p. 66.

136   "He was a homespun kind of guy": Marlin Briscoe with Bob Schaller, *The First Black Quarterback* (Grand Island, NE: Cross Training Publishing, 2002), p. 150.

136 "Cheesy weezy": *Always on the Run*, p. 167.

136 "fond memories": Bill Braucher, "Exhibition Loss to Redskins Was Last for Miami," *Miami Herald*, Jan. 12, 1973, 3-SB.

136 "Shula would say Earl couldn't hit the side of a barn": Morris interview.

136 "There he is, crew cut and all" . . . "Outta sight": Bill Braucher, "Dolphins Rocking Along with Earl in an Old Chair," *Miami Herald*, Oct. 21, 1972, 2-D.

138 "Eighty thousand rude people waving handkerchiefs": Tex Maule, "No Losses, No Ties, and No Names," *Sports Illustrated*, Nov. 27, 1972.

139 "made an ass of itself": Edwin Pope, "Oºfficially, Was It Really Pro Football?," *Miami Herald*, Oct. 23, 1972, 1-D.

139 "Had to get back Shula's fifteen": *Winning Them All*, p. 67.

139 "I told them 'Screw you'" and "I don't know, I guess I was well rested": Fernandez interview.

139 "a sorehead who can't be coached" and "the quick reactions, his use of forearms": McLemore, *The Miami Dolphins*, p. 14.

140 "I can't even say adios in Spanish": Many sources. Fernandez told me it was on *The Tonight Show* with Rickles as guest host. Fernandez was Rickles's guest on March 13, 1974.

140 "developed his upper body to astonishing proportions": Cosell, *Like It Is*, p. 79.

140 "He's always got two people blocking him": Maule, "No Losses, No Ties, and No Names."

140 "Fernandez comes in and almost steals the ball": WIOD broadcast, paired with game films, at www.youtube.com/watch?v=3frvBROVEEs.

140 "I would have scored" and "frisking everybody": *Winning Them All*, p. 68.

140 "I'm not *that* blind": Fernandez interview, April 6, 2020, and Edwin Pope, "Officially, Was It Really Pro Football?," *Miami Herald*, Oct. 23, 1972, 5-D.

141 "But mostly I'd watch the road games on TV": *Always on the Run*, p. 75.

142 "A lot of my game was heart": *But We Were 17 and 0*, p. 130.

142 "walked around in Italian knit shirts": *Always on the Run*, p. 112.

142–43 "As far as I was concerned Kiick was a winner" . . . "I'm always afraid they'll quiz me on something I'm supposed to know": John Underwood, "This Joe Had Better Be Good," *Sports Illustrated*, Dec. 13, 1971, p. 58.

143 "Oh, I hated it, I hated it, certainly": *But We Were 17 and 0*, p. 130.

143 "It's a momentum thing" . . . "I'm just very disappointed": Bill Braucher, "Kiick's Pride Stung by Lack of Activity," *Miami Herald*, Sept. 21, 1972, 4-F.

144 "Well, we couldn't have played any worse": *Winning Them All*, p. 67.

145 "Moon Over Miami": Evans, *On God's Squad*, p. 118.

145 "preaching from the stages of saloons": James D. Davis, "'Chaplain of Bourbon Street' Back in the Pulpit," *South Florida Sun-Sentinel*, Dec. 6, 1997.

145 "travel[ed] with enough clergy": Gene Miller and William Montalbano, "Dolphin Fever," *Miami Herald*, Jan. 7, 1973, 20-A.

145 "There was a very relaxed attitude": Jenkins interview.

145 "You coming to chapel, Merc?": Morris interview.

145 "I roomed six or seven years with Norm": Larry Seiple telephone interview, May 29, 2020.

146 "The first rule in such a situation": Edwin Pope, "Officially, Was It Really Pro Football?," *Miami Herald*, Oct. 23, 1972, 1-D.

146 "Old Garo really came in and did it to them": Bill Braucher, "Dolphins Tip Bills in Zany Game," *Miami Herald*, Oct. 23, 1972, 4-D.

146 "Hey man, where were you?" and "That's true, I did say that": *Winning Them All*, p. 69.

146–47 "the strangest game I've seen": Bill Braucher, "Dolphins Tip Bills in Zany Game."

147 "The most ridiculous game I've ever played in": Bill Bondurant, "It's Alleyball Time—the Winner, Dolphins," *Fort Lauderdale News*, Oct. 23, 1972, 1-D.

147 "We used to have a lot of games like this," "Hey Manny, go on back," and in the kitchen for a glass of milk: *Winning Them All*, pp. 66, 68, and 69.

Seven and Oh

148 "I intend to keep Unitas": "Rosenbloom Trades Colts for LA Rams Franchise," *Herald* Wire Services, July 14, 1972, 1F.

149 "We have not agreed to any ceasefire": Winston Lord, "A Peace That Couldn't Last—Negotiating the Paris Accords on Vietnam," Association for Diplomatic Studies & Training website, adst.org/2016/01/a-peace-that-couldnt-last-negotiating-the-paris-accords-on-vietnam/.

149 "If a year or two years from now": Perlstein, *Nixonland*, p. 708.

150 "the 6–0 Dolphins cannot win them all": Braucher, "Stanfill's Hoping to Haunt Thomas," *Miami Herald*, Oct. 28, 1972, 3-D.

150 "With me they didn't have to waste money," "But I wasn't interested in just a deep threat," and "There's only one player I'm interested in": Underwood, "This Joe Had Better Be Good," pp. 51, 57–58.

151 "I put the phone down very gently": Braucher, *Promises*, p. 161.

152 "A lot of bad things were said about him": Hyde, *Still Perfect*, p. 145.

152   Thomas resigned: Joe Thomas was replaced by no fewer than seven men: Bobby Beathard, the new personnel director, plus a pro scouting director and five traveling scouts, each responsible for one region of the country.

152   "We should be right up there winning": Bill Braucher, "Appointment as Colt GM Fulfills Thomas' Dreams," *Miami Herald*, July 14, 1972, 1-F.

153   "I've had pretty good success in here as a visiting quarterback, too": Pope, "Csonka Bops Colts with Passion," *Miami Herald*, Oct. 30, 1972, 5-D.

153   "Aren't you getting a little too old for this?," "I'm still the quarterback of this team" and "if you're a horse's ass you would": *Winning Them All*, pp. 77–78.

154   "He was the first I knew of": Seiple interview.

154   "Nobody realizes what got the Dolphins to the Super Bowl": Edwin Pope, "Shula Has One-Track Mind—Championship," *Miami Herald*, Nov. 2, 1972, 1-F, and Gary Long, "Special Teams Frustrate Colts," *Miami Herald*, Jan. 12, 1973, 8-SB.

155   "You have to admire Lloyd": Gary Long, "Special Teams Frustrate Colts," *Miami Herald*, Jan. 12, 1973, 8-SB.

155   "I loved that guy": Briscoe, *The First Black Quarterback*, p. 152.

155   "Johnson gets beat five or six times every practice": Curt Gowdy, NBC telecast of Super Bowl VII, on YouTube.

155–56   "You might not realize it": *Winning Them All*, p. 82.

156   "Den Herder is playing spectacular football": Edwin Pope, "Csonka Bops Colts with Passion," *Miami Herald*, Oct. 30, 1972, 1-D.

156–57   "wants everybody to know": *Winning Them All*, p. 72.

157   "it was that or a teaching job" and "Hey I can really play against these guys": Dr. Paul B. Langevin, "A Super Bowl Winner to the Operating Room . . . An Unlikely Tale," Feb. 17, 2016, medium.com/@Plangevin/a-super-bowl -winner-to-the-operating-room-an-unlikely-tale-ff691fc35b5f.

157   "The coach up there was some kind of a Nazi": *Winning Them All*, p. 73.

157   "freaky guy" and "a free thinker": *Always on the Run*, p. 178.

157   "I could give you a few bars of 'Lord Jeffrey Amherst'": *Winning Them All*, p. 72.

157   "One of the all-time great characters": *But We Were 17 and 0*, p. 167.

157   "We had orange peels everywhere": Yepremian, *Tales from the Miami Dolphins*, p. 62.

157   "I don't dig athletes," "I couldn't believe my luck," and "Inside of Swift": *Winning Them All*, p. 73.

158   "if football was his thing": Gary Long, "Dolphins Shun Spotlight, Stress Teamwork," *Miami Herald*, Dec. 24, 1971, 1-E.

158 "comfortable with just about everyone on the team": *But We Were 17 and 0*, p. 175.

158 "And those points weren't all against the defense" . . . "what the hell does it matter?": *Winning Them All*, p. 79.

Eight and Oh

159 "We don't even talk about that": Bill Braucher, "Shula Won't Use 'Unbeaten,'" *Miami Herald*, Oct. 31, 1972, 1-C.

159–60 "What difference does that make?" and "People waiting for us to have a let-down?": Pope, "Shula Has One-Track Mind—Championship," *Miami Herald*, Nov. 2, 1972, 1-F.

159 "It's nice to think about going undefeated": Bill Braucher, "Stanfill's Hoping to Haunt Thomas," *Miami Herald*, Oct. 28, 1972, 3-D.

160 "Most people are never that committed to anything": Dave Hyde, "Almost Thirty Years Ago, Their Team Went 17-0 . . . ," *South Florida Sun-Sentinel*, March 25, 2001.

161 "Over here, Doc!" . . . "Whatever it takes": Dave Hyde, "Almost Thirty Years Ago"; Dave Hyde, *Still Perfect*, pp. 112–18; and Griese and Hyde, *Perfection*, p. 82.

161 "It's a pretty brutal game, I guess": *Winning Them All*, p. 75.

162 "as common as pregame taping": Griese and Hyde, *Perfection*, p. 86.

163 "but only because they needed bodies": Farrell, *Richard Nixon*, p. 3.

163 "Hit him, hit him, goddamnit!": Farrell, *Richard Nixon*, p. 407.

163 gave a pep talk, which some players credited: "Misunderstood on Nixon Bit, Kilmer Claims," *Miami Herald*, Dec. 6, 1972, 2-C.

163 "[Nixon]'s something else": Sally Quinn, "Billy Kilmer," *Miami Herald* (*Washington Post* Service), Dec. 5, 1972, 1-D.

164 "Bonehead of the Year": Braucher, *Promises*, p. 265.

164–65 Nixon 1972 phone call and 1969 letter: Shula, *Winning Edge*, pp. 184–85.

165 "His absorption [was] almost frightening" . . . "Pat and the girls didn't see him": Farrell, *Richard Nixon*, p. 116.

166 "I am coming to believe" . . . "the most dangerous man in America": Farrell, *Richard Nixon*, p. 255, from letter from MLK to Earl Mazo, Sept. 2, 1958, kinginstitute.stanford.edu/king-papers/documents/earl-mazo.

166 "prowling a hotel hallway": Farrell, *Richard Nixon*, p. 407.

166 "Hey Coach, notice anything?": Terry Blount, "Shula: From Colt to Thoroughbred over 30 Years," *Baltimore Sun*, Oct. 29, 1993.

167 "Dear Don": Freeman, *Undefeated*, p. 20, transcribed from White House tapes.

167 "a dismal campaign": James J. Kilpatrick, "It's Been a Dismal Campaign," *Miami Herald*, Nov. 4, 1972, 7-A.

167 "unenthusiastically": *All the President's Men*, p. 200.

168 "It is difficult for us to believe": "The President Should Disown His 'Committee to Re-elect,'" *Miami Herald*, Oct. 31, 1972, 6-A.

168 "Much ado about nothing": Melvin R. Steves, "Watergate Caper Will Be Forgotten," letter to *Miami Herald*, Nov. 1, 1972, 6-A.

168 "probably the most massive amount of bombs": Michael Getler, "Precision Is Key to B-52 Flight," *Miami Herald* (from *Washington Post*), Oct. 31, 1972, 9-A.

169 "I know you Oklahoma delegates" and "Nobody was going to let that get in the way": Twilley interview.

169 "We really never noticed [political upheaval]": Vern Den Herder telephone interview, May 20, 2020.

169 "we weren't very politically minded": Fernandez interview.

169 "Shula would never go for that kind of crap": Morris interview.

169 "We were unified because of Shula": Twilley interview.

169 "Vietnam was an unfortunate involvement": Warfield interview.

170 "You and me, baby": *Winning Them All*, p. 108.

170 "What a winner": Braucher, *Promises*, p. 184.

170 "Marv fires out like a coiled-up rattler": Evans, *On God's Squad*, p. 177.

170 "He was one of the most unselfish players": Warfield interview.

171 "an extra in one of those inscrutable Sophia Loren movies": Bill Braucher, "Nick Won't Key on Franco Harris," *Miami Herald*, Dec. 30, 1972, 1-D.

171 "You assholes!": Griese and Hyde, *Perfection*, p. 118.

171 "Nick was a little guy" . . . "I think he's also crazy": *But We Were 17 and 0*, pp. 104, 171, and 173.

172 "But the thing you can't measure": NFL Films, *Thunder and Destruction: No Name Defense*, 1:48 mark, on YouTube: www.youtube.com/watch?v =E1CvpZha_EE.

172 "He was the best athlete in the South End": Richard Sandomir, "Nick Buoniconti, 78, Dies," Associated Press, July 31, 2019.

172 "He'll run through a wall": Hyde, *Still Perfect*, p. 177.

172 "I was terribly discouraged": Edwin Pope, "Nick Vs. Joe: Mr. Brain Meets Mr. Arm," *Miami Herald*, Nov. 16, 1972, 1-E.

173 "It takes maybe eight or ten games": Tex Maule, "No Losses, No Ties, and No Names," *Sports Illustrated*, Nov. 27, 1972.

173 "Nick sort of kept an uncle's hand" and "Nick was the Daddy": *But We Were 17 and 0*, p. 175.

173 "The sun shines every day": Bill Braucher, "Nick Won't Key on Franco Harris," *Miami Herald*, Dec. 30, 1972, 6-D.

173 "I made up my mind we'd name all our boys": Edwin Pope, "Nick Vs. Joe: Mr. Brain Meets Mr. Arm," 4-E.

174 "It was synchronized, a thinking man's defense": *But We Were 17 and 0*, p. 199.

174 "I'd think: How'd he know that?": Griese and Hyde, *Perfection*, p. 146.

174 "Nick was the general": Den Herder interview.

175 "taught me how to get back up": Hyde, "Almost Thirty Years Ago, Their Team Went 17–0 . . ."

175 "It sure is fun to hit the quarterback": WTVJ Sportsfilm in the Lynn and Louis Wolfson II Florida Moving Image Archives, Can 59 (1972/Dec. 01), viewed at www.mdc.edu/archives/default.aspx.

175 He had his pickup truck outfitted": Yepremian, *Tales from the Miami Dolphins*, pp. 90–91.

175 "Nobody knew what we were doing": *But We Were 17 and 0*, p. 279.

175 "The Dolphins give you the impression": Bill Braucher, "No Names Bend, But Don't Break," *Miami Herald*, Jan. 12, 1973, 5-SB.

176 "I wanted to give it to the offensive line . . . ": Braucher, "Morris Reluctantly Takes Game Ball," *Miami Herald*, Nov. 6, 1972, 1-E.

176 "I've been concentrating" and "That's a case": Bill Braucher, "Alert Fleming Snared a Real 'Money Catch,'" *Miami Herald*, Nov. 6, 1972, 5-E.

176 "Cookie was absolutely brutal": Edwin Pope, "Nick's List of Best: Lanier, Butkus, Cookie," *Miami Herald*, Aug. 20, 1972, 3-F.

176 "It's like a hundred years ago": Terry Galvin, "Morris Finds 100 Yards Against O.J. 'Satisfying,'" *Miami Herald*, Jan. 12, 1973, 9-SB.

Nine and Oh

177 "I leave you gentlemen now.": "The Last Press Conference," Nixon Foundation, Nov. 14, 2017, www.nixonfoundation.org/2017/11/55-years -ago-last-press-conference/.

177 "I have never known a national election": William D. Montalbano, "It's a Nixon Landslide," *Miami Herald*, Nov. 8, 1972, 1-A.

177–78 "I urge you to send a message": Clark Hoyt, "Nixon Seeks a Mandate for 'Peace with Honor,'" *Miami Herald*, Nov. 7, 1972, 1-A.

179 "One of the few people in the world with whom Nixon felt comfortable":

Stephen Ambrose, *Nixon: The Triumph of a Politician, 1962–1972* (New York: Simon & Schuster, 1989), p. 226.

179   "he never brings up unpleasant subjects": Farrell, *Richard Nixon*, p. 408.

180   "Looks like [the election's] going to be a landslide": James Savage and Darrell Eiland, "Only U.S. Wants Lansky," *Miami Herald*, Nov. 8, 1972, 1-B.

181   "They killed us, 34–13" and "Realistically, I realize this could help me": Pope, "Winning Soothes Jim Kiick's Aching Pride," *Miami Herald*, Nov. 9, 1972, 1-E.

182   "used to go to all their games," "I wasn't drafted, though," and "This is a great break for me": *Winning Them All*, p. 93.

183   "Goddamnit, I told you to keep it on the ground!": *Mercury Morris: The Full Interview, Chapter 1*, 7:55 mark, www.youtube.com/watch?v=k3bAhnaNeJE.

183   "It was good for Jim to get his feet wet": Pope, "Shula's 100th: A Cakewalk," *Miami Herald*, Nov. 13, 1972, 1-E.

183   "Twilley's annual demonstration that he belongs in there somewhere": Braucher, "Dolphins Destroy Pats, 52–0," *Miami Herald*, Nov. 13, 1972, 4-E.

183   "Otto Stowe, Marlin Briscoe and Jim Mandich . . .": Pope, "Shula's 100th: A Cakewalk."

183–84   "I'm just a guy who rolls up his sleeves" and "No, thanks, the only game ball I want": Dave Anderson, "Don Shula's Century in a Decade," *New York Times*, Nov. 10, 1972, p. 27.

184   "The game ball I really want . . ." and "Hey, Big-Time . . .": Pope, "Shula's 100th: A Cakewalk."

184   "My touchdowns didn't really mean anything": *Winning Them All*, p. 94.

184   "You got Briscoe for a draft pick" . . . "in terms of winning 'em all": *Winning Them All*, pp. 31–32.

Ten and Oh

185   Robbie's press luncheon: Ed Storin, "Robbie Forgets Politics and Delivers Message," *Miami Herald*, Nov. 14, 1972, 1-D.

187   "Miami Beach audiences are the greatest in the world!": George Bourke, "Gleason's Return a Stroke of Genius," *Miami Herald*, Nov. 16, 1972, 11-C.

187   "definitely retire at thirty-three": Robin Adams Sloan, "Rock Star Jagger Says He'll Stop Rolling at 33," *Miami Herald*, Nov. 16, 1972, 10-C.

187   "the game of the century": Jay Maeder, "Dolphins' Fans Cheer for It All," *Miami Herald*, Nov. 20, 1972, 14-A.

187–88   The scene outside the Orange Bowl and "What is this, a religious service?":

Randall Poe, "Your Captain Speaking: It's 81° in Miami, the Dolphins by 6 . . . ," *New York Times*, Dec. 17, 1972, p. 1.

188 "Anyone that tries to jump over": Jay Maeder, "Dolphins' Fans Cheer for It All," *Miami Herald*, Nov. 20, 1972, 14-A.

188 "The Dolphin hierarchy alone": Bill Braucher, "Shula Can't Envision Leading Csonka in 'Hail to the Dolphins,'" *Miami Herald*, Jan. 11, 1973, 1-E.

188 "the bullshit before the game is ridiculous": *Winning Them All*, p. 76.

188–89 "It was a fine murderous Sunday afternoon in the Orange Bowl" . . . "Hah!" . . . helped Tannen off the field: Jay Maeder, "Dolphins' Fans Cheer for It All," 1-A.

189 "I weigh two thirty-five": Sahadi, *Griese/Csonka*, p. 140.

189 "I don't like getting hurt": Braucher, "Brown, O.J., Riggins—All Can Bow to Csonka," *Miami Herald*, Nov. 22, 1972, 4-D.

189 "I wouldn't want my son to grow up to be like Namath": *Winning Them All*, p. 98.

189 "Not against Joe": Edwin Pope, "Nick vs. Joe: Mr. Brain Meets Mr. Arm," 1-E.

190 "Run the fucking play!": Hyde, *Still Perfect*, pp. 175–76, and Griese and Hyde, *Perfection*, p. 147. (But both incorrectly have this sequence in the fourth quarter.)

191 "At halftime, I just felt I had things to do": Terry Galvin, "Anderson and Merc Make Amends," *Miami Herald*, Nov. 20, 1972, 5-D.

191 "That run must have taken thirty-five . . ." and "I think I ran about twenty-five yards . . .": Edwin Pope, "Anchors Aweigh for Earl of Miami," *Miami Herald*, Nov. 20, 1972, 1-D and 5-D.

193 "In those days you needed another job": Charlie Nobles, "1972 Dolphins: Undefeated on Field, Undeterred off It," *New York Times*, Feb. 3, 2008.

193 "Do not bet with this kid at anything": *Winning Them All*, p. 42.

193 "I don't think there has been a better safety combination": Dave Hyde, "Where's Jake Scott? Dave Hyde Found Him," *South Florida Sun Sentinel*, Nov. 19, 2006.

194 "I would have had a peaceful college education": *Winning Them All*, p. 43.

194 "He's the one guy no one messed with" and "Now I find out who my real friends are": Griese and Hyde, *Perfection*, p. 183.

194 "As long as you don't fall down, it's not too bad": Bill Braucher, "Scott Resigned to Another Painful Season," *Miami Herald*, Aug. 24, 1972, 1-E.

195 "And I thought I had women in New York": Griese and Hyde, *Perfection*, p. 176.

195 "He win it on class": Bill Braucher, "Dogs, Planes Keep Jake Scott on the Run," *Miami Herald*, Nov. 10, 1972, 1-E.

196 "fertile hunting grounds": Fernandez interview.

196 "the white guys would go to Lum's": Jenkins interview.

196 "Performers like Lionel Hampton": Paula Park, "Heart and Soul," *Miami New Times*, Oct. 2, 1997.

197 "shimmying and shaking": Larry Mahoney, "Chisholm—Influence for Change," *Miami Herald*, March 2, 1972, 8-A.

197 "would hold court": Jenkins interview.

197 "Yeah, I was the Jet-A-Way king": Little interview.

198 "Because I don't come across as a manly stud": Barry Meisel, "Ex-Packer Fleming: Honest, I'm Not Gay," Racine *Journal-Times*, Aug. 4, 1993.

198 "Ah, er, Fleming, interesting fellow": Edwin Pope, "McGee on Fleming: 'It's Up to Shula,'" *Miami Herald*, May 20, 1970, F-1.

198 "I was very lonely in Green Bay": UPI, "Packers Get Clancy from Miami," *Sheboygan Press*, May 19, 1970, p. 20.

198 "Mandich and I would take off for Mike's Lounge": Chris Perkins, "'More Than Perfect' Is a Movie Worth Watching," *South Florida Sun Sentinel*, Dec. 16, 2012.

198 "It was just a neighborhood shot bar," "Not you again, Jim," and Manny Fernandez: Hyde, *Still Perfect*, p. 134.

199 "It was a war, a war": Ray Crawford, "Weeb Sees 14–0 Mark for Miami," *Miami Herald*, Nov. 20, 1972, 5-D.

199 "I came straight down" . . . "Alcohol gives me a nose bleed": Sahadi, *Griese/Csonka:* p. 141.

199 "the next time I break it": Griese and Hyde, *Perfection*, p. 155.

199 "They'll go undefeated . . . ": Ray Crawford, "Weeb Sees 14–0 Mark for Miami."

199 On their honeymoon: Hyde, *Still Perfect*, p. 161.

199–200 "Every time Garo comes running," "How can Don get coaching experience," and she even took a swipe: Underwood, "Sitting on Top of the World," *Sports Illustrated*, Sept. 17, 1973, p. 122.

200 "If there's something you'd argue about" and "I like to be reminded of a hurt": *Winning Them All*, pp. 92 and 99.

Eleven and Oh

201 "It would be nice to have that" . . . "Championships are meaningful": *Winning Them All*, pp. 101–102.

202 "I tell him we'd like to go seventeen and oh": Bill Braucher, "Dolphins' Left Side No Laugher Anymore," *Miami Herald*, Nov. 25, 1972, 2-E.

202 "Everybody up!": *Winning Them All*, p. 103.

202 "I'm not down" . . . "How would you feel?": *Winning Them All*, p. 103, also in Sahadi, *Griese/Csonka*, p. 74.

203 "not a great athlete, never have been,": *But We Were 17 and 0*, p. 290.

203 "He's a tight end, running back": *Winning Them All*, p. 102.

203 "I can't stand" . . . "one of these days": Jonathan Rand, "What Counts of Seiple's Seconds," *Miami News*, Aug. 10, 1972, 3-B.

204 "Anderson has hit more foul balls," "Did you see Zonk's nose?," and "That's my outstanding statistic": *Winning Them All*, pp. 102 and 104.

204 "Langer and I had a standing bet": NFL Films, *History of the Miami Dolphins*, 33:40 mark.

205 "Where in the world is Earl going to get a flattop in Miami?": "The Male of the Species," *Miami Herald* fashion advertising section, June 9, 1972, p. 3.

205 "I don't even think about that": Edwin Pope, "Shula Will Have Choice, and Morrall Is Best Bet," *Miami Herald*, Nov. 22, 1972, 1-D.

207 "Better not come to Miami, Howie": Howard Cosell, *Cosell* (Chicago: Playboy Press, 1973), p. 353.

207 "Would you *please* tell the people of South Florida": Pope, "Cosell Calls Off Irate Dolphin Fans," *Miami Herald*, Nov. 3, 1972, 1-F.

207 "I'd hate for anything out of order to happen": "Shula Asks OB Crowd to Keep Cool," *Miami Herald*, Nov. 22, 1972, 7-D.

208 "carried himself with great personal dignity": Cosell, *Like It Is*, p. 77.

208 "Right now I rate Miami and Washington": Pope, "Cosell Does Know Dolphin Footnotes," *Miami Herald*, Nov. 29, 1972, 2-D.

209 "I took it easy on them": *Winning Them All*, p. 106.

209–10 "The Miami crowd has become quiescent" and other dialogue: ABC broadcast, *Monday Night Football*, Nov. 27, 1972, on YouTube: www.youtube.com/watch?v=traefp7Hz7E.

210–11 "You know why we were flat?" and "Don't ask me": *Winning Them All*, p. 106.

211 "They'd cut my head off": Pope, "Csonka Bops Colts with Passion," *Miami Herald*, Oct. 30, 1972, 1-D.

211 "I wouldn't have been able to live with myself": Bill Braucher, "Zonk Gets a Little Push Down the Road to 1,000," *Miami Herald*, Nov. 29, 1972, 1-D.

212 "looked like Sly Stone": Briscoe, *The First Black Quarterback*, p. 155.

Twelve and Oh

213 "When I arrived in 1970": *But We Were 17 and 0*, p. 218.

213 "When I got to Miami there was no weight program": Fernandez interview.

214 "groaning with wounded after" and "We'll go with the strength we have": Bill Braucher, "Backup Men Help Preserve Dolphins' Unbeaten Record," *Miami Herald*, Oct. 3, 1972, 4-F.

214 "We gotta lose one game": *But We Were 17 and 0*, p. 10.

214 Rest of "Not this week" story: Bob Kuechenberg, "The Perfect Season," in *The Dolphins at 50* (Chicago: Triumph Books, 2015).

215 "Don't pay my bills, my life is enough": Edna Buchanan, "Bigamist Found Dead, One Wife Strangled," *Miami Herald*, Dec. 1, 1972, 1-B.

216 "Well, isn't it a damn good thing": *Winning Them All*, p. 108.

216 Marriott story: *Always on the Run*, pp. 4–5.

217 "He threw it right to me": *Winning Them All*, p. 110.

217 "I blame Manny for tackling me": Den Herder interview.

217 "I didn't realize that guy was so tall" and "We were still in the game": Terry Galvin, "Den Herder, Stanfill Combine to Give Plunkett a Rough Day," *Miami Herald*, Jan. 12, 1973, 15-SB.

217 "I'm the ultimate No-Name": *Winning Them All*, p. 43.

218 "that do-goody Dutchman": *But We Were 17 and 0*, pp. 97, 100, and 104.

218 "It's a total body workout" and "gravitated to because we had similar ideas": Den Herder interview.

218 "Well, I've made it this far": *But We Were 17 and 0*, p. 83.

218 "I don't have real good upper-body strength": Braucher, "Den Herder Walks Softly with Big Hit," *Miami Herald*, Dec. 2, 1972, 3-E.

218 "By the end of training camp": Shula, *The Winning Edge*, p. 216.

219 "I never thought to go more than four or five": *Winning Them All*, p. 110.

220 "Of course, I'd love to get it": Terry Galvin, "Csonka Barges to 1,000 but Eyes Higher Levels," *Miami Herald*, Dec. 4, 1972, 1-E.

220 "I don't know how the runners feel about it": *Winning Them All*, p. 111.

221 "a Bunyanesque figure to his fellow iron workers": Bill Braucher, "Go to College or Be a Cannonball," *Tropic*, Oct. 22, 1972, p. 13.

221 "My dad basically said": Daniel E. Slotnik, "Bob Kuechenberg, 71, Dies; Gritty Guard With Champion Dolphins," *New York Times*, Jan. 16, 2019.

221 "older vets who felt threatened . . . and it kept me playing": *America's Game*, 16:00–17:30.

222 "Kooch!": *Winning Them All*, pp. 87–88.

222 "come off the sandlots" and "It's getting to the point": *America's Game*, 18:00 mark.

222 "I just fight": Red Smith, "For the Jets, a Tale of 5 Rejects," *New York Times*, Nov. 7, 1975.

222 "Work on your stance": Griese and Hyde, *Perfection*, p. 193.

223 "a 250-pound bundle of nerves, humor, and theory": Braucher, *Promises*, p. 166.

223 "And knowing him": Evans, *On God's Squad*, p. 145.

223 "Sure, we hope to go all the way" and "We're not 14–0": Terry Galvin, "Csonka Barges to 1,000 but Eyes Higher Levels," *Miami Herald*, Dec. 4, 1972, 5-E.

Thirteen and Oh

224 "When I came down here": Morris interview.

224 "I got a kick out of watching Armstrong": Morris, "Diary of a Rookie," *Miami News*, July 21, 1969, 1-C.

224 "In some ways we became associated with the space program": *Zonk! Zonk's NFL* video.

224 "America's last lunar explorers" and "Go . . . go . . . go!": Mike Toner, "It's Late, But Apollo's on Its Way," *Miami Herald*, Dec. 7, 1972, 1-A.

225 "airline employees ignored the magnetometer's": Don Bedwell and Edna Buchanan, "How Good Is Miami Airport's Anti-Hijack Security Setup?," *Miami Herald*, Dec. 4, 1972, 1-A.

225 "The jury is going to want to know": Lawrence Meyer, "Watergate Bugging Trial Should Probe Who Started It All, Judge Declares," *Miami Herald* (*Washington Post* Service), Dec. 5, 1972, 20-A.

226 "Losing is like death": Myra MacPherson, "George Allen: You Can't Let Up One Day Toward Winning," *Miami Herald* (*Washington Post* Service), Jan. 7, 1973, 1-D.

226 "The worst moments of my life" and "And if we win": Jeannie Morris, "Mrs. George Allen No. 1 Fan of Intense Redskins Coach," national column in *Miami Herald*, Dec. 26, 1972, 4-D.

227 "Dick is inclined to foul one off now and then": Bill Braucher, "Lothridge Booted Down to Taxi Squad," *Miami Herald*, Dec. 9, 1972, 7-E.

228 "I just can't buy that attitude": *Winning Them All*, p. 113.

228 "I'd like to see Merc get it": Bill Braucher, "Shula Likely to Activate Ailing Griese," *Miami Herald*, Dec. 5, 1972, 1-D.

228 "To those who understand": Frederick Exley, *A Fan's Notes* (New York: Harper & Row, 1968), p. 345.

229 "It's been a dream all my life to play in Yankee Stadium": *Winning Them All*, p. 113.

229 "It has to psyche you up": Edwin Pope, "Dolphins 'Sloppy'? Yeah, But . . . ," *Miami Herald*, Dec. 8, 1972, 1-E.

229 "The last time I was there was in '68": Pope, "Instant Don Shula," *Miami Herald*, Dec. 6, 1972, 1-C.

230 "If we want to stop the Dolphins" and "We were backed up to the ten-yard line": *Winning Them All*, p. 112.

230 "Merc, only a dumb Hunky": *Always on the Run*, p. 171.

231 "the ultimate in locker-room news management" . . . "but in footnotes": John Crittenden, "A Few Bad Words from Paul Warfield," *Miami News*, Aug. 24, 1972, 1-C.

231 "long-winded, forensic explanations": Bill Braucher, "Warfield Returns from Obscurity to Catch 4 Passes for 132 Yards," *Miami Herald*, Jan. 12, 1973, 16-SB.

231 "It has no place in pro football" . . . "and the long passes are gone": Crittenden, "A Few Bad Words from Paul Warfield"; Maule, "No Losses, No Ties and No Names"; and Terry Galvin, "Paul Warfield: After Super '71, a Year of Near Misses," *Miami Herald*, Dec. 6, 1972, 3-C.

231 "He personifies class": *Winning Them All*, p. 69.

232 "He's like satin": *Always on the Run*, p. 164.

232 "He just glides into the end zone": *Winning Them All*, p. 69.

232 "Even when he blocked": Jenkins interview.

232 "There were plays designed for me to block": Warfield interview.

232 "Warfield was twenty-five percent of that team": *But We Were 17 and 0*, p. 208.

233 "I said to myself, 'Oh, Lord, pull yourself together'": Hyde, *Still Perfect*, p. 153.

233 "I don't know how he did it": Morris interview.

233 "I slipped under Williams," "That last one," and "I had Paul covered": Pope, "Clever Warfield Spun a Spider's Web," *Miami Herald*, Dec. 11, 1972, 1-C.

234 "the vivid reds and oranges, the plaids and tans of autumn clothing": Exley, *A Fan's Notes*, p. 346.

234 "At first we floundered around": *But We Were 17 and 0*, pp. 171–72.

235 "That's the worst punt" and "That was a sand wedge": *Winning Them All*, p. 113.

235 "scoop gobs of mud" and "if you can find a sport foolish enough": Bill Braucher, "Garo Conquers Mud . . . and Colleagues," *Miami Herald*, Dec. 13, 1972, 4-E.

Fourteen and Oh

237   "begin talking seriously": Stanley Karnow, *Vietnam: A History* (New York: Viking, 1991), p. 652.

238   "old, half-crippled Jews": Arthur Miller, "Making Crowds," *Esquire*, Nov. 1972, p. 161.

238   "the poor and the old wandering" and "We need fewer nursing homes": Doug Clifton, "Beach Nudging Elderly out of Picture," *Miami Herald*, Dec. 16, 1972, 2-B.

239   "I think Earl will start in the playoffs": *Winning Them All*, p. 115.

239–40   "If we perform like we can" and "I'm more worried about Oakland than Miami": "Steelers' Bradshaw Has Early Itch for Dolphins," *Miami Herald* (from *Herald* Wire Services), Dec. 12, 1972, 2-C.

240   "Don't you agree there are no great teams . . . vis-à-vis New York's eleven million": Ed Storin, "Are the Dolphins a Great Team?," *Miami Herald*, Dec. 12, 1972, 1-C.

241   "Today I got more harassment" and "Usually a couple of dozen fans": Arnold Markowitz, "Dolphins, Dolfans 'Perfect' as Records and Colts Fall," *Miami Herald*, Dec. 17, 1972, 32-A.

242   "Offensive linemen don't have statistics": Gary Long, "Offensive Line Shows Way to 14–0 Season," *Miami Herald*, Jan. 12, 1973, 17-SB.

242   "Monte Clark did magic": *But We Were 17 and 0*, p. 149.

242   "we never went a day being hungry": Bill Braucher, "Skins No Worry for Larry Little After Tough Dad," *Miami Herald*, Jan. 11, 1973, 1-E.

243   "It was colder": *More Than Perfect* DVD.

243   "I finally got you," "I was getting ready to make my home," and "And though we weren't winning": Little interview, and *More Than Perfect* DVD.

243   "That's great . . . I was traded for you": *The Fish Tank* podcast, "Larry Csonka, Larry Little & Mercury Morris: Perfection."

244   "And when I lost that weight": Little interview.

244   "People didn't realize how fast he was": *Zonk! Zonk's NFL* video.

244   "the moment of truth . . . try to stay on your feet": Al Levine, "Little vs. Corner: 'No Way I Lose,'" *Miami News*, Aug. 8, 1972, 1-B.

244   "Like a tractor hitting a tree": Gary Long, "Offensive Line Shows Way to 14–0 Season," *Miami Herald*.

244   "I enjoyed knocking a man off the ball": *History of the Miami Dolphins*, 32:30 mark.

244–45 "Anytime Larry is out in front of me" and "He's a soft-spoken, easy-going guy": *Always on the Run*, p. 173.

245 "I was exposed to everything" and "I was broken up": Ray Crawford, "Little's Playing Big Guardian Role for Kids, Dolphins," *Miami Herald*, Aug. 20, 1971, 1-D.

245 "the comedian of the team": Yepremian, *Tales from the Miami Dolphins*, p. 78.

246 "except for a suspicious tremolo on the left side": *Winning Them All*, p. 84.

246 "I hated [the trade]": *But We Were 17 and 0*, pp. 43–44.

246 "a gentle giant and quiet family man": Briscoe, *The First Black Quarterback*, p. 150.

246 "a prince": Raymond A. Partsch III, "A Fading Legend: Moore's Stature Didn't Overshadow His Humility," *Beaumont Enterprise*, Dec. 9, 2013.

247 "How about Doug Crusan coming in": Edwin Pope, "Originals Prove Great Company for QB Griese," *Miami Herald*, Oct. 2, 1972, 5-C.

248 "I want to sneak in there": *Winning Them All*, p. 111.

248 "All of a sudden I see this guy" . . . "no fucking record off me today": Morris interview.

248 "Merc needs twenty-nine more": Pope, "Morrall Enjoys Irony of Record-Setting Run," *Miami Herald*, Dec. 17, 1972, 7-C.

248 "Every time I lined up": Morris interview April 23, 2020.

249 "As far as I'm concerned, Merc was denied": Terry Galvin, "'Merc Denied His 1,000 by Turf,' Csonka Claims," *Miami Herald*, Dec. 17, 1972, 7-C.

249 "carnival" and "travesty": Bill Braucher, "Surrounded by Success, Shula's Back on the Fence," *Miami Herald*, Dec. 20, 1972, 4-E.

249 "an injury perhaps needlessly sustained": NFL Films, *This Week in Pro Football, 1972 Colts at Dolphins Week 14*, 2:50 mark, on YouTube: www .youtube.com/watch?v=DI1p96hl7a4.

249 "Hell, everybody was trying to get it for me": Terry Galvin, "Disappointed Merc Feels He Let Teammates Down," *Miami Herald*, Dec. 17, 1972, 1-C.

250 "What's to be emotional about": Gary Long, "Unitas Ends 'Worst Year,' Colt Career," *Miami Herald*, Dec. 17, 1972, 6-C.

250 "I had a lump in my throat" and "No, wait one play": *Winning Them All*, p. 117.

251 "I really can't get too excited" and "Maybe we don't realize the importance of it now": Bill Braucher, "14 and 0, Three to Go As Dolphins Rip Colts," *Miami Herald*, Dec. 17, 1972, 6-C.

Fifteen and Oh

252 "At first I didn't believe him": Gary Long, "NFL Boosts Merc to 1,000," *Miami Herald*, Dec. 22, 1972, 1-E.

253 "The public response was relatively muted": Karnow, *Vietnam*, p. 653.

254 "binge" and "And now, thank God": William Hines, "End of a Crazy Business," *Chicago Sun-Times*, Dec. 21, 1972.

255 "would strongly urge the new Congress": "NFL Refuses Nixon on Playoff Blackout; Probe Is Threatened," *Miami Herald*, Dec. 21, 1972, 1-A.

255 Overnight ticket line: Jay Maeder, "'Boy Howdy, Us Dolfans Are Maniacs,'" *Miami Herald*, Dec. 18, 1972, 1-B.

256–57 "You win ten games": "Pro Bowl Shun Miffs Browns," *Miami Herald* (UPI), Dec. 21, 1972, 1-C.

257 "to have a ticket to the dance": *Winning Them All*, p. 122.

257 "I think it was one of the greatest trades": Bob Egelko, "Phipps Finally Shakes Warfield Image," *Miami Herald* (AP), Nov. 15, 1972, 4-E.

257–58 "All we heard," "If I had to pick," and "if you think about revenge": *Winning Them All*, pp. 125–26.

258 "Everybody's saying we don't have much of a chance": Gary Long, "No Chill Factor on Bob DeMarco's Return Visit," *Miami Herald*, Dec. 20, 1972, 4-E.

258 "The situation is not real good": Al Levine, "Mercury's Ankle: The Situation Is Not Good," *Miami News*, Dec. 18, 1972, 1-C.

259 "ongoing music and frivolity": "1968—NW 36 Street north of Pan Am's hangars, and the Kings Inn in Miami Springs," webpage by Don Boyd, www.pbase.com/image/80369380.

260 "Merry Christmas to the Dolphins" and "When the Dolphins play the Browns": *Miami Herald*, Dec. 27, 1972, 9-C.

260 "We were not committed to living in Miami" . . . "incident my wife experienced": Warfield interview.

260 "Not since junior high school": *Winning Them All*, p. 127.

262 "The president feels very strongly": Randy Bellows, "It's Just Workday for Nixon," *Miami Herald*, Dec. 25, 1972, 10-A.

262–63 "I don't want the smoke bothering anyone," "The big bastard isn't going to beat us," "I can't really say whether," and "At the half, we knew": *Winning Them All*, pp. 128–29, and Terry Galvin, "Skorich Blames Blocked-Punt TD," *Miami Herald*, Dec. 25, 1972, 4-D.

263 "The wind's against you!": Terry Galvin, "Garo Set to Duel Gerela," *Miami Herald*, Dec. 28, 1972, 1-E.

264 "We thought they'd choke": *Winning Them All*, p. 131.

264 "I'd have done it if I felt it would shake us up": Bill Braucher, "Kiick Made Sure He Didn't Fumble on TD," *Miami Herald*, Dec. 25, 1972, 4-D.

264 "We've got plenty of time": *Winning Them All*, p. 130.

264 "All right, this is it": Luther Evans, "Dolphins Rally to Bag Browns, 20–14," *Miami Herald*, Dec. 25, 1972, 1-D.

265 "Never let them know you're hurt": *The Fish Tank* podcast, "Nat Moore: 'We ain't supposed to score? Nah bro,'" Aug. 28, 2018: www.thefishtank81.com /all-episodes.html#/.

266 "That really had me thinking": Braucher, "Kiick Made Sure . . ."

266 "One of the greatest moments of joy": *A Football Life: The Perfect Backfield*, 28:07 mark.

267 "[Phipps] laid it right on my head," "Anderson's fumble," and "I got exhausted and fell down": Bill Braucher, "Swift and Babb: Pair of Opportunists," *Miami Herald*, Dec. 25, 1972, 1-D.

267 "That last drive": Luther Evans, "Dolphins Rally to Bag Browns."

267 "We played only as good as we had to play": Braucher, "Kiick Made Sure . . ."

267 "I was nervous and emotional": Edwin Pope, "Up-Tight Warfield Finally Gets Loose," *Miami Herald*, Dec. 25, 1972, 1-D.

267–68 "Sometimes you wonder what the hell you're doing": *Winning Them All*, p. 76.

268 "I like all the money . . . a big financial thrill": Gary Long, "'Greedy' Doug Swift Steals Phipps' Passes," *Miami Herald*, Jan. 12, 1973, 18-SB.

268 "Intercepting is the only joy a linebacker gets": Dave Anderson, "Warfield Stars in Late Drive for Score," *New York Times*, Dec. 25, 1972, p. 23.

Sixteen and Oh

270 "She doesn't go for Women's Lib": Jack McClintock, "Faith, Orange Juice, and Anita Bryant," *Tropic*, Nov. 26, 1972, p. 14.

270 "until God gives us victory" and "I declare that the door": "Despite Soviet Warning, Sadat Urges New War," *Miami Herald* (from UPI), Dec. 29, 1972, 1-A.

271 "a record of futility unmatched in professional sport": Edwin Pope, "Steelers' Rooney Has Heart of Winner," *Miami Herald*, Dec. 29, 1972, 1-C.

271 "Art Rooney is the finest person I've ever known": Dave Anderson, "Art Rooney Never Changed," *New York Times*, Aug. 26, 1988, Section B, p. 13.

271 "There was no way he was going to call it...": *Winning Them All*, p. 137.

272 "We'll beat the Dolphins": *Winning Them All*, p. 138.

273 "I got to my room and called home": Fernandez interview.

273 "I used to live on the twenty-five-yard line": Al Levine, "Mercury at Home: 3 Rivers," *Miami News*, Dec. 25, 1972, C-1.

274 "He's a superstar": *Winning Them All*, p. 139.

274 "I had a little chip on my shoulder": Little interview, May 15, 2020.

274 "We've got nothing to be proud of," "We relaxed or something," and "If they play like that": Bill Braucher, "Dolphins Brace for Expedition to Steeler City," *Miami Herald*, Dec. 26, 1972, 1-D.

275 "Three Rivers Stadium was loud": Larry Seiple, "In My Own Words: vs. Pittsburgh Steelers," Miami Dolphins website, Oct, 24, 2019, www .miamidolphins.com/news/in-my-own-words-larry-seiple-vs-pittsburgh -steelers.

275 "You know what I would like?" and "Scott really knocked me silly": *Winning Them All*, pp. 140–41.

276 "Shula and Taseff both took me aside": Seiple interview.

276 Rick Weaver told him he'd had a dream: Hyde, *Still Perfect*, p. 226.

276 "Well, it was supposed to be called by Coach Shula": Seiple, "In My Own Words."

276 "Maybe I had too much to drink . . . so I just took off": Seiple interview, May 29, 2020.

277 "I could hear the Steelers fans": *America's Game*, 3:05 mark.

277 "The offense was floundering": *But We Were 17 and 0*, p. 173.

278 "Replacing Earl was one of the toughest things I ever had to do": *America's Game*, 33:40 mark.

278 "I'm going with Bob the second half," "Griese, because that would mean they'd be behind," and "our money pattern": *Winning Them All*, pp. 142–43.

279 "If you expect to be a world championship team" and "knocked the center back like a bowling ball" (Larry Ball quote): Bill Braucher, "Fourth Down Conversions Set Up All Dolphin TDs," *Miami Herald*, Jan. 1, 1973, 4-D.

279 "When we play for the big money": *Winning Them All*, p. 144.

280 "in a deep concentration bag": Ron Reid, "Sweet 16 on a Super Trip," *Sports Illustrated*, Jan. 8, 1973.

280 "just wasn't functioning mentally": Terry Galvin, "Scott's Tackle Left Bradshaw 'Confused,'" *Miami Herald*, Jan. 1, 1973, 5-D.

280 "Brad, what's the score?" . . . "wobbling a little": Kevin Cook, *The Last Headbangers* (New York: W. W. Norton, 2012), pp. 44–45.

281 "That's what the people pay their money for": Bill Braucher, "Dolphins Heeded Griese Order to 'Shut Up,'" *Miami Herald*, Jan. 1, 1973, 3-D.

282 "Watch the offsides!" . . . "Shut up, damn it!": Bill Braucher, "Dolphins Heeded Griese," and *Winning Them All*, p. 145. Many writers have placed this incident in the third quarter, when Griese first came in, but all sources from the day it happened concur that it occurred on the final possession.

282 "Maybe it'll balance out" . . . "harder than our own junk": Bill Braucher, "Secondary Suffers Severe Blow: Scott, Foley Separate Shoulders," *Miami Herald*, Jan. 1, 1973, 5-D.

282–83 "I said before today's game": Terry Galvin, "Scott's Tackle Left Bradshaw 'Confused,'" *Miami Herald*, Jan. 1, 1973, 5-D.

283 "The kid won it for us" and "My most satisfying victory": *Winning Them All*, p. 146.

283 Scene at Miami airport: Jay Maeder, "Dolphins Make It a Sweet New Year with AFC Title and Super Bowl Berth," *Miami Herald*, Jan. 1, 1973, 1-A, and Evans, *On God's Squad*, p. 206.

284 "Hey, Eddie": Jenkins interview.

Super Bowl Pregame

285 "You don't fool around," "I feel fine, Coach," and "His eyes lit up": Shula, *Winning Edge*, p. 7.

285 "I want to play just as much": Hyde, *Still Perfect*, pp. 233–34.

286 "Nobody on the team is going to question it": *Winning Them All*, p. 152.

286 Gator story: Fernandez interview, Csonka quoted in various interviews, and many other sources.

287–88 "Come on, go to it" . . . "It might last all day": *Winning Them All*, p. 152.

288–89 "raise a little hell " and ". . . And what in the hell is a female impersonator?!": Freeman, *Undefeated*, p. 131.

289 Players' night out in L.A.: Hyde, *Still Perfect*, p. 240; *Always on the Run*, pp. 202–203; and Bill Braucher, "Dolphin Publicist Callahan in Satisfactory Condition," *Miami Herald*, Jan. 9, 1973, 2-C.

290 "Hookers are unwelcome": Edwin Pope, "Super Bowl VII Right out of Hollywood," *Miami Herald*, Jan. 12, 1973, 1-E.

290 "like walking through a room full of convicts": Edwin Pope, "Pope's Prediction: Dolphins by 20–13," *Miami Herald*, Jan. 14, 1973, 1-D.

290 "Coaching is my life": Larry Fox, "George Allen," *Miami Herald* (New York News Service), Dec. 21, 1972, 7-C.

290 "It was more fun to lose": Carlo DeVito, *Don Shula* (New York: Sports Publishing, 2018), p. 76.

291 "Your first Super Bowl" and "Gearing for pregame distraction": Edwin Pope, "Dolphins No Longer 'Star-Struck' by Super Bowl," *Miami Herald*, Jan. 7, 1973, 1-D.

291 Mercury Morris had a weight set: Jenkins interview.

291 "The Super Bowl is a game": *Winning Them All*, p. 156.

292 "You've got to be an idiot," "Last year we were glad," and "We need this one": Freeman, *Undefeated*, p. 214.

292 "walked out on me, hired behind my back": Bill Braucher, "Rosenbloom Raps Both Allen, Shula," *Miami Herald*, Jan. 12, 1973, 1-E.

292-93 "Anything that man says" and "slip the word over to George": Edwin Pope, "Shula Hasn't Time to Worry About Rosenbloom," *Miami Herald*, Jan. 13, 1973, 1-E.

293 "to be announced after we finish practice": Bill Braucher, "Shula Can't Envision Leading Csonka in 'Hail to the Dolphins,'" *Miami Herald*, Jan. 11, 1973, 3-E.

293 "No, George is handling that," "What is the attitude of the coach?," and "I've never seen Shula as uptight": *Winning Them All*, pp. 155, 160, and 161.

293 "good-natured Shula's" and "graceful humor": Hyde, *Still Perfect*, p. 246.

293 "All you guys want to do": "Redskins' Allen Blasts, Bars Press," *Miami Herald* (wire service), Oct. 7, 1972, 5-E.

293 "Yesterday thirty-one of my players": Bill Braucher, "Crush of Interviews Sours Allen's Mood," *Miami Herald*, Jan. 13, 1973, 1-E.

294 "He loves his men": Jeannie Morris, "'Skins Win Because They Think They're a Family," *Miami Herald*, Jan. 5, 1973, 3-F.

294 "to hide the taste of the whiskey," "to hide the taste," and "Fifty degrees and cloudy": Sally Quinn, "Billy Kilmer," *Miami Herald* (*Washington Post* Service), Dec. 5, 1972, 1D, 6D.

295 "I can't run anymore, though" and "I wake up at five-thirty": Bill Braucher, "Redskin QB Survived Brushes with Death and Obscurity," *Miami Herald*, Jan. 12, 1973, 1-E, and *Winning Them All*, p. 159.

295 "Today I'm convinced" and "It looks to me": Griese, "Super Bowl Diary," *Fort Lauderdale News*, Jan. 21, 1973, 9D.

296 "We had black [players], we had white": *But We Were 17 and 0*, p. 50.

296 "I'm going to take that Super Bowl check": Hyde, *Still Perfect*, p. 243.

296 Players and wives' plans for playoff bonus: Janet Chusmir, "Dolphin Wives:

Most Agree Super Bonuses Likely to Become Investments," *Miami Herald*, Jan. 12, 1973, 28-SB.

298   "I don't know why I went to Vegas": King interview.

298   King and Greek driving from Vegas: King interview and *History of the Miami Dolphins*, 28:14 mark.

298   "The prediction here is that the fearsome Redskins": Freeman, *Undefeated*, p. 230.

298   "at least ten points": Tex Maule, "It's the Top-of-the-Hill Gang," *Sports Illustrated*, Jan. 15, 1973.

299   "kids . . . in kooky tangerine-and-turquoise" to "Who's that bald-headed guy playing safety?": Jim Murray, "Dolphin 'Rubes' Don't Belong in Pro Football's High Society," *Miami Herald*, Jan. 14, 1973, 6-D.

299   "That was the first thing I saw": John Crittenden, "Dolphins Say It's Time for Recognition," *Miami News*, Jan. 15, 1973, 1-C.

299   "It was a nice affair": *Winning Them All*, p. 154.

299–300   "I wouldn't plan to see Howard" and "We've gone through some hard times": Jeannie Morris, "Dolphins Outmaneuver 'Skins in Game Plan for Happy Wives," *Miami Herald*, Jan. 12, 1973, 4-E.

300   "I was throwing the ball thirty-five yards": Yepremian, *Tales from the Miami Dolphins*, p. 32.

300   "Taylor never made any big plays off me," "I like the way Kilmer throws," and "What do you expect him to say?": Bill Braucher, "Shula Can't Envision Leading Csonka in 'Hail to the Dolphins,'" *Miami Herald*, Jan. 11, 1973, 3-E.

300   "This is going to be one of my biggest games": Edwin Pope, "Super Bowl VII Right out of Hollywood," *Miami Herald*, Jan. 12, 1973, 1-E.

301   "I wouldn't want to be Griese on Sunday": Luther Evans, "Dolphins Rule Football World," *Miami Herald*, Jan. 15, 1973, 6-D.

301   "began betting heavily on Miami": Hunter S. Thompson, "Fear and Loathing at the Super Bowl," *Rolling Stone*, Feb. 15, 1973.

302   "Good morning, Larry": King interview, and Griese, "Super Bowl Diary," *Fort Lauderdale News*, Jan. 21, 1973, 9D.

302   "He'd get us together at breakfast": Jenkins interview.

302   "You worried about going down as the losingest coach": Numerous sources, confirmed in Hyde, "Where's Jake Scott? Dave Hyde Found Him," *South Florida Sun Sentinel*, Nov. 19, 2006.

Seventeen and Oh: Super Bowl VII

303 "We had gone sixteen and oh": Evans, *On God's Squad*, p. 214.

303 "We had them when we walked on the field": Al Levine, "Super Dolphins Greatest Ever—Just Ask Them," *Miami News*, Jan. 15, 1973, 2-C.

304 "I soon realized I was having problems": Yepremian, *Tales from the Miami Dolphins*, p. 33.

304 "It was pretty quiet" and "But his voice was cracking": *Zonk! Zonk's NFL* video. Also *Always on the Run*, pp. 214–15.

305 "I know it sounds strange": Freeman, *Undefeated*, p. 236.

306 "Take it in, offense!": Evans, *On God's Squad*, p. 217.

306 "watching the two little men on this side" and all Gowdy and DeRogatis quotes: NBC telecast of Super Bowl VII, on YouTube.

306 "Before Bob uttered a single syllable": Howard Twilley unpublished memoir.

306 "We probably ran that a hundred times": Twilley interview.

306 "had me convinced he wanted to stay inside": Terry Galvin, "Kilmer Accepts Losers' Guilt After 3 Misfires," *Miami Herald*, Jan. 15, 1973, 4-D.

306 "I'm in!": Bill Bondurant, *Fort Lauderdale News*, Jan. 19, 1973, 4B.

307 "Usually, I know where I want to throw": Bill Braucher, "Kilmer Beat Heavy Odds," *Miami Herald*, Jan. 12, 1973, 3-E.

307 "You talk about reckless abandon": Gary Long, "No Bones About It, Scott's Hands Soft," *Miami Herald*, July 22, 1972, 2-F.

308 "Arnsparger changed the whole defense" and "Manny was too quick for them": Jake Scott, "In My Own Words: Super Bowl VII," Dolphins website, Oct 10, 2019, www.miamidolphins.com/news/in-my-own-words-super-bowl-vii-jake-scott-vs-washington-redskins.

308 "I never did make a Pro Bowl": Fernandez interview.

309 "I imagine the president must have given George some coverages": John Crittenden, "Dolphins Say It's Time for Recognition," *Miami News*, Jan. 15, 1973, 2-C.

310 "Just get set! What the hell are you doing?": *America's Game*, 3:55 mark.

311 Lying on the ground . . . Butch's helmet: John Crittenden, "A Typical Dolphin game," *Miami News*, Jan. 15, 1973, 10-C, and *Always on the Run*, p. 216.

311 "Time's on our side": Evans, *On God's Squad*, pp. 218–19.

314 "We needed at least three": Bill Bondurant, "Final Countdown to a Super Season: Super Bowl Diary with Bob Griese," *Fort Lauderdale News*, Jan. 21, 1973, 9-D.

315 "I guess I got a concussion": Fernandez interview. Also see *Winning Them All*, p. 163.

315 "I can't get greedy": Bill Braucher, "Kilmer Beat Heavy Odds," *Miami Herald*, Jan. 12, 1973, 3-E.

316 "Field goal makes it seventeen oh": *America's Game*, 39:00 mark.

317 "As soon as I picked up the ball": Yepremian, *Tales from the Miami Dolphins*, p. 34.

318 "it made you sick to think about it": *Winning Them All*, p. 166.

318 "wasn't man enough": *But We Were 17 and 0*, pp. 13–14.

318 "If he ever gets the ball again": *More Than Perfect* DVD.

318 "Nobody panicked . . . would have haunted me forever": Bill Braucher, "'Quarterback' Garo Prayed After Pass Ended in Disaster," *Miami Herald*, Jan. 15, 1973, 5-D, and Brian D'Ambrosio, "Garo Yepremian on Super Bowl Gaffe," Huffington Post, Jan. 17, 2014.

319 "Everybody remembers Garo's guffaw": Briscoe interview.

321 "I remember going outside": *More Than Perfect* DVD.

321 "Has peace been declared?": Darrell Eiland, "'Has Peace Been Declared?,'" *Miami Herald*, Jan. 15, 1973, 1-A.

321 "I think we were in shock": Seiple interview.

322 "No one seems to realize": Scott, "In My Own Words: Super Bowl VII."

322 "If I didn't know better": Evans, *On God's Squad*, p. 226.

322 "That's the level of maturity": Warfield interview.

322 "It was just the mindset of that team": Crusan interview.

322 Shula-Arnsparger hug: King interview.

322 "It was the first time ever": *Always on the Run*, p. 6.

322 "Let the record speak for itself": *Winning Them All*, p. 167.

322 "I just want to go to sleep": Bill Braucher, "Mixmaster Griese Calls Canceled TD 'Upsetting' but Not Spirit-Breaking," *Miami Herald*, Jan. 15, 1973, 5-D.

322 "Garo thought he was a quarterback": Jerry Green, "Lions Had Kicking Woes Back in Garo's Era, Too," *Detroit News*, Sept. 20, 2014.

322 "I've got to work with Garo": Braucher, "'Quarterback' Garo Prayed After Pass Ended in Disaster," *Miami Herald*, Jan. 15, 1973, 5-D, and *Winning Them All*, p. 167.

322 "This is the first time": Barry Jackson, "Miami Dolphins Legendary Kicker Garo Yepremian Dies at 70," *Miami Herald*, May 16, 2015.

322 "That championship ring will hang heavy on my hand": Tex Maule, "17-0-0," *Sports Illustrated*, Jan. 22, 1973.

323 Hunter S. Thompson bets: Freeman, *Undefeated*, p. 239.

323 "I don't remember the last nine, ten minutes": Fernandez interview.

323 "The best Super Bowl I ever saw a defensive lineman have": *Zonk! Zonk's NFL* video.

323–24 "Maybe I should have shared the MVP": Scott, "In My Own Words: Super Bowl VII."

324 "We didn't think about fourteen and oh": Luther Evans, "Dolphins Rule Football World."

324 "By the way, you're not getting out of here": Jenkins interview.

325 "Can you believe it?": Evans, *On God's Squad*, p. 226.

Past Perfect

327 "This is everything I ever dreamed of": Underwood, "Sitting on Top of the World," *Sports Illustrated*, Sept. 17, 1973, p. 132.

328 "Now, our objective this season": *Zonk! Zonk's NFL* video.

328 "Csonka, Kiick, and Warfield Switch Teams": Advertisement, *Miami Herald*, Oct. 9, 1972, 3-C.

329 "throwing beer bottles" and "We literally had to swing": Jason Cole, "Don't Get Too Close to Fans in Oakland," *Fort Lauderdale Sun Sentinel*, Dec. 1, 1996.

331 "Miami's skid row": Mario Alejandro Ariza, *Disposable City: Miami's Future on the Shores of Climate Catastrophe* (New York: PublicAffairs, 2020), p. 201.

331 "I have never met a finer person": Raymond A. Partsch III, "A Fading Legend: Moore's Stature Didn't Overshadow His Humility," *Beaumont Enterprise*, Dec. 9, 2013.

332 "President Nixon suggested": Matt Crossman, "I Remember . . . Garo Yepremian Reflects on Perfect '72 Dolphins," *Sporting News*, Jan. 17, 2011, www.sportingnews.com/us/nfl/news/175372-i-remember-garo-yepremian -reflects-on-perfect-72-dolphins. Also see Hyde, *Still Perfect*, p. 282.

332 "Hey, look who's coming": Briscoe, *The First Black Quarterback*, p. 17.

333 "He had them so wrapped up": Jenkins interview.

334 "Sure, we were lucky": Morris interview.

334 "Go ask the Patriots": "Mercury Morris: Props to Panthers," *TMZ*, www.tmz .com/2015/12/08/mercury-morris-panthers-dolphins-undefeated/.

334 "We finish the game": Ron Kantowski, "Jake Scott, Super Bowl Forgotten Hero, Resurfaces at Las Vegas Drag Race," *Las Vegas Review-Journal*, May 2, 2016.

335 "I live the simplest life": Dave Hyde, "Where's Jake Scott? Dave Hyde Found Him," *South Florida Sun Sentinel*, Nov. 19, 2006.

335 "I can deal with the pain": Ken Belson, "The Perfect '72 Dolphins and Football's Ultimate Toll," *New York Times*, Jan. 30, 2020.

335 "Bill had a hundred and twenty": Fernandez interview.

337 "They say they'll pay for it": S. L. Price, "'I Feel Lost. I Feel Like a Child': The Complicated Decline of Nick Buoniconti," *Sports Illustrated*, May 15, 2017.

337 "have quietly dealt with cognitive impairment": Adam H. Beasley, Armando Salguero, and Linda Robertson, "Football's Toll: At Least Eight Members of 1972 Dolphins Affected by Cognitive Impairment," *Miami Herald*, May 13, 2017.

337 "Every Sunday was a dream come true": Dave Hyde, "Almost Thirty Years Ago, Their Team Went 17–0 . . . ," *South Florida Sun Sentinel*, March 25, 2001.

338 "I got dizzy" and "He has holes in his brain": S. L. Price, "How Jim Kiick Fell Through the Cracks," *Sports Illustrated*, May 9, 2017.

338 "We made a great running back together": Dave Hyde, "Ex-Dolphins Kiick, Morris Form a Backfield, and Bond, Far Beyond Football, *South Florida Sun Sentinel*, Dec. 7, 2018.

338–39 "I got on my hands and knees," "I feel lost," "Football kept rewarding me" . . . "Everybody pays the piper": S. L. Price, "'I Feel Lost. I Feel Like a Child': The Complicated Decline of Nick Buoniconti," *Sports Illustrated*, May 15, 2017.

340 "to keep [his] brain fresh" . . . "I loved playing the game": Beasley, Salguero, and Robertson, "Football's Toll."

340 "I will remember him": Tom Brew, "Don Shula Was Always More Than Just a Coach to Bob Griese," *Sports Illustrated*, May 5, 2020: www.si.com/college /purdue/football/purdue-bob-griese-mourns-loss-don-shula.

341 "Just kind of old-folks pains": Beasley, Salguero, and Robertson, "Football's Toll."

341 "nobody could get close enough to him to hurt him": Hyde, "Almost Thirty Years Ago . . ."

341 "My headaches went away": Cooper Rollow, "Csonka Laughs His Way to Hall," *Chicago Tribune*, Aug. 2, 1987.

341 "Was that the same fellow": Gerald Eskenazi, "Csonka Can Go Home Again, and the Dolphins Are Winning," *New York Times*, Sept. 30, 1979.

342 "My left leg is turning yellow": *Winning Them All*, p. 11.

342 "He was so obsessed with winning": Dave Hyde, "Happy Birthday, Don Shula—No One Could Hold a Candle (Much Less 90) to You," *Fort Lauderdale Sun Sentinel*, Jan. 3, 2020.

342 "I've spent the last thirty years": Janie Campbell, "Dolphins Throw 80th Birthday Party for Shula," NBC 6 South Florida, Jan. 3, 2010, www.nbcmiami.com/news/sports/dolphins-throw-80th-birthday-for-shula/2050265/.

342 "It was the first time we ever saw him" . . . "I guess I thought he'd live forever": Ken Willis, "Larry Csonka Got 50 Years with Don Shula and Thought There'd Be Many More," *Daytona Beach News-Journal*, May 9, 2020.

342 "Because can you picture a world": Dave Hyde, "We'll Never See the Likes of Don Shula Again," *South Florida Sun Sentinel*, May 4, 2020.

343 "we love football": Mark Fainaru-Wada and Steve Fainaru, *League of Denial: The NFL, Concussions and the Battle for Truth* (New York: Crown, 2013), p. 346.

344 "Seventeen and oh just happened": *America's Game*, 42:00 mark.

345 "We were lucky": Morris interview.

345 "That's what makes it really fun": *Zonk! Zonk's NFL* video.

345 "The fact of the matter is": *America's Game*, 39:00–42:30.

345 "I'm eighty-six now": King interview.

346 "The only thing I miss about football": *Zonk! Zonk's NFL* video.

346 "Isn't it great, Mad Dog?": Hyde, *Still Perfect*, p. 88.

INDEX